The Stopsley Book

James Dyer was born in Stopsley in 1934 and educated at Stopsley Infant and Junior Schools, followed by Luton Grammar School. After National Service in the R.A.F. and Teacher Training at St John's College, York, he obtained a Masters degree in archaeology at Leicester University. Eight years teaching at Farley and Stopsley Junior Schools was followed by ten years as Principal Lecturer in history and archaeology at Putteridge Bury College of Education. In 1976 he returned to teaching at Harlington Upper School in Bedfordshire where he specialised in geography and archaeology. He has excavated in many parts of Britain, as well as Denmark and Greenland, and is the author of numerous books on archaeology. For more than thirty years he has been archaeological editor for Shire Publications, with special responsibility for the Shire Archaeology series of books. Between 1966 and 1974 he also edited the *Bedfordshire Magazine*. Now retired from full-time teaching, he continues to lecture and broadcast on archaeological and local history topics. Co-author of the highly successful *Story of Luton*, he has for the past thirty years been researching the history of Stopsley. He has been a governor of the Stopsley Infant and Junior schools since 1968, and has also served on the governing body of Putteridge Infant and Junior schools. He was elected a Fellow of the Society of Antiquaries of London in 1969, and has served on the councils of the Royal Archaeological Institute and the Bedfordshire Historical Record Society.

The
Stopsley
Book

BY JAMES DYER

The
Book
Castle

For my Parents,
who made it possible
for me to be born
in
Stopsley

First published October 1998
by
The Book Castle
12 Church Street
Dunstable
Bedfordshire LU5 4RU

ISBN 1 871199 24 7 (hardback)
ISBN 1 871199 04 2 (paperback)

Typeset by the Author.
Printed in Great Britain by Antony Rowe Ltd.,
Chippenham, Wiltshire.

Contents

Photographs

Maps

Introduction

There have been Dyers living in Stopsley for more than four hundred years, though my family only moved to the village in 1931. My interest in local history was first aroused in my infant school days, when at Christmas I was given a new penny by the former village headmaster, Charles Breed, and I wondered why?

During 1965, I led a group of Stopsley folk who met together at the High School for a term, to try and record our memories of life in the village in earlier days. We collected together old photographs and tape-recorded interviews with people like George Souster and Maud Stronell. At last some of their findings are published here.

For eleven years since 1987 I have written a monthly article about village history for the St Thomas' Church magazine *The Stopsley Signpost*. The interest that these articles have engendered has persuaded me that there is scope for a closer look at Stopsley's past. This book is the result. Whilst at all times I have tried to be as accurate as possible, I must point out that my subject spans that precarious gulf where memory and history meet. I have talked to many elderly villagers, and sometimes details have become a little blurred. If we have erred, we beg forgiveness!

Although the earlier chapters of this book are written in broadly chronological order, it was not my intention that it should be read in its entirety as a continuous narrative. For ease of reference the later chapters are dealt with as self-contained subjects: farms, churches, education, etc. Inevitably this means that some topics may occur in more than one chapter. In those cases it should be possible to follow them using the index on page 192.

A Select Bibliography appears on page 191, but many subjects covered by this book remain largely unpublished or were recorded only in the pages of *The Luton News*. With one exception, the Wills described in Chapter 4 have not previously been described, and the account books of Ramridge End Farm are an untapped source of agricultural information (though the present whereabouts of the original books is unknown to the author). The School Log books (at the schools), Stopsley Parish Council Minute Books and Luton Borough Council Minute Books (Luton Museum) and Church Registers (at the churches) are the major primary sources.

James Dyer: May 1998

Acknowledgements

A work such as this relies on the help of dozens of people and organisations, some of whom have not lived long enough to see it completed. I thank all of them sincerely and list their names below. With research spread over more than thirty years it is inevitable that some names will have been overlooked. For this I apologise.

A few people must be singled out for special thanks for granting me access to their own unpublished research. Betty Shaw has permitted me to incorporate her work on the history of Manor and Whitehill Farms. The late Jean Sewell provided almost all the information concerning Sir Samuel Starling. Former County Archivist Patricia Bell transcribed seventy Stopsley wills for me and offered much good advice. Barbara Benson has freely exchanged information concerning Round Green and discussed many other local matters with me. My former colleague at Putteridge Bury College, William L. Gates, has redrawn most of the maps. Walter Rainbow has copied and printed many difficult photographs. Over the years *The Luton News* has accumulated thousands of local photographs. These have now been placed in Luton Museum, and I am deeply indebted to Chris Grabham of the Museum staff for making prints, and John Buckledee, the Editor, for allowing me to use so many of them.

I gratefully acknowledge the help of all the following for providing me with information or photographs:

Revd. David Alexander; the late Revd. Arthur B. Allen; Eva Allen; the late Ellen Barber; the staff of the Bedfordshire County Record Office; Marge Bierton; Ann Boddy; R.H. Bristow; Anne Buck; the late Walter F. Burgess; Dr Lindsay Burton; Basil and Rachel Cheverton; Leslie Church; Ray Clements; Mrs J.R.Clutterbuck; Sister Columba; Leo Covey-Crump; Myrtle Cox; Kath Crampton; Revd. Cecil Dawes; Frederick Dyer; Philip Eden; Margery Ekins; Kath Endersby; Canon F.A. Estdale; Joan Evans; Jack Farrer; David Farish; John Foster; Sue Fuller; David Garrattt; Chris Grabham; Brin Griffiths; Eunice and Gerry Hale; Anthony J. Hales; Mary Hall; Peter Haydock; Marie Heath; The *Herald and Post*; Muriel Hill; Angela Hillyard; Tilly Hodgson; the late Ronald A. Hopkins; Simon Houfe; Margaret Large; Colin Lathwell; the late Walter Lawrence; Bishop Ken Leslie; John Lunn; the staff of Luton Central Reference Library; the staff of Luton Museum; *The Luton News*, Tom Madigan; Norma Major; John Manning; Mick Marsh; Jean Miller; A.J. Mowbray; Ken and Pat Munslow; Dr H. M. Murray; Revd. John Neal; John M. Newbury; Bob Norman; Barbara Peters; Alan Pickles; Norman and Freda Pinney; Canon C.F. Pollard; Jeanne Powell; Josefine Pugh; Reading University Library; Walter R.Rainbow; John Rowlands; Dr Walter Roy; Bob Rumble; Les Sammons; Revd. R.E. Sargent; David Scrimshire; John Shaw; the late Pat Shaw; Ann Smith; Stuart Smith; the late George C. Souster; the late Maud Stronell; Stroud Public Library; Pat Tansley; Alan Thayne; Jenny Walsh; Michael Webb; Fay Weighell; R.D. Whalley; Peter White; Hugh Wright; Patricia Yates; Jill Yorke.

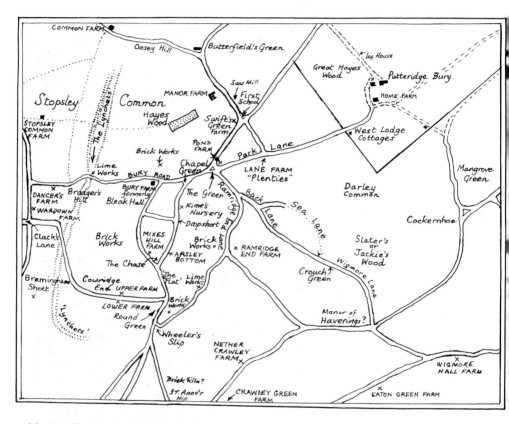

Map 1: The location of old Stopsley place-names, most of which were still in use in 1930, or could be confirmed by reference to earlier maps. The roads are those of about 1930.

Chapter 1

Setting the Scene

The civil parish of Stopsley, as it was defined between 1861 and 1933, lies on the north-eastern side of Luton in Bedfordshire. It occupies a ridge of the Chiltern Hills that drops gently from north to south. The north-western edge is marked by Galley Hill and Warden Hill, rising 187 and 195 metres respectively above sea level. From Whitehill Farm at 178 metres the ground drops to 167 metres at Swifts Green and 164 metres at Jansel House. The ridge is at its lowest, 157 metres, close to the traffic roundabout at the junction of the Hitchin Road and Vauxhall Way (Arsley Bottom - or Arsey Bottom). The eastern side of the parish drops gently into Hertfordshire. On the west the chalk escarpment of Bradgers Hill creates a dramatic fall of 35 metres in a distance of 300 metres, to finish at 108 metres above sea level beside the river Lea at Mud Arches (the junction of Kingsdown Avenue and New Bedford Road).

The boundary of Stopsley has often changed over the centuries and in recent years has reflected both the ecclesiastical and political whims of the times. In each case, it has been subdivided by the creation of new churches (St Christopher's, St Francis and Bushmead) and electoral divisions (Putteridge, Wigmore, Crawley and part of Icknield ward). Only on the east has the boundary been established for centuries, since it also forms the county boundary with Hertfordshire. To the north Whitehill Farm and its fields have always been historically part of Stopsley, although it is now administratively part of Streatley parish. For the purpose of this book I shall consider Whitehill Farm and the South Bedfordshire Golf Club, and the land as far north as the Icknield Way, as within the historic parish of Stopsley. West of Warden Hill the Old Bedford Road and the river Lea formed the boundary as far south as Stockingstone Road, where the boundary of 'stakes-and-stones' looped east up the hill and, until it became part of Luton in 1928, included Round Green. The edge of the parish then followed the crest of the chalk escarpment south to Crawley Green and St Ann's Hill, and east to include Eaton Green and Falconer's Hall (the latter now destroyed by the runway of Luton Airport). Numerous early documents, right up to the 1924 edition of Kelly's *Directory*, also include Someries Farm and the Spittlesea Isolation Hospital within Stopsley parish.

Geomorphology

The whole ridge upon which Stopsley stands is composed of upper chalk, liberally covered with a layer of clay-with-flints (in places up to 9 metres thick) and a capping of plateau drift. This drift covered at irregular intervals a large number of dolines: hollows usually formed through dissolution and collapse of the chalk and akin to swallow holes. These were filled with an almost stone-free, loess-like, silty sediment known as brickearth. Until 1939 this earth was frequently quarried for brickmaking in the Stopsley area, and gave rise to a minor industry, (see page 184).

At least one ice-sheet reached the foot of the chalk escarpment at Barton-in-the-Clay, three miles beyond the northern edge of our parish, during the Anglian period, perhaps 500,000 years ago. The resultant meltwater rushed down the Lea valley and through the neighbouring Hitchin - Stevenage gap, and forced glacial debris onto the plateau, covering many of the dolines, although glaciers did not penetrate the uplands and scour the site of the future Stopsley. Whilst ploughing in the late 1950s farmer Pat Shaw of Whitehill Farm struck a large rectangular erratic boulder some 1.5 metres long and 0.6 metres wide on Stopsley Common (at TL:098243). It appeared to be composed of micaceous sandstone (unconfirmed). Defying all efforts to remove it with farm machinery, it was reburied.

Stopsley soils are notoriously heavy and tenacious, giving rise to ponds and mud in winter, and drying out to rock-hard conditions, often resulting in flash-floods in the summer. The natural water supply in the parish was entirely from ponds filled with surface water, supplemented by deep wells. The ponds, numerous on the Tithe Map of 1844, have almost all disappeared, due to modern drainage and wholesale building. Writing of Eaton Green Farm near the Airport in 1911, William Austin observed:

'In the meadow at the rear of these buildings is a large pond. How far the water is supplied by rainfall, and how much by condensation, is a matter of conjecture, but the situation seems to us to be too high for the supply to come from surface drainage. Most of the farmhouses and cottages on the high lands within the parish of Stopsley in early times were almost entirely dependent on similar reservoirs for their water-supply for the inhabitants and the animals on the farms. The wells sunk at great cost on many farms and Luton Water Company's water-supply in the village and even on many of the farms have made the people and the farmers independent of pond water, and so the ponds are neglected and gradually dry up. When ponds were a real necessity they were kept in a sound condition by regular use: animals daily entering them and walking through them, kept the clay well puddled (trampled), and some farmers annually had a stampede of animals through the pond for the purpose. A little trampling will keep a pond in working order for unlimited seasons.'

Stopsley's impermeable clay-with-flints has always created drainage problems, some of which still persist today. As the village has grown, old ponds and water courses have been forgotten and tarmaced over, only to suddenly reappear after heavy rain. The two ponds in front of Pond Farm now flood the forecourt of Jansel House. The Lane Farm pond floods Putteridge Road in front of the Putteridge Parade shops, as does another in the corner of the Putteridge High School playground every time we have a massive downpour.

Surface water, which once dispersed into field ditches on what are now the 'prairie plains' of the Lothair Road playing fields, has nowhere to go after heavy rain. Some of it used to find its way into the ponds at Manor Farm and in front of the present vicarage (Dyer's pond), but the ditches were filled in, and the dual carriageway blocked all chance of escape in that direction. After exceptional rain in September 1968, for example, the gardens and foundations of 667 and 669 Hitchin Road were flooded by water draining off the playing fields. 'The prolonged intensity of the rain was such that the water couldn't percolate through the clay soil quickly enough, and consequently it flooded over the field surface to the lowest points.' Something similar happened the previous January when rain fell on top of frozen snow. Deep flood ditches have since been dug and have eased but not cured the problem. When man interferes with nature and destroys established drainage patterns without making adequate provision for emergencies, then disasters will invariably happen.

All the local farms and each group of houses had at least one well, some fitted with simple pumping equipment. Records of their depths are sparse and unreliable. Frederick Davis (1874) records that the well at Whitehill Farm was the deepest in the parish at 76 metres (250 feet). When the 17th century well-head from Tithe Cottage (north-east of present day Jansel House) was presented to Luton Museum in the 1930s, it was estimated that the well may have been 60 metres (200 feet) deep, necessitating a hefty lifting device, which included a large oak turning wheel and two cogged wheels, housed in its own barn. It is now displayed in Stockwood Park Museum. A number of wells were filled-in on the site of Pond Farm (Jansel House) when it was demolished in 1958, and another was observed beneath the kitchen floor of Bury Farm. There were many others in the immediate vicinity, some of which may still be accidentally discovered. The *Luton Reporter* for 8th July 1874 recorded that four cottages belonging to Mr Ainsworth at Stopsley had no adequate water supply. It was suggested that a well in the village, the property of Trinity College, Oxford, might be used until storage tanks could be built. (This was probably at Pond Farm). The main communal village well on Chapel Green was sealed by a stone slab in October 1901, and is now covered by the village War Memorial. A photograph taken in 1897 shows it covered by a well-built wooden shed with a corrugated iron roof. Water was drawn from it with the aid of two buckets of equal weight, one ascending and the other descending at the same time.

Towards the end of the nineteenth century the springs in the Luton area began to run low, and in 1898 all the wells in Stopsley ran dry, although there was still water in the Luton reservoir. The Stopsley Schoolmaster wrote on 28th June: 'The drinking water in the village is exhausted and our tank water is too filthy to touch'. Since this was the worst of a number of occasions on which the calamity had occurred, the Luton Water Company was persuaded by pressure from the Parish and Luton Town Councils to build a water tower in 1900 beside the reservoir at Hart Hill to supply Stopsley with water. Mains water reached the centre of the village on 7th June, 1901. (see page 73).

'Come wind, come weather'

The weather is always with us, and as with so many things that are familiar, we tend to ignore it. In writing about the past it is seldom mentioned and yet it is often the governing factor in the success of events, be it a wedding or fête, a football match or the harvest. In our part of the world we can never be sure of the weather. We can feel the change of the seasons and wonder as we cross the frosty park wrapped in our furs, how four months before we were wearing T-shirt and shorts.

We can notice more subtle climate changes too: what meteorologists call micro-climatology. This may give us clues as to why Stopsley is sited where it is. It may tell us why frost and fog occur in Arsley Bottom, or why the windiest spot in the village is beside Jansel House.

Take a walk from the village centre, across the Lothair Road playing fields towards Butterfield's Green and notice the temperature differences. On a bright spring morning, the chill breeze hits you and you adjust your scarf and button the collar of your coat. As you approach the steeper slope of Bradgers Hill and Stopsley Common the wind gains strength and the wind chill factor reaches its 'depths'. When you turn back into the housing after the stimulating exercise, cross the Hitchin Road and move into Cannon Lane, the sudden mildness is a welcome relief.

This temperature variation is one element of micro-climate which Stopsley exhibits. The location of the old village centre may be used to demonstrate the wisdom of the early settlers and the nature of the micro-climate of those days. Stopsley avoids the sharp slope of Stopsley Common, as does Caddington further west. This is not the cliff-hugging vista of an Italian hill-top town, but a settlement lodged beyond the scarp where a dip in the ground will give that little extra shelter. Fog, too, lingers on the highest ground. Whitehill Farm, and Warden Hill beyond, is often surrounded by fog, long after it has cleared away from Stopsley village.

Stopsley's micro-climate varies from that at Luton which is situated in a valley 60 metres below. It is most noticeable on those clear, cold days when frost is prevalent and sinking cold air collects in the valley creating a frost pocket. This is particularly noticeable in Vauxhall Way and at Arsley Bottom.

Woodland, too, presents a different range of temperatures and humidity. Warmer out of the wind, cooler in the shade, drier when it rains but damper as the rain ceases and the drip off leaves continues for hours afterwards. Most of Stopsley's woodland has gone, but it certainly influenced the siting of the village in Saxon times.

We have no detailed figures that that tell us about Stopsley's weather in past centuries. Every now and again there are references to extremes in the vicinity which are of more than passing interest. Frederick Davis in *Luton, Past and Present* (1874) recorded that in 1789 'In this year happened the hardest frost and deepest snow ever known. It continued fifteen weeks; the roads and hedges were buried, and the wagons and carts went over the fields - any where for the nearest way; and so hard was the snow frozen that their track could not be seen.' Davis also noted that in 1805 'A deep snow began December 26th, and lasted twelve weeks.' The Northampton *Mercury* for 13th February 1808 reported a great fall of snow with snowdrifts on Chalk Hill near Dunstable where 21 sheep were dug out. In the summer of 1808 haymakers at Leighton Buzzard were so overpowered by the heat as to lose the use of every faculty, and had to be carried home.

The earliest Stopsley School Log Books contain numerous references to the weather, and when checked against scientific records, there can be little doubt that towards the end of the nineteenth century, winters were marginally colder than today. Many casual remarks are recorded like 'fearful weather' or 'very hot today'. Sometimes they are sufficiently important to reflect national trends. For example, on 16th July 1875, the Log records 'Attendance still low through wet weather.' On 23rd July 'The weather still worse and for two days some of the roads were impassable for children.' On 30th July, perhaps because of the weather: 'attack of fever in village.' National figures show that the average monthly rainfall for July in the late 19th century was 69.5 mm. but in July 1875 it reached 142.7 mm. It was the wettest July since 1840. Across Cambridgeshire and Bedfordshire constant heavy rain fell, but without thunder; brooks were flooded, crops ruined and sickness followed.

1881 is recognised as the worst winter of the nineteenth century in south-eastern England. The School Log for Wednesday 19th January reads 'I was compelled to close the School this morning - the snow being so deep as to hinder the children from coming to school. Snow as high as the hedge on the Hitchin Road.' Monday 31st: 'Punished [four boys] for throwing snowballs at the assistant mistress on Friday last'! The Leighton Buzzard to Dunstable railway was blocked with 3 to 4 feet (0.9 to 1.2 m.) drifts from 8 pm on the 18th until noon on the 21st. Between Luton and Leagrave there were 2 to 3 feet (0.6 to 0.9 m.) drifts on the railway and goods traffic was delayed by several hours on the 19th. On the morning of the 20th a temperature of 5 degrees Fahrenheit was recorded at Hitchin.

On Shrove Tuesday, 14th February 1888, deep snow fell in Stopsley and lay for a fortnight. A Buckinghamshire observer noted that the snow began to fall early in the morning and was 6 inches deep (15 cm.) by 11 am. By 10 pm. it was 12 inches deep (30 cm.). William Lucas at Hitchin described it as 'the coldest winter but one since the Crimean winter of 1855.' The snow had thawed by 8th March, and on 14th another overnight fall melted in the morning. The summer of 1888 was also one of the coldest on record, with temperatures in June 1.4 degrees below normal, July 2.5 degrees below normal and August 1.9 degrees below normal. At Stopsley the harvest was delayed until mid-September.

1900 was also a year of exceptional weather. Nine inches (23 cm.) of snow fell on 2nd February. It was so cold in London on the 3rd that Big Ben froze at 1.30 am. On 5th February 'a heavy snow storm spoilt the [Stopsley] school attendance.' By Tuesday 13th light engines had to be kept running to and fro on the Luton to Hertford branch lines to stop them from freezing. The London and Midland Railway trains were much impeded by drifts up to 6 feet deep (1.8 m.) north of Leagrave at Chalton. At Baldock 12 inches (30 cm.) of snow lay, driven by an easterly gale. During that Tuesday night 'a severe snow storm had covered the roads [at Stopsley] to a great depth. At 9 am there were no infants or infant teacher at school and about 4 or 5 boys whose shoes and stockings were soaked. Temperature 35 degrees F. School was dismissed for the day.' By Thursday 15th 'an even worse storm came on this morning,' there was a 'violent south-easterly gale with driving snow' and later the same day a 'furious gale from the south-east.' It was appreciably worse in the north Midlands and Scotland. Then there was a rapid thaw. On Friday 16th 'about six boys were in a miserable state as the roads were all flooded and the yard had 6 inches of slush in it up to the doors of the lobbies. Temperature at school 40 degrees F.'.

By midsummer 1900 there was a complete change. A great heat wave began, lasting from the 10th to 27th July, with frequent thunder and hailstorms. It was hottest in London with temperatures reaching 93.4 degrees F. in Camden Square and 92.4 degrees F. in Kensington. At Stopsley from 23rd to 25th July the Headmaster wrote 'The heat is terrific. We started these three mornings at 81 degrees F. before the children entered.' William Lucas at Hitchin observed: 'Hottest day, hottest night and hottest month in records lasting over 50 years.' (It was not to be surpassed until 1995). The heat turned milk sour, butter and cheese rancid and fresh food could not be kept. In many places small children and the elderly became ill and even died, though fortunately not in Stopsley.

There are fewer details of the weather in the Log Books after 1900, but heavy winter snow was frequently recorded until about 1930. Following heavy snow on 28th and 29th January 1919 Wigmore Lane became flooded and a school teacher (Miss Newall) could not get through. In December of the same year, snow was followed by heavy rain which flooded the school boiler house, [present Infant School] extinguishing the boilers. All the children were sent home.

A hamlet of Luton

Historically Stopsley was a daughter hamlet of the King's Manor of Luton, of which there were once five: Limbury, Leagrave, Hyde, Biscot and Stopsley. Loosely speaking hamlets were all small villages without churches. At the time of the Tithe Commutation Award of 1844, when tithes in kind were finally replaced by fixed rent charges apportioned on individual plots of land, Stopsley was officially assessed as a hamlet of the town and included in Luton's Poor Rate. At the same time, it was assessed as a separate rating area for Land Tax, highway rates, etc. With the Local Government Act of 1894 the five hamlets of Luton were formed into the civil parish of Luton Rural. Finding this difficult to administer, the County Council agreed in 1895 to divide Luton Rural into the four separate civil parishes of Stopsley, Leagrave, Limbury and Hyde. As a result, Stopsley had its own Parish Council from April 1896 until 1st April 1933. At that time the village was incorporated into the Borough of Luton. Round Green had been taken into the Borough on 1st October 1928.

The establishment of an ecclesiastical District of Stopsley in 1861, with an area of approximately 2,710 acres, effectively fixed the bounds for St Thomas' church. However, with the building of St Christoper's church at Round Green in 1937, St Francis church in Carteret Road in 1960 and the formation of the conventional district of Bushmead in 1993, the area served by St Thomas' decreased considerably, although by then the population had increased dramatically. The building of the Wesleyan chapel in 1846, the Baptist church in 1870 and the Sacred Heart Roman Catholic church in 1950 had no effect on parish boundaries.

The definition of the ecclesiastical District of St Thomas' church dated 4th February, 1861 is as follows:

> 'All that part of the hamlet of Stopsley in the parish of Luton, in the county of Bedford and diocese of Ely, wherein the present incumbent of such parish now possesses the exclusive care of souls which is situate to the north of an imaginary line commencing upon the boundary dividing the said hamlet of Stopsley from the township of Luton within the same parish at a point in the middle of the road leading from Luton past Turner's Knoll to Ramridge End, and extending thence north-eastwards along the middle of the said road as far as a point opposite to the middle of the northern end end of another road leading from Ramridge End aforesaid to Cockernhoe and Mangrove, and extending thence in a direction generally south-eastward to and along the middle of the last mentioned road [Crawley Green Road] as far as a point opposite to the middle of the southern end of an occupation road leading therefrom past Hostler's Wood to Putteridge Bury, and extending thence first northward and then north-eastward to and along the middle of the occupation road as far as the boundary dividing the said parish of Luton from the parish of Offley, in the county of Hertford and diocese of Rochester.'

Old Names

The first recorded reference to Stopsley appears in a *Feet of Fines* dating from 1199 when a law suite involving John de Stoppelee was heard at Westminster. It involved the ownership of land at Heihovre [High Over ?], an unidentified place, possibly in Bedfordshire. In 1207 John was again in dispute, this time over 'lands in

Stoppesle', and in 1219 Juliana Balle claimed a number of strips of land in Stoppeslega, together with a messuage (that is a house with garden), the ditch around it, and 1½ acres of land adjoining. By 1276 the name Stopesleye occurs: spelt almost the same as today. The origin of the village name is discussed on pages 15-16.

Variations of spelling were very common when most people were unable to read or write. There was no standardisation at that time and names had to be taken down phonetically by clerks often unfamiliar with the local district names or dialect. When Fred Shoosmith became Headmaster of Stopsley school in January 1887 he experienced a great difficulty in making himself understood. He found that the children spoke a broad *patois* or dialect. Fifty years later it had all but disappeared, submerged beneath a veneer of careless Lutonian and Cockney.

Two names of ornithological origin are Ramridge and Crawley Green. Ramridge has been variously spelt *Ramrugg* (1227) and *Ramrigge* (1240); it derives from raven-ridge. Crawley was *Craulea* in 1196, meaning a crow-clearing or wood favoured by crows. The Green was added much later. A further ancient Stopsley name is Mixes Hill, or Mixies Hill, originally a farm and row of labourers' cottages where the road called Englefield now runs. In an Assize Roll dated 1276 this was referred to as *Mixeweye*, which has the unromantic meaning of 'dung-road', probably a road along which manure was carted to the open fields.

Some local names have disappeared altogether, but we know their location from Bryant's *Map of Bedfordshire*, published in 1826. The new Baptist church in St Thomas' Road stands on the site of Bleak Hall. The road widened out in front of the Hall to form Bleak Hall Green, from where a track made its way south to Mixes Hill. The Green must have disappeared when the first clay pits were dug for the brickworks (now under the municipal caravan site, established in 1963), and Bleak Hall was rebuilt as Bury Farm, giving its name to Bury Road (renamed St Thomas' Road in 1933). Bury Farm house was demolished in 1959, by which time its barns were being used by Stopsley High School as a rural studies centre. They continued to be used as classrooms until they were demolished in 1974.

Along the Hitchin Road (sometimes called Main Road) between Stopsley and Round Green was Dropshort, where the Kime's had their Nursery Gardens (almost opposite the junction of Hitchin Road and Lynwood Avenue). Further west in the hollow was Arsley Bottom, marked today by the traffic roundabout at the junction of the Hitchin Road and Vauxhall Way. The Chase was a private house, later used as a nursing home, on the open space at the Hitchin Road - Birchen Grove corner. The Flat was the stretch of the Hitchin Road that ran from the Chase to *The Jolly Topers*. Turner's Knoll (reputedly named after a suicide) was called Wheeler's Slip in 1844.

Between the row of cottages at Butterfield's Green and Whitehill Farm stood Old Farm, also known as Little Whitehill, with adjoining labourers' cottages. Thomas Butterfield (died 1722) was the head of a yeoman family with a house in the vicinity. Whitehill refers to the colour of the soil, when the underlying chalk has been disturbed.

Wigmore (both Hall and Lane) derives from its connection with the great Welsh Marches dynasty of the Mortimers, who built a large castle and abbey at Wigmore in Herefordshire. Members of the family held land at East Hyde in the 13th and 14th centuries, some of which may have extended to the site of the present Wigmore Hall Hotel. It was later absorbed into the Manor of Luton. Wigmore Lane, which leads to the Hall, was also known as Wigmore Road and Back Lane. It was a grassy bridleway with lots of small holdings on its eastern side until the 1950s. It widened out where the Someries Schools stand today into an area known as Crouch Green.

An old bridle-road ran off Wigmore Lane in a loop which today is followed by Green Lane, and then curved back to meet Wigmore Lane opposite the present Someries Infant School. This completely forgotten road was known as Sea Lane. From the top of Sowerby Avenue through Eastfield Close and on to the Putteridge High School playing field was a stretch of common land known as Darley Common. H.C. Janes gave part of the common off Wandon Close, as a public recreation ground. In 1826 Slaughter's Wood (or Jackie's Wood) was known as Slater's Wood. Part of it survives around the Girl Guides' Haverings Recreation Centre. There was once a much larger wood called Horsley Wood close to Wigmore Primary School. Another small wood in the same area was Stiles Wood, between Ashcroft High School and Buckingham Drive. At the top of Stockingstone Hill, just east of its junction with Richmond Hill, were a group of farm cottages known as Scourge End in 1629. In 1196 the adjacent area was known as Cowridge End, of which more later. (see pages 139-40). The western end of Stockingstone Road by the Wardown Cricket Ground was known as Clack's Lane where it forded the river Lea.

Some roads changed their names when Stopsley was incorporated into the Borough of Luton in 1933 as confusion might have arisen with existing Luton names. Bury Road became St Thomas' Road and Ramridge End Lane changed to Ashcroft Road. Putteridge Road was formerly Park Road as far as approximately Hawthorn Avenue, and Park Lane as it led to Putteridge Park. Delcot Close, created after the 1st World War, ostensibly to provide homes for ex-servicemen, began its existence as Park Lane Close. Three older roads with unusual names are Venetia, Lothair and Tancred, named after novels by the Victorian Prime Minister, Benjamin Disraeli. Lynwood Avenue is named after Lynda Woodfield. Her father, Arthur Woodfield of Bury Farm, owned the land on which it was built. Stronnell Close, off Turner's Road, is miss-spelt. It is named after the Stronell family who originally lived by the village Green.

After the 2nd World War many new roads in the Ramridge and Putteridge areas of Stopsley were named after old field names. Whilst some are situated fairly close to the original fields, like the Severalls and Littlefield Road, others have become quite separate: for example, Bray's Road and Bray's Close field which lay beside Stopsley Fire Station; Rye Croft was where the Ramridge Schools now stand, and Swifts Green Road is some distance from Swift's Green, where the old Stopsley School stood at the entrance to the crematorium cemetery in Butterfield's Green Road. Rickyard Close reminds us that Ramridge End Farm once stood there.

The Natural Landscape

A striking feature of early photographs of Stopsley are the number of trees they show, especially beech, oak, elm and ash. Uprooting hedgerows, the felling of woodland and the devastation caused by the elm beetle in the 1960s has had a catastrophic effect on the arboreal appearance of the parish. The beech was by far the most common tree, followed closely by the elm, whose consequent demise has impoverished the landscape beyond belief and probably beyond the recognition of Victorian inhabitants. Almost every road and bridleway had its hedgerows, dominated by hawthorn bushes and brambles: a source of heartless bird-nesting in the spring months, blackberrying in the autumn, and school nature rambles throughout the year.

Hays or Hayes Wood (TL:102243) was once a major wood with its own gamekeeper, lying between the village and Manor Farm. It was famous for its oak trees, harvested each year for the acorns they provided for pig fodder. Once considerably more extensive, the wood was clear felled prior to the 1st World War. What remains is a pathetic, regenerated relic in a poor state of conservation. Bluebells have survived there, despite overpicking by enthusiastic, but ill-informed, school children.

Slaughter's Wood (TL:117230) at Haverings, is of the oak-hornbeam type more characteristic of Hertfordshire. It is another traditional Stopsley wood, still full of some of the finest bluebells in the parish. At Butterfield's Green, Whitehill Wood (TL:103257) and Upshot Wood (TL:103251) are small woods with rich vegetation. Whitehill Wood and the small Whitehill Spinney to the east were joined together by planting early in the 20th century. The division between the old and new can be clearly seen by the limit of bluebell growth in the older areas. Upshot Wood is of more recent age and contains evidence of planted conifers and the rare dwarf cherry.

Former cultivated farmland at Arsley Bottom (TL:100233) between Mixes Hill Road and Sunningdale was designated for Luton's eastern by-pass in the 1930s. Due to extended delays in planning decisions an area of secondary woodland has evolved, some of which would be worth retaining if the by-pass is ever constructed.

The most interesting area of natural vegetation in Stopsley is Bradgers Hill (TL:096243), marked by the longest stretch of strip lynchets in the county (see page 15). The northern section is privately owned, but the southern part, 'Nail's Hill Common', belongs to the Borough of Luton. Since the 1950s the hills have been invaded by scrub which has done much to destroy the undergrowing vegetation. The Donys' in *The Wild Flowers of Luton* (1991) regretted the appearance of two grass species, California Brome and Tor-grass, which were invading the northern area and smothering smaller plants. As a boy in the pre-scrub days, the author recalls the shorter grass and his pleasure at finding the first pyramidal and bee orchids of the year. They are just surviving, but harder to find now.

Warden Hill (TL:091261) and Galley Hill (TL:092270) are on the northern edge of the old parish of Stopsley. They are owned by Luton Borough Council although they now lie in Streatley parish. They are both situated within the Chiltern Area of Outstanding Natural Beauty (AONB) as designated by the Countryside Commission. In 1951 they were also designated Sites of Special Scientific Interest (SSSIs) and were renotified in 1986 as 'calcareous improved grassland developed on the middle chalk with a characteristic downland flora including locally uncommon species and a nationally rare plant'. The latter, the purple milk-vetch *(Astragalus danicus)* was common on Bradgers Hill sixty years ago, but is now difficult to find. It can also be found as a rarity on near-by Lilley Hoo.

The *Bedfordshire Regional Planning Report* of 1937 said that

> 'the whole of the chalk escarpment from Dagnall ..... to Dunstable.....and the Warden and Galley Hills should form a belt of open country in perpetuity. It is of considerable importance not only to the town of Luton, but to the County and Greater London that the hills should be preserved as an open space from Stopsley Common northwards to include Warden Hill and Galley Hill above the Icknield Way, which has no immediate road access and should, therefore, be readily preserved.'

Admirable sentiments in 1937. Sixty years later a quarter of the area designated on the south-west of Stopsley Common has already been destroyed by housing, and more south of Whitehill Farm will follow if some local politicians get their way.

Since the publication of the *Bedfordshire County Structure Plan* in 1977 (approved 1980) much of the area known as Butterfield's Green, lying north-west of the A505 trunk road and the Vale crematorium, and south of Whitehill Farm, has been threatened by building development. Bound on the east by the county boundary, and less clearly on the west where it merges into the playing fields of the Regional Sports Centre west of Manor Farm and the designated Area of Outstanding Natural Beauty.

Initially Luton Borough Council recognised that in due course some 4,000 dwellings would have to be built in the Stopsley and Wigmore areas. Later it changed its mind with regard to the Butterfield's Green area and modified its *North-East Luton Plan* saying that Stopsley Common, the Playing Fields and the area of countryside around Butterfield's Green north of the A505 should be kept free of development and any further building to preserve it for the enjoyment of all Luton people and future generations. The Butterfield residents raised a petition carrying 4,400 signatures in support of the Council's new viewpoint. Unfortunately, as a consequence, the Bedfordshire County Council's Environment Services Committee refused to certify the *North-East Luton Plan* and the Secretary of State directed the Borough Council to make provision for approximately 2,000 dwellings in north-east Luton. The Borough Council reluctantly amended their plan to comply with the directive.

The Department of Transport announced its intention to build a Thame-Stevenage Link Road (linking the A1, M1 and M40) across the northern extremity of the Butterfield area, and Luton Borough Council now proposed to infil the remaining area with approximately 1,100 houses, an Infant and Primary School, local shopping facilities, and two open space and play areas, all to be completed within ten years.

Not surprisingly there was considerable local opposition to what was seen as the destruction of the last surviving green lung of countryside in Luton. Following a public meeting on 30th January 1986 a Butterfield Preservation Group (BPG) was formed. Meanwhile a Public Inquiry into the whole of the *North-East Luton Plan* was scheduled to commence on 16th April 1986. The Butterfield section ran from 29th April to 15th May. A number of other organisations and individuals, as well as the BPG, lodged objections to the proposals, including the Hertfordshire County Council, the North Herts. District Council, the Lilley Parish Council, the South Bedfordshire Preservation Society and the Ramblers' Association. After deliberating for some months the Inspector's 25 page Report concluded:

> 'A decision is therefore required now as to the long-term future of this land. If that decision is that there are such strong environmental objections to the development of the land that it can never be acceptable for it to be developed, the site should be included in the green belt. That, however, is not my view ..... I can see no strong environmental or other objections to the development of the land.' He proposed a moratorium on any development at Butterfield's Green for ten years.

Unfortunately the matter was not allowed to remain there. In 1989-90 a quite outrageous land use strategy was prepared for the Luton Borough Council in which practically the whole of the north side of Stopsley would be smothered by development. Vast areas were earmarked for a further leisure complex (Stopsley already had two large Leisure Centres) and a stadium for Luton Town Football Club, as well as housing and commercial developments. Nowhere in the plan were the positive needs of Stopsley given any consideration. A massive 'Keep Butterfield Green' campaign was launched through 1990-91 by the local Liberal Councillors. A vast public meeting of supporters held at Stopsley High School overflowed into the yard outside, and two huge petitions made the villagers feelings very clear. In consequence the Borough Council withdrew its proposals and Stopsley breathed again.

The land that the Stopsley Parish Council had guarded so jealously for the enjoyment of the villagers until its demise in 1933, was by 1996 burning a hole in the pocket of the Luton Borough Council. It had to be developed at all costs. In 1996 yet another scheme 'The Borough Plan' was drawn up in an effort to destroy 'the built and natural environment' of Butterfield's Green. By that time the Government had abandoned (temporarily ?) the proposed Thame-Stevenage Link Road.

Smaller in scale than the previous plans, 'The Borough Plan' still took no account of Stopsley's particular needs (e.g. a Community Centre, new Library, car park). Instead it proposed to build a Third Campus for the University of Luton on the western side of Butterfield's Green Road, opposite the Manor Farm buildings and the medieval site of Swift's Green. A Technology Village was also proposed to the north and east of the Vale cemetery, with an adjacent hotel complex and Park-and-Ride car-park. There the matter rests at the time of writing this book.

Chapter 2

In the Beginning

The Stopsley area has been occupied sporadically by man from the earliest times, but it would be quite wrong to suggest that there was any continuity between those first inhabitants and the present occupants of the parish. There were vast periods of time when tundra and forest conditions prevailed, when human beings never entered our area at all.

Perhaps 500,000 years ago, debris from glaciers that flowed some 3 miles to the north-east of Stopsley, covered our area with plateau drift. Thousands of years later, under more moderate climatic conditions, wide funnel-shaped dolines or swallow holes formed and filled with fine sediments and water. Beside these shallow, marshy lakes itinerant bands of lower palaeolithic hominids camped and made tools and weapons of wood and stone. They preyed on the deer which came in large herds to drink, and occasionally elephant and rhinoceros appeared. In summer blackberries and raspberries enlivened a diet of bog bean, hazelnuts, pine seeds, lettuce and salad burnet. From time to time small groups of early humans collected together piles of flints and shaped them into tools and weapons. This might have happened about 300,000 years ago during the warmer Hoxnian interglacial period. As time went by wind and water erosion caused sediments to slowly fill the swallow holes with a deposit of loess or brickearth, and then a mass movement of melting soil at the end of a cold period completely buried them, together with all traces of our early ancestors.

Early in 1886 the Dunstable antiquarian, Worthington G. Smith, visited a newly opened clay pit (beneath Birchen Grove and Sunningdale) at Mixes Hill near Round Green. At a depth of 12 feet (3.6 metres) he noticed a dark-coloured horizontal layer running through the grey brickearth which contained numerous bones and antlers of red deer. At the bottom of the pit, 20 feet down (6 metres) he found a scatter of sharp-edged palaeolithic (or old stone age) flint flakes. Smith was told that the pit had contained numerous other bones, but that these had been taken away by the workmen. When he returned to the pit after an absence of some months, he found the brickfield abandoned, the pit partially filled in, and the men moved to other brickworks. With some difficulty he traced Joseph Ford who had worked at Mixes Hill. He told Smith that "at a depth of about 22 feet (6.7 metres) a complete human skeleton had been found with all its bones in place; it was extended on its right side with its head - which he described as slightly flattened - to the south-west. The length of the skeleton was 5 feet 6 inches (168 cm.). The bones were dark brown and crumbly, and the men took away the best preserved examples, including the skull, which fell to pieces. Ford took a lower arm bone. The great depth at which the skeleton was found and the [unbroken] horizontal stratification of the brickearth precluded any idea of a [more recent] burial". There can be little doubt that if the skeleton had survived we would have the remains of an extremely ancient inhabitant of the Stopsley region.

At the Ramridge End clay pits eleven palaeolithic (old stone age) flint handaxes of oval and pear-shaped types were found, together with friable extinct animal bones. Numerous flint flakes show that the tools were made on the spot.   In spite of their 19th century name, we really do not know what these 'axes' were used for: probably for killing and skinning animals, they certainly were not for chopping down trees!

The best documented discoveries are from the Turner's Knoll (Mardle's) clay pits at Round Green.   Smith had been quietly exploring these for 27 years.   It was necessary to keep his work secret, otherwise, as he wrote "members of local scientific, literary and philosophical societies would have visited the place like a swarm of locusts and totally destroyed all my work."   Mardle's brickfield lay behind (south of) the *Shepherd and Flock* and east of the present Methodist chapel at Round Green, and is now completely built over.   There had been a large swallow hole on top of the hill at 530 feet above sea level (161 metres).   Smith recognised that for a very brief period in palaeolithic times this would have formed a pond, at the side of which men would have camped, using the local flint to make hunting equipment for use in the surrounding deciduous forests.   During his years of searching at Round Green, Smith found the actual land surface on which men had sat and made flint tools.   He recovered 21 well-shaped flint implements, 9 sharp knife forms and more than 280 flakes.   These are all now stored in the British Museum.   George Souster, the Stopsley brickmaker, recalled, in 1965, being paid between 1/- and 1/6d (5p and 7p) for finding 'old stones' for Worthington Smith, when he worked at the clay pits in Caddington, but not at those in Stopsley

During the ensuing centuries Britain was separated from continental Europe. Small bands of mesolithic hunters passed across our area, occasionally leaving evidence of their presence in the form of a few flint weapons and tools. Examples have been found at Butterfield's Green. They seem to have camped beside the source of the river Lea at Leagrave.

Later Prehistoric Times

The heavy clay lands of the Stopsley area would not have proved very attractive to the early farmers of the neolithic period (new stone age), although they would certainly have hunted in the forests which covered the southern two-thirds of the parish. Such activity is illustrated, for example, by the finding of a fine leaf-shaped flint arrowhead, 2 inches long (5 cm.), in the back garden of 30 Lothair Road, beside the former Harris Lane footpath.

The northern boundary of our historic parish is marked by the Icknield Way, which ran across a belt of open countryside, providing an east-west corridor between East Anglia and Wessex from at least 4,000 BC until the beginning of the 20th century. Only the lighter soils close to the Icknield Way and the chalk escarpment are likely to have been cultivated, with grazing on the slopes of the Galley, Warden and Bradgers hills. On the marginal land between the cultivated fields and the forest edge small settlements may have been established, although they have not yet been identified. Some of about a dozen scattered religious monuments and burial mounds of the neolithic and bronze ages have been found and excavated between Galley Hill and Lilley Hoo.

In the 1970s, in the north-eastern corner of the parish, half a mile east of Galley Hill, (TL 100269), the author photographed a dark circle showing up in a field of growing corn. Upon excavation in 1983 and 1984 the ploughed-out remains of an early bronze age ring-ditch, some 65 feet (20 metres) in diameter, were revealed. The ditch had once surrounded a burial mound, at the centre of which an inverted collared or cremation urn had been buried in a shallow pit. Amongst the burnt bones was what archaeologists describe as a broken blue quoit-shaped faience bead; that is, a finger-ring shaped bead made of a vitreous glass-like material which can be dated somewhere between 2,000 and 1,700 BC. Around the urn, five roughly rectangular hollows had been dug into the chalk. Three of these held the skeletons of women variously aged between 17 and 40, and the fourth contained a young person, possibly male, of between 15 and 17 years. One of the women had been buried in a wooden coffin. If anything had been placed with the dead, it had not survived. Some centuries later four cremation burials were inserted into the barrow, and its surrounding ditch redug, to give it more height and perhaps whiten its appearance. A disc-headed bronze pin suggests that the later additions were made in the late bronze age - between 1,000 and 800 BC. Two similar burial mounds, each containing a circle of five or six graves, were uncovered by Worthington G. Smith on Dunstable Downs in 1887. Whether all the burials in each mound were contemporary is open to debate.

Two other burial mounds on the summit of Galley Hill were excavated by the writer in 1961 and 1962. Both barrows had been very badly damaged and the burials for which they were originally built had been removed. The most northerly of the two had been roughly kidney-shaped in plan. In a shallow hollow were the disturbed remains of two young men and numerous joints of oxen, probably of neolithic date. The barrow's surface had been used in the 4th century AD as an haphazard cemetery for more than a dozen Romano-British burials, some clearly slaughter victims. In the middle ages half a dozen people, hanged from a gallows, had been buried on the western side of the mound. This event probably gave the hill its name. The second barrow had been used as a military dug-out during the 2nd World War. Its burial had clearly been found, since when the trench was abandoned and backfilled, some humorist had carefully left part of the skull and two crossed leg bones, together with a milk-bottle containing part of a newspaper dated 1940. The only ancient dating materials were scraps of iron age pottery

Worthington G. Smith wrote in 1894 of seeing the hollows of possible iron age huts on the sides of Warden and Galley Hills. Unfortunately these have become confused by the growth of rough grass and scrub, and the cutting of forgotten golf bunkers in the 1890s. Aerial photographs show an unexcavated circular enclosure of probable iron age date on the southern slope of Galley Hill

There is nothing to suggest that the clay-with-flints soils of Stopsley proved more attractive to settlers in the late iron age, although pottery of that period has been found on the gravels of the river Lea in New Bedford Road. A gold coin of the Belgic tribe from Gaul known as the 'Morini' was found by a schoolboy in a garden in Cannon Lane in 1949. Again, this should not be taken as evidence of anything more than a hole in a wandering tribesman's breeches pocket.

There are a few suggestions of a Romano-British presence in the Stopsley area, (i.e. Britons influenced by the Romans). Fragments of Roman pottery have been found at Butterfield's Green, close to the site of Little Whitehill Farm. Excavations across the course of the Icknield Way in 1971, near the South Bedfordshire Golf Club House, showed that although the road's surface had never been metalled, it had frequently been used by traffic in Roman and later times. Fragments of a dozen horseshoes could well be of Roman manufacture although it is difficult to be sure. We are on safer ground with a Romano-British cooking pot found at Turner's Knoll, Round Green in

1921, and a number of domestic vessels, apparently accompanying cremation burials found between Richmond Hill and Colin Road, close to Stockingstone Road, in 1926. They suggest that there may have been a Romano-British settlement of mid to late 1st century AD date in the Round Green area, but wherever it was has almost certainly been destroyed by building development. These Roman discoveries are now in Luton Museum. Mention has already been made of burials of Romano-British folk of the 4th century AD excavated on Galley Hill in 1961, who may have come from a small settlement, destroyed by fire, in the vicinity of Runfold Avenue. The manner of their burial suggests that some, at least, were the victims of a massacre. This may have been the result of marauding Saxons passing along the Icknield Way.

On the south-eastern edge of the parish between Wigmore Park and Winch Hill Farm, sherds of iron age and Romano-British pottery scattered on the modern field surface, suggest an area of substantial settlement in an early forest clearing.

Saxon Agriculture

There is a slight possibility that the strip lynchets or 'linces' that once stretched intermittently for about 1½ miles from People's Park, northwards along the chalk escarpment to Stockingstone Hill, Bradgers Hill and Stopsley Common, might have originated in the late iron age. It is more likely that they are of Saxon date. These giant 'steps' on the hillside were cultivation terraces, which formed when simple single-coulter ploughs cut a single furrow backwards and forwards along the slope or 'tread' of the hill. Gradually they dug into the chalk on the upper side of the hill and wind and rain erosion carried soil down the slope until it was stopped by an obstruction - perhaps a fence or hedge. Gradually it built up into a step or 'riser'. The ploughman with his oxen or horses could get from one terrace to another using an approach lynchet, such as the one that still sweeps up as a footpath from what is now the Fairford Avenue-Bushmead Avenue roundabout. Sadly, the lynchets that run north from Bradgers Hill Road are the last remnants of one of the longest runs in England, and even they are threatened by road building. In the 19th century some of the lynchets had individual names, such as Nails Hill Common and Dancer's Lynch. A photograph taken by Sir Cyril Fox about 1922 shows the treads of the lynchets ploughed, with light scrub on the risers. By 1945 scrub was still only on the risers, and during the snowy winter, R. M. Stump, a Swiss art master teaching at the Luton Grammar School (now Sixth Form College) made a number of dramatic ski-runs down the hill slope.

The presence of the lynchets on the western edge of Stopsley suggest that settlement was not far away, but no trace has been found. Pagan Saxon cemeteries are known in the vicinity of Biscot Mill (Argyll Avenue), well above the flood plain of the river Lea. By AD 700 a small wooden church may have existed in that same area. A house for the Bishop of Mercia, in whose vast diocese both Biscot and Stopsley lay, was built about AD 800. The Bishop's house or 'cote' became Bishopscote and later Biscot.

'The Clearing in the Wood'

Most place-name experts are agreed that the name of our village is made up of two elements: *Stopp* and *ley*. The ending comes from the Old English word *leah*, meaning a wood or clearing in a wood. This indicates the presence in the middle Saxon period (*c.* AD 750-*c.* AD 950) of woodland in our area which the Anglo-Saxons recognised as ancient. The *Stopp* element represents a personal name. We can therefore assume that sometime before the Norman Conquest a wood or clearing belonging to someone called Stopp was already recognised as Stopp's leah. To the south of Stopsley we find another *leah* - Crawley Green. In 1196 this was *Craulea* - a crow clearing or wood favoured by crows: the Green was added later. Eastwards, in Hertfordshire, are our neighbouring villages of Lilley and Offley, probably meaning respectively, a 'clearing where flax was grown' and 'Offa's clearing'. This gives us a picture of continuous woodland, broken by a number of clearings or 'assarts' containing small settlements and linked together by a series of trackways.

In the ninth century Britain was the subject of frequent attacks by Viking marauders. By AD 871 practically the whole country was under their control. Prolonged guerrilla warfare between the English king Alfred and the Danish king Guthrum ended in AD 886 with the signing of a peace treaty dividing the country between them. Alfred was to hold Wessex and much of western England. Guthrum held the east, north of the Thames. The boundary between them ran:-

'up the Thames, and then up the Lea, and along the Lea to its source,

then in a straight line to Bedford, then up the Ouse to Watling Street.'

The treaty forbade people to cross the boundary except for reasons of trade. All the lands east of the boundary were known as the Danelaw and were under Danish occupation.

Stopsley found itself within the Danelaw, whilst Luton and the other hamlets were west of the river Lea and in Wessex. There is no evidence to suggest that the boundary was ever continuously guarded or that free passage from one side to the other was seriously restricted. There would have been insufficient troops to patrol more than token stretches of the boundary. Most Stopsley people would have had relatives and friends beyond the river, and in all probability knew little of the political inclinations of their rulers. There were undoubtedly military camps within the Danelaw, at Bedford and Northampton, and perhaps smaller local bases at Shillington and Beeston; but this is a subject that needs urgent study by historians and archaeologists. Stopsley and our region were under the control of a Danish *jarl* (or earl) called Thurcatel, who was based at Bedford, and eventually submitted to Edward the Elder in 915.

During the 10th century, with the temporary withdrawal of the Danes, new administrative areas came into existence, which were eventually called 'shires'. They were largely based on the Danish administrative areas, and were placed under the charge of the shire-reeve or sheriff; officers who were third in precedence beneath the earls and bishops. In their turn the shires were sub-divided into 'hundreds'. Bedfordshire contained nine of these, with Stopsley and Luton in the hundred called Flitt, after the river of that name. Every four weeks it held an open-air court, usually in a central place. The Flitt court may have met somewhere between Streatley and Barton, perhaps near the spot later marked by Jeremiah's Tree (*c.* TL:083295).

At the end of the 10th century a fresh wave of Danish invasions swept across England and in 1009 raids occurred in north Bedfordshire, with many incursions into the south. The accession of the Danish king Cnut in 1016 restored order. Without evidence to the contrary, we must assume that Stopsley safely weathered the storm.

The death of Edward the Confessor on 6th January 1066 marked the beginning of yet another period of political unrest. Whilst the Witan accepted Harold I as king of

England, the Norman, Duke William lay claim to the country for himself. After his success at the Battle of Hastings on 14th October, he was not immediately accepted as king. In consequence he led his army on a circuitous rampage, living off the country, and marching up the Thames valley, around the Chilterns and then east along the Icknield Way into Bedfordshire, where it split into two columns. One branch continued to pillage through central and eastern Bedfordshire, Cambridgeshire, and south to Hertford. The other moved more cautiously through the royal manors of Leighton, Houghton Regis and Luton, allowing William, who was with them, to see what he would inherit. On 25th December 1066 he was crowned King in Westminster Abbey.

Luton survived the devastation caused by William and his army. Biscot was less lucky. There is no reference at all to Stopsley, so we are probably safe to believe that it went unscathed, safely tucked amongst some of the densest woodland in the county. William appointed Ralf Tallebosc to be Sheriff of Bedfordshire; his predecessor, Godric, having been killed at Hastings. In 1070 the king granted Luton Church to William the Chamberlain, and in due course it passed to his son, also called William.

The compilers of *Domesday Book* in 1086 made no mention of Stopsley. It is not surprising, if as in future centuries, it was made up of scattered farmsteads and tiny hamlets in forest clearings. As a daughter settlement of the royal manor of Luton, any records for Stopsley would have been incorporated into the assessment for the whole manor. We learn that there were 101 villeins, 51 cottars and 6 serfs or slaves living within the area of the present Borough of Luton. These figures do not include women and children. This suggests a population well in excess of 700. William Austin (1928) has indicated that Luton was clearly a prosperous royal manor. Each villein held on average 117 acres of land, a house with farm buildings, shares in meadow land and common land, and pannage for his pigs. This was considerably larger than many Stopsley farms in the 19th century. Cottars or cottagers had 3 to 5 acres of land with common rights and a cottage. Both villeins and cottars were subject to labour service for the Lord of the Manor, whilst the serfs had no legal rights and were seen as the property of the Manor.

Particularly revealing is the Domesday record of enough woodland to feed 2,050 swine. Dr G.H. Fowler, writing in 1922, cautiously suggests that his was some 3,100 acres - about the size of the Borough of Luton in 1890. Clearly, most of this was on the hilltops in the Stopsley area. Woodland to the south-west around Caddington (some 300 acres) is recorded separately. This only serves to emphasise the wooded nature of the settlements on top of the Chiltern plateau. By contrast, the Domesday figures for arable land in Luton are remarkably low.

The Manor of Luton

It was probably in 1121 that King Henry I gave his Manor of Luton to his illegitimate son, Robert Fitzroy, Earl of Gloucester. Robert began the building of a new church at Luton, dedicated to St Mary, possibly using architects and artificers from the recently completed Abbey at St Albans.

In 1138 Earl Robert opposed King Stephen, and supported his half-sister Lady Matilda. In consequence, he was stripped of all his English possessions. The Manor of Luton and the advowson of the church were given to a foreign mercenary, Robert de Waudari, who, expecting local opposition, immediately set about building a castle in Luton. Constructed in wood, it stood for only fifteen years, before being pulled down in 1154. Its earthworks in Castle Street could still be traced in the 1960s, but have now been demolished or built over.

After the treaty of Wallingford in 1153 Waudari was banished and the Manor of Luton was restored to William, son of Robert Earl of Gloucester. In due course Luton Church was transferred to St Albans Abbey on certain conditions, which included using some of the church's surplus wealth to pay for the entertainment of visitors to the Abbey and pilgrims visiting the Shrine of St Alban. Annual processions to the Shrine began about this time, and were a binding obligation for the people of Luton and Stopsley.

The Church held extensive lands around Luton which were mentioned in the Domesday survey. The historian William Austin deduced that this included some 43 acres in Stopsley at Crawley Green. There, on the edge of the downs, the Abbot of St Albans built himself a summer palace of stone, between 1121 and 1131, with extensive views westwards across the water-meadows of the river Lea to Luton and Houghton Regis. The palace had its own chapel, dedicated to St Anne. It stood on the hillside now occupied by Rutland Crescent, and having fallen into ruins, was demolished in 1689. In 1910 an allotment holder on St Anne's Hill uncovered the foundations of a building composed of large blocks of Totternhoe stone interspersed with brickwork of Norman construction. According to William Austin a carved pillar capital was identified as early 12th century work.

On his accession in 1155 Henry II reclaimed all the land that had once belonged to his predecessors, including the Manor of Luton. It was not until 1190 that his successor, Richard I, granted Luton Manor to one of his crusading allies, Earl Baldwin de Bethune for £80. Soon afterwards, according to a surviving Deed of Confirmation, a dispute seems to have arisen between the Lord of the Manor of Luton and the Abbot of St Albans concerning certain rights which they both claimed. These centred on the annual fair held in Luton, but also included ownership of the Stopsley lands at Crawley Green, and woodland stretching north along the Hart Lane ridge to Cowridge End (Colin Road - Stockingstone Road junction). After an enquiry, Earl Baldwin accepted Abbot John's claims and the matter was amicably settled.

There was little provision for the sick and infirm in Norman England. About 1160 Archbishop Thomas à Becket founded a hospital on the southern edge of Stopsley parish under what is now the north-western edge of Luton Airport. Known as 'The House of God, of the Virgin Mary and St Mary Magdalene', it was administered by the brethren and sisters of the Augustinian order for the care of the sick and diseased. The adjoining land called Spittlesea was probably part of the same endowment. Always in need of money and gifts, the hospital received a grant of land from Roger Groneway in 1377, and in 1465 a petition for a licence to collect alms to support it, was prepared by the most important local land-owners, Lord Wenlock, Thomas Hoo, John Ackworth and John Lammer. The later fortunes of the hospital are unknown. The flint and rubble foundations of the building were found in the 1830s when Samuel Crawley removed Hassex Wood. They have now been built over.

Ia: The Green at the junction of Ramridge End Lane (Ashcroft Road) and Park Road (Putteridge Road) about 1910.   The village pond gave its name to Pond Farm.   Overflow water was piped past the Cottages, and then flowed in an open ditch along Ramridge End Lane and Wigmore Lane until 1938.   Beyond the row of Cottages stand 19-21 Ashcroft Road and in the distance 55-61 Ashcroft Road.   The latter were demolished to make way for a Service station.   Boulter's Meadow is behind the hedge on the right.   Stopsley Green Surgery stands there today.   (*Author's Collection*)

Ib: Part of the western boundary of Stopsley was marked by the river Lea and Stockingstone Road. The latter, also known as Clack's Lane, crossed the Lea by means of the ford, seen in this photograph taken about 1910.   In the distance is the North Lodge of Wardown Park, and on the skyline a solitary tree marks the site of present day Wendover Way.   (*A. C. Jordan Collection*)

IIa: Flooding in Putteridge Road on 13th March 1937.   On the right is the junction with Stapleford Road and Reg. Markie's 'Newsagents and Confectioners'.   Before the road surface was raised and pavements laid, rain water always collected around the large pond which stood beside the wall of the Lane Farm barns on the right.   Even today after heavy rain, water still floods this spot in front of the Putteridge Parade shops.   A gas man collects money on the left. (*Luton News*: *Luton Museum Colln.*)

IIb: Flood water in the back garden of 667 Hitchin Road in September 1968.   The water had drained off the rock-hard clay of Lothair Road playing field after heavy rain.   Originally it would have made its way into field ditches and Dyer's pond, on the opposite side of the Hitchin Road.   Extensive building and wide expanses of impenetrable tarmac surfaces prevents the water from escaping, hence the resultant temporary flooding here and in the forecourt of Jansel House. (*Margaret Large*)

III: This old oak well-head stood in a barn at the rear of *Tithe Cottage*, and served a well estimated to have been 60 metres (200 feet) deep. Probably dating from the 17th century, it has now been re-erected at the Stockwood Park Craft Museum. (*Bagshawe Collection, Luton Museum*)

IVa: Saxon strip-lynchets or cultivation terraces can be seen on the side of Bradgers Hill and Nail's Hill Common in this photograph of 1959. The terraces are cut diagonally by the old bridle road to Manor Farm. The hillside is still relatively free from the scrub invasion which followed the decimation of the rabbit population by myxomatosis in the early 1960s. Bradgers may be a corruption of Badgers' Hill, though Headmaster Charles Breed spelt it Bradge's Hill. (*James Dyer*)

IVb: One of the lynchets on Bradgers Hill about 1923. Only the riser is scrub covered. The level treads are ploughed for cultivation as they would have been in Saxon times. Common Farm can be seen in the distance. In 1845 it was proposed to build a railway to Hitchin from Dunstable across the low ground in the picture, passing into a tunnel beneath the hill on the distant right. (*Sir Cyril Fox*)

Va: Vestige woodland. Hayes Wood was one of the largest woods in Stopsley during the medieval period, and part of it extended south to present-day Lothair Road. In the nineteenth century if warranted its own gamekeepers. It was clear felled prior to the 2nd World War and has slowly regenerated. It has sadly received little care and attention in recent years. (*James Dyer*)

Vb: The National Cross-Country Championships of 1975, held at the Stopsley Sports' Centre. The picture shows the open nature of Stopsley Common at that time, viewed from Bradgers Hill. In the middle distance can be seen Common Farm and its barns, with Warden Hill beyond. The bridleway running from the farm towards the Golf Course was known as the Driftway, whilst that from left to right across the picture was the Hexton Highway. Oosey Hill linked the farm to Butterfield's Green. Bushmead covers some of the land on the left of the picture where medieval strip fields survived into the 1850s. (*James Dyer*)

VIa: Alfred Mardle's brickworks at Round Green in 1908, looking north. In the background is a circular domed down-draught kiln and square chimney. On the right are hacks under which the green bricks were dried before firing. The antiquary Worthington G. Smith can be seen in the pit in the centre examining the gravel layer in which he found palaeolithic flint tools some 125,000 years old. The pits were back-filled with Luton's refuse. (Photo: *Arthur E. Smith, Luton Museum*)

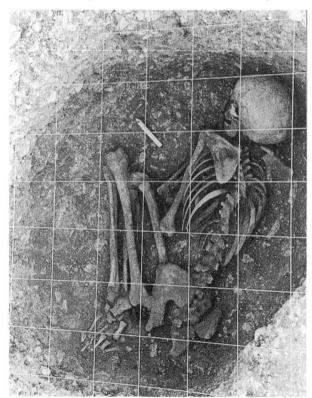

VIb: This crouched burial of a teenage boy was one of four placed within a ring-ditch about 1700 BC. It formed part of a line of bronze age burial sites stretching from Galley Hill to Lilley Hoo. It was excavated in 1983-4. (*Hugh Sheppard*)

VIIa: A trench cut across the Icknield Way near the South Bedfordshire Golf Club House in 1971. It shows the rutted surface of the road which had sunk into a hollow in the chalk. A number of Roman and later horseshoes were found embedded in the ruts. (*James Dyer*)

VIIb: Daniel Brace's 'way to Hexton' excavated in Grovefield to the north of Whitehill Farm in 1966. The cobbled road surface lies between the white pegs. The uneven nature of the field indicated the presence of medieval house platforms. The area has since been levelled by infilling the hollows. (*James Dyer*)

VIIIa: The present Manor Farm, built about 1870, stands on the site of Haye Manor. The scene has changed little since this photograph was taken in 1922. The pond, fed by surface drainage, provided water for the livestock and general farming purposes. Drinking water came from a still existent well in an outbuilding. (*Helen Farr*)

VIIIb: This vaulted chamber, some 1·2 metres high and 3 metres square, was discovered when the car park beside the playing fields in Butterfield's Green Road was constructed in 1973. On the site of Swift's Farm, its function is uncertain, though it may have been a water cistern. Charred timbers seem to have supported the roof of a low alcove, above which is a blocked opening in the wall. It was back-filled with rubble and reburied (*James Dyer*)

Chapter 3

Stopsley in Medieval Times

The Manors of Stopsley

I have said that Stopsley probably originated as one of a number of scattered farmsteads in broken forest land during the middle Saxon period (c.750-950 AD). It did not approach minor village status much before the eighteenth century. From time immemorial the Manor of Luton has claimed rights over the whole of the ancient parish of Luton, which included Stopsley amongst its daughter hamlets.

Between 1086 and 1300 England witnessed a period of intense economic and population growth. Pressure on the land reached its zenith in the 13th century resulting in frequent 'assarting' - the clearing of farmland from woodland and waste (from the French *essarter*, to clear or grub up). Huts or cottages, set up on the edge of seasonal grazing, would in time emerge as peasant farming units, eventually becoming the 'Ends' and 'Greens' so common in Bedfordshire and the Chilterns.

Already by the 12th century we have to envisage unmetalled tracks through woodland with open-fields here and there, and tiny groups of one or two-roomed cottages, constructed of wattle-and-daub, with barns, stock enclosures and a pond. Larger timber-framed farm houses might acquire the title of manor, though their owners were invariably subservient to the Lord of the Manor of Luton who held his living from the King. Consequently, the story of Stopsley is almost inextricably tied to the history of Luton and should be considered in tandem with it. Some of the smaller manors, which frequently changed ownership, were probably manorial only in name and the pride of their occupants.

One of the first manors in Stopsley of which we hear mention is that of Haye and Hoo-Barn which derived its name from a family called 'de la Haye'. It belonged to them from at least as early as 1198. In that year John de Sandon [Sundon?] transferred a quarter virgate of land in Luton to Reginald de la Haye. In 1319 and 1320 John de la Haye was summoned to parliament as a landowner by Edward II, as was Geoffrey de la Haye in 1332 and Thomas de la Haye in 1333 by Edward III. Manor Farm in Butterfield's Green Road stands on the site of Haye Manor and it will be discussed again later. The name Hayes survives in Hayes Wood, now reduced in size, between Manor Farm and the Regional Sports' Centre. John Sybley hanged himself in the wood on 8th May 1589 'near the path from the house leading towards Biscot.'

The Manor of Haverings was one of the most extensive manors and stood north-west of the junction of Crawley Green Road and Wigmore Lane, and comprised some 700 acres. It was owned by Richard de Havering and his wife Lucy in 1258. Ninety years later Sir Richard de Havering obtained a charter giving him the right to hunt any small game on his home farmland in Stopsley. During the reign of Henry VI Haverings was described as 'a moiety (half) of the Manor of Stopsley'. In 1402 the manor was

19

acquired by the Butler family, and in 1534 sold to Richard Fermor. His 'transgressions and contempts of the King' led to it reverting back to the Crown. A rent-roll of the Manor of Haverings exists for 1544. At that time the Manor belonged to Thomas Barnardiston. The roll is incomplete, but it lists the names of seven tenants and the properties they held in Stopsley (see page 124). In 1568 Haverings became the property of another prominent local family, the Crawleys. At that time it was still described as a moiety (half) of the Manor of Stopsley and consisted of 'two dwelling houses, two gardens, 300 acres of arable land, 100 acres of meadowland, 200 acres of pasture, 100 acres of woodland, in all 700 acres' In 1708 the Crawleys purchased Stockwood Farm, and 32 years later built Stockwood House surrounded by a fine park. There is no evidence to show that any Crawleys actually lived at Haverings and for much of its existence the Haverings lands seem to have been rented out to a number of small tenants. The house was pulled down in the early 19th century. According to William Austin (1928) it was 'held of the Manor of Luton' up to the middle of the nineteenth century, but it does not appear on the 1st edition of the Ordnance Survey of 1834.

Henry Cobbe (1899) tells us that at Eaton Green 'in Stoppesley, near Falconer's Hall, originally stood a house and small *chapel*, the foundations of which may still be seen, the whole surrounded by a moat. The place is still called "Chapel Field" (or Little Chapel Close) and the land next to it, Chapel Common.' There was also a 'chapel coppice' of three acres somewhere close by in 1543. Austin identified this site with the house called Haverings Holy. It was quite distinct from Haverings Manor.

Falconer's Hall [sometimes Faulkener's] was built towards the end of the 16th century. Its site now lies within Luton Airport (c.TL 124212). It seems to have been constructed by William Crawley or his son about 1612. In 1647 the property belonged to Sir Francis Crawley, the judge. He bequeathed it to his son Francis and daughter-in-law Elizabeth Rotherham and their children. Francis Bigge, an early Quaker, died at Falconer's Hall in 1664. Frederick Davis (1824) wrote: 'On rising ground [is] a very lofty mansion, with thick walls of brick with a porch of Totternhoe stone, fronting eastwards; the windows were cased with the same. On the porch was scratched 1612. There was a court yard in front, surrounded by a ditch. The building is now (1874) converted into two cottages, and the land added to Eaton Green Farm.'

The Manors of Stopsley and Norwood are something of a mystery. They belonged to the Hoo family in the 13th century, but a hundred years later only Norwood remained in their possession. The names of Alexander Stopsley and his descendants occupy a prominent place in local history and it is reasonable to assume that they were Lords of the Manor until 1416 when it passed to John Gedney. In 1573 Thomas Catesby owned the manors of Hayes, Stopsley and Norwood, and the latter two were amalgamated. Thomas Docwra of Putteridge Bury held the Manor of Stopsley in 1617 and it later passed to the Crawley family. It was part of the marriage settlement between John Crawley and Susanna Sambrooke in May 1740. After 1772 it received no further mention. (In 1291 a charter of Edward I granted Robert de Hoo the right of free warren on his Stopsley estate. This meant that he had the sole right to hunt pheasant, partridge, hare and rabbit. This was reconfirmed in 1338, and again by James II in 1617). Norwood may derive from Northwode: Robert de Northwode of Stopsley was a juror at Bedford Assizes in 1247. William Austin provisionally identified Norwood with Bury Farm, which stood on the site of the new Stopsley Baptist Church in St Thomas's Road.

The so-called 'Manor' of Bennetts belonged to Thomas Rotherham in 1504. Seventy years later it was sold to John Franklin. In 1797 it became the property of the Sowerby family who held Putteridge Bury, and it was absorbed into that estate. It is believed to survive as Whitehill Farm at Butterfield's Green. (see pages 131-3)

Similarly the Manor of Plenties is of dubious manorial origin. Its site has been identified with that of Lane Farm which stood in Putteridge Road opposite Cannon Lane. (see page 137). It is first mentioned in the will of John Crawley, dated 24th May 1519, (though he did not die until 1578), in which he makes the bequest 'To my wife Joan, my house that I dwell in called Plentisse till Richard my son comes of age at 23 years, paying to his mother 20 shillings yearly.' In due course Richard left it to his son William, who in turn sold it in 1568 to Robert Woolley, a draper from St Albans, for £300. At that time it was described in a deed as 'The manor or capital messuage called 'Plentyes', one dovecot, one garden, one orchard, 224 acres of land, 5 acres of pasture, 8 acres of wood and 9 shillings rent.' The estate remained in the Woolley family for ninety years. By then the manor had been divided into two separate houses, each with its own garden and orchard. There were also 120 acres of land, 20 acres of hay meadow, 60 acres of pasture and 20 acres of woodland. Robert's son Richard Woolley sold Plenties in 1656 to Henry Knight, and sixteen years later Michael Knight gave it to his daughter on her marriage to the Rev. Guy Hillersden. In 1709 Richard Crawley bought it back from Hillersden and it remained in the Crawley family until about 1922. After that it was divided between various smallholders.

In 1537 Richard Crawley purchased a house and land at Stopsley called 'Bradways.' Its position is unknown, but it had belonged to a family of that name for many years. It was described as "All that messuage [dwelling house and surrounding buildings], dove-house, garden, orchard, two closes of pasture and 70 acres of land". William Austin observed that the presence of a dove-house suggested that it was a manor house. It is just conceivable that this property later became Swifts Farm (see pages 128-9).

The Tax Payers

It was in the late 12th century that taxation on personal property, or 'taxation of movable' as it was called, first reared its ugly head in England. The system was based on levying a fixed fraction of the total value of the tax payers stock, crops, household or trade goods. In a detailed study of the taxation of Bedfordshire in 1297, the author, A.T. Gaydon, points out that such taxes were always regarded as an extraordinary source of income for the Crown. In that year they were needed to finance Edward I's expedition to Flanders. As royal demands for tax became more frequent, so they became more and more unpopular and subject to nation-wide protest. In 1297 two chief taxers were specially appointed from outside Bedfordshire to oversee the taxation: namely Walter de Molesworth and William de Wassingle: both were from Huntingdonshire. The goods of each tax payer were assessed separately at one ninth. Stopsley tax payers were included with those from the rest of Luton and we can only specifically pick out a dozen whose names include their hamlet of origin; others, like John le Newman could have come from any part of the Luton parish. The Luton tax return begins by declaring the names of six lesser taxers who were sworn to assess the vill [town] of Luton. They included Alexander, son of Maurice of Stopsley and John de Ramerugge [Ramridge]. Amongst the tax payers listed, we find:

Lucia de Stoppesleye:	4 quarters wheat; 1 qr. drage; 6 qr.oats; 1 affer, 4 shillings; 2 oxen; 2 cows; 4 pigs, 8s. Total 60s.2d Ninth 6s.8¼d.
John son of Walter de Stoppesleye:	1 qr. wheat; 1 qr. barley; 1 qr. oats; 1 cow. Total 12s.10d Ninth 17¼d.
Agnes de Mixweye [Mixes Hill]:	2 qr. wheat; 1 qr. drage; 1qr. peas and vetches; 1 qr. oats; 1 affer. 4s.; 1 cow; 5 sheep. Total 27s.2d. Ninth 3s. ¼d.
William de Ramerugge [Ramridge]:	1½ qr. wheat; 2 qr. oats; 1 affer, 3s.; 1 cow, 3 pigs, each 16d. Total 20s. Ninth 2s. 2¾d.
John de Courugg' [Cowridge]:	1 qr. wheat; 2 qr. oats; 1 affer, 2s.; 1 ox; 1 cow; 1 piglet, 2s.6d. Total 22s. 6d. Ninth 2s.6d.

[Drage was an inferior form of barley: with wheat and rye it was used for making bread. An affer was a small draught horse worth roughly half as much as a cart horse].

Law and Order

There was no organised police force for the prevention or detection of crime in the early middle ages. It was the responsibility of every man and woman to report any irregularities to the appropriate authority: the bailiff, coroner or sheriff. As a result local justice was haphazard and often unfair. In an attempt to standardise the law, *Eyres* or 'journeys' were undertaken by the King's Justices, who sat rather infrequently at County Courts to hear Crown pleas.

The *Eyres* are often most interesting today because they give us the names of inhabitants and properties in our parish. Often the results of the hearings are not recorded.

During the fourth year of King John in 1202 the Justices in Eyre sat at Bedford on 20th October. Only one case bore direct relevance to Stopsley. It concerned a question of inheritance or an 'assise of mort d'ancestor'. Robert Clark of Caddington challenged the right of Ralph de Oakley to own half a virgate of land with appurtenances at Stopsley. [A virgate of land was a measure between 14 and 50 acres, which varied in different part of the country].

In December 1227, Alice, the wife of Roger de Stopel', who was suspected of theft, pleaded her innocence to the Justices and put herself at their mercy 'for good and ill'. The Jury said that she was not guilty, and was therefore dismissed.

Just before Michelmas Day, 1247, the Justices, coming from Northampton, were met on the county boundary by the Sheriff and an armed guard. They were escorted to Bedford, where the court was probably held in the nave of St Paul's church. The castle would have been more appropriate, but it had been slighted in 1224 and not rebuilt. For almost four weeks the court listened to 850 cases, requiring the attendance during that time of more than 1000 men and women. As it is reported that there were only 98 decent houses in the county town at that time, one can only wonder where they bought food and drink, stabled their horses, or found lodgings for the night.

Of the cases that were heard, two in particular interest us.

'Evildoers unknown burgled the house of Walter de la Hide in Stopeslegh and carried off the goods there found, and so wounded John Modde and Richard de Rindele who were in the house that they died 6 days after.'

No witnesses from Stopsley turned up at the hearing, though four were required by law, to support the Coroner. The Coroner, and Roger his clerk and bailiff, were amerced for failing to produce the servants who were in the house at the time. That means that they were placed at the mercy of King Henry III for failing to do their duty. They were probably made to pay a small fine.

At the same court 'Matilda de Beynhal accused Roger de Beynhal of coming on her at the vesper hour on Thursday before the feast of St James at the east end of Stoppeslega with a premeditated assault, breaking her left arm with a stick, and striking a blow of 3 thumbs length on the left side of the head; and robbing her of a wimple priced at 10 pence and a silver buckle priced 3 pence.' [A wimple was a linen head-covering similar to those worn by nuns.] She also accused Roger's son Herbert of taking part in the same attack. Both men flatly denied the charge. Matilda then decided to withdraw her allegation and was committed to gaol. Those who had supported her (Thomas de la Egge and Richard de la Mare) were placed at the King's mercy. The Jury, however, were convinced that Roger *had* given her 'the blows aforesaid' and requested that 'he therefore be guarded'. Being guarded in this case meant that he had to pay an unrecorded fine. As common folk seldom had any coined money available, two friends, Alan de Bremhelhangre [Bramingham] and Roger Lauwys [Lewsey], stood surety to pay the fine within five months. Another case at the same court referred to a scuffle breaking out when 'the whole countryside met at the chapel at Limbury for sports.' One wonders if any Stopsley folk participated.

It becomes clear from these court records, of which only a tiny proportion have survived, that life in Stopsley in the 13th century (bearing in mind a very much smaller population) was just as violent as it is today.

Let us return to the village during the reign of Edward Ist. On the night of 24th April 1275, Thomas de Barton and his three daughters were sleeping in their house at Stopsley. About midnight thieves broke into the building and woke Thomas, demanding to know where he kept his valuables. They tied him up and hit him on the head with a pick-axe, leaving a deep wound from which he died soon after lunch the next day. Then they attacked his three young daughters, wounding Cecily and Agnes. Twelve years old Joan was so badly injured that her brain was visible through a hole in her skull. She lay speechless for six days before dying on 30th April. The thieves ransacked the house and took away everything of value. At dawn Agnes managed to stagger to the house of a neighbour, Richard de Sedefold, and raise the alarm. By that time the thieves were well away. Richard called a hue and cry in which all the neighbours joined to search for the villains, but no trace could be found of them, and the girls were too distressed to identify anyone.

At an inquest at the County Court on 13th May 1257 the Coroner, Geoffrey Rouland, passed a verdict of unlawful killing by felons unknown. Amongst those present in the court were nearly a dozen Stopsley people. These are some of the earliest names that we have for inhabitants of the village: Richard de Sedefold, Ralph North, John de la Hay, William of the Pit (*de puteo*), John Aeymere, Robert le Gaunter and Ralph Tebold.

The name of Alexander de Stoppesleye (who held the Manor of Stopsley) and his wife Matilda occurs in a *Calendar of Fines* for 3rd February 1306 - 'the Morrow of the Purification of the Blessed Mary'. The case, which is complicated, concerns the renting out of the land on the Manor of Clapham (near Bedford) which had been given to them as a wedding present by Matilda's parents. It was agreed that Simon de Baiocis and his wife Isabel could rent the land for life, on payment of a rose each Midsummer and by carrying out certain feudal services.

Early in the 14th century a national trade recession was having a detrimental effect on agriculture in Bedfordshire and this was particularly reflected in the prosperity of the larger towns. In 1309 Luton and its hamlets paid £19.18s. in tax, compared with Bedford at £20. 0s., Dunstable at £22. 4s. and Leighton at £18. 0s. In 1332 Luton's tax payment was the only one to have risen, to £21.17s.; whilst Bedford, Dunstable and Leighton had fallen to £19. 11s., £13. 13s., and £15. 10s. respectively. All the towns show a decline in the number of people required to pay tax: Luton from 163 to 112, Bedford 116 to 72, Dunstable 170 to 114 and Leighton 147 to 134. Some caution must be applied to these comparisons: Bedford and Dunstable were essentially trading centres; whereas the figures for Luton include its hamlets, as do those for Leighton (though excluding Stanbridge), and consequently a considerably larger area of agricultural land was involved.

In 1314 and 1315 there was a severe famine throughout England, the result of six successive years of bad harvest. Wheat cost an exorbitant 10 shillings a bushel. In London people were reduced to eating the flesh of dogs and horses. A number of people around Luton died of starvation. In 1316, in contrast, an early harvest resulted in wheat in Bedfordshire selling at 10 pence a bushel. The following year a murrain (or plague - perhaps foot-and-mouth disease) broke out amongst the cattle of the neighbourhood, and hundreds of beasts around Stopsley died.

Early in 1336 a fire started in one of the houses in Luton. Fanned by strong winds it rapidly spread through the closely spaced buildings of the town centre, where most of them were made of wood, and thatched with straw or reeds. Everything in its path was destroyed including barns and implements, seed and stock. In a short time several hundred families were made homeless. When Simon Croyser and Hugh del Croft, the tax assessors, visited the town in July 1336, they were instructed to give the inhabitants a respite until Michelmas Day (29th September) on account of the damage caused by the late fire. Four years later two hundred houses were still uninhabited, and about 720 acres of land (292 hectares) had not been cultivated. Faced with a catastrophe of this magnitude we can be certain that many of the homeless fled to stay with relatives and friends in the neighbouring hamlets of Biscot, Limbury and Stopsley. It is not hard to imagine the depredation and squalor that must have resulted when whole families, bereft of most of their possessions, tried to squeeze into already overcrowded and inadequate accommodation, or were forced to make temporary homes in barns and hedgerows.

Before the battle of Crecy in 1346 King Edward III instructed the Sheriff of Bedfordshire and Buckinghamshire to urgently command all those persons owning land worth more than a hundred shillings a year 'to have, at Portsmouth on the Sunday

in mid Lent next to be, men at arms, hobelars and bowmen, ready to set out with Us at Our charges.'

Failure to do so could involve forfeiture of life and limbs, land, goods and chattels. Hobelars were troops who travelled on horseback but fought on foot. The Bedfordshire list gave the names of eight landowners from the Luton area, including another Alexander de Stoppesle and Richard de Havering, both of whom were required to supply one bowman. We do not know who they sent, or whether the two men actually came from our village. If they did, and survived the victorious battle, one wonders what stories they told in Stopsley on their return. Roger de Loring of Luton and his cousin Sir Nigel Loring of Chalgrave near Toddington also took part in the battle of Crecy.

The French war was brought to a standstill in the autumn of 1347 when the bubonic plague, 'the Black Death', began to spread across western Europe. By the winter of 1348 it had reached London. It peaked in Bedfordshire between March and August of 1349 when about a third of the population died. Carried by fleas which inhabited black rats, it was always worst amongst the poor in congested towns where buildings were crowded together, and in Luton perhaps it killed a thousand people. There are no figures for Stopsley where it may have been a little under a hundred. The plague recurred on numerous occasions during the next two hundred years.

Boccaccio in *The Decameron* described the manifestation in Florence. People 'fell sick by their thousands...some died in the streets, some in their houses, and then only the smell of decomposition told others of their doom. There was no one to follow, no one to mourn, for men's lives were considered of no greater value than the beasts'. At St Albans more than forty monks died within a few weeks. The vicar of Luton, John de Luton, died at the beginning of 1349. His successor Andrew Power died suddenly during the autumn, and Richard de Rochelle who followed him, resigned before the end of the year. There are no burial registers or records to give us the names or numbers of those local folk that died, nor was there any consecrated ground in Stopsley in which to bury the dead. It was far too dangerous to carry the putrefying corpses to St Mary's churchyard in Luton for burial. In most cases plague victims were interred in communal pits. If these existed around Stopsley, they could have been anywhere away from habitation. None are known to have been found.

After the Black Death there was an enormous shortage of labour, creating a great demand for manpower. The peasantry were quick to take advantage of the situation. There is a record of two villeins from Streatley who took jobs in Luton for inflated wages and were prosecuted. Many peasants began to demand a better standard of living with higher wages, and a series of spontaneous revolts broke out in different parts of the country, including St Albans and Dunstable. Although most of these were put down, often with drastic punishments for the leaders: the peasants had made their strength felt. In many areas men siezed the strip fields of their dead neighbours and combined them with their own, until they grew large enough for them to employ labour and form a Yeoman class. This may well have happened in the Stopsley area where many of the strip fields seem to have disappeared at quite an early period.

When William Wenlock, a Canon of St Paul's and Master of Farley Hospital, died in 1392, he left benefactions to Luton Church, and various residents. Amongst these was Hugh de Stoppusley, to whom he left money and his black horse. His kinswoman, Dennis Stoppusley, he made his executrix. Bequests were also made to Hugh's four sons, including £6.13s.4d. to put Hugh's son, William de Stoppusley to school. It is known that Hugh owned a watermill, presumably on the Lea in Luton.

One of the most famous members of the Hay family of Hayes Manor and Hoo Barn (Manor Farm), Stopsley, was John Hay, who died in 1455. The *Return of the Gentry of Bedfordshire* of 1433 informs us that Johannes-atte-Hay, (John Hay) who was possibly a lawyer, was a great benefactor of St Mary's church in Luton, where he carried out major repair works, transforming its architecture from the Decorated to

Perpendicular styles, largely at his own expense. For thirty years he was the seneschal (or steward) of four successive Archbishops of Canterbury. After his burial in St Mary's, a tablet was placed in the north aisle commemorating his work, and also his two wives and three children.

The Guild of the Holy Trinity

Sir Thomas Rotherham was born in 1423 in Yorkshire and rose to become Archbishop of York in 1480 and a Cardinal. In 1468 he had been made Bishop of Lincoln, and on that accession had been granted the Manor of Luton and a number of other estates in Bedfordshire and Hertfordshire that had been forfeited by Lord Wenlock. On 12th May 1474 Bishop Rotherham obtained a Licence from King Edward IV allowing him to found a religious Guild in connection with St Mary's church in Luton. The Licence, which cost £72, was addressed to the Bishop and twelve other founder members of the Guild, who included Richard Stopisley, William Bradwey and John Welle, all of Stopsley.

The Guild of the Holy Trinity as it was called, was one of seventeen similar bodies in Bedfordshire, formed, in order that every day two priests would say masses for the souls of its members, both living and dead. It would help those brethren who fell sick, had fallen on hard times or were too old to work. Members were also expected to contribute funds for the upkeep of a school, (though here is doubt as to whether this materialised). The Guild was administered by a Master and two Wardens who were elected annually on the Feast of St Michael the Archangel (29th September). Social activities were held in a Guild Hall known as 'Brothersed House' which stood at the corner of Castle Street and George Street, Luton, where the *Red Lion* stands today. Membership was for life, and the Brethren consisted of men, their wives and sometimes their children. The beautifully illuminated *Register* of the Guild, containing more than 6,000 names, collected between 1474 and 1546, is preserved in Luton Museum.

Amongst the names recorded in the *Guild Register* are Richard Stoppesley, who was chosen as Master of the Guild for 1484. Ordinary members from Stopsley included: 1474 Richard Stopisley and Agnes his wife; 1475 Edward Hylle; 1492 Richard Stoppusley, son of Richard; 1495 Simon Hylle and Margaret his wife; 1501 Thomas Stoppusley, and Richard and Margaret his parents, deceased. 1509 Henry Stoppustey and Parnell his wife; 1514 John Sawnder and Joan his wife; 1516 Thomas Gaunfilde and Joan his wife; 1519 Thomas Hylle and Anne his wife; 1521 Richard Lonsdale; 1525 Joan Stoppisley, spinster; 1528 Valentine Stoppysley; Margaret Stoppisley, spinster; 1530 Robert Grauley; William Beche and Margaret; John Jak and Margaret; 1531 Richard Stoppisley and Elizabeth of Luton; 1533 John Cooke and Agnes. 1544 Agnes Stoppysley wife of John. From Ramridge came: 1475 William Ramrige and Alice his wife; John Ramrige and Joan his wife; and fourteen other entries. From Crawley Green: 1514 Cudyffe Crawley; 1531 John Nures, bachelor, and many others.

Events of national history seldom disturbed the quiet of Stopsley, though it did happen once more in February 1461. During the Wars of the Roses, the Lancastrian army, led by Queen Margaret of Anjou, passed across the north of the parish as they marched along the Icknield Way from Royston to Dunstable on 16th February. The following day they fought the second Battle of St Albans, where Margaret defeated

Richard Neville 'the Kingmaker', and liberated her husband, Henry VI. Sadly for her, she failed to capture London and achieve a final victory.

Sir Samuel Starling

Although he was probably Stopsley's most colourful son, Samuel Starling was also one of its most elusive. He claimed to have been born in Stopsley about 1628, although no records have been found that record his baptism, or that of his two brothers and three sisters. His family also held property in Whitechapel, London, and it is there that they grew up.

Samuel's father, also called Samuel, may have started his working life in Luton, perhaps in the Malting industry. By the time of young Samuel's birth, he was a member of 'The Worshipful Company and Mysterie of Brewers', and seems to have owned a Malthouse and Brewhouse in Parrett Alley, Whitechapel. He became Master of the Brewers' Company in 1655. There is some difficulty in tracing the movements of the Starlings since they often used the surname Starnoll and also Sterling. It may have survived as the local name Stronell.

Samuel junior was apprenticed to his father in September 1640, when he was about twelve or thirteen years old. In 1643 he entered Cambridge University, where he remained for three years. As a Royalist he refused to take the Covenant in 1645 and, the following year, left the University without a degree. For four years from April 1646 he attended Grays Inn, but could not be admitted to the Bar since he utterly refused to subscribe to the 'cursed Ingagement'.

About 1650 he married Mary Garford, daughter of Richard Garford, a stationer in Holy Trinity Minories in the City of London: again no record of the marriage can be traced. A 'settlement before marriage' between Samuel and Mary, dated May 1649, (and now in the Bedfordshire County Record Office) shows that their parents each gave about £1,000 towards the purchase of an estate for the young couple, with land scattered around Luton. In June 1652 Samuel paid Francis Crawley (son and heir of Sir Francis Crawley) £1,080 for another estate which was largely at Chiltern Green, and included Gillhams Farm. The latter was occupied by Edward Wilson, who remained the tenant for the next twenty years. The sale also included the Manor of Hayes at Stopsley which had been 'lately occupied' by Richard Lacey senior. Research suggests that this may have been the Captain Richard Lacey who served in Colonel Hollis's Regiment and fought on the Parliamentary side under Robert, Earl of Essex, the Captain General, during the Civil War. As well as the estate in Luton, Starling also owned property in Enfield and a town house near Samuel Pepys in Seething Lane, London.

Samuel worked with his father in their London Brewery, and in October 1647 was admitted to the Brewers' Company. His father died in 1661 and was buried in St Mary's Church, Luton on 15th June. Two months later on 21st August 1661 'Samuel Starnoll, Alderman and Sheriff Elect for the City of London' was sworn in, as Master of the Brewers' Company.

With the restoration of the monarchy in 1660 Starling began to take a more active part in the affairs of the City, and gave much of his time to its administration; being rewarded with a knighthood on 21st October 1667. Samuel Pepys thought less favourably of him. Writing in his *Diary* of the misery and havoc caused by the Great Fire of London, he recorded on 8th September 1666:

'Then to Sir W. Batten's, and took my brother with me, and there dined with a great company of neighbours, and much good discourse; among others of the low spirits of some rich men in the City, in sparing any encouragement to the poor people that wrought for the saving their houses. Among others, Alderman Starling, a very rich man, without children, the fire at next door to him in our lane, after our men had saved his house, did give 2s.6d [one penny each] among thirty of them, and did quarrel with some that would remove the rubbish out of the way of the fire, saying that they come to steal.'

On the feast of St Simon and St Jude, October 28th, 1669, Sir Samuel Starling became Lord Mayor and Chief Magistrate of the City of London. It was normal at that time for the Lord Mayor to come from one of the twelve great Livery Companies. Since the Brewers' was not one of these, he translated to the Drapers' Company early in 1669. They would have borne the expenses of the Lord Mayor's show or pageant, of which few details survive. We know that it cost £271.13s.6d. It would normally have been much more, but owing to the Plague and the Fire 'the inauguration of the City Magistrate' wrote F.W. Fairholt (1843) 'was thrown on its beams.'

Starling moved to Guiltspurr Street on the western side of the city, where he could better entertain his fellow Aldermen. In due course he was elected to the office of Master Draper.

There is no direct evidence to tell if Samuel actually visited Stopsley and lived at Hayes Manor during the period of his Mayorality. It would be quite reasonable to imagine Mary coming to stay there whilst the great Plague raged in London. Certainly he paid tax on eight hearths in the manor house in 1671.

The Starlings had no children, but Samuel made provision for his many relations, especially his nephews and nieces. It has been estimated that at the time of his death in Enfield, in August 1674, his estate was valued at around £40,000. He arranged for the bulk of his property, including Hayes Manor, to be administered by the Brewers' Company. As by right, his body lay overnight in the Drapers' Hall. On the following day, the 27th August, the funeral procession, accompanied by the Master, Wardens. livery and almsmen, made its way to All Hallows-by-the-Tower for the burial.

All Hallows, Barking, was almost totally destroyed by enemy action in 1940. To-day, only a small, faded piece of glass set into a window in the north aisle, survives to commemorate him. It bear the arms granted in 1661 to "Samuel Starling of the hamlet of Stoppesley in the parish of Luton in the County of Bedford: Argent, on a bend azure three square buckles or" (three gold buckles on a blue diagonal, on a white background).

The Hayes estate passed to Samuel's brother, Richard, and then to Richard's daughter Jane, who was his 'heir general'. In 1693 she married Anthony Ettrick of Bishop Wearmouth, and they lived at Hayes Manor until her death in 1700. Ettrick remarried and sold the property to Benjamin Morris of Buntingford in 1716. John Morris Ashforth sold it to Colonel George Sowerby of Putteridge Bury about 1866.

The Growing Parish

At the beginning of the 17th century Luton seems to have been a flourishing little town with some good houses, an important corn market and a well-established malting industry. Many of the larger houses in the main street, including a number owned by minor members of the Crawley family, had malthouses attached to them, in which they could produce their own ale.   Stopsley farmers would have supplied them with quantities of barley, helping to provide work for many of the townsfolk in some sixty separate malthouses.   We know that Anne Spufford's house at Stopsley had a malthouse in the 1630s.   It should be remembered that ale had been the most important family drink for centuries.   It was often much safer than well water.

In 1618 a number of the smaller householders in the centre of Luton began to divide their large houses into tenements, or replace them with a number of smaller cottages, which they let to poor tenants, usually with large families and little chance of employment.   This may have been a partially philanthropic act to provide urgently needed accommodation for the poor.   However, it caused an outcry from two of the principal landowners in Luton, Sir Robert Napier of Luton Hoo and Francis Crawley, who saw the problems of bringing too many unemployed people into the town.   They petitioned the Lords of the Privy Council to intervene.   Unfortunately, we do not know the outcome of the petition.   The document still exists listing the names of the properties concerned and their nineteen owners.   One of these was William Howe of Cowridge End, Stopsley (and a cousin of Francis Crawley), who 'depopulated a fayre howse' and turned it into a cottage.   That he genuinely cared for the poor is shown by his Will; when he died ten years later he left a gift of 10 shillings to be distributed amongst 30 poor widows of Luton.

We do not know what effect the Civil War had on the common people of Stopsley. Only the names of major land holders, like the staunchly royalist Crawleys, occur in official records.   Even so, there were many lesser members of the Crawley family living in and around Stopsley and Luton, and their senior brethrens' allegiance to the Crown must to some extent have rubbed off on them.

Thomas Crawley of Someries and Nether Crawley had died in 1629 and his property passed to his son Francis, who had been made a Serjeant-at-law in 1623 and knighted by Charles I a month later.   He was one of the twelve judges who advised the impecunious King on the legality of imposing a Ship Money tax in peacetime.   In the Long Parliament of November 1640 the Commons proceeded to impeach Sir Francis and five other judges who had advised the King on the legality of the Ship Money.   Fortunately for Sir Francis the impeachment was not pressed to a conclusion at that time.   On New Year's Day 1643 whilst Sir Francis was at Someries, he received a summons to join the King in Oxford: the Civil War had begun and the King must be obeyed.   In November 1645 Parliament decreed that Sir Francis Crawley and four other judges should 'cease from being Judges as though they were dead.'   Sir Francis and his son (another Francis), his cousin John Crawley of Falconer's Hall, and Sir Robert Napier at Luton Hoo were all classed as 'delinquents' by Parliament and their estates were sequestrated.   For some months these were occupied by Roundhead troops.   Lady Crawley, left alone at Someries, was in particular subjected to great inconvenience and considerable expense.

After the surrender of Oxford in 1646 Sir Francis Crawley was permitted to return to Someries where he immediately began to petition for compensation and the return of all his property, which included 'divers messuages, lands and tenements, lying and being in Eaten Greene Farme, Nether Crawley ..... and Ramridge End.'   John Crawley of Falconer's Hall died at the beginning of 1645 and was buried on 3rd January inside St Mary's church at Luton.   He left his estate to his son John, but it seems to have been almost immediately transferred to Sir Francis Crawley, since in a deed dated October 1647 he, in turn, gave it to his 27 year old son, yet another Francis Crawley, probably on the occasion of his marriage to Mary Clutterbuck of London. No further references to the Crawleys at Falconer's Hall occur after that date.

The burial of John Crawley, mentioned above, may have been a cause of some friction between the Revd. Samuel Austin, newly appointed by Parliament, and the Crawley family who desired to have him buried inside the church, and the Prayer-book service for the dead read over him. Samuel Austin seems to have found the parish fiercely divided between supporters of the King and of the Commonwealth, and his position rapidly became untenable. He resigned the living after only a few months.

The great schism that developed in the parish continued for a further sixteen years, during the incumbencies of the next three 'intruded' ministers, Thomas Attwood Rotherham, Mr Carey and Thomas Jessop. The Crawleys again caused problems in 1650 when Lady Crawley, widow of Judge Crawley, died and the family wanted her buried in the Someries Chapel at St Mary's, and the *Book of Common Prayer* service for the dead read over her body. When Thomas Jessop refused permission, her younger son Thomas Crawley called the Vicar 'a scoundrell, a jacke and a clown', and forced entry into the church and read the burial service himself. Mr Jessop petitioned Cromwell's Council and the sergeant-at-arms was ordered to take Thomas Crawley into custody. The event was overtaken by the death of Cromwell, and nothing more is recorded of the affair.

With the Restoration Mr Jessop was replaced in 1660 by Thomas Pomfret, an episcopally ordained clergyman. By then the Commonwealth had stamped its mark on the future of worship in southern Bedfordshire. Cromwell had repealed those statutes which made attendance at the parish church obligatory each Sunday. Many Luton folk flocked to Kensworth to hear the preaching of Edward Harrison, a charismatic leader, who rejected infant baptism and preached that the church must consist only of believers. Thus was the Baptist movement born in south Bedfordshire.

In 1655 George Fox, the founder of the Society of Friends (the Quakers), visited John Crook at his house in Park Square, Luton, and met with a number of local gentry to discus 'God's eternal truth.'. Three years later the first yearly meeting of the Society of Friends was held at Beckerings Park, Crook's country estate near Ridgmont. The gathering, which lasted three days, was so large that the assembly had to meet in the orchard. It was some time before a Meeting House was registered in Luton, but meetings in private houses flourished.

With the Restoration came a period of persecution for those who dissented from the Church of England. Toleration did not come until 1689. The Baptists weathered the storm, and came through strongly into the twentieth century. In Stopsley they have held their own for 180 years. The Quakers, with land holdings in Stopsley, have been represented at the Luton Meeting since the beginning of the 18th century. Both groups were to have considerable influence on the development of Luton in the 18th and 19th centuries.

There has been an obligation for parishes to provide men, weapons and equipment for the defence of the realm since Anglo-Saxon times. By the 17th century such troops were only called together when there was local unrest or a fear of foreign invasion. After the Restoration in 1660 threats of rebellion led to the passing of a number of Militia Acts. In Bedfordshire, Huntingdonshire and Cambridgeshire a militia horse, consisting of 8 companies of some 60 men each, under one commander, was set up. A permanent peace-keeping force of some 20 men from each county was also formed. Only one Bedfordshire muster roll from about the year1683 survives and has recently been transcribed by Nigel Lutt. Under *Flitt Hundred Militia Foote, Capt.*

Palmers Company are listed 53 men from the Hundred. Stopsley was required to provide 3 muskets and 2 corslets (light half-armour for the upper body including an open helmet). The five men enlisted from the village were Thomas How, Thomas Smith, William How, Thomas Piggott and Nicholas Taylor.

It is difficult to try and imagine the number of people who were living in Stopsley by the middle of the 17th century. Small isolated groups of dwellings were scattered through a parish that covered about six square miles. One way that we can try to get an idea of the size of the larger properties in the community is by looking at the Hearth Tax returns which are available for 1671. From 1662 to 1688 Parliament imposed an insidious tax on domestic heating. 'Every dwelling and other house, edifice and all lodgings ..... shall be chargeable for every firehearth and stove the sum of two shillings by the yeare', payable in two half yearly instalments on Lady Day and at Michelmas. Anyone whose property was valued at less than 20 shillings per year was exempt. Householders were responsible for providing the parish Constable with an accurate list of the number of hearths in their houses, and the Constable was responsible for collecting the tax. He had the power to confiscate goods from any householder who refused to pay. Later, specially appointed Collectors or 'chimney men' took over, but the Constables still assisted in the inspections and confiscations. They often suffered violence and abuse, which was punishable by a month's imprisonment. If stuffed-up chimneys were discovered the householders were taxed double.

In 1671 Stopesley [*sic*] was inspected by a Collector called William Staunton, accompanied by John Dyer, the village Constable. The head of every household was listed. Of fifty-two householders, forty-four were taxed and eight qualified for exemption. If we assume an average of 5 persons per household we can estimate a population of around 260. That is almost certainly an underestimate. The major householder in the parish was Sir Francis Crawley at Someries who had 23 hearths, (for comparison Luton Hoo had 60 and Wrest Park 52). Sir Samuel Starling at Hayes Manor had 8 hearths, as did William Kilby. Farmer Thomas Pigott, Richard Wackett, Richard Lacy and Daniel Burt each had 5 hearths. Four houses are recorded with 4 hearths, six with 3, four with 2 and the remaining twenty-three with 1 each. William Staunton drew up the register and John Dyer added his mark, a 'K', signifying both that the document was correct and, incidentally, that the Constable, not surprisingly, was illiterate and unable to write his name. He was honest enough to declare that he had 2 hearths! The Hearth Tax was repealed in 1688 as an act of grace on the accession of William and Mary.

HEARTH TAX RETURN FOR STOPSLEY: 1671
(preceded by number of hearths)

1	John Ward	1	Widow Farr	1	Edw. Sevaine
1	Fra. Pigott	5	Ric. Wackett	1	Will. Rolfe
1	John Streete	1	Edw. Wells	1	Will Beane
5	Tho. Pigott	3	Will. How	2	Widow Beane
1	Geo. Sanders	4	Tho. Jaques		(Noe Distres)
2	John Dyer	1	Will. Goodwin	1	Widow Holmes
4	Widow Gazeley	1	Widow Groome	1	Geo. Collins
1	Widow Cotton	3	Tho. How	1	Widow Young
1	Ric. Moores	1	John Welsh	1	Fra. Curtis
3	Edw. Roberts	3	Geo. Clarke	5	Ric. Lacy

1	Will. Young	1	Ric Streete	5	Dan. Burt
1	Ralph How	2	Will. Waple	4	Tho. Smith
3	Widow How	2	Will. Day	8	Will. Kilby
1	Nic. Taylor	1	Rob. Brewer	3	Will Crawley
4	Edward. [sic]	8	Sir Sam. Starling		

23   Summeris in the occupacion of Francis Crawley Esqr.

[Sum of the hearths - 124]

Discharged by Certificate from paying Hearth Tax

1	Rob. Norman	1	Ric. Waple	1	Widow Ward
1	John Tyler	1	John Whittamore	1	Widow Farey
1	Rob.Gilbert	2	John Day		

In his study of *The Rural Population of Bedfordshire, 1671-1921*, (1934), L.M. Marshall uses the above figures to estimate the population of Stopsley in 1671 as 221. Although a number of the people listed are widows and presumably some widowers, this figure seems to the present author to be too small.

Chapter 4

Some Stopsley Wills: 1526 - 1844

Some seventy wills made by former Stopsley folk are preserved in the County Record Office at Bedford. Each begins with the name of the testator (the maker of the will) and his or her place of abode, followed by the date when the will was made and later proved. All the earlier ones begin with a religious preamble, of which the following example, made in 1602 by William Bigg, one of the sons of Richard Bigg, a yeoman of Stopsley, is typical:-

> 'I leave my Soul to almighty God, beseeching mercy to receive the same, trusting that by and thro' the only precious death and passion of our Lord and Saviour, only to be saved and thereby to have and enjoy eternal life for ever and my body to be buried in the earth in the hope of resurrection at the coming of our Lord and saviour Christ to judgement.'

In almost all cases the testators could expect to be buried in the churchyard of St Mary's church in Luton. In a surprisingly large number of cases the testators asked to be buried *inside* Luton church, something that would have proved quite expensive. Since no records survive of these earlier internal graves, we do not know if they got their wishes. In 1519 John Crawley asked to be buried in Luton church near his father, and requested his executors to buy two marble stones, one for his father and one for him 'to ly over us'. Richard Laudisdale (1526) specified burial 'within the north Ile', and Elizabeth Longe (1636) of Scourge End (Round Green) asked to be buried in the church as near her husband as possible. Edmund Clark, also of Scourge End, (1649) particularly requested burial in the chancel of Luton church, a position involving considerable expense and normally reserved for persons of particular importance.

Spiritual legacies involving gifts to St Mary's church and the diocesan cathedral at Lincoln normally took the form of money. When Thomas Shelbourne of Stopsley died in 1533 he left 'to the mother church of Lincoln cathedral' 2 pence, and to the high altar of Luton 12 pence. He went on to request '3 masses on his burial day and 3 masses on his month day'. Elizabeth Long, a Stopsley widow who died in 1550 left 2 pence to Lincoln, and 'to the high altar for tithes forgotten the price of a bushel of malt'. Richard Laudisdale (1526) asked his executors 'to bryng my bodie to Cristen buryall to kepe my monethis mynd yere mynd* and to pay my dettes and to kepe an honest prest a quarter of a yere to syng and pray for me and such other of my frendes as I am specially bowndyn to pray for and otherwise to dispose for my sowle as they shall thynk most expedient in tyme comyng'. *[requiem masses celebrated on the 30th day after burial and a year after the same]. Richard Crawley (1578) left a mark (6s.8d.) for repairs to the church roof.

It was customary for the well-off to leave money for the poor of Luton and 'to every poore body in Stoppesley wiche be howseholders 4 pence a piece' (Elizabeth Long, 1551). John Crawley of Plenties (Lane Farm) instructed his son in 1519 to keep an obit for his grandparents and father with the whole choir of Luton church, and to distribute 6s 8d to the poor for twelve years. Francis Bigge (1596) left 'to poor of Stopsley 12 pence each to everie one of them which my father used at Christmas to give grayne unto', and in 1555 Christopher Piggot left 'to every one of my pore naybors in Stopysley a bushell of Barlye a pece where most nede is.' William Bigg (1602) left 12 pence a house to the poor of Stopsley, Robert Little (1656) left 40 shillings to the poor of the hamlet of Stopsley, and Thomas Jacques (1676) 'to poor neighbours at Stopsley 20 shillings.' In 1628 William Howe of Cowridge End left 'to 30 poor widows of Luton 10 shillings among them to be distributed by Mr Bird, vicar of Luton who is also to be my executor. To Mr Bird 5 shillings to preach at my burial.'

Alan Cirket in his Bedfordshire Historical Record Society book *English Wills, 1498-1526* points out that modern wills have evolved from two separate legal documents: the testament and the will. In a will a person (the *testator*) regulated the disposal of his land and property, whilst his testament was concerned with debts and the disposal of personal goods and chattels.

Although the testators all lived in Stopsley, it is seldom possible to pin them down to precise locations. Mixes Hill, Falconer's Hall, White Hill, Plenties and Cowridge End are all mentioned, but the actual houses have long been removed. Occasionally a field name can be identified, such as Darley in Putteridge Road, or John Sibley's five acres at Ramridge End (north of Sibley Close). Others are intriguing: there is mention of pasture called Butts Close with a barn on it, in 1660. This was presumably where the local men practised their archery (a statutory requirement for men between the ages of 16 and 60 until the mid 17th century). No trace of the small man-made hill or butt has been recognised today. Bartholomew How (1665) owned Red Crosse Close containing 5 acres, and probably between present day Deep Denes and Moreton Road near Round Green. The name may be a corruption of Red Croft. How also owned a field called Oxse, now the south-eastern end of Stopsley High School playing field.

The testator's house and land was usually left to his wife or eldest son. In 1551 Richard Crawley left 'to son William the house testator lives in called 'Plenties' (Lane Farm) with all land. To wife Joan £40 and her chamber, to live with William until he is of age.' In 1621 Peter Stringer left 'to son John Stringer house and land at Stopesley after death of testator's wife Elizabeth.' Christopher Pigott (1555) left all his houses and lands in the town and fields of Luton to his son Thomas, clearly indicating that his land was scattered amongst the open fields. Similarly William Howe (1628) includes 'an acre of land in Bridgefield next to the highway leading from Luton to Stopsley,' and 'a half acre of land in Sewell field'. When Anne (Agnes) Spufford, a spinster, died in 1639, she left her house and land in Stopsley to her two godsons on their reaching the age of 14. One hopes that it proved an harmonious division:-

> 'To godson Abraham Dickes 'all that parte of my dwellinge howse in Stopeslye ..... which is lofted over. That part of the kichin extendinge from the greate beame goeing over the middle therof towards the entrye. The Haule howse and three Loftes over the same togither with the foryard and the Little barne standing at the further side of the sayd foryard (next adioyninge to the Pare tree wicke [field] and alsoe the one halfe of the orchard to lye next unto the Partree wicke ..... also that close of arable land lying in Stopesly commonly called Grove Close'.

'To godson William Beane 'the other part of my house in Stopsley aforesaid, viz. the Maulte howse, maulte shoppe, kyllhowse [*malt house, malt shop, kiln*] togither with the Gardner next to the Kinges Highewaye and that part of the kytchin next unto the killhowse to the Great beame goeing over the same and also that part of the orchard lyeing next unto the wicke adioyning over the same.' '....the part of the orchard adjoining the Maulte howse and also the Wicke which is now sown with wheat and contains 4 acres.'

The references to the malthouse, malt shop and kiln assure us that Stopsley, like Luton, was growing rich on barley for malt. Malting was a common profession for women on a small domestic scale.

In some cases husbands left property to their wives provided that they did not remarry. Richard Bigge (died 1597) left 'Nothing to wife Alice if she remarries except £50' and a lengthy list of household 'goods she brought with her', but 'if Alice does not remarry she shall have a Chamber and meat and drink' in the farmhouse left to his sons William and Thomas. There were no such conditions for Dorothy, wife of John Day, (died 1645) who was 'to have the use of one chamber over the Hall for her natural life with right of ingress and egress through the Hall' and 'to take the benefitt of the Fier in the Hall when she please'.

Frequently money was left for children and grandchildren on their coming of age or marriage, 'To Mary Gazeley £50 at age 21 or marriage day.' 'If William How reaches his full age he to pay his sister Elizabeth £20 when she reaches age 21.' 'To Catherine How's great-granddaughter Elizabeth Heath ... £10 at age 21, a gold ring, a large silver spoon, three teaspoons, half my linen and the corner cupboard and all that is in it at the time of my decease,' (i.e. 1748). Christopher Pigott (1555) left 'to son Christopher 40 sheep 'as they runne' and 20 quarters of Barley, these to remain in his mother's hands until he comes to the age of discretion.' In order to have enough money to look after her son until he came of age, John Crawley (1660) gave permission for his wife Elizabeth to fell some of the trees on his land in Stopsley. John Ward (1721) wrote: 'I doe desire my said wife Frances to doe what she can conveniently part with towards the maintenance of my daughter Alice and no more.'

In 1722 Thomas Butterfield was at pains to make provision for the welfare of his handicapped son, charging his wife Sarah for life 'for and towards the support and maintenance of Thomas Butterfield, my son, being imperfect in his senses,' then on her death leaving 'his friends John Bigg of White Hill in Luton, gent. and John Chalkley, brickmaker in trust for support of his son Thomas, during his natural life.'

Richard Jakes was charged to look after his grandfather in 1547, paying him 20 pence a week for as long as he lived, providing as much firewood as he needed and caring for the old man's mylche cow. Richard Crawley remembered 'Everyone who is or has been a yearly servant 12 pence if they come to fetch it.'

Thomas Pigott's wife Judith was to receive £100 and all the goods she brought in her dowry, 'my biggest chest standing in the parlor whear I doe lye, my standing bedsteed wherin I doe use to lye, with all fringes belonging unto it, my best cover lid, a pair of my best blankets, my best fether bed, my best mattrice, a pair of my best sheets, my best boulster, ij (2) of my best pillows and the vallance and curtains'.

One of the most interesting bequests was made by Richard Crawley to his favourite daughter Alice in 1551 of 'an honest brydcarte'. This appears to be by far the earliest recorded reference in Britain to what the *Oxford English Dictionary* refers to as a 'bridewain', a northern dialect word for a cart or wagon on which a bride's 'providing' or dowry was sent from her father's house to that of her bridegroom. A chest was placed on the cart containing her 'providing', her 'bottom drawer' and her wedding presents. The *Dictionary* quotes the example of a cart in Lancashire that was surmounted by a spinning wheel decorated with blue ribbons. One can imagine the stir such a cart would have caused as it rattled along the rutted lanes of Stopsley, from the Crawley's house at 'Plenties' (Lane Farm in Putteridge Road) to Alice's new home. It is interesting to note that none of the examples quoted in the *Dictionary* are earlier that 1800. This seems to be a Stopsley custom that took 250 years to creep north from the more inventive south.

It is just possible that Alice Crawley married Richard Bigge (died 1597) mentioned above. If that were the case then some of those 'goods she brought with her' may have travelled in the bridecart. These included 'a cupboard ..., the great chest in the parlour, the great coffer and little coffer by the door in the loft which she brought with her, a dozen pewter platters, a brass pot, a brass pan, 4 candlesticks (2 pewter and 2 latten), 2 salt cellars, the bedstead in the loft, the feather bed she brought with her, 2 mattresses, 2 bolsters, 2 pillows, testator's best coverlet, 2 blankets, 6 pairs best sheets, 2 pair pillow beres, 6 table napkins, 2 tablecloths, one of best towels, the second best cow, a spit, a pair of cob-irons, 3 cushions, 2 joined stools, 6 hens and a cock, 6 ducks and one drake.'

In 1628 William Howe of Coweridge End farm left his eldest son Thomas 'the joined standing bedstead in the chamber over the Hall, and all the benches, bench boards, painted cloths and hangings in the Hall, and also 'my Longe Ladder'. Examples of similar painted cloths and wall hangings, 'poor mens' tapestries', rescued from a house in Church Street, Luton, are now displayed in Wardown Park museum. Howe also left his son William his Bible, and his loving daughter Alice Cocke ' a book titled *Mr Barrowes meathod of visicke.'* This would have been *The methode of the phisicke, conteyning the causes, signes and cures on inward diseases in mans body from the head to the foote* by Philip Barrough, first published in 1583, and reissued without many changes until 1652. By possessing such a book Alice would have found herself the village's medical authority! In 1696 widow Susanna Groome left her granddaughter one great brass pot, one great kettle, one little kettle and a warming pan.

Susanna Groome also left clothes to her daughter-in-law Ann Groome 'one green Hodde, one greene Cotte, one brown Cullerd cloth waskotte.' In 1705 Mary Chalton received from her grandmother Mary Burt, her 'best gold ring, a feather bed, 2 feather bolsters, 3 feather pillows, 'six yards of Flanders Lace, stuff for a Gown and Petticoat not made up, a silk faradine Petticoat and my best laced handkercher and my best plain handkercher.' Another grandchild, Sarah Chalton, received her other gold ring, next best gown, 3 petticoats, black silk scarff with rest of linen and wearing apparell. In 1526 Richard Laudisdale left his best coat, sword and buckler to Richard Crawley. Fifty years later Laudisdale's godson, another Richard Crawley, gave his brother William his 'chamlett Jackett, green silk doublet and a quarter of barley.' In 1602 William Bigg left his russet cloak to William Cartwright (John Crawley's shepherd). More unusual is the case of William Wattes, described as a labourer, who in 1618 was sufficiently literate to write his own will, and leave his son Thomas his best doublet, sword and dagger, a pewter platter and 2 shillings. Edward Greene, (1739) one of the early Stopsley Baptists, endeavoured to be equally fair to each of his sons, leaving one his watch, another his gold ring, a third his silver buckles, and the youngest 'half a guinea to buy a pair of shoe buckles'.

Early photographs of Stopsley show an ample supply of elm trees. As timber these have always proved a valuable source of wealth to the village for building, furniture, carts, etc. However, they had to be treated with care. Joan Crawley, at 'Plenties', (Lane Farm) was cautioned by her husband John in 1519 'to make no wast of tymber'. When Richard Bigge died in 1597 he bequeathed large quantities of wood to his sons John and Robert, leaving both 'an elm plank to make him a table' and 100 foot of elm board lying in the hovel at the gate.

As well as his house and lands, John Crawley (1660) left his son Thomas 'the table and cupboard in the hall, and the great cast iron cauldron in the chechen, (kitchen).' The widow Elizabeth How left her daughter Elizabeth 'one presse Cobert that stanes in the Halle and one Bedstead and Curtenes and Valnens and feather bead and all of the beden belongen to that bead and one Joyned Chest and all my linen excepten three pare of sheattes.' Francis Young left Thomas, his son, his Great Chest in 1723.

Many of the people represented in their wills were reasonably wealthy farmers, or what today we might call small-holders. Consequently agricultural implements and animals are frequently mentioned. It is a noticeable sign of wealth that horses and horse equipment, and never oxen, are frequently recorded. John Crawley, in the earliest will, dated 1519, left each of his daughters, Joan and Alice, 20 sheep 'owt of the wolle' (after shearing). Thomas Shelbourne (1533) left his wife Clemens a plough and carts, horses and harnesses for husbandry; half his beasts and sheep and all his 'fellwoll that ys in spening with all the cloth'. In 1660 Peter Prudden's son Peter received a red cow bullock, and William Camfeeld 'a ewe sheep of the best sort'. Eleven years later Richard Dyer could only offer his three daughters 'one swarme of bees each, after the death of my wife', with the footnote 'provided if the bees stand sufficient to discharge them or ells not'. William How (1628) left his 3 grandchildren a 'wendling' calfe to be bred up by their father (probably a weaning calf). John Day of Crawley Green left two horses, dungcarts, carts and ploughs and implements to his son John in 1645. The village blacksmith in 1736, Thomas Love, left 'much of the stock and tools in the blacksmith's trade as shall amount to £14' to his son Edward. Both Francis Pigott (1745) and Thomas Surrey (1750) bequeathed their farming stock and implement to their sons. A later Francis Pigott of White Hill (1837) left all horses used for farming purposes and all wagons, carts, ploughs and other implements of husbandry, and all household furniture, plate, linen, books, china and glass to his wife for life.

Although it is clear that sons take precedence over daughters, and unborn males over females, the divisions are seldom very marked in the Stopsley wills. It was clearly expected that all daughters would marry, although quite a number did not do so. In many cases girls received a lump sum 'at day of marriage'.

When all legacies had been paid and 'all debts forgiven' the residue was usually left to the executors and trustees. These were usually friends of the testator, and it was quite usual for them to receive a small gift for their services. 'William Chawkley of Cruchmore 10 shillings and a pair of gloves'. 'Thomas Browne of Crawley Green, gent. to whom pair of gloves'. Catherine How's trustees included Richard Brown of Luton, a maltster and Quaker, and Charles Pryor, a Stopsley farmer. They were instructed to sell the residue, and to pay half the product to Richard Turner of Scourge End, a weaver, and then to invest the other half and pay the interest to Catherine's sister Martha Litchfield, exclusive of her husband, who was not to benefit in any way.

The witnesses to the will were also usually friends of the testator, priests, servants or visitors present when the will was being prepared. The presence of a priest as a witness is usually denoted by the polite use of 'sir' (with a small 's') before his name. e.g. 'sir Richard Fissher, sir Robert Bysshope'. Occasionally the testator wrote his or her own will, but more often this was done by a clergyman or professional scrivener. Examples include 'John Atwood, scrivener; Robert Steppinge, scrivener; Francis Olney the writer hereof;' and in the case of William Wattes 'In wittnes whereof I have written it with my owne hande the 9th daie of September Anno 1618 by me William Wattes'.

N.B. Dates in brackets in this chapter indicate the year that the Will was proved, and not necessarily the year in which it was written or that the testator died.

IXa: Green Farm stood beside the village Green at the rear of the present Elf Garage .   Of brick and timber construction, the house probably dated from the early 17th century.   A large farmyard at the rear was surrounded by barns.   A long hedged vegetable garden fronted onto the Hitchin Road.   The Farm had ceased to operate as a viable unit by about 1910.   (*Ellen Barber: Author's Collection*)

IXb and c: It is ironic that the oldest known photographs of Stopsley residents should be of prisoners in Bedford gaol.   These photographs, amongst the first to be taken by any prison (in 1867), show Levi Welch (aged 40) of Green Farm, who was charged with highway robbery at Round Green, and his son Reuben (aged 17) charged with theft of a double barrelled gun in Luton.   (*Bedfordshire and Luton Archives and Record Service*)

Xa: *The Sportsman* in 1938, with the Methodist Chapel and War Memorial.   This is Stopsley's oldest surviving public house, and dates from the 1830s, when James Darley was the first recorded innkeeper.   Like the other Stopsley public houses, it was given a face lift by its owners, J. W. Green's, in the 1930s, when the bay windows were added.   (*Author's Collection*)

Xb: A young man with a horse and cart outside *The Sportsman* and Wesleyan Chapel around the turn of the century.   The cart has solid iron wheels and seems to consist of an iron body.   It was possibly a water cart, though it appears to be rather small.   It could have been connected with the drought of 1898 when all the village wells ran dry.   (*John Grayson*)

XIa: Elizabeth Hucklesby's Store and Post Office in Bury Road (13 St Thomas' Road). Elizabeth was the Sub-Postmistress for Stopsley until her death in 1910. She left the shop to her niece Sarah, who ran it with her husband Percy Smith Kime. This photograph was probably taken during the 1st World War, and shows Percy standing in the doorway with a telegram boy. (*Luton News*)

XIb and c: Rags and riches. William Boasting, foreman of the scything gang at Manor Farm, about 1902 when he was 71. Although born in Streatley, for most of his adult life he lived in a cottage at Butterfield's Green, with his wife Mary. Asher J. Hucklesby, born in Stopsley in 1845, became Luton's leading hat manufacturer, and Mayor of Luton on five occasions. He lived in *The Chase* at Round Green for some years. (Boasting: *Helen Farr;* Hucklesby: *Luton Museum*)

XIIa: The south front of Putteridge Bury House in 1966. The building has altered little since it was built for Thomas Clutterbuck between 1908-11, although outhouses and stables to the left (out of the picture), were replaced in 1968 by a refectory for the College of Education. (*James Dyer*)

XIIb: A water-colour painting of Home Farm, Putteridge Bury, at the end of the 19th century. Today the house has been divided into three separate dwellings. On the right is the dovecote with its louvered roof-turret (now missing). All the buildings were cement rendered about 1880, and bear the Sowerby lion crest. The duck pond on the left seldom contains water nowadays Beyond it is the gated road to the Bury. (*Cassel family*)

XIIIa: The ballroom at Putteridge Bury during the 1st World War. It was also used by the Clutterbucks' as a music room, as the grand piano, timpani and gramophone bear witness. (*Mrs. J.R. Clutterbuck*)

XIIIb: Captain Thomas Meadows Clutterbuck (1850-1919) with his wife Blanche and their four oldest children: Thomas (born 1884), Viola (1886), Aubrey (1892) and Rosamund (1894). The two younger children both died of appendicitis. (*Mrs J.R. Clutterbuck*)

XIVa: Smiles are at a premium in this photograph of the St Thomas' Church "Mothers' Meeting" taken in 1910. The Vicar, Walter Covey-Crump, looks most uncomfortable, surrounded by so many village matrons in wonderful hats, each decorated with a plethora of flowers, fruit and fowls. The Vicar's wife is holding their youngest son, Leo. Next to her is Mrs. Titmus. This badly damaged print was found in the coal-barn at Manor Farm and has been digitally restored. (*John Shaw*)

XIVb: From 1922 a Clinic for ante-natal and post-natal care was set-up in Stopsley. At first it was held monthly in the Old School at Swift's Green, and later fortnightly in the Church Institute. Funds were always short and every opportunity was taken to increase them, as here at a Fête about 1928. (*Barbara Peters*)

XV: The whole village celebrated Queen Victoria's Diamond Jubilee on Monday, 21st June, 1897. Dressed in their Sunday best, they gathered on the Chapel Green. Everyone wore a hat, and most men had a flower in their button hole. Two photographs were taken from an upper window of *Rose Cottage*. In the first a lady is seen in the distance running towards the group; in this, the second, she has arrived and merged into the crowd! In the back row, sixth from the left, is the village policeman. The barn on the left covered the village well-head. Behind it can be seen the sign for *The Sportsman* and the Wesleyan Chapel. Amongst the trees in the centre distance is the half-timbered end of Green Farm. To its right are the chimneys of cottages that still survive beside the Green today. The present Infant School (eleven years into the future) was to be built behind the trees on the right. It is unlikely that anyone in this picture ever set eyes on their Queen, yet two days after it was taken, Stopsley's most prosperous son, Asher J. Hucklesby, was presented to Queen Victoria at a state reception for the Mayors and Provosts of the United Kingdom, in the Throne Room of Buckingham Palace. It is sobering to realise that fifteen years after this photograph was taken, more than thirty of the boys and young men present, would die in the Great War of 1914-18, and that a War Memorial would be erected on this spot where they had been so happily pictured together. *(Author's Collection)*

XVIa: 'The Chase Nursing Home' stood close to Mixes Hill Farm, and was named after the Chase family who owned the farm. For a time it belonged to Asher J. Hucklesby (plate XIb) and later Albert Wilkinson. By 1940 it had become a nursing and maternity home, where many Stopsley residents were born. It was demolished in 1969, after Birchen Grove had been established, and is now an open space. (*W.T. Dunning for South Beds. Preservation Soc.*)

XVIb and c: Born in Biggleswade, Schoolmaster Charles Henry Breed (1864-1954) came to Stopsley in 1893 and taught at the school for 32 years. He was also the Clerk and later Chairman of the Parish Council. Ronald A. Hopkins (1910-93) was Stopsley's leading pharmacist for 60 years, and established a chain of chemist shops around Luton. (Breed: *Luton News*; Hopkins: *Christine Horden*)

Chapter 5

Stopsley in the 18th and 19th Centuries

Pitt's Militia Act of 1757 provided the country with a home guard whilst the regular army fought the Seven Years War. As a result of the Act, Parish Constables were required to prepare lists of all able-bodied men between the ages of 18 and 50 years. From the lists men were chosen by lot to serve in the militia for three years. They had the option of finding a substitute or paying a fine of £10. When the Muster Lists for the Bedfordshire Militia were drawn up in February 1763 three men were chosen from Stopsley: Jeremiah Allen, William Newland and Richard Plumber. Only the latter could afford to pay for a substitute. He was replaced by William Bull, a man who had previously served in the Regiment.

Improvements in Communications

In the 18th and early 19th centuries there were considerable improvements in communications, with the construction of turnpike roads, canals and railways, which had developed hand-in-hand with the pressures of economic expansion.

In 1723 a Turnpike Act was introduced 'for amending and repairing the Roads from Luton to Westwood'. This was roughly the route of the Old Bedford Road from Luton to Barton, and then the A6 to Clophill, Bedford and Westwood (near Souldrop on the Bedfordshire-Northamptonshire borders). A toll-gate seems to have stood near the junction of Guildford Street and Bridge Street in Luton. There was no comparable east-west turnpike road. It was relatively easy for passengers to catch a stage coach going north or south, but to travel cross-country from Luton to Cambridge (32 miles) for example, by public transport would have been a nightmare involving at least four coaches and possibly taking up to two days. It was far easier to go to London and then out again. In 1836 five stage coach services passed through Luton from London each week, one going to Ampthill, one Kettering, one 'The Peveril Peak' to Manchester, and two 'The Times' and 'The Industry' travelling thrice weekly between Luton and London, and taking 4 and 6 hours respectively. William Kent ran a carrier's wagon from Luton to Hitchin, Royston and Cambridge twice weekly in 1830. Ten years later a carrier called Seabrooks ran a wagon from Luton to Hitchin on Tuesdays and Fridays. It is assumed that both wagons passed through Stopsley.

Minor roads in the 18th and 19th centuries were usually little more than cart-tracks. They were seldom metalled and in the Stopsley area the most one could expect was a surface of puddled (compacted) flints. There was no shortage of these: they could be hand-picked from the fields as required. It was a task often given to children and the unemployed. Such a road surface was excavated beside Whitehill Farm in 1966. Within Stopsley village flints and cinders were rammed into the traffic ruts.

For gentlemen, travelling on horseback, or the villager who wished to go east from Luton towards Hitchin there were numerous choices of route. All involved steep hills, making a difficult climb for horses, particularly in wet and icy conditions. For those with local deliveries to make, the road through High Town, Round Green, then to Dropshort and Stopsley Green would have been normal. At that point travellers wishing to continue towards Hitchin could pass around the northern boundary of Putteridge Park, down Beech Hill to Dog Kennel Farm at Lilley, and on to Little Offley and Great Offley. Alternatively on leaving Stopsley Green they could take Park Lane (Putteridge Road) passing Lane Farm and follow the bridle-road that now runs through Putteridge Park directly to Great Offley. In the 1840s this road marked the southern boundary of the Park, which was later expanded to its present circumference. A longer but less hilly route, avoided Stopsley village altogether, and followed the Old Bedford Road and Icknield Way to Hitchin, deepening the already ancient traffic ruts on Telegraph Hill. Travellers may have stopped on Lilley Hoo to enjoy the horse racing which took place there between 1690 and 1780. This was the favoured route of long-distance carriers with broad wheeled wagons, travelling between Oxford and Cambridge for instance. A network of minor trackways allowed access to distant fields and hamlets.

Broad roads with grassy verges and thick hedges provided convenient passage for drovers from Scotland and the north of England to drive their cattle, sheep, turkeys and geese to the markets of the south. At intervals these drove roads widened out to provide triangular passing places, with room for overnight camping (e.g. north-west of Lilley at TL:106281). Sometimes they arranged with local farmers to graze their animals on the succulent local pastures for a few days, so that they would be in the best condition for sale to the London meat markets. It is interesting to observe on a local scale that cattle were still being driven on foot from Copt Hall (1 km. south-east of Someries Farm) through the centre of Luton to market in Bedford as recently as 1934.

The same roads were used by families of gypsies, tinkers and vagrants. The former were usually blamed for every disaster that happened in their vicinity. With their dark skin, black hair and bright, though often shabby clothes, they were a familiar sight in south Bedfordshire. They were extremely versatile, and could turn their hands to almost any kind of work. One of the last surviving true gypsy families, the Smiths, had established an encampment of traditional caravans in Wigmore Lane, Stopsley by the 1930s. Some of their descendants live there still, though no longer in caravans.

In 1845 Joseph Locke prepared plans for an Oxford to Cambridge railway line which would pass through northern Stopsley. It was intended to follow the existing Leighton Buzzard line to Dunstable (North) Station. From there the line ran due east to cross the Dunstable Road near its junction with Crawley Road. It then passed over the Moor and turned north across People's Park in the direction of Wardown Crescent, Wychwood Avenue and the Sixth Form College. It continued north over Hancock Drive and west of the former Common Farm. It then swung north-east and was intended to pass through a tunnel 330 yards long which would emerge near Lilley church. Here it was proposed to build a railway station. It then entered an even longer tunnel under Offley Hill, and on emerging proceeded to Hitchin to join the railway line to Cambridge. Locke's scheme attracted insufficient subscribers, and considerable opposition from local landowners, including the Sowerby family at Putteridge Bury and the Crawley's of Stockwood Park, seems to have defeated it. The plans still exist in the Bedfordshire and Luton Record Office at Bedford.

Demographic changes

We tend to think of village communities as being fairly static before the coming of improved road travel facilities and the railways. The new Bedford Road was completed in 1832, and the Luton, Dunstable and Welwyn Railway opened in 1858, with fairly frequent trains each day to King's Cross from Luton. Neither seems to have had much effect on the migration of the population to and from Stopsley.

In using figures from Census Returns for Stopsley, we have to acknowledge that boundaries prior to the creation of the ecclesiastical parish of 1861 fluctuated, and we cannot therefore be certain that we are covering identical areas with each Census. When we examine the 1851 Census Returns we find a total of 580 people living in 'greater' Stopsley. Of those, 280 were born outside the Stopsley-Luton town area, *i.e.* 36%. Forty years later in 1891 the greater village population had grown to 756, of which 236 or 31% were not born in Stopsley or Luton town. The majority came from within six miles of Stopsley.

If figures for 1851 and 1891 are compared, they show the following places of birth:

1851		**1891**		
Lilley	34	Lilley	43	
Offley	⎫	Offley	11	⎫
Cockernhoe	⎬ 36	Cockernhoe	13	⎬ 33
Mangrove	⎪	Mangrove	8	⎪
Tea Green	⎭	Tea Green	1	⎭
Hitchin	10	Hitchin	0	
Biscot	6	Barton	12	
Flamstead	6	London area	10	
Kimpton	5	Leagrave	9	
Hertford	5	Shillington	8	
Barton	4	Eaton Bray	7	
Caddington	4	Streatley	6	
London area	4			
and 44 other locations		*and 59 other locations*		

More distant places of origin included:

1851		**1891**	
Clacton, Essex	1	Isle of Wight	1
Ditchingham, Norfolk	1	Leeds, Yorkshire	2
Eastbourne, Sussex	1	Lincolnshire	3
Farnham, Essex	3	Ramsgate, Kent	1
Heathfield, Sussex	1	Scotland	1
Shipton, Yorkshire	2	Ulverston, Lancs.	1
Bledlow, Bucks.	2	Winsley, Wiltshire	1

In contrast the Census Returns for Offley in 1851 and 1891 show only two (different) people born in Stopsley in each return.

What work was available to Stopsley menfolk in the nineteenth century? For 80% the answer was 'on the land'. Generally speaking farmers employed labourers with impunity. They were an expendable commodity, paid at the bottom of the wage scale. A 3-tier system operated within most parishes, divided between landowner, farmer and labourer.

The Crawley and Sowerby families formed an upper echelon who held much of the power and property in Stopsley with little challenge from those below them. There were also a few non-resident small landowners in the parish. Only Elizabeth Pigott at Little Whitehill farm was an owner-occupier farming what she owned. The remaining landowners drew rent from their tenants. The 1851 Census records 18 farmers within 'greater' Stopsley, 13 of them men and 5 of them women: 6% and 3% of the adult population respectively. The same Census shows 146 agricultural workers (70%) who were dependent on their weekly wage for their family's livelihood. Although most labourers developed many skills essential to farming, their wages were as nothing compared to some of their peers engaged in industry, who had taken apprenticeships and had trades unions to represent their rights. Even so, very few Stopsley men were attracted to work further away from the parish than Luton.

As far as Stopsley labourers were concerned in 1800, there was little alternative employment. What there was, was subject to seasonal fluctuations and a saturated market. The farmers deliberately kept the wages low, knowing that when necessary, the parish would subsidise them with allowances out of the rates. When no farm work was available, the parish overseers set gangs of men to work on the roads for 3s. to 5s. (15p. to 25p.) a week. Not surprisingly, numbers on poor relief rose, costing about £1 a head every year. This was the period of the Speenhamland system, to be replaced in 1834 by the iniquitous Poor Law Act. After that date all those in need were directed to the workhouses.

Pigot's *Directory* for 1839 records the names of the first four Stopsley tradesmen. These are Thomas Lawrence, aged 53, a straw hat manufacturer; James Darley, publican at *The Sportsman*; Edward Parrott, a wheelwright, and Samuel Holdstock (38), a blacksmith, whose forge was at the junction of Ashcroft Road and Hitchin Road (now under the dual carriageway). At that time Holdstock's 15 year old son Joseph was training as a blacksmith with his father. John Squires also had a smithy at Dyer's Cottages opposite the present vicarage. The 1841 Census lists Joseph Dawes (45) and James Crawley (24) as wheelwrights at Round Green. The same Census records Samuel Smith, aged 30, as a gardener, George Barnwell (25) as a gamekeeper living in the Keeper's Cottage near Whitehill Farm, and Edward Dimmock (65) as a carrier. William Plummer (25) and William Hill (20) were the only men directly employed in the hat industry as bonnet pressers. William Lawrence (70) was a thatcher. Sixty-six men were listed as agricultural workers. Of women in Stopsley, six were straw plaiters and 2 bonnet sewers. Many other casual plaiters must have gone unrecorded.

Straw plaiting was the saviour of many local families, keeping them just above the bread line. The report of *The Royal Commission on the Employment of Children, Young Persons and Women in Agriculture (1867)* observed: 'Speaking generally... in south Bedfordshire... all the females, and not a few boys and men, are engaged in Plaiting straw. Farm labourers in the plait district send their children, both male and female, to plait schools, where for a payment of from 2 to 3 pence per week, a master or mistress (generally a mistress) teaches them to plait, and sees that they execute the task set them by their parents, who buy the straw and sell the plait when made'. Even unemployed men were not above plaiting if the need arose. In the first decade of the 19th century straw plaiting could be more profitable than agricultural labouring, since prices paid were at their highest. By 1834 the prices slumped to only a fifth of that 20 years earlier. The straw plaiters response was to try and produce more plait to make up for the deficit in their earnings. By 1851 the hat industry (as opposed to plaiting) absorbed 8 men from Stopsley (4%): six were plait dealers and two were hat blockers. Only 8% (17) of the male population found any other alternative employment.

1851: Publicans 3, Blacksmiths 3*, Grocers 2, Shepherds 2, Thatcher 1, Wheelwright 1, Shoemaker 1, Brickmaker 1, Gamekeeper 1, Glover 1, Horse clipper 1, Gardener 1.
(A further 8.5% were retired, infirm or unemployed)
[* One was a woman: Sarah Holdstock]

These trades made the village almost self-sufficient, and Luton was only 2 miles away if other services were required.

Family finances were helped considerably by female contributions. In 1851 some 54 women (31%) were employed as straw plaiters and 30 (17%) as bonnet sewers in the hat industry. 17 (10%) were engaged in agricultural work - including farmers' wives. 20 (11%) were involved in some kind of domestic service, 30 (17%) were mothers of very young children and 23 (13%) including the old and infirm had no recorded occupation. Only two families were entirely dependant on straw plaiting for their income.

About a quarter of the arable land in Stopsley was used for growing wheat. Being on chalky soil, it also produced the best straw for plaiting. Thomas Batchelor in his *General View of the Agriculture of the County of Bedford* (1808) wrote 'straw plaiting was formerly confined to the chalky part of the county; but has been so much encouraged... that it has spread over the whole southern district.' Tales were told of people earning a guinea a week [£1.1s.]. 'Children of ten or a dozen years of age are ... capable of earning 6s. or 7s. per week and even as high as 12s. or 14s.' 'Very young children seem more capable of learning plaiting than reading or writing'.

Plait work was popular since it could be done at home whenever time was available. Indeed, in order that enough plait was produced, every spare moment from dawn to dusk was utilised, the women working as they walked in the street or rocked the cradle. They were often rebuked for paying more attention to plaiting than to the welfare of their families. As soon as their fingers were strong enough the smallest children were taught to plait and help supplement the family income. As recorded above many south Bedfordshire children attended plait schools, but there is no record of such an establishment in Stopsley. Once the School Board was established children were expected to attend full-time day school, which usually meant the demise of plaiting schools. By 1891 imports of cheap Japanese plait posed a disastrous threat to the local industry and demand was at its lowest ebb. In response, in November 1892, the Luton School Board tried to boost the ailing hat industry by adding plaiting to the curriculum of all its schools. Mr Breed, the Stopsley Headmaster, pointed out that since neither he nor any of his staff could plait, an additional teacher would be required. The matter was not mentioned again.

Plait was sold by its length in 'scores' (20 yards or 18 metres) to itinerant plait dealers who called at outlying houses, although most Stopsley women would sell their own produce at the Plait Market in Luton. This was held on Mondays, and mothers would walk to market leaving one of their older children at home to look after the babies, causing excessive school absenteeism at the beginning of each week. They would sell to whichever dealer offered the highest price (possibly one of the six dealers from Stopsley). As the hat work was seasonal, from December to May, money would be short later in the year. However, the harvest period provided work for all during part of the slack season. Bonnet sewing was sometimes outwork, but more often required attendance at one of the new Luton factories with the latest sewing machines. The 1871 Census records two sisters, Sarah and Selina Pedder, aged 8 and 10 as hat sewers. Single girls from the country, engaged in hat work, often lodged with Stopsley families during the week, returning to their homes at the weekend. Their tiny lodging payments were another welcome contribution to family budgets. Often these girls courted and married Stopsley boys and came to live in Stopsley.

By the 1860s towns were offering higher wages, which attracted a few workers away from Stopsley to seek employment with the police, railways or in the building trades. Poor housing in the village also led to the movement of some families to newer houses in Luton or more distant towns. There is not much evidence for higher wages or better housing in Stopsley before the end of the nineteenth century. The farmer landowners did little to improve the homes of their employees, some of which were described as 'wretched' and 'not fit for human habitation'. A report in the *Bedfordshire Times* of 20 December, 1873, described John Sambrook Crawley of Stockwood Park, Luton, who owned property in Stopsley, as one of the bad landlords. He had a number of poor cottages destroyed, but not replaced, causing a shortage of accommodation.

The 1891 Census Returns show a greater diversity of occupations amongst the men of Stopsley, although agriculture still dominated. There were 109 labourers (agricultural and general) out of an adult male population of 234, (47%). That was a drop of 23% since 1851, perhaps due to more efficient farming methods and the introduction of machinery. There were 6 farmers in the parish at that time. In the hat industry 29 men (12%) had found some form of employment. Other occupations included:

    Publicans 3, Carpenters 5, Bricklayers 3, Brickmakers 3, Grocery trade 3,
    Shoemakers 2, Blacksmiths 3, Railway work 3, Coalmen 2, Gamekeepers 5,
    Nurserymen 2, Painters 2.
There were also 1 each of Vicar, Constable, Baker, Thatcher, Sawyer, Poultry breeder,
    Herdsman, Horsekeeper, Groom, Shepherd, Cowkeeper, Gardener, Milkman,
    Stockman and Engineer.
There are only two instances of continuity from 1851 to 1891. John Lawrence was thatching throughout the period, and shoemaker Thomas Cain passed on his trade to his son Cornelius Cain. Shortly after the 1861 Census, Robert Hucklesby and William Harris took over their respective Grocers' shops, which remained in their families well into the 20th century.

A great change was evident in womens' hat work by 1891. Straw plaiting had almost died out due to the decline in demand for English plait, and compulsory education which prevented young girls from learning the trade. Out of 110 engaged in the hat industry, only 10 were still plaiters; the remainder were sewers and trimmers. Of the 7 women employed as domestic servants, all were under 19 years of age. Three dressmakers are recorded, and one Laundress, Washerwoman, Charwoman, Teacher, Pupil Teacher, School Caretaker, Postmistress-grocer and Publican.

The Parish Constables

The earliest record of the appointment of a parish constable for Stopsley occured in 1534, when Thomas Shilborn held the office. The constable, who was appointed for a year, was the link between the Lord of the Manor and his tenants. Normally elected on a rotation basis from the better-off members of the community, he was unpaid. He was responsible for collecting taxes, keeping parochial accounts and dealing with petty law. He was required to make a general report on the state of the parish at the Assizes. This was usually 'All well'. The office could become very time-consuming, but the officer was not compensated for his loss of earnings. John Crawley was constable in 1535, John Dyer in 1671 and later in 1715 the name of John Bigg is recorded. From the mid 18th century the Stopsley constable was one of seven serving Luton. Two were appointed for the town itself, and one each for the hamlets of Limbury, Leagrave, East Hyde, West Hyde and Stopsley. Each was responsible to the High Constable of Flitt Hundred.

Information about the Stopsley constables and other residents comes from a variety of sources. In the County Record Office at Bedford are a number of lists of people who were qualified to serve on juries from 1780 onwards. Eligible jurors were men between the ages of 21 and 70 who possessed freehold, copyhold or life-tenure property worth £10 or more, and long-term leaseholders of property valued at £20 or more. After 1825 the age limit was lowered to 60 years. The earliest lists were prepared by the parish constable, who was not always proficient in the spelling of surnames, placenames or occupations The extent Stopsley lists, transcribed by the Revd. J.E. Brown in 1917, are as follows, with their original spelling:

1780
James Gutteridge, William Cox, William Thrussell: - John Heath, constable.
1785
William Cox, Thomas Pigott [farmer, Little Whitehill]; - the mark X of William Brewer, constable.
1791
Thomas Pigott, William Smith, John Fowler [Whitehill Farm]; - Charles Tomson, constable [Nether Crawley Farm].
1798
John Fowler, Thomas Picket [Pigott ?], George Lines; - Thomas Young, constable.
1800
Thomas Pigott [Little Whitehill Farm], George Lines; - the mark of William Lunmus, constable.
1810
James Gutteridge, gentleman; John Bean, wheelwright; George Lines, yeoman; William Davis, yeoman; Francis Pigott, farmer; - George Lines, constable.
1820
Francis Pigott; William Davis; Thomas Smith [Crawley Green Farm]; William Ewer; - Thomas Hedges, constable.
1830
Daniel Davis, farmer; Daniel Gutteridge, farmer [Whitehill]; James Pryor, farmer; Thomas Smith, farmer [Crawley Green Farm]; John Swift, farmer [Swift's Green], John Tomson, farmer [Nether Crawley].

Professional Policing Begins

The Bedfordshire Constabulary came into being on 21st March 1840. It was composed of a Chief Constable, (Captain Edward Boultbee), six superintendents and forty officers. The force was divided into six operational divisions. At Luton a superintendent was responsible for six constables, two of whom were stationed in the town, with the others at Barton, Dunstable, Eaton Bray and Markyate. Stopsley was patrolled from Luton, where a lock-up was provided in Park Street. Petty Sessional Courts were held in the George Hotel until the Town Hall was built in 1847. In 1858 a purpose-built Court was opened on the corner of Stuart Street and Dunstable Place. The initial concerns of the new police force were the prevention and detection of crime, the maintenance of public order, enforcement of licensing regulations and the investigation of sudden death on behalf of the coroner. Constables were expected to be 'perfectly acquainted with all villages and places on their beats' and to be aware of all local people likely to commit offences. The constables patrolled their beats on foot, and frequently covered twenty miles each day. They were on duty for ten to twelve hours for seven days. When not on duty they were expected to be at home in case they were suddenly needed. The men were paid between 17s. and 23s a week depending on their seniority or length of service.

In 1864 the Luton police area was divided into two divisions: Luton and Luton Rural. By 1874 a police house had been established in Stopsley, beside the Hitchin Road, halfway between *The First and Last* and Rose Cottage (a flower shop in 1998). It was occupied by Constable John Nottingham (aged 29) and his wife Eliza, a dressmaker. In 1881 William Tatman (aged 27) from Great Barford lived there with his wife and baby son.

This is perhaps the place to record a murder that took place on the edge of the parish in 1867. It concerns the Welch family who lived at Green Farm in the centre of Stopsley. Joseph Welch and his wife Charlotte were the farmers. Their son, Levi, lived in a cottage next door, with his wife Ann and sons Reuben and Frederick. Levi had been a labourer for his father, but later found work in Luton as a hat blocker. He was frequently in trouble with the law, and had five times been imprisoned in Bedford gaol for offences concerning the game laws. In March 1864 he had received 15 months for poaching, and within a fortnight of his release in 1865 was caught again, and served a further three months. His young son, Reuben, had been gaoled for three months for household theft when he was 15.

In August 1867 Levi, aged 49, was lodging at 83 Burr Street in High Town. Late on the night of Saturday 3rd August, 1867, Levi Welch, William Worsley of Duke Street and James Day of Back Street, all hat blockers, were drinking together in *The Royal Oak* at Round Green. Around midnight they set out along the Hitchin Road towards Stopsley with the intention of poaching on the Putteridge Bury estate.

At the same time William Bradberry was walking home to Lilley, having been to Luton to buy clothes, followed by an evening spent at the *Old English Gentleman* in High Town. He was a few yards ahead of Welch and his friends, and somewhat the worse for drink.

A hundred yards along the 'straight' [The Flat] beyond Round Green, James Day pulled some tobacco from his pocket, and in the process dropped a sixpence. It being too dark to find the coin, he returned to the *Royal Oak* for a light. When he got back to the spot he heard Worsley say "Here's a man lays drunk". The light showed a man lying unconscious and bleeding profusely, apparently from a wound in the temple. "He was making a curious noise in his throat like one being strangled", Worsley later observed. Day dashed back to the nearest pub, *The Jolly Toper* [sic], and a number of men with lamps hurried to the scene. When he was turned over, it was clear that the man had suffered a massive blow to the back of his skull, and that he had been robbed, his pockets having been cut out of his clothes. He was carried back to *The Jolly Toper*, and died at about 8 o'clock in the morning. He was identified as William Bradberry, a labourer from Lilley, who worked for George Sowerby at Putteridge Bury.

A witness called Kilby had passed Welch and Worsley at midnight, and heard a scuffle. He said that Day was not with them at the time. The Constable was called and Welch and Worsley almost immediately fell under suspicion, particularly when certain items known to have been in Bradberry's possession, were found at Welch's lodging. Worsley was known to have been carrying an iron winch, which was later identified as the murder weapon.

The three men were arrested, but Day was released without trial. Welch and Worsley were tried at the Lent Assizes, which began in Bedford on 13th March, 1868. Levi Welch turned Queen's evidence, and swore that Worsley had struck the fatal blow. He was acquitted of murder but sentenced to fourteen years penal servitude for aiding and abetting. Worsley was found guilty of murder and sentenced to death. He was hanged in Bedford on 31st March, 1868: the last public execution in Bedfordshire. Levi Welch was sent to Pentonville Prison in April 1868, where his 17 year old son, Reuben, was serving his third sentence, this time one of seven years for stealing a double barrelled shot gun from Edmund Swain of Luton. Levi was only at Pentonville for three months before he was granted a free pardon, having provided the information which led to Worsley's conviction. He was living at Round Green in 1877 when he signed the Register at his younger son Frederick's wedding. His parents lived at Green Farm until their death in 1871, when they were both buried in St Thomas' churchyard. It is a curious irony that the two earliest known photographs connected with Stopsley are those of Levi and Reuben, taken at Bedford gaol in 1867.

In September 1876 the Luton Borough Police Force came into being, but Stopsley, along with Hyde, Leagrave and Limbury remained under the control of the County Force. As mentioned above, the Stopsley constable had a house in the centre of the village where he could keep an eye on most misdemeanours, ranging from small starving boys scrumping apples to their bigger hungry brothers poaching. All crimes were taken very seriously. For example, in 1891 the tenant of *The Sportsman* was John Hancock. At 9.45pm on 11th August in that year his wife sold a pint of beer to Arthur Allen, a 30 year old farm labourer who lived in Mixes Hill. The village policeman P.C. George Lansberry, was outside the inn at the time, talking to Samuel Pates, a carpenter who lived in 'St Peter's' cottage behind *The Sportsman*. Both men declared that they saw Allen stagger into *The Sportsman* from the direction of *The Brickmakers' Arms*. He was clearly drunk. As it was illegal to sell alcohol to any drunken person, the publican was reported to the Luton Magistrates, who fined him £2 and endorsed his licence. In January 1892 Hancock appealed to the Bedfordshire Quarter sessions, claiming that the witness Samuel Pates bore him a grudge. Two farm labourers, James Smith and Charles Crick had both been customers at *The Sportsman* and said that in their opinions Allen was not drunk. Annie Hawkins, licensee of *The Brickmakers' Arms* said that she had that evening served Allen two pints of beer, but that he was quite sober and quiet when he left her inn. The Bedford Magistrates upheld the fine of £2, but removed the endorsement, allowing *The Sportsman* to remain open.

The village was briefly without a resident policeman in 1899, due to problems with the police house, but a new residence was found by the end of the year. The County Force served Stopsley until the village was incorporated into the Borough of Luton in April 1933.

Jimmy Low was the village policeman at the turn of the century. Ellen Barber recalled her father driving from Stopsley to Preston (Herts.) via Putteridge Park one night in his dog cart. He was stopped by Low who told him to light the candles on his cart. 'Right', he said 'I've seen them lighted, now you can blow them out!'.

Care of the Sick and Elderly

In Chapter 4 mention was made of the wealthier Stopsley folk leaving money in their Wills to support the poor of the village, and of Thomas Butterfield's efforts in 1722 to make provision for his son who was 'imperfect in his senses'. The Poor Law Acts of 1601 and 1662 compelled the parishes of England to provide for their sick and poor, the responsibility falling on annually appointed overseers, who had the authority to levy a poor rate. Those receiving Poor Law relief had to be cared for and restored to health as quickly as possible, otherwise they became an unwelcome drain on the parish resources. Work was to be made available for the able-bodied in workhouses. Little could be done for those who were terminally sick or mentally ill: the latter usually derided as village idiots. Quacks and 'wise women' provided herbal remedies with varying degrees of success. Sometimes barber-surgeons, such as Cornelius Bigland of Luton (died 1673), were available to practice their skills.

Many physicians lacked detailed knowledge of the working of the human body, and there was much legal and ecclesiastical objection to human dissection. As a consequence ressurectionists and body-snatchers secretly rifled the graves of the newly buried and sold the corpses to unscrupulous surgeons. St Mary's churchyard in Luton was not exempt from this obnoxious practice. The body of Ann Webb, a young straw plaiter, was removed from her grave in 1823. In spite of the passing of the Anatomy Act (1832) which legalised dissection, Luton General Cemetery Company appointed night watchmen as recently as 1854 to prevent the graves of the newly dead being disturbed.

It was the job of the Overseer of the Poor for each parish to see that the chronically sick and infirm, the old, the orphans and those of unsound mind, were cared for. If relatives or neighbours could not look after them (even with financial help from the parish rates) then Stopsley folk went to the Luton workhouse, situated in Castle Street until 1766, after which it was moved to Park Street, opposite the University. The Overseers were quite happy to contract the running of the workhouse out to anyone who would undertake responsibility for the upkeep and labour of the destitute: often with disastrous results. Straw plaiting and hat making were both seen as workhouse trades.

Efforts were made to control epidemics of contagious diseases such as smallpox, by the provision of pest houses. Luton had one on the Great Moor, built in 1724, and another for private patients at Cowridge End near Round Green about 1795. *The Merchants Miscellany*, published in 1785, records the names of Robert Kirby and Samuel Chase and Sons of Luton, who were practising surgeons, apothecaries and men-midwives, and in 1830 Pigot's *Directory* lists John Chase and son, William Dyer and Thomas Waller as Luton surgeons.

There was no hospital in Luton at the beginning of the nineteenth century. Fortunately the Samuel Whitbreads (father and son) provided an Infirmary (1803) and Asylum (1812) at Bedford, and Luton took out a subscription which allowed those seriously ill to be carried there by horse and carriage or cart: a bumpy journey that can scarcely have helped the patients' recovery. In 1834 the old Elizabethan Poor Law was scrapped, and a new Poor Law Amendment Act came into force. It was intended to end outdoor relief. Instead of paying money to support paupers in their own home villages, those who could not or would not work were to be transferred to large Union Workhouses under the control of a Board of Guardians, in the belief that if the workhouse was sufficiently unpleasant, people would be discouraged from seeking help. Thomas Carlyle cynically remarked 'If paupers are made miserable, paupers will needs decline in multitude. It is a secret known to all rat-catchers'. The destitute and those too sick to go anywhere else, were forced into the workhouse as a last resort.

In Luton a new, purpose-built workhouse opened on the edge of the town in Dunstable Road in March 1836. It was divided into separate blocks for men, women, boys and girls. Members of all families were separated from each other. It contained an infirmary intended for those who were chronically ill or dying, and for girls in trouble. There was no one on the staff with specialist medical knowledge to look after them. The services of a local General Practitioner were retained as a part-time Medical Officer. A Relieving Officer was appointed to visit all the parishes in the Luton Poor Law Union which covered south-east Bedfordshire, to 'examine personally every individual receiving out of door permanent relief' and to admit to the workhouse paupers and their families who were unable to support themselves due to age or infirmity. This is not the place to write of the Dickensian conditions in the Union Workhouse in Luton. Described as 'a miserable pauper prison', they have been documented in detail in Margaret Currie's book: *Hospitals in Luton and Dunstable* (1982). More than a dozen Stopsley folk ended their days in the Luton Workhouse. Their names are recorded in the St Thomas' Church Burial Register. Suffice to say that for 150 years all elderly Stopsley folk dreaded the possibility of dying in the workhouse and heaved a sigh of relief when the building was finally demolished in 1995.

Dr Edward Woakes, the Medical Officer of the Board of Health, was responsible for setting up the Luton Cottage Hospital which opened in May 1872. It stood in High Town Road, opposite its junction with Duke Street, and was financed entirely by voluntary subscriptions from Luton's middle classes. To gain admission patients required letters from a subscriber. It initially had four beds, which were later increased to eight. The Hospital *Rules* stipulated that it was for the use of the Artisan class, and that whenever possible patients were expected to contribute towards the cost of their stay: 2/6d. for children and 5/- for adults per week (12½p. and 25p.). Visitors were permitted between the hours of 1 and 5 p.m. on Sundays and between 2 and 4 p.m. on Tuesdays and Fridays. To increase funds 'Hospital Saturdays' were regularly held in Luton, Stopsley and the surrounding district, when Friends of the Cottage Hospital collected money in the streets.

As the population of Luton and its hamlets increased, so it rapidly outgrew the Cottage Hospital. In 1879 the Trustees of the Marquess of Bute gave a plot of land on the corner of Dunstable Road and Grove Road (adjoining the Workhouse) for a replacement. In 1882 the Bute Hospital was opened. It had been built by public subscription, supported by numerous fund raising projects. By popular demand it retained the unofficial name of the Cottage Hospital until the mid-1890s. The Stopsley School Log Book for 26th October 1887 records 'a sad occurrence during playtime. Maria Smith, who was away for several weeks with a broken arm after Harvest vacation, was unfortunate enough to fall heavily, and re-break the bone. The poor little thing has been conveyed to the Cottage Hospital, where she will remain, in all probability for three weeks or a month.' An accident in October 1897 had a more serious ending. The roads around Stopsley were under repair, with heaps of stones lying on the verges. A spate of stone throwing ensued, and a 7 years old girl, Ethel Ward of Ramridge End, had her eyeball completely smashed by a stone thrown by a boy at Round Green, (not a Stopsley schoolboy). The Bute Hospital was unable to do anything for her, and a fortnight later she had to have the eye removed at a London hospital.

The new hospitals were not suitable for contagious diseases. Stopsley School had to be closed for a fortnight in March 1877 in an effort to stem an outbreak of measles that had spread to most of the pupils. An outbreak of whooping cough in Stopsley in July 1884 had to be nursed in individual homes. The warm, sultry weather and closure of the school for the Harvest vacation helped to contain the epidemic. Partly as a result, Spittlesea Isolation Hospital was opened in 1892 on the southern boundary of Stopsley parish, close to where the medieval hospital of 'The House of God, of the Virgin Mary and St Mary Magdalene' had stood at Hassex Wood. It was administered by Luton Corporation through its Sanitary Committee. A hutted building of corrugated iron and wood, it contained two simple wards, and was originally intended 'for the isolation of cholera and to prevent panic in the populace'. It was run by a staff of nurses and helpers. A doctor called regularly but was not resident. Children with diphtheria and scarlet fever seem to have been the main users.

The Stopsley Burial Register can be used to show that there was little improvement in health care before the 1930s. In particular it highlights the problem of infant mortality. In the first full year of recording, 1863, there were 15 burials in St Thomas' churchyard: 7 of them children under five years.

	Children under 5 years.	Total annual burials.
1863	7	15
1873	4	7
1883	10	20
1893	8	15
1903	5	11
1913	8	15
1923	6	14

Between 1862 and 1921 there were 701 burials in St Thomas' churchyard: of those 278 were children of 5 years or under; that is 40% or an average of 4·6 per year! During the same period it is worth noting that 134 people (19%) lived to be over 70 years old (36 over 80, and 5 over 90).

It became clear once compulsory schooling was established, that many children were severely under-nourished and when ill, could only be nursed at home, often in over-crowded, insanitary conditions. In November 1884, William Johnston, the Headmaster of Stopsley School wrote 'many of the people of Stopsley are in a state of semi-starvation', and two years later 'there are many cases of dire poverty in the village'.   George Souster from Mixes Hill recalled hearing a lady at that time asking the village butcher for '2 penn'orth of beef' to make a pudding. 'It comes to tuppence h'penny'. 'That's too much, cut a bit off'.

In 1889 Alfred P. Welch, a philanthropic hat manufacturer, paid for a Children's Sick and Convalescent Home, which was set up in a house on the corner of North Street and Havelock Road in High Town.   It was run to a very high standard and achieved remarkably successful results.   Fees ranged from 1/- to 5/- a week (5p.-25p.), although many children were treated free of charge.   The Hospital soon proved too small, and in 1894 a new, purpose-built Children's Hospital was opened in London Road.   Again Alfred P. Welch paid the entire cost of the building estimated at £2,250, and was rewarded with the Freedom of the Borough.

Stopsley and the Boer War

An issue of the *St Thomas' Church Magazine* for February 1900 carried an anonymous article on the Cape War: the Boer War of 1899-1902.   At the time the article was written the Boers had achieved a series of successes with British garrisons besieged in Ladysmith, Mafeking and Kimberley.

'The series of reverses which at first befell our armies have had the effect of stirring up a feeling of enthusiastic patriotism throughout the length and breadth of our land which has had no equal for 100 years past and which some thought had been killed by the spirit of modern business and trade.   Three volunteers have gone from our parish and one other member of a Stopsley family is serving at the Cape.   The volunteers [all neighbours from Bury Road] are Alfred Plummer, [born 1881], William Waller, [born 1883] and Sydney Whittemore [born 1880].   The one already serving is Private Wilson of Stopsley Common.   Local history tells us that Stopsley has always been represented where hard fighting was going on.   Stopsley helped to win the great victory of Trafalgar in the person of Plummer of Mixes Hill who fell on the deck of *The Victory* by the side of his Admiral; and one of the distinguished officers of the Crimean Campaign was Dr Dymond who lived in what are now College Cottages.'

The Boer War volunteers were almost certainly with the 6th Division 2nd Battalion of the Bedfordshire Regiment which sailed for South Africa on the *S. S. Sumatra* on 16th December 1899.   Sydney Whittemore was to die at Ypres in 1914, aged 34. Sadly a search of the Muster Roll of *H.M.S. Victory* shows that no one named Plummer served in that ship at the time of Trafalgar, although it is quite possible that he served as a rating in one of the other 32 British ships which were present at Trafalgar.   The Census Returns have failed to provide any evidence of Dr Dymond in Stopsley, or to identify 'College Cottages'.

Ending the chapter on a lighter note, we know that in the mid-19th century Stopsley had cricket and football teams, loosely attached to the church and chapels. Where the games were played is not known, though probably on meadows close to the village centre.   Some villagers walked to Luton where they could watch cricket on the Great Moor each year.   A marquee was set-up as a changing room, and in 1822 petty thieving was reported there.   Others supported the Luton Town Football and Athletic Club, formed in 1885 after the amalgamation of a number of lesser teams.   Public baths opened in 1872 in Waller Street, consisting of separate small recreational swimming pools for men and women, and a series of much needed washing baths.   It was not until the Putteridge Recreational Centre opened in 1977 that Stopsley got its own swimming pool. Many local men and boys were involved in hunting and shooting on the local farms and at Putteridge Bury. Poaching was also a regular pastime, keeping the local game keepers and constabulary on their toes, inspite of a Night Poaching Act which came into force in 1844 with dire penalties. Guy Fawkes Night on November 5th was celebrated with a bonfire on the village green and fireworks. Unlike Luton, where such celebrations were notoriously famous for getting out of hand, especially in the 1820s; the Stopsley revellers seem to have behaved with admirable decorum!

The Hucklesby family

Mention must be made of the Hucklesby family whose influence in the village and beyond was paramount. Robert and Hannah Hucklesby moved from Luton to live in Bury Road, Stopsley, during the 1840s. They had eight children, three girls and five boys, six of whom were born in the village. The three oldest boys all held posts of responsibility.

At the time Robert came to Stopsley he was employed as a hat blocker and Hannah was a plait maker. They had saved sufficient money to open a small grocer's shop in the front room of their cottage, which must have been very crowded as their children grew up. In August 1861 Robert bought a plot of land in Bury Road from Francis Foster, a brickmaker. On this he built a new grocer's shop and house, complete with a cellar, accessible from the street. (This house is now 13 St Thomas' Road). The brick frontage of the house was smartly built in Flemish bond with tuck pointing, in marked contrast to the rougher brickwork at the sides and rear. The upper part of the frontage was symmetrical with two tall sash windows. The ground floor frontage was quite irregular with a sash window, a larger shop window (its surround painted to imitate marble), and two doors: one to the shop and one to the house. Above the shop door hung a large glass lantern containing an oil lamp, later replaced by a gas light. Some time in the 1880s part of the shop was taken over as the post office, and a posting box was inserted into the front wall.

When Robert Hucklesby died in 1872 he left the shop to his eldest son, Asher John Hucklesby, who immediately sold it to his sister-in-law Elizabeth for £300 (although no legal deed of conveyance was drawn up until 1901). Elizabeth was married to Robert's second son, Eliah, and she ran the shop for more than thirty years. By 1885 Eliah was registered as the Receiver of Letters for Stopsley. Sadly, following a carriage accident, he spent the last 20 years of his life in the Three Counties Mental Hospital at Arlesey, prior to his death in December 1910. For many years Elizabeth ran the shop with the assistance of her niece Sarah Ann Godwin. When she died in October 1910 she bequeathed the shop to Sarah, who, with her husband Percy Smith Kime, performed the roles of village grocer and post master until the 1930s.

Asher John Hucklesby was Robert's eldest son, born in 1845. As there was no Stopsley school at that time, he attended the British School in Langley Street, Luton, until he was 13. He was then sent to work for C. J. Rosson, a hat manufacturer. He worked hard and by the time he was 20 and ready to marry, had reached the position of office clerk. His wife was Ellen Barber, the 19 years old daughter of Joseph Barber of Ramridge End Farm. In 1873 Asher started his own straw hat and plait business in George Street, Luton. It grew to become one of the largest hat and plait manufacturers in the town, concentrating on the international market, where the name of 'A. Hucklesby and Co.' became world famous. Asher was a J.P. and Liberal County and Town Councillor from 1888 until his death in 1908. He was elected Mayor of Luton on five occasions, and is best remembered for enabling the town to acquire Wardown Park. He was a loyal and regular member of the Congregational Church in King Street, Luton and a life-long Temperance worker. As a philanthropist he liberally supported many local causes concerned with health and the church. When he died at his house 'Leaside' in New Bedford Road, he owned estates in Suffolk and Yorkshire and left £165,000 after probate. He was buried in Rothesay Road cemetery. His was the largest funeral ever seen in Luton, but curiously, he has no memorial in the town. (See *Bedfordshire Magazine*, (1997-8), Vol. 26, 135).

The third Hucklesby son was Arthur, born in 1849. Like his elder brother Asher, he attended Langley Street School. For 38 years he worked for his brother as a plait warehouseman. Unlike Asher he continued to live in Stopsley all his life. For some years he was Chairman of the Parish Council, and represented Stopsley on the Luton Rural District Council and Board of Guardians. He regularly attended St Thomas' church from its inception and was a founder member of the Parochial Church Council. He was particularly fond of cricket and renowned in the local folklore of the game. With Asher he followed the Hertfordshire hunt for many years. He was also a popular singer and entertainer in many local villages. Roy Darby recalled him entertaining in his 70s at Lilley Cricket Club, singing comedy songs at the piano. His two party pieces were 'The Village Pump' and a song about a donkey. In 1868 he married his wife Caroline from Anstey in Hertfordshire and they lived in a cottage in Park Road (opposite Pond Farm). There they raised nine children, seven girls and two boys. The latter were both employed in the hat industry. Of the girls, two, Maud and Gertrude, became Stopsley school teachers. In later life he built and lived in Jutland House, 618 Hitchin Road. Arthur died in 1928 and was buried in St Thomas' churchyard.

It should be noted that the separate family of James and Hannah Hucklesby also originated in Stopsley at the end of the 18th century, predating the arrival of Robert and Hannah Hucklesby by some fifty years. The two families may have been slightly related to each other, and this can cause confusion when trying to trace individual members. Most of James Hucklesby's family had left Stopsley before the 1891 census, by which time it seems possible that Arthur had acquired James' old house in Park Road.

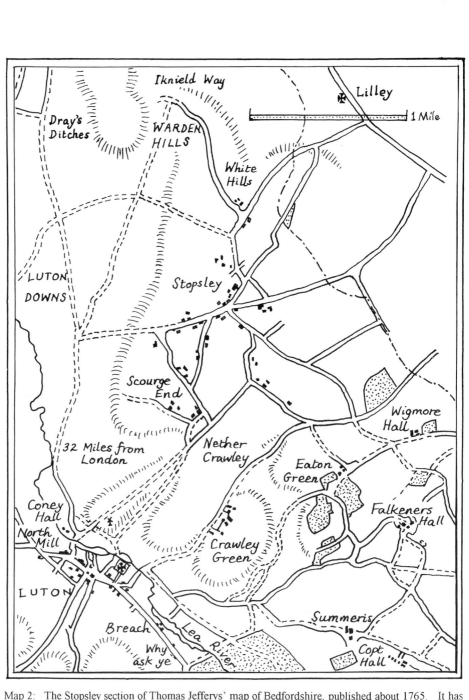

Map 2: The Stopsley section of Thomas Jefferys' map of Bedfordshire, published about 1765. It has been redrawn to approximately the same scale as Bryant's map, opposite, for comparative purposes.

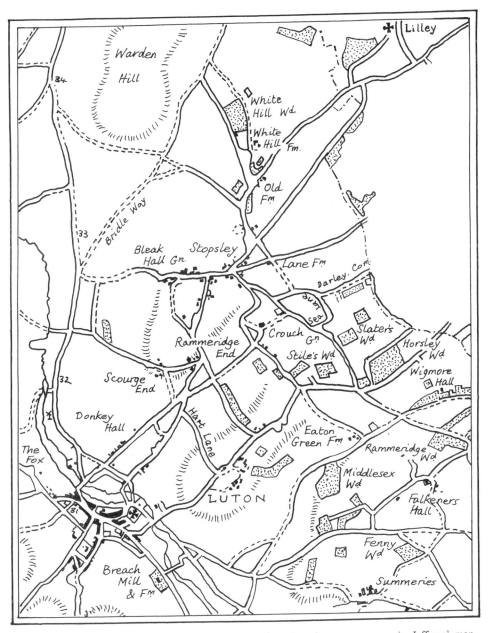

Map 3: A copy of Andrew Bryant's map of 1826, covering the same area as in Jefferys' map. Putteridge Bury was not surveyed for this map.

Chapter 6

At the Big House

Almost every village had its associated 'big house', where an influential local land owner dominated his tenants. Since for centuries Stopsley was a daughter hamlet of Luton the Lord of the Manor of Luton assumed that role. The owner of the title changed with the fortunes of the Manor. The Crawley family at Haverings and later Stockwood were the most influential to hold the title. Even so, they were not geographically close to Stopsley, and the discipline that the folk at the big house often imposed on a settlement, whilst it *did* exist, seems to have been somewhat lacking.

Instead, Stopsley adopted a 'big house' that was not only outside the parish, but also outside the county. Putteridge Bury stands in Offley parish in Hertfordshire, and is less than two miles from Stopsley village Green. There is no doubt that in earlier days Putteridge Bury had much closer ties with the village of Lilley, from whence came most of its domestic staff and in whose church, most of its owners were buried. But its long western drive, known as Park Lane, ran directly into the centre of Stopsley, and in the nineteenth and twentieth centuries half the land in the parish belonged to the owners of Putteridge Bury.

Called at various times Puderig' (1207), Puderugge Bury (1240), Potheriggebury (1365) or Putrechesbury (1411), the Manor of Putteridge Bury was possibly a mesne manor of Delamers before the Norman Conquest, which at the time of the Domesday Survey possessed sufficient woodland to support forty hogs. It later appears to have belonged to the Royal Manor of Hitchin, and was held then by three vassals of Earl Algar. In 1239 it was held by Nicholas de Puderugge, and passed through various hands in the course of time. Thomas and Elizabeth Chelrey paid an annual rent of half a pound of pepper and a pound of cinnamon for the estate in 1407.

In 1968 Mr W. L. Gates made a detailed (unpublished) study of the history of the house, and he has kindly allowed me access to items which have some relevance to the history of Stopsley.

Putteridge Bury eventually came into the possession of Richard Lyster, Solicitor to King Henry VII, and Chief Justice of the King's Bench. In 1525 he sold it to John Docwra, a member of an ancient and important family from Westmoreland, who was nephew and heir to Sir Thomas Docwra, the Lord Prior of the Order of the Knights of St John of Jerusalem. John Docwra's son, Thomas, added the Manor and Advowson of Lilley to his Putteridge estates in 1555, and the ownership of the two manors remained in tandem until fairly recent times. Thomas died on 14th July, 1602, and is buried in Lilley church, where a monument beneath the tower records 'He died in his house at Putteridge (by him built) in ye 84th yeare of his age'.

Thomas Docwra's grandson settled his estates at Lilley, Putteridge, Huckwellbury at Offley, and Lindsey in Pirton, on his grandson, Sir George Warburton. In turn Sir George conveyed them to Charles Cavendish, third son of the 2nd Duke of Devonshire, in 1729. These estates were then resold, in 1738, to Sir Benjamin

Rawling, a former Sheriff of the City of London. He came to live at Putteridge Bury, and died there on 2nd December, 1775, aged 99. He, too, lies in Lilley church, and the property then passed to his aunt's children, Rebecca Nicholson and Sarah Corney, who sold it in 1788 to John Sowerby of Hatton Garden.

Sowerby was the younger son of a Cumberland farm labourer who, 'by a lucky speculation gained a sizeable fortune' and progressed by his own efforts to become a wealthy citizen of London. He settled at Putteridge Bury at the age of 43, and in 1796 became High Sheriff of Hertfordshire.

On 25th February, 1808, a serious fire destroyed the entire mansion and most of the furnishings. It is recorded that Johann Kellerman, of Lilley, 'the last of the Alchemists,' was present and helped to save some of the effects. A new house, in the Regency style, was built, half a mile to the north of the old one, on the present site. The grounds were laid out by the well-known Scottish horticulturist and landscape designer, J.C. Loudon (1783-1843). A tree in an avenue on the south side of the park had been planted in 1820 on the evidence of its rings, when it was cut down in 1970.

John Sowerby died on 20th January 1823, aged 78, and was succeeded by his sons, William, Thomas and George. William died unmarried in 1838. Thomas, who was in the Coldstream Guards and fought at Waterloo, also had no issue and died in 1864, aged 75. He held the advowson and patronage of the new St Thomas' church in Stopsley. His brother George had four children, the oldest of whom, another George, succeeded him in 1868 when he was 35.

The Census returns make it possible for us to compare the Household kept by the bachelor Thomas Sowerby in 1851, with that of his married nephew George in 1871. Thomas employed John Wadman and his wife Mary as his senior House Servants, assisted by five maids, a manservant, and two stablemen. In 1871 George Sowerby and his wife Emily had three children, Anne (6), Thomas George (4) and Harry (3). They employed a staff of twenty-six. These comprised a house keeper and assistant, lady's maid, butler and under butler, footman, two under footmen, children's nurse and under nurse, coachman, groom, two stablemen, an upper laundry maid and two under laundrymaids, an upper housemaid, 2nd and 3rd housemaids, kitchen maid, scullery maid, still-room maid, dairy maid, head gardener, and Land Agent.

George Sowerby, Junior, had been Colonel of the 3rd Battalion, Durham Light Infantry and had taken part in the Sudan campaign. He was a J.P. for Bedfordshire and Hertfordshire and had been High Sheriff of Hertfordshire. He was Lord of the Manor of Lilley and principal landowner in that parish and northern Stopsley. He supported and financed the Luton Cottage Hospital and was president of the Luton Choral Society. He was a keen naturalist with a museum of curiosities in his house and a small private zoo in the grounds. Children from Stopsley School were often invited to visit the park for Easter treats and to watch agricultural demonstrations: the latter particularly useful for boys likely to spend their working lives on the land. On 10th May 1887 they joined with the neighbouring villagers at a great party to celebrate the coming of age of Thomas Sowerby, George's eldest son.

A Tragic Accident

On Thursday 2nd August, 1888, Putteridge Bury witnessed a most tragic accident. During that afternoon Herbert Sworder from Buntingford and his Luton cousin, Clara Sworder, visited Colonel Sowerby, and asked if they might photograph some of his deer. As the animals were some way across the park, the Colonel suggested that they should photograph his Egyptian stag which was in a paddock not far from the house. The *Luton Times* reported that 'the stag was of uncertain temper and very dangerous to strangers, but the Colonel was accustomed to fondle it with impunity. Although small, it was a powerful beast and had antlers of great size with particularly sharp tines. The Colonel called to it, but it did not come forward, so he entered the paddock and went towards the animal. Mr Sworder was following, but the Colonel said 'Don't come, as you're a stranger', and laughing, added 'Perhaps it may run at me; but I'll bring him round, and you shall have a good view of him.' Mr Sworder proceeded to undo his camera and his cousin offered her help. This being declined, she then turned to see what the Colonel was doing. To her consternation she saw that in the moment that had elapsed, the stag had attacked him and knocked him down, for he was on the ground with the savage animal standing over him.. She screamed, 'Look, he's down!' Mr Sworder jumped over the fence, taking his tripod with him, and at the same time shouting for help. The Colonel was on his back, pinned down by the stag's antlers, with one of the tines in his thigh, and he was clutching the antlers with his stick still in his hand. He had a gash under the eye, from which blood was streaming. He seemed to lose consciousness. Mr Sworder released the Colonel's hands from the stag's antlers and got out his knife intending to stab the animal, but the Colonel revived and said in quite a natural voice 'All right, we'll manage him yet'. Those were his last words.

The stag ran away. Mr Sworder tried to get the Colonel to move but he was too exhausted and feeble. In trying to move the Colonel Mr Sworder dropped his knife, and at that moment the stag rushed again. Mr Sworder caught the stag's antlers and had a severe tussle in which he was tossed over the brute's head. The animal made two more thrusts at the dying Colonel. Mr Sworder collared the stag again and clung on to it until Miss Sworder had sent Herbert Dimmock (a gardener mowing the lawns) to his assistance. Together Mr Sworder and Mr Dimmock tried to pull the stag away from the Colonel. When two more men arrived they managed to fling the stag over the fence and it ran away into the park, where later in the day it was shot.'

The Colonel was carried into the house, where he died shortly afterwards. He was only 55 years old.

Colonel Sowerby was buried in the family mausoleum at Lilley church on 6th August, 1888. It was a military funeral led by the permanent staff and band of his regiment from Barnard Castle. His coffin was made of oak from a tree grown on the estate, by the estate carpenter.

A few days after the funeral, Princess Mary Adelaide, Duchess of Teck, who was staying at Luton Hoo wrote:

'In the afternoon Madame de Falbe [wife of the Danish Ambassador, who lived at the Hoo] and I went for a drive, and called to inquire after the poor widow of the unfortunate Colonel Sowerby. The Falbes knew the Sowerby's well. On our way there we took a roundabout route, which *aboutit* on the further side of the town of Luton, all new to me, and then ascended a steep hill, driving on some way through a nice village [Stopsley] to the Sowerby's place, which lies high, the park being all broken ground, with any number of enclosures for the pet animals the poor man loved to collect. A servant, who looked very woe-begone, and no wonder! gave us some particulars.'

After the Colonel's death, Mrs Sowerby moved to Putteridge Grange where she died in 1914, and the Bury was let to Mr George Herring, a philanthropist who was always willing to welcome parties from Stopsley School. He died in November 1906. The new squire, Lieutenant Thomas George Sowerby was following a military career, and left his domestic staff to look after Putteridge Bury. He eventually settled in Lilley Manor. The Stopsley School Log Book records that Mr Sowerby returned from the Cape on 5th December, 1900. 'The children welcomed him outside the school at 3 pm and sang 'Home, Sweet Home'. Mr Sowerby thanked them for their sweet song and welcome.' All the estate farms were decorated with welcoming banners. Thomas's youngest brother, Francis, died four months later at Kroonstad in South Africa.

In the late 19th century Home Farm at Putteridge Bury was celebrated for the quality of its cattle and crops. Up to the time of the Boer War it employed between 20 and 30 local men and boys.

Putteridge Bury was famous for its shoots, and according to the *Victoria County History of Bedfordshire* (1908) Vol. 2. Major Sowerby was instrumental in introducing 'driving' to Bedfordshire. (*i.e.* beaters, with sticks and dogs advance across the shooting area, causing game to rise and fly into the path of guns of a stationary shooting party). The best bag of 346½ brace killed in 1896 on Grubbs Bush field was a record for the county at the time. Grubbs Bush lies a kilometre north of Whitehill Farm, west of the bridleway to Lilley. The Putteridge estate was particularly remarkable for the number of pigeons killed. The total head of game killed in 1893 was 1,673 partridges, 2,626 pheasants, 232 hares, and 4,494 rabbits. In the following year 3,199 pigeons were killed, and in 1895 the totals amounted to 2,332 partridges - of which 315 brace were killed on the Grubbs Bush beat in one day by a party of seven guns - 3,103 pheasants, 273 hares, 2,589 rabbits and 1,705 pigeons.

On Saturday 18th November, 1905, Mr Breed wrote in the School Log Book: 'This evening about 25 scholars went with me to Putteridge Bury and by the kindness of Mr Taylor and Mrs Reeves, after singing a selection of songs and hymns, were regaled with hot milk, scones and oranges. They had a fine time.'

The Clutterbuck Years

Captain Thomas Meadows Clutterbuck (1850-1919) acquired Putteridge Bury in 1908. The Clutterbucks were an old Hertfordshire family dating back to at least the 16th century. Robert Clutterbuck (1772-1831) was one of the most distinguished, being the author of the 3 volume *History and Antiquities of the County of Hertford* (1815, 1821, 1827). Captain Clutterbuck was related to another branch of the family who lived at Micklefield Hall near Sarratt on the western edge of Hertfordshire. These were the brewers of Great Stanmore. There were numerous public houses named after them in Hertfordshire and Buckinghamshire.

Thomas Meadows Clutterbuck had married Blanche Mary Derbyshire in 1883. One of their five children, Aubrey, had died of appendicitis in 1905 (aged 13), and a daughter, Rosamund, died of the same complaint in 1915. Since 1902 they had rented Chequers, near Wendover, (later to become the Prime Minister's country home), to which Captain Clutterbuck had been attracted by the shooting and stalking. In January 1909 the lease of that building was acquired by Arthur Lee, the Conservative M.P. for Fareham. Mrs Clutterbuck was so enamoured with Chequers, that she insisted that Putteridge Bury should be entirely rebuilt to replicate it as closely as possible.   The firm of Sir Ernest George and Yates were engaged to design and build the new house which took until 1911.   Edward Lutyens, a pupil of Sir Ernest George, was involved in the work.   It is a very good imitation of a Tudor manor house, built chiefly of brick, with stone dressings and a roof covered with Colly Weston stone slabs.   According to one source, it cost £30,000, excluding the decoration and sanitary work.

The Clutterbuck family lived at Putteridge until Thomas's death in 1919.   Their heraldic achievement can be seen above the front entrance, on a stone panel, and shows the family's coat of arms - a rampant lion, with three scallop shells.   Above the esquire's helmet is the crest - a buck sejant, between two slips of laurel.   The arms can also be seen above the sundial on the south front of the house, and devices from it have been used to decorate the lead rainwater pipes on various parts of the building: the lion, scallop shells, the crest, entwined 'C's', and the date 1908.   Initials and this date can also be found on the plaster ceiling of the loggia   The sundial also has carvings of a cockerel and owl, representing dawn and dusk respectively.

Many of the ground-floor rooms are panelled in oak, and the door-panels show variations of the linen-fold design which make interesting comparisons.   The main staircase is especially fine, although relatively plain.   The Clutterbuck lion, holding a shield, forms the finial of the newel post.   The windows throughout the building, composed of iron casements with leaded lights and unusual stays and fastenings, are fashioned in the 16th century style, as are some of the door handles and hinges.

The ground floor contains the finest rooms in the house.   The Ball Room, behind the main staircase, is lined with white-painted panelling with Ionic pilasters, and contains a plain open fireplace with carved mantelpiece, and a fine plaster ceiling. This is decorated with a strap-work design, and bordered by an elaborate cornice filled with moulded swags of fruit and flowers, and curved perforated brackets.   The beams are decorated with cherubs and caryatids.

The Dining Room, to the right of the main entrance, has a remarkable barrel-vault plaster ceiling, with a complicated design - strapwork, great curlicues of foliage terminating in dolphin's heads, swags of silk and garlands of fruit.   The arms of Clutterbuck are represented, and also two fine plaster panels, showing cherubs playing with cymbals and a trumpet, and carrying garlands and ribands   The fireplace is exceptionally rich in its decoration.   Supporting the mantelpiece are two caryatids, each on an Ionic plinth.   One represents a woman with her hair braided, the other the pagan god Pan, with pan-pipes, horns and tiger skin.   The family arms and entwined C's are carved above.

The Billiards' Room, on the south front, is partly wainscoted in plain dark oak.   It has a fine fireplace, probably dating from the early 17th century and brought from elsewhere.   It is made up of two pairs of Ionic columns.   The cornice is enriched with egg and dart moulding, which also surrounds the central panel.   On either side of this are two renaissance arches, within each of which stands a carved oak figure.   That on the right carries a Cornucopia, and may represent the goddess Demeter.   That on the left appears to be carrying a palm-leaf.

East of the Billiards Room is the former Drawing Room, also lined with fine panelling,   It has windows inset with sixteenth century stained glass, of great interest. Much of it is continental, and heraldic, and may come from a similar source to glass at Chequers.   The Royal Arms of France can be seen - three gold lilies on a blue field - and the initials V.S. and a crown, in the window on the right.   Nearby is a panel showing a man with a bow, and a G. and L. in cipher.   Another shows a shield which has above it, for a crest, a golden duck. The arms of Daubermont, so labelled, can be seen, in association with other panels of arms, showing spread-eagles and unicorns. There are two panels showing kings (perhaps king David) playing musical instruments. Another bears the date 1593, and one other piece, dated 1540, shows a golden lion on a coat of arms, the motto '*Volo non Vales*', and pictures a cherub with a deer. A companion piece to the archer is an Arquebusier - a soldier with an early musket and a pronged stick used as a barrel-rest. Two modern pieces show in colour the arms of Clutterbuck: Azure (blue) a lion rampant or (gold), in chief three scallops argent (silver), and the crest - a silver buck, seated on its haunches between two slips of laurel leaves.

The west wing, containing the servants' quarters, kitchens and domestic offices was approached on the ground floor through a brown leather door covered with brass studs. The kitchens were tiled in white, and possessed a game larder with hooks on the ceiling, and cool store rooms shelved with black slate.

A large dome-shaped ice-house provided cold storage. This still exists about half way along the eastern side of the main drive, tucked down amongst the trees. Dudley's, the Luton fishmongers, kept it stocked with ice during the summer months. Another relic of former food provision on the estate is the dove cote, now in a parlous condition, that stands to the south of Home Farm. It was described by Jean M. Taylor in 1968:

'This octagonal cote was probably built about 1788 and is in the same style as the farm house. It is brick, covered with plaster that is falling away in places and each wall has a long window slit decorated with a plaster moulding. The walls appear to have been built with bricks recovered from an older building but the corner bricks were specially made for the purpose. The lower six courses are faced with slabs of sandstone. The door frame is of stone but the door has disappeared. The roof is covered with scalloped slates, many of which are missing, and the eaves are decorated with a wooden fretwork that has broken away in places. The top of the roof... probably originally had a decorated entrance hole.

In the centre of the cote is an old wooden beam, sawn off half way up, with radial beams to support a floor; this almost certainly was the central beam of a potence. The L-shaped nests are lightly plastered over and are in good condition, each wall has 16 rows with 5 nests to each row. The window slits take the place of six nests. In each row the first three nests turn left, and the next two nests run right. Each row has an alighting ledge made of tiles cemented to slates which is unusual. Originally there was a trap in the roof entrance, but now little remains.'

Beyond the kitchen yard, formerly containing a well 210 feet (64 metres) deep, stood the stable-yard. This was mainly Regency and was demolished to make way for the modern extensions. Parts of the structure remain, however, in particular that surmounted by the clock-turret. This contains an eight-day clock, made by Gatwards's of Hitchin in 1841, which is still in excellent working order. The cupola contains a bell, on which the hours are struck, and is surmounted by an elegant weather vane. The stables adjoin the former enclosed Kitchen Garden, (no longer part of the premises) the red-brick wall of which runs along the northern boundary of the lawn. Piercing the wall at the eastern end are doorways closed by iron gates. One of these is florid Victorian cast iron, the other, very overgrown, appears to be Georgian. The iron pergola arch crossing he path is Victorian.

On the lawns on the eastern side of the house are two large urns. These probably date back to the earlier house; a picture of it before its demolition shows one of them in the garden. Edwin Lutyens, Sir Ernest George's pupil, was asked to advise on the gardens in 1911, and he introduced Gertrude Jekyll to Putteridge Bury. Her original designs for the grounds are in the University of California Library at Berkley, but were never fully realised in her lifetime: a fact confirmed by photographs in the Clutterbuck family collection. It was not until the 1990s that an attempt was made by the Hertfordshire Garden Trust to create the layout that she had intended.

During the ten years that they lived at Putteridge Bury, the Clutterbucks probably had more influence in Lilley than in Stopsley. From time to time the Head Gardener, Mr Thorne, visited Stopsley School to give advice on gardening. In October 1909 Mr Clutterbuck joined him, to present prizes. There were celebrations in Lilley and Stopsley in 1911 when the eldest son, Thomas Rupert married Blanche Pocklington-Senhouse. They set-up home at Micklefield Hall. On 22nd May, 1912, all the Stopsley School children were taken to Putteridge Park to see the newly constructed gardens, rockery, aviary, and ponds. The Headmaster commented 'Birds and fish interest them more than flowers, I find.' In 1914 Viola Clutterbuck married Captain Thurstan Holland-Hibbert at Lilley church. Eva Pearce, a daughter of one of the estate workers and a Stopsley schoolgirl, was one of the bridesmaids. Mrs Clutterbuck was very philanthropic, providing macintoshes with hoods for the children of Lilley and Mangrove during the First World War. She also collected and donated funds for a convalescent hospital at St Leonard's-on-Sea, and sent the estate workers there, when they were ill.

Many of the workers had accompanied the Clutterbucks in their move from Chequers to Putteridge Bury. The Head Gardener, Mr Thorne, with his wife and their four children, lived in the Estate House beside the walled kitchen garden. His daughter Dorothy trained as a pupil teacher at Stopsley School. She frequently returned to Chequers to stay with her friends.

Evan Pearce with his wife Jane and three daughters lived in Gas House lodge, later renamed Stopsley Lodge. (Putteridge Bury had its own private gas supply, until the gas mains were laid from Luton. The gas works were later replaced by a blacksmith's shop. The mansion had its own electricity supply after 1908.) Evan Pearce looked after the horses. He brought his furniture from Chequers to Putteridge by horse and cart, changing horses at St Albans. His daughters were employed in the house, the youngest Eva being a seamstress. Opposite the Pearce's lived William Winston, his wife Alice and their two daughters. Winston was the dairyman and cowman, and he later moved up to Home Farm. The estate also employed half a dozen gamekeepers including two at Lilley, two in Lilley Bottom cottages and one at Mangrove.

Thomas Clutterbuck had been attracted to Chequers by the shooting and stalking, and the same applied to Putteridge Bury. He had been particularly annoyed to find that the public had rights of access to the grounds at Chequers which he could do little to prevent. At Putteridge he was determined that they would not wander through his estate, disturbing his game birds. In September 1908 he attempted to close the right of way from Putteridge Road through to Lilley Bottom and Offley. Stopsley Parish Council were incensed. Not only was the path through the park a traditional and popular Sunday afternoon walk, but a number of villagers both from Stopsley and Offley used it as a means of getting to their work. Various meetings took place between Mr Clutterbuck's solicitors and the Council. A compromise was eventually reached, in which entry tickets to the Park had to be obtained from Charles Breed, as

Clerk to the Council. In May 1913 Mr Clutterbuck instructed his horse-keeper Evan Pearce to lock the Park gates at 10 pm each night. This caused more friction with the Stopsley Parish Council, who saw it as a further restriction of their rights. They were assured that it was only a temporary measure, but it continued for some time.

After Thomas Clutterbuck's death in 1919 the house was rented by Mr Holden who worked at the Stock Exchange. He is remembered locally for hosting lavish parties which were frequented by numerous actresses and society beauties.

The Cassel Family

Sir Felix Cassel rented Putteridge Bury in 1921 and bought it the following year. A Privy Councillor, King's Counsel and Judge Advocate, he was married to Lady Helen Grimston, and their five children grew up on the estate. Like his predecessor, Sir Felix was keen on shooting. His first recorded Putteridge shoot was on 13th November, 1922, when the bag was 14 partridges, 246 pheasants, 27 hares, 10 rabbits and 4 woodcocks. The Cassels threw lavish parties and King George V and Queen Mary, often accompanied by the Prince of Wales, were occasional visitors. On 1st December 1926 the King planted an oak tree on the south lawn. Lady Helen's daughter, Mrs Josefine Pugh, recalls that her mother put the best linen sheets on the King's bed. She was mortified when he produced his own of Egyptian cotton and had the linen ones changed! On these royal occasions policemen were stationed at every gate around the Park, stopping anyone who tried to enter. Their were frequent complaints from visitors about the poor state of Park Lane leading from Stopsley to the mansion. The King attended a shoot on 4th November, 1927 which commenced in the Park and progressed towards Lilley, during which 1,001 pheasants, four hares, three rabbits and six pigeons were killed. After one shoot at which the King rode on a small pony, lunch was served at Mangrove Lodge. Unfortunately there were no cooking facilities, and the servants had to struggle to heat soup and make toast over smoking fires in the Lodge and Laundry cottages. On another occasion there was consternation when one of the princes turned up in a blue serge suit instead of a shooting outfit. It was said that his valet had laid out the wrong clothes. Lord Louis Mountbatten was also a frequent visitor, having married Sir Felix's niece Edwina Ashley in 1922.

From time to time members of the Cassel family attended functions in Stopsley. For example, on 12th January, 1927 Lady Helen Cassel opened the new Church Institute in Bury Road, and in June 1948 Sir Felix Cassel opened the present Stopsley library.

Much of the estate land in Stopsley, including Manor and Whitehill Farms, was sold to the Crown in the mid 1930s. Sir Felix Cassel died in 1953, and his son Sir Francis inherited the remainder of the estate. He is perhaps best remembered as a talented pianist who gave concerts all over Europe and hired the Albert Hall each year in order to give a recital. In his later years he kept race horses at Putteridge. He lived in a house near the Stopsley entrance to the park that had originally been built by Lady Helen for estate workers. He adapted it for his own use and died there in 1967.

During the Second World War Putteridge Bury house was requisitioned by the government for military use. Italian and German prisoners of war were housed in fourteen Nissen huts arranged in two rows in the park, west of the drive and to the north of the cricket ground. After Sir Felix Cassel's death the house was bought for use by the textile company British Celanese, who converted part of it into research laboratories, and did substantial damage to some of the fine woodwork. Much of the 4,000 acres of farmland was sold off from the Estate in the 1950s. In 1964 the mansion and 40 adjacent acres of land were acquired by Luton County Borough Council for use as a Teachers' Training College, (see page 180). Today it is part of the University of Luton. The remainder of the park, some 421.29 acres (170.56 hectares), was sold by the Cassel family to the Newcombe Estates Company Ltd. in July 1998.

XVIIa: A number of new roads were privately built in Stopsley during the 1930s, including bungalow estates with large gardens. This photograph of Lynwood Avenue shows little structural change since it was taken in 1938. Paving slabs replace tarmac, the road is better surfaced and the gas lamp has given way to electricity. There is no provision for garages or curb ramps to allow vehicle access. The cars have been updated and are certainly more prolific! (*Author's Collection*)

XVIIb: A number 11 bus parked beside the Green about 1950. To its right stands Green Farm house, considerably altered since Plate IXa was taken around 1900. Its garden has been replaced by an Esso service station and Stopsley Motor Services. Left of the bus is W. H. Cullen's grocery store, (formerly John Cox, and now the Midland Bank). In 1938 cottages were demolished leaving the waste land on the left, beside which Mrs Smith and her daughter Mrs Bird are walking. The dual carriageway now joins the Green roundabout at this point. (*Luton News: Luton Museum Collection*)

XVIIIa: The Hitchin Road or Main Road in the centre of Stopsley, looking from the Green to *Rose Cottage*, with the Wesleyan Chapel on the right and cottages on the left. This picture was taken in 1910 and looks in the opposite direction to XXIVb, taken on the same day. (*Author's collection*)

XVIIIb: The same view as above, taken in 1938. The hedged field has given way to a row of shops and garage flying the Union Jack. The end cottage on the left has been converted into A.E. Fisher's butcher's shop. A gas lamp and white telephone box have appeared. On the left a board advertises the George Hotel in Luton. Johnson's milk cart and a No.11 bus are in an otherwise empty street. (*Author's collection*)

XIXa: *Tithe Cottage* about 1880. It stood where Barratt's building now stands. No historic survey of the building was carried out before its demolition. From extant photographs it could have been a medieval aisled hall, with the aisles later cut off and floored, or a later 17th century building. By 1900 it was occupied by three separate families including the District Nurse. (*Luton Museum*)

XIXb: The eastern end of *Tithe Cottage* was partially demolished in the 1930s, and a new bay was added on the west. This became the Greenways Café and Filling Station, photographed here in 1961. After the Cottage was finally demolished in 1963 a filling station occupied the site, together with the Lee-West Bowling Alley. The latter burned down in 1967. (*James Dyer*)

XXa: It is hard to believe that these two dilapidated labourers' cottages in Butterfield's Green Road about 1920 are now the attractive *Thatched Cottage* near Manor Farm. Demolished in the 1950s, they were rebuilt as the present cottage using bricks from the Old School wall. (*Author's Collection*)

XXb: These cottages at the northern end of Ashcroft Road were photographed in 1962, a year before they were demolished. In the 1930s they were occupied by the families of Frederick Claridge, Florence Waller, John Foreman and Albert Usher. By the time this picture was taken their gardens had been sold to make room for the bungalows on the right (compare plate I). (*James Dyer*)

XXIa: Bury Road (St Thomas' Road) about 1910. Hucklesby's Grocery Shop and Post Office is on the left, with cottages scheduled for demolition in the 1930s beyond. The sign of the old *Brickmakers' Arms* is in the middle distance. On the right is the old Baptist Church, with other cottages now demolished. At the end of the road are chestnut trees and a barn belonging to Bury Farm. The barns were used as classrooms by Stopsley Secondary Modern School before being replaced by Mixes Hill Court and the new Baptist Church. (*Author's Collection*)

XXIb: George Rainbow, with his grand-daughter Jean, in the back garden of his house in Bury Road in 1931. The houses, now demolished, were just to the left of those in the picture above. The turret on the roof of the Wesleyan Chapel can be seen in the background.
(*Walter R. Rainbow*)

XXIIa: These 19th century houses in Putteridge Road still survive.   The four *Park Road Cottages* (centre) and the two *Laurel Cottages* (left) were built by Jabez Cook, the Baptist builder and grocer, in 1894.   In the 1920s Charles Fitzjohn had a poultry farm behind the Laurel Cottages.   Their original frontages have been somewhat altered.   (*James Dyer*)

XXIIb: Putteridge Road has changed little since this photograph was taken in 1938.   Thick hedges now replace the iron railings, which were taken, ostensibly for salvage, at the beginning of the War. The large tree has been cut down, and a pavement runs along the right hand side of the road.   The gas lamp has been replaced by electricity, and a multiplicity of cars now park where the hand-pushed milk cart makes its way along the road.   (*Ray Clements*)

XXIIIa: St Thomas' Church Institute was opened by Lady Helen Cassel in January 1927. It was the only large hall in Stopsley and, with its stage, provided a popular venue for concerts, socials, meetings and the fortnightly Welfare Clinic, as well as a base for Church organisations. Constructed largely of asbestos, it became a health hazard, and was demolished in 1973. It was replaced by a temporary day-centre. (*Ethel Toyer*)

XXIIIb: A concert party on the stage of the Church Institute in the mid-1920s. This was one of many productions presented by the Vicar's wife, Mrs Winifred Gilbert. (*Luton News: Luton Museum*)

XXIVa: The Wesleyan Chapel, built in 1846, with its hall of 1894 on the right, pictured in 1910. It stood opposite the present Infant School. Behind the hedge on the right was a narrow field used for fêtes and flower shows. Bury Road (St Thomas' Road) can be seen in the distance. (*Author's Colln*)

XXIVb: Looking from Bury Road in the opposite direction to XXIVa above. On the right is the newly opened Infant School of 1909. The Senior School which was built in front of it in 1912 has yet to be constructed. The signpost stands on Chapel Green, where the villagers in the Diamond Jubilee picture were photographed. All traces of the village well have disappeared. The sign for *The Sportsman* and the cottages of plates XVIIIa and b are in the distance. (*Author's Collection*)

Chapter 7

Stopsley Enters the 20th Century

The Local Government Act of 1894 established Parish Councils, composed of elected members, in rural areas where the population exceeded 300. Stopsley's population in 1881 was recorded as 741 and so qualified for a Council. William Austin, as Returning Officer, called elections for 9th March 1896, and the first General Meeting was held in the village school on 20th April. William Hartop (Senior), the Overseer for the parish, was enforced to take the chair until the meeting elected a Chairman. The nine Councillors who had been elected were: Alfred Barber (farmer: Cowridge End Farm), Jabez Cook (builder and grocer), Arthur Thomas Hucklesby (plait salesman), John Hill (bricklayer), John Impey (brickmaker), George Matthews (painter), Thomas Oliver (farmer: Lane Farm), Daniel Queensborough (farmer: Pond Farm) and George Shaw (farmer: Manor Farm). From these John Impey was elected Chairman and George Matthews Vice-Chairman. The meeting went on to elect Walter Oliver and Jabez Cook as Overseers, and co-opted Charles Breed (Schoolmaster) as Assistant Overseer. The latter was to be paid £15 per annum to collect rates, take the minutes of the Parish Council's proceedings and act as Clerk to the Parish Council. It was agreed that meetings would be held on the first Monday of each month. This was changed to the first Tuesday from May 1898 until June 1910. It then reverted to Mondays until the demise of the Council in 1933, with the exception of one year from April 1927 to April 1928 when it returned to Tuesdays. All meetings were open to the public and the press, although for most of its latter years the press were excluded, depriving many of the villagers of news of its proceedings. Sub-committees were responsible for such matters as footpaths, sanitation and water-supply.

For the most part the Parish Council was a consultative body, that reflected the opinions of most of the community. Although it had no great powers, it did bring urgent local matters to the attention of the Rural District Council and made sure that they were properly dealt with. It probably worked most effectively under the long Chairmanship of farmer Benjamin Hartop between 1915 and 1927. First elected to the Council in 1901, he was one of the three farming Hartops. He farmed at Exton Green (near Crawley Green) and later at Eaton Green. Ben was ably assisted by Arthur T. Hucklesby, who was Vice-Chairman for 14 years. (Arthur was the brother of Asher J. Hucklesby, five times Mayor of Luton). Only one Vicar of Stopsley, Walter Covey-Crump, ever became a Vice-Chairman of the Parish Council; that was in 1908.

As well as local issues, which are considered later, the Parish Council acted as spokesman for the village in responding to national events. The first of these to be recorded were the arrangements for Queen Victoria's Diamond Jubilee in June 1897, which included a week's holiday for the school children, and commemorative medals, a group photograph of the whole village, and the purchase of flags for this and future occasions. The majority of Stopsley folk were nonconformists and Liberals. This is reflected in a unique letter from the Council dated June 1898: 'The inhabitants of the parish of Stopsley do hereby express our sincere regret at the death of the right Hon. William E. Gladstone, and do most cordially express to his sorrowing widow and family our heartfelt sympathy with them in their sad bereavement and the nation's great loss.'

On 9th June, the Revd. Stephen Gladstone replied: 'The evidences of the love and trust felt all over the land for Mr Gladstone are a great comfort, I need not say, to my mother and all of us.'

In February 1901 a much simpler vote of condolence was sent to the Royal Family on the lamented death of Queen Victoria, and a reply from the Home Office on behalf of King Edward VII was duly received three weeks later.

Another letter, in 1910, was sent to Queen Alexandra and King George V expressing the Council's feelings of loss at the death of King Edward VII. By March 1911 plans were in hand to celebrate the Coronation of George V, but we have no details of what they were. The School Log Book tells us that the school closed for two days and that the children took part in a massed musical concert in Luton, and were given souvenir mugs.

At the end of the first Council meeting of the 20th century in January 1900, the Chairman, John Impey, invited all the Councillors and their wives to a hot supper at his home. 'A very pleasant evening ensued.' In June 1902 a group photograph of the whole Council was taken by Messrs. Cox and Jones, but copies cannot now be found.

The Parish Council were responsible for setting-up the village War Memorial in 1920, and for its upkeep until 1933, with the help of a devoted team of local ladies.

Health Hazards

Sanitation and water supply had been causes for concern in the village for many years. A *Report to the General Board of Health* on a preliminary inquiry into the sewerage, drainage, water supply and sanitary conditions of the town of Luton was published in 1850. Whilst it does not actually cover Stopsley, it must reflect something of the state of affairs in the village being only two miles away. It paints a horrifying picture of filth, squalor and sickness. Endemic, epidemic and contagious diseases prevailed both in and on the outskirts of Luton, particularly where the houses were crowded together, and the inhabitants numerous. The Inspector found the walls, floors and furniture of the houses literally saturated with the body-smells of the inmates, the sleeping rooms being the most pungent and obnoxious. Drainage (including human excrement) poured from many houses into open gutters. When this was directed into dumb-wells, (intended to take only surface water), which were dug down into the chalk, the water of the neighbouring draw-wells (i.e. drinking-water wells) became contaminated and undrinkable. The walls of many houses were constantly damp and covered with mould, due to their foundations standing on ground thoroughly saturated with surface drain water. Few of the houses had any ventilation and the impure air rising from cess-pools and surface drains became trapped indoors. Without the addition of any fresh air, it consequently had a detrimental effect on the health of the inmates. The Inspector also noted a considerable lack of privies (i.e. toilets), often only one between six families.

Wells, hand-operated water pumps and ponds provided most of the water supply. Often the wells were inconveniently placed, and their considerable depths (over 30 metres) made the labour of drawing the water so great, that women and children undertook the work unwillingly; consequently little if any was ever drawn for flushing purposes, the amount being limited to the absolute minimum required for domestic purposes, 'a state of things that will exist wherever there are wells'. Ponds were generally unsafe for human drinking purposes, but played an important part in providing water for household cleaning and washing, as well as for animals and gardens. The main ones in Stopsley stood conveniently by Bury Farm, Pond Farm, and Lane Farm.

In the village the privies in Ramridge End Road (Ashcroft Road) and Cannon Lane gave the Parish Council constant cause for concern. The Sanitary Committee feared an epidemic every time there was a hot summer. The Blacksmith's pond, which stood beside the Hitchin Road, outside the present Vicarage, had become little more than a cess-pool, and a case of typhoid had reputedly arisen from drinking its water.

In the summer of 1899 an epidemic of whooping cough and measles broke out at the School. The District Surveyor and Nuisance Inspector immediately drew attention to the fearful smells from the three WC's which had not been emptied for two years and were in a deplorable condition. They were swiftly cleared within two days. The School was closed in 1903 for three weeks due to a diptheria epidemic. Dr Morcom, the Medical Officer for Health, said that this was partly because the building had not been properly disinfected. In 1901 Crawley Green Road was reported to be littered with filthy offal from slaughter houses, dropped whilst being carted to Crawley Green Farm. Earlier, in 1898, the carcasses of dead horses had been found blocking the road at Mixes Hill.

In 1910 arrangements were made for a night-soil cart to visit Stopsley one night each week, to empty lavatory buckets and cart away the manure. This was emptied into Mardle's clay pit at Round Green. Prior to that sewage had either been dug into the gardens or dumped in a convenient ditch or the street. More modern closets drained into dumb-wells or cess-pits, where the tenacious local clay prevented the slurry from soaking away. These were cleaned out by Scavengers at very infrequent intervals. Numerous reports of overflowing liquid refuse are recorded into the late 1920s. After the earth-closets had been emptied it was the householder's responsibility to apply disinfectant powder. This could be obtained from Miss Clementine Pates, who stored the large bags of brown powder at the rear of her home 'St Peters', (later called 'Fern Cottage') which stood in the alleyway that ran north between the Methodist Chapel and *The Sportsman*. Marge Bierton recalled being sent by her mother each week to collect the family supply in a rusty old tin.

When Stopsley was incorporated into the Borough of Luton in April 1933 the Corporation promised that a sewerage scheme for the village would be their first priority. At that time Luton's sewage works was situated in a section of the Eaton Green Road which no longer exists, and lay under part of Vauxhall Motors, west of Airport Way. A foul-water sewer was proposed from the works to Turners Road (North) and then along Ramridge End Road (Ashcroft Road) and Hitchin Road (East) with branch sewers in Crawley Green Road, St Thomas's Road, Putteridge Road and other roads, so as to drain the whole of the Stopsley area which was approximately 1,234 acres, with provision for limited future development. A proposal to include land in Wigmore Lane was rejected as it was thought unlikely that there would be development there in the next twelve years, and there was no point in paying interest on a scheme that brought no return. As it happened, due to the intervention of the War, this proved to be correct.

The estimated cost of the sewerage scheme for Stopsley was thought to be £23,250, and an application was made to the Ministry of Health for permission to borrow the amount required, and to invite tenders for the work. The Ministry held an enquiry at Luton Library on 4th April 1934. Dr William Archibald, the Medical Officer of Health for Luton spoke of the danger of disease from the cess-pools and considered the new scheme a matter of some urgency. The Inspector was told that the sewage would flow to the disposal work wholly by gravitation, and that the works might soon reach capacity and need enlarging, especially if there was any large increase in private development. (The works moved to East Hyde in 1942). At the time of the enquiry the housing density of Stopsley was eight to the acre, but in 1933 some 934 houses had been built by private enterprise and already by April 1934 another 250 had appeared. Once the area was sewered development would increase at a greater rate, and it would then prove attractive and accessible to prospective Vauxhall workers.

Some seventeen tenders were submitted to carry out the work, the lowest being £15,730. This was well below the estimated cost, the saving being due to the cessation of emptying of cess-pools, and revenue received back from frontages. As it transpired, the scheme did not get the go-ahead until 1936, by which time the cost had risen to £26,154 16s.11d. and a tender from John Mowlem and Co. Ltd. was accepted. During the 1930s the village spread into the Chesford, Applecroft and Stapleford Road areas, along Ashcroft Road, and around Mixes Hill. A belt of open green farm land between Lynwood Avenue and Round Green still separated the village of Stopsley from the suburbs of Luton. Butterfield's Green was not sewered until 1995.

Medical Care

In Chapter 5 we saw how most medical care was provided in the home. The Bute Hospital and the Children's Hospital were available for those seriously ill, whilst Spittlesea Isolation Hospital catered for contagious diseases. In all cases fees were expected, though often waved, if the patient could not afford to pay. The first Old Age Pensions were introduced in 1908 and state Sickness and Unemployment Benefit followed in 1911. Partly as a result of the Poor Law Institutions (Nursing) Order - 1913, a new Infirmary and Nurses' Home were built at the Union Workhouse in Dunstable Road and opened in August 1913. The infirmary was expressly for the welfare of the poor sick. It had no full-time medically trained supervisor until 1927. Two year later, the Workhouse changed its name to St Mary's Hospital, in the hope of changing its image, but local people were not easily fooled. For them it would always be the Workhouse. In the 1930s tactful Stopsley Vicars' wrote '11a Dunstable Road' in the Burial Register as the address of those unfortunate enough to die in the hospital.

In 1906 'Pound Week' was inaugurated to raise funds for the Bute Hospital. The public were invited to contribute gifts weighing one pound - usually groceries - which could either be used directly by the hospital or auctioned. In spite of their own poverty Stopsley school children entered into the spirit of the scheme with alacrity. On 16th June 1913 'a number of boys and girls left school early to take to the Bute Hospital a £1 collection and 17 lbs sugar, 1 lb Quaker oats, 2 lb rice 1 lb tapioca and 1 lb oatmeal. This is 'pound day' for the Institution and affords a good lesson in Charity.' In 1915 the children collected £1.6s.3d. and 20 lbs groceries, and in 1916 £1.11s.4d. and 27 lbs rice, etc. In 1920 a cheque for £6 and 21 lbs of various articles were sent, and in 1922 they achieved a record with 83 lbs of groceries and £1 in cash.

Early in the new century St Thomas' church inaugurated a Village Nurse Association, and efforts were made to raise funds in numerous ways. In September and December 1912, for example, a jumble sale and musical evening were held in the Stopsley school hall. By January 1913 Nurse Bailey had been appointed and was attending to cases of measles in the village. She was paid £75 per annum, but this soon became a drain on resources, especially during the War.   In 1918 the County Council agreed to pay half the cost, if the village found the remainder from its Julius Wernher legacy.   There was no doctor in Stopsley until the Clinic opened in 1922.

There was a diphtheria outbreak in the Luton area in September 1913.   In Stopsley it seems to have begun in the homes of the Dawson and Brown families in Bury Road. Red crosses were painted on the house doors to warn unsuspecting visitors.   Dr Morcom, the Medical Officer and Mr Pickering, the District Surveyor, inspected the school building as a possible source of infection but found it clean and satisfactory. Gladys, Frank and Mabel Dawson and Leonard and Violet Brown all contracted the disease and some were sent to Spittlesea.   Anxious mothers, some of whose children had sore throats, congregated at the school gates, for information.   The epidemic passed and all the children recovered.   Unfortunately, two years later, in April 1915 another major diptheria epidemic struck the village and nine families were effected. The school was closed for two weeks, and a 4 year old boy, Frederick Catlin, died. Less serious was 'itchy koo', the childrens name for vitamin C deficiency which caused them to itch all over.

Stopsley's children had far better medical provision than their parents.   In 1907 a clause in the *Education (Administrative Provisions) Act* required Local Education Authorities 'to provide for the medical inspection of children immediately before, or at
>the time of, or as soon as possible after, their admission to a public elementary school, and on such other occasions as the Board of Education direct, and the power to make arrangements ..... for attending to the health and the physical condition of the children educated in public elementary schools.'

On Thursday 16th July 1908 forms for Medical Inspection were sent to all the parents of Infant children at Stopsley school, to be filled in and returned by the following day.   Three days later Dr W. J. Butcher carried out the first medical inspection of 50 children in the school's history.   These inspections were to continue, usually at yearly intervals, to the present day.   In December 1919 Mr F.S. Cooper, the Dentist, made his first visit.   In 1921, 17 Infants and five older children had teeth extracted in school.   Dr Herdman called in 1920, offering to remove tonsils at 2s.6d (12½p) a time.   Children with special problems were referred to the doctors, 'Gladys D. (consumption case specially put forward by Mr Breed for examination) ordered absence until Christmas.(1922).'   'Albert R. aged 11 years, found by Dr Herdman to be a case of 'arrested development' is transferred back to Infants for twelve months (1925).'   'Dr King examined one mentally deficient Infant child (1930)'.   Head inspections for lice also occurred regularly.   They reached epidemic proportions in the Infant school in February 1917.   By 1941 head inspections were being supervised by the local Health Visitor, known affectionately to the children as 'Nitty Norah'.   During the 2nd World War school children were subjected to a more rigorous examination.   In March 1940 Headmaster, Leonard Benson recorded: '35 children examined today ends first week of medical inspection.   The examination is the most thorough that has taken place with 1 doctor and 2 nurses in attendance.'

A new brick-built isolation hospital was opened at Spittlesea in 1925 with extensions in 1936.   Dr Fred Grundy became Medical Officer of Health for Luton in 1937.   He was horrified by the apparent apathy on the part of Luton parents to having their children immunised, and he inaugurated a massive campaign of immunisation for local school children.   At Stopsley school on 11th February 1940 'so many children had applied to be immunised against Diphtheria that it was decided to do this in the schools and it was carried out this morning by the Medical Officer at 10 am to 10.45

am.' Further injections were given a month later. A special Smallpox Hospital also stood close to Spittlesea in south Stopsley from 1928 to 1948, but it was fortunately seldom used and closed when the National Health Service began. It was later demolished to make way for the Airport.

Writing in the *Bedfordshire Magazine* in the summer of 1966 the Revd. Arthur B. Allen recalled an old Stopsley herbalist, Granny Mead, who lived by the village Green. 'There were few ailments that Granny could not cure, from warts to the relief of, if not the cure of, rheumatism. When the season was right, and the weather set fair, Granny would be away over the fields, gathering her roots and flowers, fruits and leaves, that were to be brewed into balms and lotions, pills and simples.' Granny Mead is not in the 1891 Census and may be the creation of Arthur Allen's fertile imagination, but she typifies the many country folk who drew on natural remedies for cures.

In 1934, another herbalist, Ronald Albert Hopkins, opened his Chemist shop at 615 Hitchin Road, in Stopsley. He was 24 years old at the time. His family were of labouring stock, originating at Trowley Bottom near Flamstead. Educated at Luton Modern School on Park Square, he later studied pharmacy at The Square, the London headquarters of the Royal Pharmaceutical Society, whilst being apprenticed to the Luton chemists, Duberly and White. He was admitted to the Pharmaceutical Register in 1933. He acquired a shop in Grange Road, Leagrave and the following year took over the Stopsley shop from a man called Bedford, whose chemist business was not doing very well. 'At first,' he observed in 1993, 'it was a bit like surfing, the force of the wave carried you along and you made a go of it. I was an elaborate herbalist, helping people to die comfortably.' Hopkins was fascinated by old herbal remedies, and grew many pharmaceutical plants from which he knew useful and life-enhancing drugs had been obtained, often displaying them in his shops. At first, in order to make ends meet, he also ran a small library of the latest fiction, for which he charged a modest sum. 'It paid the electricity bills,' he said. During the War his reputation grew and he became the poor man's alternative to the doctor. He could be relied upon to offer sound advice that cost nothing. With the foundation of the National Health Service in 1948 and the growth in prescriptions, the business flourished and expanded into six further branches around Luton and at Toddington. Stopsley remained the retail and wholesale headquarters, with an extensive warehouse in Venetia Road. At its height 'R. A. Hopkins Ltd.' employed more than 60 people. The Stopsley shop, which began as two tiny 'lock-up' rooms, was enlarged a number of times. Since his death in 1993, his son Brian and daughter Christine Horden, both directors of the firm, have continued Stopsley's longest running family business.

Prior to the National Health Act of 1948 all medicines and treatment had to be paid for by individuals. Some men subscribed to 'the Panel', but that did not cover wives and children. In the earlier years of the century most people walked or cycled everywhere, enjoying much more exercise. The mass development of motor cars in Luton, and the easy terms given to employees to purchase them, created the overweight, under exercised population now found all over Britain.

There was no resident doctor (general practitioner) in Stopsley before 1936. Immediately prior to that date Dr Robert Gregory, at 258, High Town Road, Round Green, dealt with most health problems in the village, including mid-wifery. In 1936 Dr Redvers Anderson from Northampton acquired Stopsley House (589 Hitchin Road) and set up a surgery in outbuildings at the rear. His sister Daisy acted as his receptionist, secretary and general assistant. Much liked by his patients, he was not very popular with his peers, at times being considered somewhat unorthodox in his methods. He employed Alfred Warren of 37 Ashcroft Road as his chauffeur. On his death his practice was acquired by Dr George E. Garratt. Born in the Midlands in 1906 Garratt spent his youth in Llandudno, where he was fascinated by ornithology. After studying at Queen's College, Cambridge and St Bartholomew's Hospital, London, he came to his only practice at Stopsley in 1947. At first Dr Garratt worked single-handed, with his wife Veronica caring for most of his secretarial needs; but later he formed an alliance with Dr Joachim to share night duties. Dr K. K. Joachim had opened a surgery at 257 Hitchin Road during the 1939-45 War and had many patients in the Stopsley area. Dr Garratt built up a large and expanding practice, which eventually exhausted him. He died whilst still working in March 1974 at the age of 68. The practice became fragmented after his death, but many of his patients passed to Dr B. Kaluarachi and are now with Dr P. S. Bath at 49 Ashcroft Road. Mrs Garratt continued to live at Stopsley House for a further four years, before moving to Hitchin. Both she and George Garratt played an active part in village affairs, often acting as President or Chairman to a number of organisations. A memorial tree in the Vale cemetery remembers them as 'servants of this community'.

In the 1920s Dr J. A. Clarke ran a Practice at 1 Union Street, Luton. On his retirement it was taken over by his son John G. R. ('Jack') Clarke, who had trained at St Thomas' Hospital in London. In the 1950s and 60s the Practice was joined by Drs. T. W. Leslie Roberts, David A. Riley and Lindsay J. Burton. Immediately prior to the War Clarke had bought a new house at 702 Hitchin Road, Stopsley (the present Vicarage) with a purpose-built surgery, from which he practised in the Stopsley area. With the rapid growth of housing in Stopsley and High Town during the post-war period, the patients in those areas soon exceeded those in the town centre. Consequently Clarke and his partners decided to close the Union Street surgery and in 1967 opened a newly built one at what is now the Stopsley Green Surgery at 26 Ashcroft Road, to which Dr Clarke's 702 Hitchin Road patients were transferred. It was subsequently necessary to enlarge the new surgery on two occasions.

Also in the early 1960s, Dr Maxwell had opened surgeries at 172 Ashcroft Road and 42 Lalleford Road to cover the Ramridge and Hart Lane estates. He was succeeded by Dr L. G. Capaldi who had a special surgery built at 172a Ashcroft Road. He practised there for a number of years until health problems forced him to retire.

The Old School at Butterfield's Green road was used as a monthly Clinic for ante- and post-natal care from 1922 at a rent of 10/- (50p) per quarter. In 1926, and now fortnightly, it moved to the new Church Institute at a cost of £6 per annum, paid by the Bedfordshire County Council. When Luton took over in 1933 they offered the Church the same rent, but wanted the hall weekly. The Church demanded, and eventually got, a higher rent! The Institute was used intermittently as a Clinic until the 1950s. Stopsley Day Nursery, opposite St Thomas' Church, opened on 27th October, 1944. Purpose-built in brick it was expected to have a long life. Miss Hadfield was the first Matron, supervising the nursery until July 1963, when she was succeeded for ten months by Mrs Price and then Mrs Norwood (1964-69). Its longest serving matron, Mrs Payne was at Stopsley from 1969 to 1994.

'The Chase Nursing Home' (at the present Hitchin Road- Birchen Grove junction) provided maternity and nursing care during and just after the 2nd World War. It had been set up by a local G.P., Dr Hegarty, who had a particular interest in midwifery. It was run by Mrs J. Healey. She is reputed to have accepted a number of military service girls who found themselves pregnant, and supplied them with food, lodging and delivery by Dr Hegarty in return for help with household chores. A large number of Stopsley children were born at 'The Chase'.

Neither Drs. Garratt or Joachim did any mid-wifery, and Dr Clarke's practice looked after most of their pregnant patients as well as his own for ante-natal care and home deliveries. Most of this ante-natal work was done at the Stopsley Infant Welfare Clinic, adjoining the Day Nursery, where the doctors were joined by the District Midwives. At one time they were delivering 360 babies a year, but by the mid 1970s home deliveries became a rarity. The emphasis was on hospital delivery and the 'flying squads' for attending emergencies during the course of home delivery were run down.

Dr Clarke retired from general practice in 1968, following a coronary thrombosis, although he continued to work for the area health authority. Leslie Roberts left the Stopsley Green Surgery shortly afterwards and emigrated to South Africa. In 1969 Drs. F. P. Adler and Michael Spira joined the practice. Tragically, David Riley died of cancer in 1972, and his place was taken by Richard Prigg. Dr Burton then became the Senior Partner. By that time Dr K. K. Joachim in Hitchin Road was finding his practice increasingly difficult to manage. He and Dr Garratt were both single-handed and covered for each other for out of hours work, night calls, etc. On the death of Dr Garratt in 1974 Joachim joined the Stopsley Green practice, seeing his own patients during the day, but being covered by the Stopsley doctors at other times. When he retired the majority of his patients remained at Stopsley. The village's first lady doctor, Krishna Sen, arrived in 1975 and in 1983 Dr Georgina Johnson joined her. In 1986 tragedy struck again when Dr Prigg died from the same type of cancer as his predecessor. He was a well-loved and respected practitioner and was sadly missed by all his patients. Dr Chris Ellis endeavoured to fill his place, and Drs Sara Warriner and Diane Seamark arrived in 1989-90. When Linsay Burton retired in January 1990, Dr Adler became the Senior Partner.

Scores of new patients from the extensive building developments in the Wigmore area caused the Stopsley Green Surgery to burst at its seams; and so with the approval of the local health authority, a new surgery was opened in the Clinic at Wigmore. Drs Johnson and Ellis moved there, and were joined by Dr Hill-Smith. In 1993 the Wigmore and Stopsley practices split and are now quite separate, although much co-operation continues between them.

A Clean Water Supply

Today when we take the provision of clean water for granted it is hard to imagine when every drop had to be drawn from a well or pump. The Luton Water Company was formed in 1865, and within five years sufficient wells had been dug and mains laid to supply the whole of Luton. But Stopsley was two miles from Luton and nearly 55 metres higher. Very expensive pipes and strong pumps would be needed to carry water to the village. Consequently, it was more convenient to leave the villagers with their own wells, and let them continue to collect water by the pailful when required. Over the previous century a number of droughts had occurred in very hot summers which had caused some of the village wells to dry up, sounding a warning of possible troubles to come.

In 1884 the Water Company considered bringing water to Stopsley. The village had 820 inhabitants at that time, and if all the householders consumed water belonging to the Company there would be revenue of £62. However, there was insufficient support and the scheme was dropped. In June 1896 the Parish Council drew up a petition asking the Water Company to extend their mains to Stopsley. It was placed in Jabez Cook's shop for the signatures of those willing to have water laid to their houses. 81 people signed, which would have provided a revenue of £40. In October the Company said that they could not risk bringing the water mains to Stopsley on the responsibility of the tenants alone. The owners of the houses must be responsible, and would have to guarantee an agreed sum for five years. Mr T. G. Sowerby of Putteridge Bury said that he would be willing to guarantee the cost if the mains were extended to Whitehill, Manor and Pond Farms.

In March 1897 the Water Company proposed a charge of £2,200 for bringing water to Stopsley; this the Parish Council found unreasonable. A separate report commissioned by the Rural District Council said that a supply of water from Luton Water Company was impracticable since most of Stopsley was at the same height as the reservoir at Hart Hill. The R.D.C. offered to dig a well at Stopsley, with a tank, winding gear pump, and mains supply to all houses for £966. The Parish Council deferred a decision.

Matters came to a head in July 1898 when every well in Stopsley ran dry. Two 1,000 gallon water carts had to be brought up to the village from Luton each evening at a cost of 3s.8d. (c.17p) a cart. The Medical Officer for Health, Dr Morcom, began an investigation. He found that sewage had seeped into some of the storage tanks and any water left was too filthy to drink It was months before some of the tanks and wells were cleaned and back in use again. The Water Company now asked for £1,000 to lay the mains, and further lengthy haggling took place.

Eventually in November 1899 a decision was reached. All the expenses of the water scheme would fall on Stopsley. A 4-inch (11 cms.) main would be laid from Hart Hill at a cost of £500; the payment of interest and cost of water adding a further £60 per year. The sum would be levied on the Rates and each cottage would pay no more than 2d. per week; the larger houses a slightly higher rate. Charles Breed, the schoolmaster, agreed to collect the revenues for the District Council.

The Parish Council accepted the proposal, and seventeen years after the scheme was first mooted, the digging of the new mains began on 22nd April 1901. The system was completed seven weeks later, with complaints that paths had not been properly relaid, and that tree roots had been damaged. A Water Tower was built at Hart Hill in 1900 to raise the head of the water supply for Stopsley. On 7th June 1901 a Turning-On Ceremony was held at a stand-pipe on Chapel Green, attended by the entire Parish Council, District Councillors, surveyors and contractors. In the School Log Book Charles Breed wrote 'Water was obtained this evening for the first time from the water taps.' These taps stood in the village street, but did not extend to the school itself. Three months later the main had been extended along Park Lane (Putteridge Road) to Putteridge Bury, and in 1906 it was taken along Ramridge End Road (Ashcroft Road) as far as the Turners Road junction. On 20th June Mr Breed wrote 'The house and school were connected with the water mains outside', and on 11th July he added 'Water available in school and house'.

Following the rapid expansion of Stopsley during the first half of the 20th century, it was decided in 1957 to construct a reservoir at Whitehill Farm (TL:105254). At a height of 178 metres above sea level, and with a capacity of one million gallons, water was pumped to it, mainly at night, from the Hart Hill reservoirs. During the day this supplied Stopsley and north Luton.

With further development, especially in the Wigmore area of Stopsley, it became necessary to increase and re-route the water supply to Whitehill Farm. In 1998 the source of the water was the Graffham Water reservoir in Huntingdonshire, where it was treated, before being pumped via the Sundon reservoir (TL:062283) to Whitehill. Most of the water was used to supply Stopsley and the airport, although some was taken from Whitehill and blended with water from boreholes at Crescent Road, Luton. This was then treated at the Hart Hill treatment works, before being supplied to central Luton.

Street Lighting

It is hard to imagine Stopsley on a dark winter evening without the orange glow of sodium street lamps. Yet in 1896 the only light to fall on the uneven roads was the candle or oil lamp-light that filtered from uncurtained cottage windows. In that year the Parish Council considered setting oil lamps on wooden standards around the village, but nothing seems to have come of it. The first building to be lit by gas-light was Putteridge Bury House, which had its own private gas works, situated in the spinney at the end of Putteridge Road beside the High School. Workmen digging trenches at Putteridge Bury College or in the Park often come across old lead gas pipes.

The Luton Gas Company had laid its pipes to the Borough boundary by 1904. After discussions with the Parish Council in 1906 the Company agreed to bring gas to Stopsley if 30 or 40 consumers could be found. By February 1907 some 58 people had agreed to use gas. The Company then began delaying tactics, and it was not until early in 1912 that a gas main reached the village. A number of private houses, chapels and the school soon installed gas lighting.

It was another ten years before any action was taken on gas street lighting. In September 1922 the Parish Council held a public meeting to consider the advisability of adopting the new Street Lighting Act. As a result the Gas Company was asked to erect gas lamps at the Village Green, the War Memorial, Marsom Place and Arsley Bottom (the roundabout at the junction of Hitchin Road and Vauxhall Way). The lamps did not work automatically. Sidney Peacock was appointed the first lamplighter at a salary of 6 shillings (30p.) a week. An iron bracket protruded from the top of the cast iron lamp standards. Mr Peacock rested his ladder against this as he climbed up to clean the glass or change the gas mantle. He used a long pole to turn on the Stopsley lamps. They were lit for the first time on 7th December 1923 and were an immediate success. By the following September sixteen lamps had been set up around the village.

George Fensome took over as lamplighter in September 1927. His annual conditions of employment stated: 'The Lamplighter to light, extinguish and clean the lamps from the 1st October 1927 to 31st March 1928. That the lamps be lighted at a reasonable hour and extinguished on dark nights at 10.30 pm. When the moon is bright no lamp need be lighted.' In September 1929 a lamp erected at the corner of Park Road (Putteridge-Ashcroft) was knocked down by a cow! By 1932 the spread of lamps indicated the growth of new housing in the village to Sowerby Avenue, Cannon Lane, Lothair Road, Bradgers Hill and Lynwood Avenue.

On 1st September 1939 all street lamps were extinguished for the duration of the War. From the 1950s the gas lamps were slowly replaced by orange sodium electric lights, using cheaper off-peak electricity.

Highways and Byways

For the majority of Stopsley people at the beginning of the 20th century the only means of transport was on foot. Consequently footpaths were more important to rural folk than roads. Paths tended to follow traditional routes from one point of importance to another. This was normally the most direct route to work or to the neighbouring villages. Stopsley was criss-crossed with a network of such tracks. The Parish Council investigated numerous unsuccessful attempts by landowners to block them. Not least, that of Captain Clutterbuck at Putteridge Bury (page 62). As the village has been built up, old paths have been diverted or have vanished, though vestiges of them can still be found. For example, Cannon Lane was originally the continuation of a footpath that ran from Butterfield's Green to Ramridge Road. Because of building, it dog-legs in Putteridge Road and forms the alleyway linking Hawthorn Avenue, Hazelwood Close and Wigmore Lane, passing behind a service station to reach Ramridge End Lane (Ashcroft Road). A second lost branch ran through Lane Farm and out towards Mangrove and Cockernhoe.

Stopsley was not on a regular stage-coach route though coaches stopped at the *White Horse* from time to time. It was the carriers' carts of the late 19th century that called for a direct road from Luton to Hitchin. This passed through Stopsley via Whitehill Farm and Lilley. Maps show a move to the present line of the A505 from around 1900. There was a blacksmith's workshop beside Dyer's Cottages (behind 769 Hitchin Road), well placed to attend to cast horseshoes, farm machinery or carriage repairs. Another stood beside Green Farm, later becoming a garage for tractor and car repairs. Most 19th century traffic took the form of farm animals, carts and machinery. All the roads were narrow, often with passing places. They were frequently deeply rutted with surfaces of rubble, flints and clay. In wet weather they were almost impossible to negotiate. One of the worst was Bradgers Hill where farmers needed three horses to drag one cart up the hill in 1896. The village centre was little better. At times it resembled a farmyard, with ducks, chickens and geese scratching for titbits, and dogs wandering freely. In September 1900 the Parish Council noted that 'the footpaths and channels [gutters] of the village have been neglected of late, and no one has attended to them. The main path of the village and the path leading to the school [at Swift's Green] need great repair, the former being the worst kept path in the village'. It was proposed that 10 cart loads of ashes be laid in the worst spots at a cost of 4 pence per load of ashes and 1/3d. (7p.) carting and laying. In 1904 the Stopsley to Round Green Road (known locally as the Main Road) was considered sufficiently dangerous as to need widening to 21 feet (6.4 metres) at a cost of £95. George Powdrill, the farmer at Crawley Green Farm, acquired a traction engine in 1904 and this did considerable damage to the unmettalled road surface in the area which would cost £15 to repair. 'Mr Powdrill's engine has smashed up the roads very much.' These extremely heavy steam engines, primarily used for driving threshing machines, continued in use well into the post 1939-45 war period. The writer's uncle, Noah Day of Higham Gobion, (having survived the Great War) was killed when one that he had been driving, ran backwards over him on Eaton Green Road hill (beside Luton Airport) in 1921.

A new problem emerged in 1907 when the county surveyor, William Leete, was asked to erect danger signals for motorists in the village. The problem was exacerbated by the proximity of Vauxhall Motors, who had begun constructing motor cars in Luton in that year. On some busy weekends as many as five cars a day had been seen in the village! As nothing had been done by the following March, Mr Leete received a letter, 'calling his attention to the sharp corners in the village, and urging that steps be taken to erect signals at such places, calling the attention of motorists to the necessity of driving carefully so as to avoid danger to the public.' In 1912 and 1927 requests were made for traffic signs warning of the sharp corner near the school. A crossing marked by Belisha beacons was laid out opposite the school gates in 1938.

The Parish Council also received complaints of the excessive speed of motor vehicles passing along the Main Road. Four dogs were killed during one summer, but requests for a speed limit were opposed by the motoring organisations. Inevitably it took a fatal accident before anything was done. Tragically, at 8.50 am on 25th April, 1917, six years old Frederick Armitage was knocked down and killed by a motor cycle on his way to school. The Infant School Headmistress, Charlotte Nott, and six of Frederick's fellow pupils attended the funeral on 30th April, whilst the older children lined the footpath as the cortége passed the front of the school. Another Stopsley School child, Millicent Day, aged 9, of Moreton Road, was knocked down and killed by a motor car at Round Green in January 1923.

It was during the 1920s that a number of new roads were constructed in Stopsley, mainly by private contractors. On various occasions the Parish Council was asked to consider the diversion or closure of popular footpaths close to the village centre. Their places would be taken by the new roads, some of which, such as Lothair Road and Lynwood Avenue, were not adopted by the Rural District Council or the Luton Borough Council until the late 1930s. It was at that time that a Petrol Station opened in front of Green Farm with a Garage in the adjoining workshop. It was to be the first of a long series or repair shops, showrooms and filling stations on the site.

In January 1928 Luton Rural District Council expressed concern at the increase in traffic passing through Luton, and considered the possibility of the Ministry of Transport constructing a by-pass south from Stopsley along Wigmore Lane to Eaton Green, Dane End and the London Road, and another from Stopsley west to the New Bedford Road, so that all heavy traffic could avoid the town. Sadly, like most good schemes, nothing came of it.

The Bedfordshire Regional Planning Report (1937) proposed a somewhat similar route, 120 feet wide, running north-east from the London Road (A6) at Bull's Wood to the south-east of the Vauxhall Works, across Kimpton Road, through the old sewerage works and up the valley past Nether Crawley Farm. It joined the Hitchin Road east of The Chase at Arsley Bottom, then proceeded north-west to cross St Thomas's Road at Bradgers Hill, and joined the New Bedford Road north of the Icknield Way intersection. In 1939 preliminary survey work on this route (along the present Airport and Vauxhall Ways) came to a sudden halt due to the outbreak of War.

It was not until 12th October 1978 that Vauxhall Way (the eastern section), and November 1985 that Airport Way (the south section), linked the A6 south of Luton to the Hitchin Road (A505). The urgently needed link between the Hitchin Road at Arsley Bottom and the New Bedford Road (A6) south of Streatley seems no closer, sixty years after it was first planned. The proposed east-west Trunk Road (TP29) from Stopsley, across Bradgers Hill to Bushmead Road, begun in 1937, was never completed (see page 134).

From 1908 to 1932 a tram service ran from Luton to Round Green, but no closer to Stopsley. It made the journeys into Luton that much easier and was particularly popular with hat workers. On dark winter evenings the girls returning to Stopsley from Luton would group together, afraid to walk on their own under the fir trees between The Chase and Dropshort. It was there on the bank at Arsley Bottom that the tramps congregated to light their fires and boil their billy cans.

In 1912, Thomas Attree began a bus service from Luton, through Stopsley to Hitchin and Letchworth. From Whit Monday of that year he ran three buses a day to Hitchin, with extra ones on Tuesdays (Market Day). The journey took 1¾ hours and cost 1s. 3d. In 1925 Attree sold his buses and routes to the National Bus Company. About 1930 William Brain ran an old Commer Cars bus with solid tyres from Luton to Stopsley and Breachwood Green, twice a day. In 1932 the Parish Council requested Luton Corporation to extend its bus service to Stopsley. The National Bus Company continued to operate a long distance service from Luton to Stopsley, Hitchin, Letchworth, Arlesey, Norton, Baldock and Stotfold, and a new local service from Luton to Stopsley and Ramridge End. The bus stops were situated at Dropshort, the War Memorial, the Infant School and the old school at Swift's Green (the Crematorium). For a time during and after the 2nd World War the terminus for the No. 11 bus which ran directly from Williamson Street, Luton to Stopsley was beside the Police Box in the centre of the village Green. With the post-war growth of the village new Corporation Bus routes appeared; in particular the No. 4 from Park Square, via Hart Lane to the Ramridge estate, and along Ashcroft Road to Stopsley Green.

The Emergency Services

The Bedfordshire County Constabulary acquired a new Police House at 29 Lothair Road during the late 1920s. This was occupied by P.C. Minney until the Luton Borough Police Force took it over in 1933. At that time P.C. Christopher Fryer and his family moved in. His daughter, Fay Weighell recalls that 'at that time Lothair Road was 'unadopted' and a sea of mud in winter and baked into deep, hard ruts in the summer. There was a metal sign over the door saying 'POLICE HOUSE' which eventually fell off and was never replaced. The House was used as the local Police Office and everything and everybody from stray dogs to battered wives appeared at the door, all round the clock. Police Officers' wives were not supposed to take up employment, so that there was always someone at home to take messages, render first-aid, comfort the distressed and give general help. Tramps, walking from one 'casual ward' to another (St Margaret's Home at Bramingham was the nearest) were given mugs of tea and a sandwich, and one 'regular' used to call once a year for an old pair of father's stout police boots. These tramps were decent men, victims of the 30's economic depression. 'Casual wards' were state hostels, spaced out across the country, roughly one day's walk apart. The homeless, workless could get a hot bath, a meal and a bed and breakfast before setting off on another day's measured walk, in all weathers, carrying all they owned in a sack.'

The Police House was 'tied' and was, in effect, rented from the Borough Council, which was responsible for repairs, decoration and maintenance. A major underpinning of the front corner was carried out in the 1930s when it collapsed, due to subsidence.

During 1937 a dark blue Police Box with emergency telephone for public use was set-up on the village Green. A blue light flashed on top of the box when a constable was wanted urgently by the Luton Police Headquarters. The constables patrolled their beats, between one box and another, usually on bicycles. They also varied their times and routes to fool criminals relying on their regularity. During the War the flashing light was screened so that it was not visible from aircraft flying above.

The history of the Luton police force is detailed in T. J. Madigan's book *The Men Who Wore Straw Helmets: Policing Luton 1840-1974* (1993) and does not need to be repeated here. Suffice to say that the days of the foot-patrolling policemen, once a common sight in Stopsley, are now largely forgotten. Motor transport is the order of today. Community policemen and women are sparse on the ground and are expected to cover an impossibly large territory. One Constable patrols the same area as P.C. Fryer did in 1933. The only difference is that the population of that same area has increased a hundred fold!

The Luton Fire Brigade, formed in 1844, was taken over by the Board of Health in 1864. As it was originally a purely voluntary brigade, it is unlikely that its horse-drawn engine would have ventured up to Stopsley, unless there was a major conflagration, such as that at Stopsley Lane Farm in 1860 or Mixes Hill Farm in 1881. A Luton Fire Station was built in Church Street in 1876, but its officers still served on a voluntary basis until 1914. In that year the first full-time firemen were recruited and motor engines introduced. In 1940 the Church Street Station was replaced by one in Park Street, and by 1956 the present Studley Road Station had taken its place. The rapid post-war growth of Stopsley meant that fire-cover on the eastern side of Luton was under strength. On 16th May, 1984, Lord Elton, Minister of State at the Home Office opened the Stopsley Fire Station in Stopsley Way. Independent of the Luton Station, it has its own pump engine and rescue vehicle, and receives its emergency calls direct from the central County Control at Kempston.

Housing Problems

With the exception of some of the Farms, a large number of houses in Stopsley towards the end of the nineteenth century were old and inferior cottages. Many were timber framed with brick or daub fillings and tiled roofs: a few were thatched. They were essentially labourers' cottages, often consisting of little more than a single all-purpose ground-floor room, with another in the roof. Even the pretentious timber-framed 'Thatched Cottage' in Butterfield's Green Road, consisted in the 1920s of two semi-detached labourers cottages, possibly built about 1760, one with a tiled roof and the other with thatch. These were knocked into one cottage in the late 1930s. In the 1950s it was demolished by its owner, Frank Cox, who designed and rebuilt the present 'cottage' from its foundations, using many of the bricks from the walls of the old Swift's Green School. Cox later exchanged the cottage with Jack Jepps, who had been born in one of the former cottages, and who laid out the gardens.

The larger 'Tithe' or 'Tythe Cottage' (Barratts, 668 Hitchin Road) probably dated from about 1600. It was the property of Daniel Queensborough of Pond Farm at the end of the 19th century. He bequeathed it to Sidney Allen in 1911, and it passed via his son's guardian, Gertrude Langdale, to Arthur B. Allen in 1932. It, too, had a timber frame with brick nogging and wattle-and-daub infilling. At one time part of it had served as Miss Menlove's School. Early in the 20th century it was divided into three separate houses occupied by the Ward family, the District Nurse and the Allen's. It later became the 'Greenways Café and Garage', with the original Stopsley Working Mens' Club in a hut beside it. In 1963 the last remains of the Cottage were demolished leaving the garage on its own. Lee-West opened a ten-pin bowling alley beside it in

1964, which was gutted by fire in an alleged arson attack three years later. The cause of the fire was never resolved.

Quite a lot of building took place in the village soon after 1860. The old Post Office in Bury Road and the *First and Last* building are from that time. By 1880 a row of four cottages had been built at the corner of Putteridge and Ashcroft Road. Elm House (671 Hitchin Road), was built by Joseph Weatherhead 'a man of private means' about 1888. The Baptist builder, Jabez Cook, erected a block of four terrace houses on the north side of the village Green. These were pulled down in the 1960s to extend the Garage forecourt. A second row of three that once included a shop (beside Harris's Lane), still survives. Cook was also responsible for the four Park Road Cottages and the two Laurel Cottages (1894) in Putteridge Road. Other terraces were built in Hitchin Road opposite Venetia Road (Sommerfield site), and in Ramridge End Road (67 to 97 Ashcroft Road). George Duberly of Bury Farm built the Marsom Place terraces in St Thomas's Road in 1903. Other private houses of the period still standing include Stopsley House (589 Hitchin Road), Rose Cottage (1 St Thomas's Road), Jutland House, built in 1916 (618 Hitchin Road), and an unnamed house (21 Ashcroft Road).

The General Election of 1918 promised 'Homes fit for Heroes'. A Government inspired inquiry the previous year had asked the Parish Council how many additional working mens' houses it considered the village needed. It had replied '12'. Unlimited Council building of 'Homes for the Working Classes' began in Putteridge Road about 1924 with the parish liable to a fixed rate of 1 penny. Anger surfaced when the District Council allocated many of the new houses to outsiders and refused Stopsley applicants. By 1930 the Parish Council was writing to the Rural District Council requesting them to build even more houses. In December 1931 they wrote again 'that this Council looks with disfavour on the Housing Committee's action in allowing one of the Council Houses at Stopsley to be let to a person from another County when people in Stopsley for whom the houses were built, are in fear of being turned out of their homes through them being condemned'.

This situation had arisen as a result of the Rural District Council implementing the Housing Act, 1930. The council had reviewed 31 houses in Stopsley which the Medical Officer of Health and the Sanitary Inspector considered unfit for human habitation. In February 1931 demolition orders were issued for six houses in Bury Road (St Thomas's Road) known as Toyer's Cottages, one of a block of four cottages near the disused clay-pit in Bury Road, six cottages known as Dyer's Cottages (at the rear of the present 679 Hitchin Road) and two cottages known as Lane Farm cottages in Putteridge Road. A number of others, also in Bury Road, were condemned later in the year.

Reports by the Medical Officer, Dr. J. Rollings, revealed a terrible state of affairs, the cottages being in a tumble-down, unhealthy and in some cases dangerous state. Describing the six cottages in Bury Lane, reputedly built about 1870, Dr Rollings said the walls, floors, ceilings and windows were defective, the staircases were ill-lighted, and the small bedrooms inadequately ventilated. There were no places for storing food. The communal yard was in a most foul and insanitary state. The paving and the shared outside pail-closet and barn were very defective. The houses were incapable of repair at a reasonable cost. Two rooms measured 11 feet by 10 feet (3.35 m. by 3.05 m.), and two 8 feet by 7 feet (2.44 m. by 2.13 m.), and the ceilings were about 6 feet 10 ins. (2.08 m.) high. The owner of the cottages claimed that his tenants were quite happy, one having just bought a beautiful new gas stove. Dr Rollings suggested that one day he might suffocate from the fumes!

The Medical Officer described 'Toyer's Cottages' as 'absolutely impossible' and urged that they should be condemned. He pointed out that the stairs were unsafe, the treads being only 4 inches (11cms.) wide, and there were ropes so that people could pull themselves upstairs. In one house an old ladder was used as a means of access to the bedrooms. The houses contained little furniture since the tenants couldn't get it in. They did their best to keep the houses clean. They papered the walls to cover the defects, but 'some of the walls are black with mould and damp and you would be hard put to it to know whether there was any wallpaper or not. Plaster ceilings are bulging, and in some places dangerous. In some great pieces are down.' The rents varied from 4 shillings to 8 shillings (20p. to 40p.).

Dyer's Cottages were a row of six tiny houses opposite the present Vicarage in Hitchin Road. They were set well back from the road behind a large front garden, but they were in a deplorable condition and had been up for sale for many years. In 1881 there had been 12 adults and 10 children living there, sharing one pail-closet between the six cottages. One had been occupied by the village blacksmith, John Squire, in 1851, and early maps show his smithy near the road. In 1891 they were owned by Joseph Weatherhead of Elm House (671 Hitchin Road), and were occupied by the families of Charles Crick, William Whittemore, Alfred Toyer, Jesse Peters and Susan Young. Weatherhead used the sixth as a wash house and out building. In 1894 he sold Elm House and the cottages to William Dyer, a straw plait dealer from Offley. It was due to him that they were known as Dyer's cottages. In 1931 the owner proposed to build two or three houses in their place with the help of a housing subsidy (£11 for 40 years), and demolition was agreed. At the time of demolition most of them were vacant. By 1939 almost all of the village's sub-standard housing had been raised to the ground.

Gardens for All!

Most of the cottages in Stopsley had tiny gardens, comprising a rod or two of land in front, and the same quantity forming a small yard at the back. (A rod was about 5 metres). The soil was usually rich and black, the result of burying years of toilet waste. However, such small gardens were inadequate when required to provide fresh food for large growing families. 'Under such circumstances, the want of a garden is well supplied by the allotment system' wrote Samuel Beeton, husband of the Victorian cook, in his *Dictionary of Every-Day Gardening* (c.1870).

It is not clear when Stopsley had its first allotments, but it seems to have been about the same time as Mr Beeton published his *Dictionary*. The allotments were situated at Dropshort, in fields where Stopsley Way, Langford Drive and Forrest Crescent now lie. They covered some 10 acres (4.05 hectares) and were individually divided into plots of a quarter acre each (about 25 x 40 metres). The land was rented from the Lords of the Manor, the Crawley family, at Stockwood Park. The original rental charge is unknown, but it was raised to £4 an acre around 1875 to stop tenants sub-letting.

A supply of water from a pond or stream was a requisiste for good allotments. The nearest pond was on the private land of Kime's Nursery Gardens on the Hitchin Road, close to Lynwood Avenue. Mr Kime would have needed most of the water for his

XXVa: Although Stopsley had football teams for most of the 20th century, early pictures are very hard to find.   A number of the unnamed young men in this picture of the Baptist Football Club team of 1912-13 probably lost their lives three or four years later during the Great War.   (*Author's Colln.*)

XXVb: After the 2nd World War Stopsley Football Club played on Shaw's Field beside Lothair Road, where two ex-army huts provided changing rooms.   This photograph of the 1951-52 team typifies many.   *Back row:* Ron Toyer (Asst. Manager); Jack Horn; Tom Adair; David Scrimshire; Peter Brandham; Gordon Brown; Dick Halloran; Jack Groom (Trainer); *Front row:* Jack Manton; Peter McGrath; Bill Weston; Bob Manton; Billy Pugh.   (*Luton News*)

XXVIa: Stopsley had a cricket team from the middle of the 19th century, and there was considerable rivalry with teams in Lilley and Offley, who played by invitation at Putteridge Bury. This picture of the Stopsley team dates from 1920. Where it was taken is uncertain, but houses in the distance suggest not far from the village centre. The first three men in the front row are Fred Wicks, Charles Goodship and Walter Miller. Mr Crick is first in the back row. (*Freda Pinney, née Miller*)

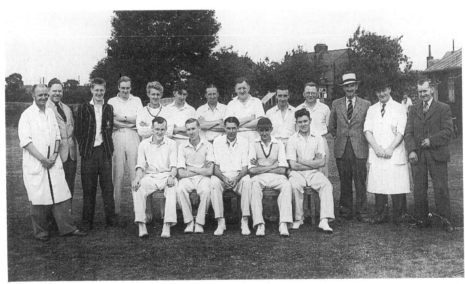

XXVIb: The Stopsley Cricket Club was dormant during the 2nd World War. It reformed in 1947, at the instigation of Harry Lowrie of the *First and Last,* and combined pub players and boys from the Youth Club. Due to poor pitch maintenance and vandalism at Lothair Road, and lack of players, the Stopsley and Offley teams combined for the first time in 1998 at Offley. Stopsley's 1952 Cricket Team: *Standing:* Dick Edwards, Harry Lowrie, David Burgess, Alan Gibbs, Ron Kavanagh, Peter Clorley, Les Burgess, 'Nobby' Clark, Albert Teasdale, Jim Sewell, Bill Walker, Jack Groom, Fred Clarke. *Sitting:* Brin Griffiths, Arthur Gunner, Bill Targett, David Scrimshire, John Massey.

XXVIIa: Part of the Ashcroft Road Recreation Ground in 1989. The Bowling Green was originally laid out by the Stopsley Working Mens' Club in the 1950s. The pavilion beside the green is the only survivor of four built in the park in 1938. The semi-circular area beside the path in the foreground was intended for seats, which never materialised due to the War. In the far distance and left of centre is the Hart Hill water tower, erected to aid the water supply to Stopsley in 1900. (*James Dyer*)

XXVIIb and c: Two of Stopsley's leading athletes. Tony Simmons (1288) won the National Cross-Country Championships at Stopsley Regional Sports Centre in 1975 and was 2nd in the World Championships the following year. (Steve Ovett won the Junior title at Stopsley in the 1975 races). The gold medal for the marathon in the Commonwealth Games in Auckland in 1974 was won by Ian Thompson, (right), who attended Stopsley Junior School and Luton Grammar School. (*James Dyer*)

XXVIIIa: The north side of the village Green on the eve of the Great War. Tithe Cottage is on the right. Most of the cottages on the left have been demolished to make way for the Service Station. At the right hand end of the row stood the *White Horse* public house, and in the centre was Harris' baker's shop. Beside it ran Harris Lane to what is now Lothair Road and the playing fields beyond. Oak and elm trees are abundant. A traffic sign stands at the end of the Green. (*Author's Collection*)

XXVIIIb: Looking west from outside Jansel House towards the old village centre (1992). Stopsley Court, on the right, is on the site of the *White Horse*. Its modern arched entrance echoes the original stable yard entrance of the 19th century. The cottage with the boarded-up bay-window was Harris' bakery, and Harris Lane ran beside the wall beyond it. (*James Dyer*)

XXIXa: The *First and Last* (in 1972) was built as a private house about 1860 and converted into a public house by the brewer, William Lucas of Hitchin, some ten years later. Modernised in the 1930s, it ceased to trade in 1997 and is now the Luton Conservative Club. Next door stands Stopsley House, possibly the first Vicarage in the village, and later the boyhood home of Arthur B. Allen, and the surgery of Dr George Garratt. (*James Dyer*)

XXIXb: Workmen preparing the first flower beds on the Green in 1948. With its prettification came the first sounds of the death knell of Stopsley as a village. The local policeman reported at intervals to the dark blue police box with its public emergency telephone. The pole above it supported the air raid siren throughout the War. On the right is Pond Farm, the pond filled in and supporting electrical equipment. The hilltop in Putteridge Road is dominated by St Thomas' Vicarage, demolished in 1972. The No. 11 bus waits at its terminus for passengers. (*Luton News: Luton Museum Collection*)

XXXa: *The Brickmakers' Arms* in St Thomas' Road seems to have begun as *The Stopsley Arms* around 1860. By the 1870s its owner, Edward Fordham the Ashwell brewer, changed its name to reflect the local industry, This picture, taken about 1920, shows the landlord George Bennett and his wife, outside the old building. There is a Navy recruitment poster on the wall. (*Kath. Crampton*)

XXXb: By the 1930s *The Brickmakers' Arms* had been largely rebuilt, and was the only local pub to offer its clients an attractive garden. Its fortunes diminished by the 1990s and it closed in 1997. In March 1998 it was gutted by fire and later demolished. This picture dates from 1972. (*James Dyer*)

XXXIa: *The Sportsman*, with the War Memorial and Methodist Chapel in 1972. Stopsley's oldest surviving public house dates from the 1830s when James Darley was the first recorded innkeeper. Like the other village centre pubs, it was given a face-lift in the 1930s, when the bay-windows were fitted, (compare plate Xb). (*James Dyer*)

XXXIb: The Bennetts' at *The Brickmakers' Arms* were keen gardeners. They celebrated their own harvest festival each year in the small room above the double doors in plate XXXa.
(*Kath. Crampton*)

XXXIIa: This old National Fire Service hut beside Greenways Café was the original home of the Stopsley Working Mens' Club which began here in October 1946. (*Stopsley Working Mens' Club*)

XXXIIb: Stopsley Library has had three homes since it first opened in 1933. Originally in a shop at 605 Hitchin Road, it moved to the corner of Lothair Road and St Thomas' Road in 1941. The present prefabricated building was opened by Sir Felix Cassel in 1948. The Council had purchased the site in 1937 for £440, but building was delayed by the War. (*James Dyer*)

own use, so the source of supply remains a mystery until a stand-pipe was set-up on the Hitchin Road in 1901.

In 1907 the Rural District Council tested the demand for small holdings in Stopsley and was surprised to get requests from ten residents for about 80 acres of land. Quite a number were disappointed as only 40 acres (16 hectares) were available, on the eastern side of Wigmore Lane and south of Darley Lane (Sowerby Avenue). Many of these were still occupied in the 1950s; some with corrugated iron shacks upon them.

A Board of Agriculture return for January 1915 recorded 66.3 acres (26.8 ha.) of allotments and small holdings in Stopsley. The County War Agricultural Committee made quantities of seed potatoes available in 1917: *Arran Chief, Up-to-Date* and *Dalhrusie* being sold at £12.10s. a ton. Mr Jesse Boulter of Pond Farm agreed to distribute them. With many men away at War, wives and grandparents were left to manage the allotments, and some found it beyond them. Mrs Cain, Mrs Church, Mr Cole and Mr Waller needed help, and Mr Breed sent some of the senior boys from the school to assist them.

With the War over, everyone wanted a garden, and in 1919 the Parish Council began negotiations to try to find more room for allotments. In Stopsley 40 new applicants, 14 of them ex-servicemen, each required 20 poles of land (110 yards or 100 metres). At that time Lane Farm in Putteridge Road was beginning to run down due to the prospect of encroaching housing, and the Parish Council pressed the County Council Small Holdings Committee to begin negotiations for 6 acres (2.4 ha.) of land. 'The field with the dip through it', part of Great Haycroft adjoining Putteridge Road, being chosen as the most suitable 'on account of its proximity to the village'. An Allotments Sub-Committee composed of Arthur Hucklesby, Thomas Willford, George Cain and Harry Warner was set up to administer the scheme. In July 1920 a further 7 acres (3 ha.) was acquired from Lane Farm at an annual rental of £18.15s. (£18.75). These new allotments in the field called Four Coat ran between the future Hawthorn Avenue and Wigmore Lane and were bounded by Green Lane and the footpath running from 13 Wigmore Lane to 50 Hawthorn Avenue.

During the late 1930s Luton Town Council had plans to sell off some of the allotment land to build houses. There was an outcry in the village and in 1937 the Stopsley Allotment Association, ably led by its spokesman, Headmaster Tom Whalley, put up a stout and largely successful resistance.

By the 2nd World War allotments had appeared behind Lynwood Avenue, Mixes Hill Road and opposite the present Vicarage. Today they are almost forgotten, and most are covered by the streets and houses of present day Stopsley. On the eastern edge of the parish at Round Green one group of allotments extended south-east of Turners Road and Somerset Avenue, whilst another lay west of the Hitchin Road roughly between The Chase, Birchen Grove and Heywood Drive. New roads had begun to encroach in that area from 1927 with the construction of Northview Road

It may be convenient here to mention beekeeping in Stopsley. Honey provided the only means of sweetening until sugar was imported in the sixteenth century. It was easier to obtain and far cheaper than sugar, and consequently most farmers and many individuals kept bees. Charles Breed, the schoolmaster, was a keen beekeeper, and considered it important that country boys and girls should know how to handle them. When a swarm settled in an apple tree in the school garden in June 1910, Breed donned suitable clothing, and showed the boys how to take the swarm and place it in an empty hive. In May 1914 he wrote 'I took the 1st class to help swarm and drive some bees. Some boys and girls got over their fears and began to handle the bees.'

In 1903 William Herrod-Hempsall and his brother Joseph moved to *The Apiary* and *Sternthorpe* in Stockingstone Road, where they set-up an apiary and a school of beekeeping, which was popular with visitors from all over the world. Their beehives were ranged in rows along the lynchet below Stockingstone Hill. William was secretary of the British Beekeepers' Association, and lectured at Swanley College, Kent. At one time he edited *The British Bee Journal*, and was a technical adviser to the Ministry of Agriculture. The brothers set up the popular observation beehive, formerly at Luton Museum and now at Stockwood Museum. Joseph Herrod-Hempsall is buried in St Thomas' churchyard. In Stopsley village, Harry Gouldthorpe and his wife were the best known beekeepers, with their apiary first in St Thomas' Road, and later at 665 Hitchin Road. Harry was a familiar figure, often seen in mask and gloves, dashing off to investigate a swarm in someone's garden.

Postal Services

It is not clear when the Post Office was first established in Stopsley. Robert Hucklesby purchased a plot of land in Bury Road (13 St Thomas' Road) from Francis Foster, a grocer and brickmaker, in August 1861, on which he built a new grocer's shop. After his death in 1872 the shop passed to his second son, Eliah, who was recorded as the Receiver for letters in 1885, At that time letters arrived in the village from the new Cheapside Post Office in Luton at 6.45 am and were dispatched at 6 pm. At first the letters were brought up to Stopsley by a postman on foot, and later by bicycle, and then distributed all over the parish. The Postman was so regular that it was claimed that you could tell the time by him. Parcels were brought up to the village in a red horse-drawn cart or coach that went on to Offley and Hitchin.

From 1900 Stopsley Post Office issued Money Orders and in 1901 became a Savings Bank. In 1903 the Parish Council requested two deliveries of letters each day. These arrived at the Post Office at 7 am and 5 pm, and there were collections at 11.20 am and 6.20 pm. On Sundays letters arrived at 7 am and were collected at 9.50 am. The second delivery did not cover all outlying parts of the parish. Houses were unnumbered until 1932. The Post Office opened on Sundays from 7.15 am to 9.55 am, but this changed in 1909 from 9.00 am to 10.00 am. In 1911 Wednesday afternoon closing was introduced. Eli Hucklesby died following a long illness, in the Three Counties Asylum near Arlesey, in December 1910; his wife Elizabeth had predeceased him in October of the same year. Their niece, Sarah Ann Kime (née Godwin) had been running the grocery shop for some years and her husband Percy Smith Kime had become the Sub-Postmaster. (Sarah Ann Kime was, incidentally, the only lady to have held the post of Vicar's Warden and Institute Secretary at St Thomas' Church).

The Parish Council made numerous enquiries between 1908 and 1924 concerning the possibility of setting up a telegraph service for the village, but all estimates were too costly. (A telegraph line from Luton to Offley had passed through the village since 1900). The Luton Telephone Exchange was opened in 1923 with a capacity for 4,000 subscribers. In October 1924 the Parish Council looked in detail at the costs for bringing a public telephone service to Stopsley. It would be required to guarantee £16 for seven years. There would be a public call-phone in the Post Office, and emergency calls could be made free of charge at the Postmaster's discretion. Private subscribers within 1 mile of the Luton Exchange would be charged 27s.6d. per quarter (£1.38p), and business subscribers 35s. plus 10s. per quarter (£2.25p). Mr William Arthur Kime, the Nurseryman, was one of the first known local subscribers.

The Post Office moved from Bury Road to Hitchin Road (opposite Venetia Road) in the 1930s, where it was run by Henry S. Beckitt as part of his General Stores. Donald Thomson owned it in 1939, and at the end of the War it was run by Kenneth W. Fryer, who gave up the Post Office in 1946. In 1948 Robert (Bob) Yeomans took over the Stores. R.W. (Bob) Warner became the Post Master in 1946 and acquired a lock-up shop on the opposite side of the road (No. 605) as a Post Office. Invalided out of the army after being wounded by a mortar shell, Bob had been with the allied troops who landed by glider at Pegasus Bridge in Normandy on 6th June 1944 and was shot during the advance. In 1954 the larger Jutland House (618 Hitchin Road), next door to the Infants' School became available, and Mr and Mrs Warner transferred the Post Office there, together with a confectionery, stationery and wool shop. The Post Office moved to Jansel House in 1974.

The first (white) public telephone box was set up between the Garage and Cox's Grocery Store (now the Midland Bank) about 1930. Two years later it was illuminated at night. About 1938, and now painted red, it was moved to a more prominent position in front of Hopkins' Chemist Shop, where it remained until 1954. During the War it was painted grey with blacked-out windows. Its weekly cleaning was the responsibility of the village Post Master, Bob Warner, who was paid a minute sum to clean and disinfect it. In 1954 it was moved to Jutland House, and then to its present position outside Jansel House in 1974. Other early phone boxes stood at the corner of Putteridge and Stapleford roads, and at the Ashcroft and Turners road junctions.

The Demise of the Parish Council

The demise of the Parish Council was first intimated in January 1911 when plans to incorporate Stopsley with the Borough of Luton were discussed. These were more or less forgotten during the upheaval of the First World War. They re-emerged in June 1925 when the Borough extension at Round Green was discussed, and the tenants of Kenneth Road presented a petition 'against incorporation and wishing to stay in Stopsley'. By 1927 the Parish Council had 'no objection to the proposal of incorporation provided Luton Corporation also included the main inhabited portion of the parish.'

When Charles Breed became Chairman in 1928 incorporation seemed to be a *fait accompli*. Anger arose in 1932, however, when it was proposed to split the parish into two, and the Parish Council expressed 'to the Bedfordshire County Council their **Most Emphatic** objection to the merging of Stopsley into two separate wards of Luton, which have their centres a considerable distance from the population of Stopsley. In their opinion Stopsley should have a separate ward unity as its population now and in the near future demands. Since the last Census builders have provided for a considerably increased number of people and in the very near future, much building will be done, and it is incumbent that the people should have a ward representation, as has been allowed to Limbury and Leagrave so that Stopsley's interests are not overridden.' Charles Breed and Tom Whalley represented the Parish Council at an inquiry in May 1932 which reviewed the future County Districts, and the outcome seems to have been acceptable to most Stopsley people. On 1st April 1933 Stopsley became a part of the Borough of Luton, but with a strong individual identity, which has lost little of its fervour, more than sixty-five years later.

The final full Parish Council meeting was held on 6th March, 1933, 'when valedictory cigars, cigarettes and sandwiches were passed amongst the Councillors.' They were Charles Breed (Chairman), Miss Maud Hucklesby (Vice Chairman), James Titchmarsh, Harry Warner, Albert Cook, Frank Summerfield, W. J. Hutchings, H. J. Beckett, R. Tom Whalley and Arthur Cain (Clerk).

Charles Breed had been associated with the Parish Council since its inception in 1896, first as Clerk until 1928, and then as Chairman. At the final meeting he recalled John Impey, the first Chairman, as 'a rugged, plain, homely personality, whose only question about anything was "Is it for the good of Stopsley? If so, we must have it, or try to have it."' Looking back on what the Council had achieved in 37 years, Breed recalled that it could pride itself on the provision of good footpaths in the village centre and to Round Green. When it began, children could not go to school properly washed as their parents had insufficient water to wash them. Thanks to the Parish Council Stopsley now had a water supply pumped into the village from Luton mains since June 1901. After the water came a supply of gas for the houses transforming the dingy-looking cottage interiors 'into flaring palaces'.

The Council's Accounts closed with a balance of £1.3s.6d (£1.18p). Enough, it was suggested, to provide a supper for the members. Unfortunately the balance had to be handed over to the Luton Borough Treasurer!

'I'm all right, Jack!'

The 1920s and 30s were the years of industrial depression and the General Strike, yet as John Dony has written about Luton 'There was comparatively little unemployment in the town. It is probably true to say that Luton was the most prosperous - or least depressed - town in Britain between the wars. There were two reasons .....Luton enjoyed diversity of industry ..... and there was an increasing demand for the goods which Luton made.'

In the 1920s there was something of a post-war building boom, with council and private houses being built in many parts of Luton and the surrounding hamlets - the 'homes fit for heroes!'. In Stopsley there were Council houses on the north side of Park Lane (Putteridge Road), Dellcot Close, Hayes Close, and Cannon Lane. The various Stopsley brickworks were at their busiest. Ex-army officers spent their gratuities on small enterprises, of which the most successful locally were probably egg farms. Other Stopsley folk followed suit, though on a much smaller scale. Charles Fitzjohn had his Laurel Cottages poultry farm in Putteridge Road, Thomas Croxton had another at Mobley (now in Forrest Crescent), the Angell's had one at the rear of 104 Ashcroft Road, and there were more beside. In Butterfield's Green Road and at Tithe Cottage Frederick Jepps, Arthur Ward and Stanley Ward were all higglers or egg dealers: collecting eggs (and anything else saleable) from the farms and selling them at competitive prices at the local markets.

In October 1936 the employment figures for Luton were:

Men	31,489	Women	14,798	Total	46,287
Unemployed:					
Men	942	Women	845	Total	1,787

Less than 4% were unemployed. In Jarrow in County Durham the figure was about 80%. It was not surprising, therefore, that when news of Luton's 'prosperity' spread, thousands left the depressed Merseyside and north-eastern areas and made for Luton. Vauxhall Motors, the Davis Gas Stove Co., George Kent, Electrolux and Skefko were but a few of the local factories who chose to employ them, sometimes in preference to local men. The straw hat industry had suffered a set-back as a result of the 1914-18 War, but it now began a revival, specialising in felt hats and millinery for out-workers (women who decorated hats at home). Most Stopsley men were in work, though many of the traditional agricultural jobs had given way to light engineering. The village was becoming a dormitory for Vauxhall employees. Even so, there **was** unemployment in Stopsley and in Luton. The sheer desperation of those who longed to work, but were unable to find employment, in spite of good qualifications, is hard to imagine. A letter in the *Luton News* for 8 October, 1936 read:

> 'Sir. I am writing you on how an unemployed man seeks work in a town where every other person exclaims, 'Oh, there's plenty of work if only you look for it.'. I am 35 - smart - fairly well educated - will take anything - but no success. H.A.'

The arrival in Luton of the Jarrow Marchers on Wednesday 28th October, 1936, was reported in 15 lines in the local press. It was, perhaps, unfortunate that it coincided with the opening of the new Town Hall by the Duke of Kent, whose visit warranted six pages plus two of photographs. The 200 marchers arrived from Bedford in the pouring rain shortly before 6 o'clock, where they were met by their M.P. Ellen Wilkinson and were briefly welcomed in the Winter Assembly Hall by the Mayor, Alderman C. C. Dillingham, before he left for the Civic Reception for the Duke. The marchers were provided with hot meals, baths, and free tickets for the local cinema, and spent the night in the Assembly Hall. This was the only stop on their march where there was no public meeting and no gifts from local firms as in other towns. Luton did no more than courtesy required: Luton had no major employment problems!

In Stopsley, the 28th October 1936 was marked by celebrations for the Duke of Kent's visit. The senior school closed all day and four double-decker buses carried the older children to Old Bedford Road to view the procession. They were brought back at 3.30 pm, and 298 of them sat down with the infants for a tea in the school hall.

Chapter 8

Social Life and Leisure in Stopsley

In 1900 Stopsley lacked two of the main requisites of rural life, a village hall and a recreation ground. A century later there is still no village hall, but we do appear to have a surfeit of recreation grounds.

The only halls of any size prior to 1927 were to be found at the schools and the Methodist Chapel. The old school at Swift's Green was not altogether suitable, being too far from the centre of the village on dark, cold winter nights. The new school of 1912 (the present Infant School) was in a much better position, well lit and heated, with plenty of space for dances and concerts. The first *Register of Lettings* kept by the Caretaker, George Cain, still survives. The major users were the church and chapels who booked it for Sunday School and socials. The Labour, Liberal and Conservative parties held electioneering meetings at regular intervals, and on many occasions it was and still is, used as a Polling Station. The Register includes bookings for whist drives, the Odd Fellows Club, Stopsley Cricket Club dinners and dances, the Small Holders' Association, the Boy Scouts and Girl Guides, the Red Cross, the International Bible Students' Association and many others. Hire charges in the 1920s averaged 7s.6d. (38p.) for 2 hours, with additional costs of 1s. each (5p.) for fires and lights, 5s. (25p.) for use of the piano and 2s. (10p.) for the Caretaker to clean up afterwards.

The Methodist Chapel had a hall built in 1894. It was certainly used for secular functions as well as Sunday School and chapel meetings. Apart from reference to concerts in which the village children took part, there are no records of how it was used. It did provide overflow classrooms when the school opposite was full to saturation point in the 1930s and the immediate post-war years. During the Second World War it was used as an emergency station by the Civil Defence organisations.

In 1890 the Revd. Paul Walker set up a St Thomas's Church Hall building fund. Very little money was collected until a determined effort under the Revd. G. H. Shorting during the 1st World War brought in £300. In February 1917 Mr Lempriere gave the Church a building plot in Bury Road, and in the same month the Parochial Church Council bought the adjoining plot. A further purchase in 1922 created a total area of 518 sq. metres. Building prices were prohibitively high in the 1920s, and because of a pressing need for a new organ in the church, funds were temporarily diverted towards that cause. Hopes of building a hall in brick were dashed when estimates between £1,317 and £2,625 were submitted. A series of fêtes, bazaars and even a limerick writing competition were rapidly organised to raise funds. In July 1926 the Church's architect, Mr Shaw, was instructed to design a building of creosoted timber and asbestos sheeting. This he did, and a contract for its construction at a cost of £906 was signed by Mr Denby Gilbert, the Vicar, in September 1926. On 12th January, 1927, the Church Institute as it was called, was opened by Lady Helen Cassel of Putteridge Bury, who described the hall as 'a great ornament to the village'. Canon Shorting recalled how two village boys, both recently killed in the Great War, had donated their pocket money to the Hall fund. One of them, Sidney Peters, who had been a member of the Sunday School and Church choir, had left money in his Post Office account for the new building.

From the beginning the gas radiators were inadequate to heat the Institute, and the piano suffered badly from damp. Consequently an instrument had to be brought by cart from Round Green whenever one was needed. In April 1935 electric light and heating were installed.

Mr Percy Kime was the first Caretaker. Eva Allen recalled that he would march into the Institute at midnight, waving a large alarm clock, and stop whatever event was in progress. The Institute had a variety of users, including the Mothers' Union, the Young Peoples' Fellowship, Church Lads' Brigade, Guides and Scouts, British Legion and the local Health Clinic. It was regularly used as a Polling Station, and political parties were permitted to use it so long as no political speeches were made. It was the venue for what was possibly the first film show in the village on 21st January 1938. The Hall was often used for amateur dramatics by village groups directed by Mrs Winifred Gilbert, or the Stopsley Ladies' Association. Other would-be thespians used St John's Church Hall at Round Green, and later St Christopher's Hall, home of the St Christopher Players. During the 1939-45 War many local groups provided a host of morale-boosting entertainments, often in aid of charity. During 1942 the Bishop of St Albans sanctioned the use of the Institute for the celebration of Mass for the Roman Catholics in the village by a Priest from Luton.

The Hall served the Church and Stopsley well, but eventually it became unsafe and uneconomic, and the use of asbestos in its fabric made it a health hazard. Consequently it was necessary to demolish the building in June 1973.

A temporary 'Day Centre' erected on the site of the Church Institute is quite inadequate for the present needs of Stopsley. The old village cries out for a Community Centre, combining a public library, day centre, assembly and lecture rooms, refreshment lounge and perhaps a police station. This should be high on the agenda of every local politician who genuinely seeks to represent the community.

The Baptist Church Hall was opened in September 1954, and catered primarily for its own organisations. The new Baptist Church of 1995 provides a venue for many activities, with its ample auditorium and meeting rooms, catering for large scale musical concerts and a wide range of conferences and rallies, as well as serving the needs of the local community 'from the cradle to the grave'.

Recreational Needs

As soon as it was formed in 1896 the Parish Council were asked to consider the need for a proper cricket field. There was a fine one at Putteridge Bury, but it was privately owned and was usually considered to be the preserve of the Lilley village team. Council member, Arthur Hucklesby, an ardent cricket player, proposed writing to the County Council asking for the provision of 'a recreation ground of not less than three acres in extent as we cannot loan one or hire one'. In 1908 the local policeman was considered to have over-reacted when he stopped cricket being played on the village Green!

At about that time 'Stopsley and District Football Club' played its matches on Smith's Meadow. This was formerly 'The Field' on the west side of Cannon Lane, roughly between Greenways and the Hitchin Road. Later the team was renamed 'Stopsley United' and moved to Shaw's Meadow, (formerly Cox Croft on the Tithe map), between Lothair Road and Manor Farm.

Smith's Meadow was also the field where the lads from Stopsley School played their home matches. The boys were expected to provide their own shorts, socks and boots, but the shirts were hired each week from G. A. Wild's Sports' Shop at 14 Manchester Street, Luton. These shirts were a faded blue colour and had been laundered many times. A boy was sent from the school to collect them on Friday afternoons and return them on Monday mornings.

It was 1919 before negotiations began, to obtain a small part of Lane Farm for a recreation ground. A field on the eastern corner of Cannon Lane and Putteridge Road was briefly used for cricket. It disappeared with the implementation of the 'Houses for the Working Classes' scheme in 1928-29. Stopsley Tennis Club had grass courts at the entrance to what is now Hayes Close until they were lost to the same scheme about 1932. In 1925 Parish Councillor Frank Summerfield spoke of the need for 10 or 12 acres of land in the middle of the village for recreation. That would have meant an outlay of about £1,600 at a time when the annual expenditure of the village was already £2,160. A sub-committee of the Parish Council was formed in 1929 which made serious attempts to obtain a playing field. In 1932 it began negotiations with Sir Felix Cassel of Putteridge Bury for a piece of land, but events were overtaken by the incorporation of Stopsley into the Borough of Luton in April 1933.

In the meantime Stopsley Cricket Club had been using land belonging to Benjamin Hartop at Eaton Green Farm. Stopsley's cricketing vicar, Mr E. D. Gilbert, tried to persuade Luton Council to develop the area as a general recreation ground. The Town Councillors had their hearts set on using the land as a municipal airport, and it was agreed to provide an alternative playing field at the northern end of Ashcroft Road. Two fields, Brays Croft and a small part of Lower Brays Croft, were purchased, comprising about 10 acres. Stopsley Athletic Football Club had been playing by private arrangement on Brays Croft for some time, whilst the Vauxhall Rugby and Football Clubs had used part of Lower Brays Croft, where they were joined by the Old Luton Modernians' R.U.F.C. The Cricket Club became defunct during the War years.

The Ashcroft Road Recreation Ground or 'Rec' as it is affectionately called, began to take shape in 1938. Almost rectangular in plan, it was surrounded by green-painted iron railings. The entrance gates, emblazoned with the Borough coat-of-arms, stood in Ashcroft Road, and borders of flowering shrubs led up into the park. At the top of the drive was a drinking fountain. To the left was a play area containing a see-saw, two sets of swings, a joy-slide, roundabout and 'umbrella'. To the right was a large oval paddling pool, with a central fountain. (The pool was closed early in the War as a precaution against poliomyelitis, and never reinstated). Beyond was the playing field with its football pitches, used by the school. An asphalt path ran around the perimeter, leading to a small gate on the far (western) side. Semi-circular areas, intended for seats, were never completed. There were four brick-built pavilions with wooden seating. Only one still survives in the Bowling Green enclosure. The only public toilets in the village were situated in the Park. Behind the pavilion in the south-eastern corner was accommodation for a Park Keeper and his maintenance equipment. Older folk remember with affection Keepers like Basil Mills and Fred Clarke who made sure that the children played safely, and lent a friendly hand if an accident occurred. They saw that both gates were locked at dusk. The War intervened before the Park was completed: no cricket table or changing rooms materialised. It did have its own air-raid shelters: they still survive under the low banks between the swings and empty paddling pool and the gardens in Ashcroft Road. Today the pavilions and toilets have been pulled down, and the Bowling Green has been constructed. More of Lower

Brays Croft field has been added to the Park on the south side. The dual-carriageway has cut off the Park from the Junior School, although the strip of grass land between the Bowling Green and the road still belongs to the school. The Bowling Green, with its South Downs turf was laid out by the Working Mens' Club in the late 1950s. It was taken over by the Parks Department of the Borough Council, and is the home of Stopsley Bowling Club.

Shortly before the 2nd World War the Borough Council purchased Shaw's Meadow (or Cox Croft) and Bean Croft, two fields situated between Hayes Wood, Lothair Road and Hitchin Road, for use as playing fields. A wooden pavilion with changing rooms for football and cricket was installed. The village Cricket Club was reformed in 1947. In 1965 the Council acquired almost all the fields north of Stopsley and west of Manor Farm for development as the Stopsley Sports Centre. It rapidly became a popular venue for a wide variety of local team games and gymnastics, and its easy access to open countryside made it ideal for major athletic events like the National and English Schools Cross-Country Championships. After enlargement the Centre was upgraded as the Stopsley Regional Sports' Centre, and was opened by Denis Howell MP., Minister of State for Sport and Recreation on 11th September 1976.

The oldest established sporting institution in Stopsley parish is the South Bedfordshire Golf Club, formed in 1891 as the Warden Hill Golf Club, with William Austin as its first secretary. The first 9-hole Golf Course came into play on and around the south-west side of Warden Hill in 1892. A wooden Clubhouse with a thatched roof, situated in Home Field (now Wybourne Drive) was opened on 12th October 1895. It contained a Gentlemen's Room with lockers and a corner fireplace, a Men's Dressing Room, and a Ladies' Room 'a charming little chamber...with dainty chairs and a little table with a little lamp all to itself'.

During the First World War a rifle range was established on the northern part of the Golf course at the foot of Galley Hill. Spent bullets are still dug-up there from time to time.

The Club fell foul of Stopsley Parish Council in 1914 when it attempted to block part of the bridle-road known as Driftway that ran between the Clubhouse and the foot of Warden Hill. In June 1931 the Club sought the Council's aid, when builders put gates across the common-road access leading from New Bedford Road to Warden Hill, causing the public to trespass on the Clubhouse grounds when lawfully proceeding to Warden Hill. On the evening of Thursday 8th July, 1931, with the support of the Footpaths and Commons Preservation Society and the knowledge that they were in the right, the Stopsley Parish Council *en masse* marched to the Golf Club and removed the obstructions.

The Golf Club moved into a new Clubhouse with panoramic views of Warden and Galley Hills in 1976. By that time a new 18-hole course, considered by many players to be the hardest in the county, stretched beside the Icknield Way and parish boundary, around the northern end of Galley Hill. A detailed history of the Golf Club was published in 1992.

For a brief period from the end of 1929 Stopsley had its own unlicensed Greyhound Racing Track. It was situated between Ashcroft Road and Hawthorn Avenue, at the rear of houses in Putteridge Road. The Track was run by Jack Gates and his son Freddy. It was alleged that they had been barred from professional racing due to a dispute now long forgotten. The course was a long, straight one, as there was insufficient room for the usual oval shape. Cyril Draper helped to construct a Heath-Robinson apparatus which, with the aid of a length of wire and an upturned bicycle, trailed a rabbit skin in front of the dogs. Punters came from the surrounding villages. In 1981 Stanley Bunker from Mangrove recalled betting on the fastest dog he had ever seen. 'It was black, bigger than a normal greyhound, and called Sefay. It was seven to one favourite, and won by at least ten yards'! By January 1931 the land on which the track stood had been sold for development, and Mr Gates moved to a new site at Henlow Camp.

Lee-West opened a ten-pin bowling alley on the site of the Tithe Cottage in 1964. It burned down in somewhat mysterious circumstances in 1967 and was not rebuilt.

A section on Stopsley's sporting associations cannot end without mentioning marathon runner Ian Thompson, who won a gold medal in the 1974 Commonwealth Games in Auckland. Ian lived at 38 Hawthorn Avenue and had attended Stopsley Junior School and Luton Grammar School. The football player-manager Bruce Rioch attended Stopsley High School until 1963 and lived for a time during the early 1960s in a flat at Jansel House, where his father was the first Caretaker. His contemporary at the High School (and a former Ramridge pupil) was fellow professional footballer Alan Slough, who played for Luton Town, Fulham and Peterborough.

The Public Houses

The 1861 Census shows that nearly 140 men in Stopsley belonged to the labouring classes. For relaxation, many turned to the local public houses, where women were not admitted. The earliest hostelry in Stopsley of which we have a record is the *Red Lion*, probably beside the village Green, which was licensed in 1824, 1825 and 1826 to Thomas Young; Thomas Hill standing the surety. A Jury List of 1798 records Thomas Young of Stopsley as also being a Constable. It would seem likely that they were one and the same person. The Census returns lists Edward Young (aged 32 and possibly Thomas' son) and his wife Sarah as publicans in 1841 and beer sellers in 1851, and living beside the Green.. The 1844 Tithe Map shows 'Public House Garden' on the opposite side of the road near Tithe Cottage. No inn is mentioned by name in 1851. The Youngs' lived some eight doors east of Green Farm where in 1841 Joseph Welch was listed as a farmer and publican. By 1861 there is firm evidence that *The White Horse* stood beside the village Green, where Stopsley Court (630 Hitchin Road) now stands. At that time the inn keeper was George Bodsworth, who lived there with his wife Rachel and five children. He employed George Hare as a general assistant. By the 1881 Census it had ceased to trade and become a private house. Maud Stronell (née Webster) was born there in 1884. It was pulled down about 1970. An archway at the end of the original building gave access to stables beyond. The architect of the present building has incorporated an archway in a similar position.

In the 1861 Census we get the first mention of the *Stopsley Public House* in Bury Road (St Thomas's Road). It was run by a widow, Mary Davis, with the help of her 16 year old son, William, who also worked as a labourer. Mary took in lodgers, doubtless to supplement her meagre income. By 1871 it had changed its name to *The Brickmakers' Arms*, and was owned by Edward Fordham, the Ashwell brewer. The tenants were James Hawkins and his wife Fanny. They also took four lodgers. After James death in 1888, Fanny retained the licence for some years. Subsequent tenants were Samuel Wren, Harry Tidnam and by 1918 George Bennett who was a keen rose gardener. There was a large room at the east end, over the stable, which was used for darts matches. Once a year the Bennetts' used it for a secular harvest festival. *The Brickmakers' Arms* was largely rebuilt in the 1930s, when a number of condemned houses in St Thomas' Road were demolished. Ownership passed to J. W. Green's in 1952 and then to Whitbread's. It was put up for sale in 1997 and the inside was gutted by fire in March 1998. The pub stood close to the Stopsley brickworks which gave it its name. The 1891 Census (probably mistakenly) listed it as *The Bricklayers' Arms*.

The First and Last, rebuilt around 1930, stands on land next to St Thomas's churchyard. This land which ran from Hitchin Road to Bury Road belonged to John Chase, Esquire, of Luton, who died in 1843. His widow, Frances, drew rent from three cottages which had three roods of land at the rear. When she died her son Frederick (a solicitor) inherited the property, and sold it all to William Fisher of Inions Farm at Caddington, who in turn sold it to Francis Foster, a brickmaker of Stopsley. Some years before 1860, Foster built a house on part of the land which he occupied, and afterward leased to Samuel Cumming (first vicar of Stopsley) and then Samuel Impey. On 14th March 1868 Francis Foster sold the property to William Lucas, a Brewer of Hitchin, for £450. Lucas converted the house into *The First and Last* public house shortly afterwards. The original building was already registered as a beer house in 1885 when Henry Smith and his wife Sarah were the tenants. When Maud Stronell worked there about 1903 it was still owned by W. and S. Lucas Ltd., the Hitchin brewers. (They were acquired by J. W. Green in 1921). By that time the landlord was Arthur Godfrey. He was followed by Jack Waller, who declared that he hated pub work, and ran a theatrical costumier business as a side line. Landlord Harry Lowrie reformed the Stopsley Cricket Club in 1947 with players from the pub team and boys from the village Youth Club. *The First and Last* closed in 1997 and was acquired by the Luton Conservative Party who opened it as a social club in April 1998.

The Sportsman is the village's only surviving 19th century hostelry. Piggott's 1839 *Directory* lists James Darley as the innkeeper. In a deed relating to the Methodist Chapel dated 19 August 1844 the inn is labelled on an architect's plan as *The Green Man*. Ann Clarke, a widow aged 63, was listed as the publican in 1851. The 1861 Census gives William Plummer as the tenant. He also acted as the local carter, taking heavy goods to the markets at Luton and Hitchin. His wife supplemented the family income by sewing bonnets. They had eight children: a baby, five at school and two plaiting straw and sewing bonnets. By 1876 the brewer James Mardall of Harpenden owned *The Sportsman*, and William Ransome was the tenant; he was also a blacksmith. Another widow, Mary Wainwright, aged 50, was the licensee in 1881. In 1891 the tenant was John Hancock. Glover and Sons of Harpenden bought Mardall's brewery in 1898 and owned *The Sportsman* until 1919, when J. W. Green acquired the property. It was about that time that bay windows were added to the front of the building. There is no truth in a story by Arthur B. Allen printed in *The Bedfordshire Magazine*, (Vol. 13, (1973) 327) that King George V and the Prince of Wales drank in *The Sportsman* whilst visiting Putteridge Bury, or that their glasses were on display. The Royal party confined their activities to the Putteridge estate and Lilley village. Official visitors avoided using the Park Lane approach from Stopsley due to its narrowness and poor state of repair. E. J. W. Egan, landlord in 1934, stood for election as a Luton town councillor, but failed to gain enough votes. J. W. Green merged with Flowers in 1954 and were taken over by Whitbread in 1962.

The rapid growth of post-war Stopsley led to the building of a number of other public houses including *The Hansom Cab* in Wigmore Lane in 1959, *The Double Barrel*, [later *The Barrels*] Cannon Lane (1962), *The King Harry*, Fermore Crescent (1968), *The Straw Plaiters*, [later *The Moon and Sixpence*] Ashcroft Road (1968) and the *Wigmore Arms*, Wigmore Lane (1991).

The ability to buy a drink at any reasonable time was the primary reason for the formation of the Stopsley Working Mens' Club on 15th October 1946. The instigator was Percy Bowler, a well-known character in Stopsley during the middle years of the 20th century. Born in 1906, he had been taught at Stopsley School by Charles Breed. As a young man he had been kicked by a bullock, resulting in the loss of a leg. This did not prevent him from leading a more than active life as a cattle drover and slaughterman. He frequently drove cattle from Hitchin to Luton market, picking some up at farms on the way. They were given lairage in Fisher's Field where *The Barrels* now stands. When the 1939 War began he was directed to work in a London slaughterhouse, travelling by train every day to the capital. The work continued for some time after the war ended. On his way home from Luton Station, dirty and tired, one evening in the autumn of 1946, Percy met-up with some mates and they called at *The First and Last* for a drink and some cigarettes. Perhaps because of the lateness of the hour, their untidy and smelly clothing, or boisterous behaviour, the landlord refused to serve them.. They were so angry that they left, vowing never to set foot in the pub again. They decided to start a club for themselves. This was to be non-political and called the Stopsley Working Mens' Club. It began on the 15th October 1946 in an old National Fire Service hut situated next door to Greenways Café (on the north side of Jansel House, where the Barratt building now stands). It belonged to a local builder, W. Holland, and was rented for £78 per year. The original joining fee was 2/- (10p) and annual subscription 5/- (25p). The club was essentially for men: any women visitors had to be accompanied. By the end of 1946 there were 159 members. Women were admitted as full members in 1958-60. The first brick building in Putteridge Road was completed in 1956 at a cost of £11,000, followed by a dance hall in 1963 and lounge bar in 1971. In 1992 a further extension costing £350,000 included a steward's flat and committee room. The Club now attracts almost 3,000 members, many from outside the immediate parish, and a large number of Irish descent.

Other Leisure Activities

The most popular leisure activity in Stopsley for most of the 20th century was reading, and as a measure of its importance Library provision was always prominent. The earliest recorded library was set up in the School in 1892. Mr Fred Shoosmith, the Headmaster, commented that 'school work would be the easier for the children and pleasanter for the teachers if the children would do some home reading.' There was little need for an adult library at that time since less than 5% of the villagers could read. In 1894 the school children put on a concert in aid of the library fund and collected £2. Shortly afterwards there were fifty books available for borrowing.

On 26th October 1900 the first Stopsley village library came into being, though only briefly. The Parish Council received a box of fifty books from the Director of Education, F. K. Spooner for the use of anyone in the village. They were placed in the care of Arthur Hucklesby and were possibly made available from his General Store and Post Office. They were recalled in July 1901 for no known reason.

Six weeks after Stopsley became incorporated into Luton in 1933, a Public Library was opened in a shop at 605 Hitchin Road (currently Alan Bartram Travel), by the Mayor, Councillor G. Wistow Walker, with Joan Cox, daughter of John Cox, the Stopsley Grocer, as Librarian. Only one room at the front of the shop was occupied, and at first it opened for ten and a half hours each week. In 1936 it began to open daily, either in the afternoon or evening. When the lease ran out in 1941 the library moved to a slightly larger shop on the eastern corner of Lothair and St Thomas's roads. During the War years between 1939 and 1945 the number of books issued annually increased from 32,000 to 82,500. On 16th June 1948 the present prefabricated library opened with rows of brand new books reflected in the highly polished floor. Initially there were 6,000 for adults and 4,000 for children. Sir Felix Cassel of Putteridge Bury performed the opening ceremony, and was presented with a set of Churchill's *Marlborough: his life and times*. In 1994, after nearly half a century of constant use, and a number of closure threats, the public area was extensively refurbished, but financial restraints severely limited the number of books.

Before the days of motor-cars and electronic entertainment Stopsley people amused themselves in a variety of simple ways. Games could be played in the streets which seldom saw transport faster than a farm cart. Children would lie with an ear to the ground and hear the mail coach coming from Luton to Hitchin. At the corner of the village Green opposite a hoarding advertising the George Hotel in Luton stood a lamp-post around which the children would swing, singing:-

'Sally go round the sun, Sally go round the moon,
Sally go round the chimney pot on a Sunday afternoon.'

In the light of the lamp, boys would bowl marbles across the street, whilst others played conkers. Whip-tops were always popular, but in February 1914 Mr Breed vetoed them at the school as two windows had been broken. In January 1886 twelve boys were caned for arriving late at school: they had been sliding on the ice on the 'Drinkers' - the flooded clay pits in Bury Road.

About 1912 a small airship with 'Bovril' written on its sides came down low over the village Green trailing a rope and anchor. The children thought it wanted to land and hitched the rope to a sign-post. A sudden gust of wind took the vessel back up into the air, with the sign-post trailing below. It was never seen again. The airship R101, from Cardington, flew over the village on a number of trial runs during the summer of 1930.

Youth Organisations

Arthur B. Allen was responsible for bringing Scouting to Stopsley. In 1914 he wrote to Haydn Dimmock, editor of *The Scout*, asking for details of becoming a Lone Scout. Teaching himself all that he needed for Tenderfoot and Second Class Badges, Allen was passed in both grades, and proudly appeared in Stopsley in uniform. Soon, joined by his two brothers and one or two village boys they formed the first Lone Patrol. This expanded into three patrols and became the 79th Bedfordshire Lone Scout Troop (13th Luton) by 1916. Dolphin Marlow, a foreman bricklayer at Putteridge Bury became the Scout Leader. Meetings were held at the old School, and amongst other things the boys learnt to dance! The Scouts volunteered for work at Manor Farm and were put alongside German prisoners of war, with whom they soon made friends, under the wary eyes of two Cockney guards. The 79th Bedfordshire Troop abruptly disbanded when Allen went to college in 1920. It was revived in 1923 and functioned until 1933: the boys sporting familiar grey neck scarves. In 1928 a Scout entertainment raised 30 shillings (£1.50p) to help pay off the Church Institute debt.

The 72nd Bedfordshire - 33rd Luton Wolf Cub Pack (Stopsley and Round Green) started in 1950 at Stopsley High School, with a distinctive chocolate brown scarf, edged with blue. The 77th Bedfordshire - 38th Luton Wolf Cubs met in Stopsley

Junior School from 1954 until 1962, then moved to Home Farm, Putteridge Bury in 1962. They wore a royal blue and yellow scarf. The 72nd and 77th Troops amalgamated with the 127th (St Ninian's) in 1970 to form the 1st Someries Scouts, based at Ross Park. With their black bordered, gold scarves, they are still flourishing.

Ross Park (Peartree Road) was given to the Scout Movement by Leslie B. Sell in 1962. The first Scout building was a prefabricated house from South Wales, which was gutted, dismantled, carted and re-erected at Ross Park by a Luton Rover Crew. The second building re-erected on the site dates from World War I. Leslie B. Sell was Deputy Chairman of H. C. Janes Ltd. and Assistant Commissioner for the Bedfordshire Boy Scouts' Association, with a considerable involvement in youth activities.

The 42nd Luton (Ramridge School, now defunct) and 26th Luton (Sacred Heart) Troops have both been active in Stopsley.

The 1st Stopsley (St Thomas') Girl Guide Company registered on 28th April 1939 was originally led by village librarian Joan Cox, and flourished during the War, helping with garden fetes and concerts. An unfortunate rift developed in 1950 and a rival company was formed at Stopsley High School. Gladys Clements and Tilly Hodgson led the 1st Stopsley Brownies.

In 1969 Mr Leslie B. Sell offered the Luton Division of the Girl Guides Association an 8 acre site off Handcross Road as a Guide Training Centre. The ground was a remnant of Slaughter's Wood and part of the land of the manor of Haverings. The ground was offered to the Guides on a 99 year lease, and a rental of an annual bunch of roses for the wife of the Chairman of the Leslie Sell Youth Trust. The land was gratefully accepted, and plans were quickly made to raise funds for a brick-built training centre and five camp sites, each with water and drainage. As Slaughter's Wood is a protected area, site clearance and the removal of trees required careful supervision, paying particular attention to the preservation of a number of hornbeams. Building, by H. C. Janes, began on 5th May 1970 and cost £10,000. The Guides raised another £10,000 for equipment. All was paid for by 19th September, 1970, when the Centre was officially opened by Lady Patience Baden-Powell, accompanied by her husband Robert, grandson of the founders of the Scout and Guide Movement, Olave and Robert Baden-Powell. In deference to its historic origins the Centre is known as 'Haverings'.

The 15th Luton Boys' Brigade Company attached to Stopsley Baptist Church was formed on 25th July, 1941 under the Captaincy of Hubert Leslie Hulland, with the Rev. E. H. Robertson as Chaplain. It held its meetings in Stopsley Junior School Hall. As it only catered for boys over the age of 11, a branch of the Lifeboys, for the 8 to 11 year olds, was formed on 9 February 1945. This met in the old Baptist Chapel. Both organisations were disbanded in July 1957. The Boys' Brigade was later restructured and in May 1972 the Juniors were formed (8 to 11), followed by the Company (over 11s) in March 1973 and Anchor Boys (5 to 7) in January 1979.

Also attached to Stopsley Baptist Church were the 11th Luton Company, Girls' Life Brigade, formed in October 1941. The name was later changed to the Girls' Brigade, and apart from a short break during the War, it continued in Stopsley until July 1988. The first Captain was Winifred Rudd. She was succeeded in 1944 by Kath. Endersby, who ran the Company, with her sister Freda Pinney, until its closure.

Most local youth organisations were linked together during the 1939-45 War by the Stopsley Youth Council, which had the Vicar of Stopsley, A. H. W. Cleaver as its Chairman and George C. Souster of the Baptist Church as its Secretary. In February 1942 St Thomas' church was packed to capacity for a joint Youth Council service addressed by the Rev. Ernest Scott, Deputy County Scout Commissioner for Bedfordshire. In June 1942 a recruitment campaign took place in the Ashcroft Road recreation ground during which the various groups demonstrated figure marching, physical training, dancing, games and a 'camp fire'.

A somewhat erratic Boys' Club was active in the village in the late 1930s and was revived from time to time, as were the 1st Stopsley Company Church Lads' Brigade (leaders S. Smith and Staveley Knight) and various Youth Fellowships. A Toc H Boys' and Girls' Club was organised for a time by schoolmaster John Bavister. Headmaster, Leonard Benson and some of his staff ran a successful Youth Club at the village school from 1943 to 1963. The Girls' and Boys' Club was started at the end of the War by Tilly Hodgson and proved very popular. In 1947 the childrens' mothers asked if an organisation could be started for them, and the Stopsley Ladies' Association began (1947 - 1995), sometimes combining with the children for social and fund raising events. The Stopsley Ladies' Association raised large sums of money for charity, and befriended such organisations as the Ampthill Cheshire Home, the Sue Ryder Home at Segenhoe and Moggerhanger Hospital. Stopsley Ladies' Lifeboat Guild began in 1957 and still flourishes today as the Stopsley Branch R.N.L.I.

A Stopsley and District Branch of the British Legion was formed on 26th November 1946. Lieut. Comdr. W. R. Smith was elected first Chairman, with the Rev. H. T. Pimm, padre, and Dr G. E. Garratt, President. Many prominent local men held office in the formative years including John A. Cox, Jack Peters, Bob Warner and J. Mc Laughlin. In March 1947 a women's section was formed under the Chairmanship of the indefatigable Tilly Hodgson, with Mrs H. T. Pimm as Vice-Chairman, Miss P. Holloway, Secretary and Mrs J. Cox, Treasurer.

Every autumn, except during the 2nd World War, Stopsley children carried branches and boxes, old furniture and garden waste, to build a large bonfire on the village Green. There, on November 5th they celebrated Guy Fawkes Night with a band, and almost the whole village congregated to enjoy the fireworks with crowds coming up from Luton. This custom sadly came to and end when the Green was prettified and suffered the indignity of becoming a traffic roundabout. For a short time an alternative Guy Fawkes Night procession went from the *First and Last* via the Green to the Ashcroft Recreation Ground, but the bonfire there was not popular and the village celebration lapsed.

Empire Day, 24th May, was commemorated with Church services. On 11th May 1908 a new Union Jack was sent to the School by the Lord of the Manor, Francis Crawley. On the following day a flag-pole was set-up and the flag hoisted. 'On Friday 22nd Empire Day was celebrated for the first time with suitable songs and lessons.' The 1936 Empire Day saw the school children saluting the flag in the playground and singing the National Anthem. On the eve of war in 1939, after saluting the flag, the children performed a play illustrating Empire, in the school yard. When the writer taught at the village school in 1964 Empire Day had become a distant memory. It had been replaced by a luke-warm Commonwealth Day in May 1959.

In 1923 and 1924 the Vicar's wife, Winifred Gilbert, tried to introduce May Day celebrations to Stopsley, but the idea did not catch on. In the first year there was a procession through the village, followed by the crowning of the May Queen, Lillian Toyer, in the Vicarage garden. During the War in 1943 and 1944 further attempts were made to start a May Day tradition in the village. The Stopsley Youth Council under the direction of George Souster asked the older school pupils to vote for a May Queen. In 1943 this was Fay Fryer and in the following year, Joyce Tavener was chosen. They were both crowned by the Mayoress of Luton, Mrs John Burgoyne. A fancy dress procession, led by the Air Training Corp's Band, moved from the Ashcroft Road Recreation Ground to the School playground, where there was maypole dancing and a physical training display by the Boys' Brigade and Church Lads' Brigade.

Stopsley people were good at providing their own entertainment. A number of organisations sponsored dances, whist-drives and concerts during the long winter months and garden parties and sales of work in the summer, often at the Vicarage or in Boulter's Meadow. Amateur theatricals thrived on the stage of the Church Institute, instilling a sense of excitement in an audience for whom the wireless was the nearest they ever got to the living theatre. An extract from a *Luton News* report of 1928, almost certainly written by Arthur B. Allen, gives the flavour of a Fancy Dress Ball:-

> 'The Council Schools formed the rendezvous of the Old and the New, of the Weird and the Mystical, of the Humorous and of the Serious, an atmosphere of joy and happiness pervaded the hall, and all was well with the world. As the evening drew on apace one found Harlene waltzing with the Cowboy, Night fox-trotting with Winter, Gypsy one-stepping with Japan - all was merry and bright. The Snowball dance was perhaps the most popular of the stunts, but the climax was reached when the cracker dance, surrounded by an air of mystery, compelled even the most innocent victims to perform the necessary functions under the mistletoe.'

Arthur Bruce Allen has been mentioned a number of times in this book. He was born in Tithe Cottage, Stopsley on 12th February 1903, and was the oldest of four brothers. From the age of 7 he lived with his guardian, Gertrude Langdale, and aunt Emma Queensborough at Stopsley House (589 Hitchin Road). A favourite pupil of Charles Breed, he had a varied career, which included school teaching for 27 years, and culminated in ordination in 1951. He was in turn Rector of Goathurst and Enmore in Somerset, then Vicar of Selsley, Bisley, and finally Moreton Valence in Gloucestershire. He was the author of a wide and varied range of books from *A Pageant of English Literature, 1900-1950;* to *Rural Education* and *Psychology of Punishment* (at one time he taught prisoners in Wandsworth Prison.) He never forgot his school days in Stopsley and contributed articles about the village to the *Bedfordshire Magazine.* In his latter years, he often visited his brother Roland (owner of Roland Allen and Co. Ltd, distributors of catering equipment, 235 North Street, Luton) who lived in Putteridge Road, and found time to talk to local schoolchildren (and the author) about his boyhood in the village. He was a strong and at times outspoken character, a born *raconteur.* He never tired of a good-humoured argument with his great friend Wally Lawrence, the village shoemaker, usually about their contemporaries. He died at Stroud on 17th January 1975.

For those of a more serious disposition, evening classes might appeal. About a quarter of Bedfordshire villages and towns had some provision by the 1870s. From 5th March 1875 a night school was opened at Stopsley School attended by 16 boys on the first evening and 25 on the second. The classes lasted from 6 till 8 pm. Thomas Tennant, the Headmaster, concentrated on the three Rs, helping the boys to improve on what they had formerly learnt in day school. It was far from easy for the lads after a hard day's work on the land, and many fell asleep, unless they were kept busy by writing. Frequent changes of teachers did not help the night schools to prosper and they languished in the 1880s.

When Charles Breed became Headmaster in 1893 he was ready to give a fresh start to anyone in the village. In October 1895 twenty-two scholars enrolled for classes in agriculture, with readings from Longfellow's poems for light relief. By 1902 the scholars were studying history and a play by Shakespeare. It wasn't all work: on 30th December they held a Christmas social. In 1905 some of the pupils gained awards in an art exam, and visited museums in London together. The evening classes were not free: usually a charge of 2 pence a night was made. On 8th February 1907 a Friends' Adult School was formed at Stopsley - for men only.

Fairly soon after the end of the 2nd World War (c.1950) Evening Institutes began at Stopsley and Challney Secondary Schools, each offering a small range of evening classes for adults on 3 or 4 evenings each week. Subjects ranged from French to photography and were very popular. Later, with the creation of Barnfield College, a supervising tutor from the College took overall control of Adult Education at Stopsley, Challney and what was then Stockwood High School. The 1973 *Russell Report* recommended the establishment of dedicated Adult Education Centres, with some purpose-built facilities, in existing educational buildings. Bedfordshire was amongst the first counties to set-up these Community Colleges, and Stopsley School was opened as one in 1975. It had a full-time Adult Education Tutor, who also spent some time working on a 'school commitment', ostensibly to forge links between the school and the community. A separate daytime and evening programme was arranged, and students were provided with a purpose-built lounge, and later a crèche and play-group facilities. By 1979 over 80 courses were available at Stopsley. The following year Stopsley combined with Putteridge Community College for the purposes of administering adult education, whilst at the same time retaining their own identities. By the mid-80s the two were also responsible for courses at Ashcroft and South Luton High Schools and some daytime courses at Charles Street: in total some 200 courses for more than 2,000 students. Languages, arts and humanities were all covered, together with a wide range of vocational subjects as diverse as cake decoration and car maintenance. When Stopsley High School became grant maintained in 1993, it separated from Putteridge, and both schools existed as Community Colleges on their own, both continuing to offer a wide range of courses.

Early in the century the Church and Chapels provided much of the social life of the village, with musical concerts, recitations and coffee evenings, and ever-popular magic lantern shows. T. G. Hobbs offered a range of illustrated lectures, all with a temperance theme, like' Sewing and Sowing', 'Little Joy's Mission' and 'Friendless Bob'. During the winter Mr Breed presented a monthly slide show for children with popular story themes such as 'Robinson Crusoe', Hiawatha' and 'The Water Babies'. Of a more general nature were the Revd. E. G. Alderson's pictures of his journey to the 'Fjords of Norway'. Although the Salvation Army had no branch in the village, its presence was felt on Sundays at the turn of the century when the band played on the village Green, and mothers and children sat round it, joining in the hymns and continuing their straw plaiting.

National and Village Politics

In complete contrast the political parties were beginning to make their mark on the working classes. Electioneering meetings proved very popular entertainment and were usually held in one of the school halls. Stopsley, with its large nonconformist population, enjoyed a long tradition of being a Liberal stronghold.

7th July, 1886 was Election day. The School was closed for polling, and the Wesleyans took the opportunity to hold their Sunday School Treat. The Liberal candidate for Luton and South Bedfordshire was Cyril Flower who won the seat comfortably, and took it again in 1892. In the 1895 election, another Liberal, Thomas Gair Ashton from Macclesfield, won by a very narrow majority, the problem of alcohol being the main issue. The declaration of the result was followed by severe rioting in Luton and the Metropolitan Police had to be brought in to restore order.

In 1910 Charles Breed saw an opportunity to introduce Social Studies into the school curriculum. A General Election was to be held on Tuesday 25th January. On the preceding Thursday the two top classes held their own election. Mr Breed was the Returning Officer for the village, so he was able to prime the children on electoral procedure, and to provide them with replica voting papers. A screened voting booth was set up, with a sealed ballot box. The outcome of the 'election' is not recorded, though most of the children copied their parents (and pleased Mr Breed) by voting Liberal.

T. G. Ashton held the Luton seat for 16 years and remained M.P. until 1911, when he was created Lord Ashton of Hyde and moved to the Lords. His elevation caused a by-election, and another Liberal, Cecil Harmsworth (brother of Lord Northcliffe) took his place, and later served in the wartime Coalition government.

The General Election of 1918 promised a new and better country for returning heroes. All men and women now had the vote. At Stopsley canvassing was brisk, and Charles Breed was very active. The Luton Labour Party put forward its very first candidate, Willet Ball, a trade union journalist, who spoke at Stopsley School on 9th December 'with more bitterness than persuasion'. The next evening it was the turn of the Coalition Liberal party, with Charles Colchin speaking on behalf of an absent Cecil Harmsworth. The Conservatives did not bother to field a candidate. Saturday 14th December was Election Day and the school Polling Station was busy all day. Cecil Harmsworth again swept to victory, eventually serving Luton and Stopsley for eleven years.

The Liberals lost Luton to the Conservatives in 1922, but regained it the following year. In 1924 a Conservative, Terrence O'Connor won the seat, but the Liberals returned to power with Dr Leslie Burgin from 1929 to 1945. He was well liked in Luton, and worked hard for the town. Burgin was the first Luton M.P. to join the Cabinet, as Minister of Supply in 1939. In a footnote to his *English History 1914 - 1945* the historian, A. J. P. Taylor, has commented: 'This was not a dynamic appointment, rather another horse from Caligula's well-stocked stable!'

The Labour Party won the first post-war election, and in Luton William Warbey was returned as Member. On 15th June 1948 thirty-one senior boys and girls from Stopsley School, accompanied by Mr Benson, Mrs Froud and Mr Moyle, visited London by motor coach to be shown over the Houses of Parliament by Mr Warbey.

In the 1950 election there was a public outcry when a very large poster appeared on the end wall of Pond Farm overlooking Stopsley Green, proclaiming 'Vote for the Radio Doctor'. This was Charles Hill, whose Agent was ordered to have it rapidly removed, since Hill was considered to be taking an unfair advantage of his popularity as a well-known wartime broadcaster. Like Leslie Burgin before him, Hill also achieved Cabinet rank. He was to hold the Luton seat for the Conservatives for thirteen years, before going to the House of Lords as Lord Hill of Luton in 1963.

Once Stopsley was incorporated into the Borough of Luton in 1933 it was entitled to elect its own Town Councillors. The first of these was Mrs E. M. Hartop, a Conservative and wife of a former Chairman of the Parish Council and a local farmer. She was joined by S. Impey in 1935 and H. S. Hewson in 1936. It would be invidious to pick out particular Councillors, but one of note was George Souster who represented the interests of the village as a Liberal-Conservative for fourteen years from 1946. Geoffrey W. Dillingham represented Stopsley Ward as a Conservative from 1976-91 and was Deputy Mayor during 1986-87. His great-grandfather Charles Dillingham had been Mayor of Luton in 1917. Geoffrey was also a County Councillor between 1989 and 1993. The Liberal Democrat husband and wife team, Jenny and Roy Davies, came to Stopsley in 1975. They were elected together for the County Council Ward of Stopsley in 1981 and in 1983 for the Borough Council Wards of Stopsley (Jenny) and Putteridge (Roy). They lost their Borough Council seats in 1987 but regained them in 1991. Jenny Davies remained a County Councillor for 16 years until Luton gained Unitary status in April 1997. Roy resigned from the County Council in 1993 due to pressure of work, but remained on the Luton Borough Council.

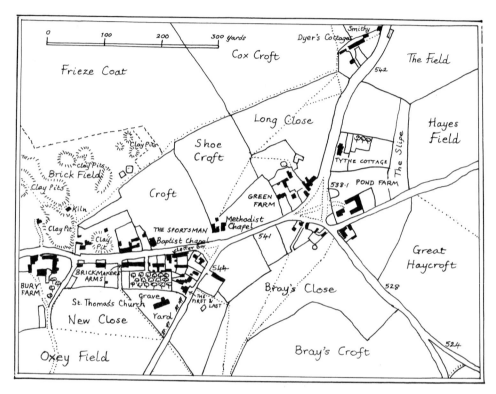

Map 4: The centre of Stopsley village, redrawn from the Ordnance Survey map of 1881, with the addition of field names.

Chapter 9

Stopsley and the Great War
1914-1918

The summer of 1914 had been extremely hot. School broke up on 31st July for five weeks holiday. Four days later War was declared. On Friday 14th August, Territorials of the 3rd, 4th and 5th North Midland Batteries, Royal Artillery, marched into the village and took over the old and new schools. The new school was occupied until Friday 11th September; the old school at Swift's Green until 16th November.

Arthur B. Allen recalled the arrival of the troops. 'On they came, the horses and the guns, the ammunition wagons, the supply wagons, the mounted men on innumerable horses. The first entered the village at eight in the morning and they were still coming in at nightfall. My aunt said to me, "I never knew there were so many men in all the world".'

'The farmers soon found every meadow and every field not down to corn, smothered with horse-lines, guns and tents, and before long we grew accustomed to the cavalry bugle-calls. Farm buildings were requisitioned and billeting began in the village.' 'Stopsley House' (589 Hitchin Road) where Arthur Allen lived with his Aunts was at first exempt from billeting since Arthur (aged 11) was the only man in the house. Later a jolly Major and his wife had to be accommodated. The stables housed two horses, and the officer's batman became one of the family. A field telephone linked the house to camp headquarters. Other Staff cars and motor cycles were housed in the barns at Tithe Cottage and various farms.

Most of the soldiers were camped in Cox Croft and Frieze Coat fields south of Hays Wood, all now part of the Regional Sports Centre Playing Fields. Here, the Vicar of Stopsley, Revd. G. H. Shorting held open air services for the men, to which the local people were invited. Not surprisingly, the church Marriages Register shows a spate of weddings towards the end of 1914 of Stopsley boys leaving for the Front.

The exhausted local clay pits at the St Thomas's Road Brickworks were 4 or 5 metres deep and filled with water. The Royal Engineers used these to practice building bridges and pontoons and to launch a great raft. The children were forbidden to go anywhere near. 'We watched until the military went away then we rushed onto the bridges and piled upon the raft, overloading it until we were over our ankles with water before we began to move across the pond!'

The village school was available for lessons once more on Monday 14th September. The children had enjoyed an extra week's holiday. Now the teachers found the building in such a muddle and mess that the pupils had to be sent home for a further day whilst the staff tried to get it back into order. The Territorials had done considerable damage and it took many months before any compensation was received.

The children sent parcels of socks, mittens and Christmas puddings to the troops. By January 1915 the girls were knitting khaki scarves, wristlets and socks with wool supplied by the Government. The boys were helping around the village by looking after the gardens of men serving in the war. Almost every week there was a collection for some war-related charity. In February 1915, for example, Mr Breed was able to send £5.1s.8d (£5.08) to the British and Foreign Sailors' Society and in December a concert raised £3.6s.0d (£3.30) for 'our soldier boys' fund. Arthur Allen again: 'We brought pennies and ha'pennies each week to buy chocolate and cigarettes to be made up into parcels to send to the village boys on active service. Each week these little parcels were packed and addressed by one of the senior children. Each parcel contained a letter from the school. The letters we received in acknowledgement were all posted in the school hall so that we could see and read them.' Lessons reflected what was happening on the War Fronts. Wall maps hung in the classrooms and coloured pins were moved to mark the position of the fighting forces each day, according to the progress of the War. From time to time, old boys, wounded in the War, would call at the school to see Mr Breed. On 20th October 1916, Lance-Corporal George Webb of the East Anglian Engineers and a former School Captain visited. He had lost his left eye on the Somme. A fortnight earlier (5th October) the whole school had paraded in front of the building to witness the passing of the funeral of William Hawkes, killed by a bomb dropped from a Zeppelin airship as it passed over a training camp at Willian near Hitchin. 'As the procession with its flag-covered gun-carriage and military escort marched slowly through the village, Mr Breed lowered the school flag to half-mast, the girls all curtsied, and we boys stood rigidly at salute.'

Arthur Hucklesby became the oldest Special Constable in the Luton Division, joining up at the beginning of the War at the age of 64. When the conflict was over he received a special medal in recognition of his faithful service.

With so many young men on active service, young women began to take their places in the local factories. Munitions factories appeared almost overnight, and many girls from Stopsley made the journey to Dallow Road and Chaul End, where they spent the day filling shells. They could be easily recognised as the chemical they used turned their hands and faces bright orange-yellow. Others built aircraft parts in Messrs Hewlett and Blondeaus Omnia Works in Oakley Road at Leagrave (later Electrolux site). The hat industry continued to employ older women, whilst young mothers concentrated on out-work.

Women of all ages worked on the farms, and the first members of the Women's Land Army were seen at Manor Farm in 1917. They were joined by schoolchildren during harvest periods and when work was urgent. School holiday dates were flexible, to account for fluctuations in the weather. Towards the end of the War, German prisoners worked on local farms, employed by the Bedfordshire War Agricultural Executive Committee. The time-sheet of Private G. Price who was in charge of a gang of prisoners at Lane Farm, Stopsley, is preserved in the County Record Office. The farmer, Morris Titmus, found 'ordinary' work for five men (139 hours) from the 28th to 31st October 1918. Hugh Shaw at Manor Farm, employed four men for the same period. Arthur Allen records working with as many as fourteen men and two Cockney guards at Manor Farm in 1917. Many of them were skilled farm workers back in Germany.

The end of the War was marred in Stopsley by the almost world-wide, great influenza epidemic. On 31st October 91 children were absent from school out of a possible 187. Monday 11th November (Armistice Day) Mr Breed recorded 'I came to school and found *no assistants* present and hardly 20 children and *no caretaker* and *no fires*. I sent the children home for another week and the medical officer subsequently confirmed our action. - Peace Day.'

This is not the place to write a history of the First World War. Suffice to say that this bloody conflict decimated a whole generation of Stopsley youth from which the village as a community never recovered. Many village girls remained spinsters throughout their lives or took the unusual step of marrying outside the parish.

The Volunteers

By the end of 1914 almost two dozen boys had enlisted for military service. Whilst a few may have joined before the outbreak of war, the majority volunteered within the first few weeks, Sometimes this involved whole families, like the four Church brothers from Ramridge End (71 Ashcroft Road), or school friends living next door to each other.

One of those who was immediately posted to France was Corporal Charlie Burkett of 121 Battery, Royal Field Artillery, who distinguished himself in the retreat from Mons. He was mentioned in General French's first despatch and awarded the Military Medal for gallantry on the Field. Sydney Whittemore, having served as a Volunteer in the Boer War was killed in the first Battle of Ypres (12 Oct - 17 Nov), whilst his cousin George Whittemore lost his left eye, and Arthur Phillips, Charlie Sansom and William Waller, all serving in the Bedfordshire Regiment, suffered leg wounds.

Arthur Heighton, Albert Smith and P. Smith from Stopsley Green and Horace and Frederick Goodship from Ramridge End all served with the 1st Battalion of the 5th Bedfordshire Regiment (Territorial Force). They enlisted pied-piper like outside Luton Corn Exchange in September 1914 and marched to Luton Station from where they travelled by train to Bedford, to do their initial training. They then moved on to successive barracks at Bury St Edmunds, Norwich and St Albans. In six months they were transformed from scruffy schoolboys to an efficient, if untried, military force; capable of marching in full kit from St Albans, via Dunstable and Toddington to Bedford, and back through Ampthill and Luton.

The 1st/5th Bedfordshire's were dispatched to Gallipoli in 1915 in order to support the Australian and New Zealand troops who had been there since the 25 April. Their destination was Suvla Bay, a bleak, dry landscape of steep, scrub-covered gullies and ridges, dotted with enormous boulders, and with no cover from the fierce Mediterranean sun. The diary of a Luton man, Private Harold Scott, tells us that the 1st/5th Bedfordshire's arrived early on 11 th August:-

> 'Once ashore we went about half a mile inland and deposited our goods and chattels in practically open country. It did not take us long to realise that we were at last on Active Service and shortly we had our first sample of 'iron rations' - bully beef and biscuits. We turned into out blankets as soon as it was dark, and I believe slept soundly, in spite of the fact that the Turks were endeavouring to shell our ships, whilst our batteries and naval guns were answering frequently.

> **Friday 13th** - Found us trench digging which proved rather exciting. We were treated to a few rounds of rapid fire from somewhere in front, but fortunately none was hurt until we were coming back, when one officer and a man got hit.

> **Saturday 14th** - again out with the intention of finishing trenches, but we did not make much progress owing to the severe peppering we had from the Turks. Most of the time we lay huddled behind the earth we had thrown up

before, and early in the morning. almost tired out, we returned to our line and tried to sleep.

Sunday 15th - was *the day* for our battalion, when great yet terrible things happened.'

The battalion was ordered into action, their object to capture Kidney Hill which was very strongly held. When the battalion 'moved forward it came suddenly into a zone swept by an enfilade of shrapnel fire. Then shell after shell fell into the Bedford's, some dropped on top of the Headquarters Section and the place became a shambles. All wounded men crawled towards Headquarters, and for some time to come so quickly one could hardly move.'

After firing for hours the day began to wane and the work was still not done, but eventually the Bedfords reached the crest of Kidney Hill where both the musketry and machine gun fire was terrific. Many gallant officers and men died. As night fell British soldiers from three Battalions were mixed-up around the hill. The weary men had to dig themselves in, sort out the remnants of platoons, collect tools, sandbags, barbed wire, food and water, whilst others collected the wounded and got them to the field ambulances. At dawn on Monday 16th August the Turkish firing resumed. Soon shrapnel shells were bursting all round. One killed Horace Goodship - the first Stopsley man to die in the Dardanelles conflict. The news reached the village school on 8th September.

The Bedfords remained entrenched on Kidney Hill until 22nd August when they were relieved by the 29th Division. The British troops were hopelessly outnumbered and could make no useful gains. Food supplies were scarce and water desperately short. Dysentery spread rapidly through the men. Many died, including Arthur Heighton. News of his death reached Mr Breed on 18th November. Frederick Goodship contracted dysentery, was sent home and spent 12 months in hospital. Albert Smith was wounded, contracted dysentery and was invalided home. His cousin, P. Smith was also sent home to England with fever. When they were considered to have recovered, all three were returned to France. The Bedfords were evacuated from the Dardanelles on the night of the 19th-20th December.

In France, on the Western Front, matters were no better. Elderly Generals directing operations from the comfort of chateaux, well back from the front line seemed not to grasp the appalling destructive power of the weaponry now being used and sacrificed their soldiers with the battlefield tactics of a past age. General Joffre, the French Commander-in-Chief, planned an autumn offensive in 1915, which included a British attack on the coal-mining town of Loos held by the Germans. It was there that poisonous gas, used against the enemy, blew back into the faces of the British troops. Joseph Woollard was a Stopsley man enrolled in the 6th Bedfordshire Regiment who survived the battle which totally flattened the town and which cost the British army 2,407 officers and 57,985 other ranks killed, wounded or missing. Sadly Woollard was to die the following June in one of a number of battles preparatory to the offensive on the Somme.

The Final Sacrifice

So many Bedfordshire and Stopsley men were involved in the long, bloody Somme conflict that one can do little more than list the names of those who died. Cousins Horace and Arthur Fensome, Ernest Furr, W. Impey and Sidney Peters lost their lives during 1916. In the following year the Battle of Arras took George Davis, and

William Souster (wounded on the first day of the battle) died of his injuries a month later. Albert Dawson, Bernard Angel and John Bangs were killed in action during the early summer. Walter Brazier was to fall at Chatiais Wood in his first engagement on the first day of the Third Battle of Ypres. He was followed a few days later by his school friends Albert Cooper, Gerald Bigmore and H.J. Bigmore. 1918 saw memorial services held in St Thomas' church for Arthur Cain and Joseph Whittemore, both killed at Cambrai, Frederick Goodship at Kemmel Ridge and E.L. Godbehere near Ypres. Both Corporal Arthur Ward and Thomas Collier were brought home to die of their injuries in English hospitals. They were the only two 1st World War soldiers to be buried in St Thomas' churchyard. Other Stopsley men suffered terrible wounds, from the effects of which some never fully recovered. Tom Church was wounded at Passchendaele, his brother Horace took part in a number of engagements and was wounded three times. George Webb lost an eye in the Somme offensive. Hugh Farnham was wounded and taken prisoner during the retreat of March 1918, and Walter B. Stronell (Stronnell) was wounded at Ypres in the closing days of the war.

Beside those serving in the army, mention must also be made of Fred Church, who served throughout the war in the Royal Navy, mainly on patrol duties in the North Sea. Flight-Sergeant T.R. Perry was a sergeant-instructor at various British aerodromes, firstly in the Royal Flying Corps, and after April 1918 in the Royal Air Force, where he remained after the war had finally ended.

The Stopsley Parish Council called a public meeting on 12th July 1920 to consider setting up a Memorial to the soldiers who had died in the war. On Sunday 14th November 1920 it was dedicated by the Vicar of Stopsley, Revd. E.T. Leslie, who had himself served as an army padre during the conflict. The Memorial seems to have been erected with undue haste. Only 24 names are recorded upon it, although the writer has traced the names of almost 40 local men who lost their lives. A memorial plaque set up in the old Baptist Church included three names not on the village Memorial. One in St Thomas' church gives an additional name. The Church Service book mentions others. An oak memorial Board displayed in the village school, and paid for by Charles Breed, lists 21 names, only 14 of which occur on the village Memorial. From this we can deduce that 10 of the boys on the village Memorial did not attend the village school. On the other hand, Mr Breed would have been hurt if all his old boys name had not been recorded somewhere together, hence his personal desire to commemorate them at the school. His non-denominational Board was set-up on 11th November 1922 in the presence of relatives of the dead, with speeches by Frederick Clark (School Manager), Arthur T. Hucklesby (Vice-Chairman, Parish Council) and Charles Breed (Headmaster). The Board hung in Stopsley Infant School until the school was remodelled in 1973, after which it was deposited for safe keeping in Luton Museum.

Care of the village War Memorial, which had been erected over the disused village well on Chapel Green, was in the hands of the Parish Council, until that body ceased to exist in March 1933. A Parish Council minute of November 1922 records that the surrounding railings should be painted an 'ecclesiastical brown'! At the instigation of the Stopsley Ladies' Association, two wooden seats were placed beside the Memorial in 1952 to commemorate the Coronation of Queen Elizabeth II.

The Great War Dead

This list contains the names of all the known Stopsley men who died in the First World War. It has been compiled from various sources and is not necessarily complete.

Andrews, William, Private
Angel, E. Bernard, Private, died of wounds, Memorial service,10 June 1917
Bangs, John, Private, died of wounds, Memorial service, 10 June 1917
Bigmore, Gerald, Private, killed in action at St Gene, 28 Oct 1917
Brazier, Walter, Private, Northamptonshire Regt., killed in action at Ypres, 31 July 1917
Cain, Arthur Thomas, Private, 10 March 1918
Chamberlain, Ernest
Chapman, Ernest William
Collier, Thomas, Private, R.A.V.C., 9 October 1918, aged 28
Cooper, Albert, Private, Lancashire Fusiliers, killed in action at Ypres, 6 Sept 1917
Crick, Ernest Sidney
Davis, George, Private, 7th Norfolk Regt., killed in action at Monchy, 28 April 1917
Dawson, Albert, Private, Royal Fusiliers, killed in action, 28 May 1917
Day, Frank
Fensome, Arthur William, Memorial service, 4 Oct 1916
Fensome, Horace Memorial service, 4 Oct 1916
Fensome, Sidney
Furr, Ernest W. Private, 7th Bedfordshire Regt., killed in action, 27 Sept 1916
Godbehere, E. L. Private, Beds. and Essex Regts., killed in action at Ypres, 22 May 1918
Goodship, Frederick H., Private, 1/5th Bedfordshire Regt., killed in action, Kemmel Ridge, 15 April 1918
Goodship, Horace Private, 1/5th Bedfordshire Regt., killed in action, Suvla Bay, 16 August 1915
Hawkes, William, Private, Royal Defence Corps., died 1 Oct 1916, aged 56
Heighton, Arthur, Private, died at Gallipoli, 18 Nov 1915
Hurrell, William R.
Impey, W. Private, Bedfordshire Regt., killed in action on the Somme, 12 Oct 1916
Peters, Sidney, Private, died in France, Memorial Service 4 Oct 1916
Pike, Nelson Thomas
Sims, Alec
Souster, William, Private, 8th East Lancs. Regt., died of injuries sustained at Arras, 2 May 1917
Ward, Arthur, Corporal, 19/39 2nd Beds. Regt., died 2 April 1918, aged 33
Whittemore, Joseph, Private, Memorial service, 10 March 1918
Whittemore, Sidney, Private, killed at Ypres, December 1914
Woollard, Joseph
Worboys, S. C. April 1917
Worsley, Frederick
Young, George

XXXIIIa and b: The first Women's Land Army came into being during 1917, prompted by the severe lack of male labour and a bad harvest. The rare pictures on this page show seven members wearing the official-issue coats, operating a threshing machine, assisted by an elderly man and a boy, at Common Farm, Stopsley. The W.L.A. was disbanded in 1919. (*Shaw family*)

XXXIVa: Stopsley schoolboys watching an unidentified troop of soldiers marching past Chapel Green on the way to their camp in the fields off Lothair Road in 1914. In the background the shape of the old Baptist Chapel in Bury Road can just be recognised. In 1920 the Memorial to the war dead would be built on this spot. (*Author's collection*)

XXXIVb: Church Parade for the Staff Royal Field Artillery in 1914 in a corner of the present Lothair Road playing field. The service was conducted by the Vicar of Stopsley, the Revd. G.H.C. Shorting. The identity of the lone lady is unknown. (*Author's collection*)

XXXVa: 'Representing all the young men of Stopsley who died in the Great War. This studio picture shows Walter Brazier, with his father and brother (both named Frederick), shortly before he left for France. Walter died at Ypres on 31st July, 1917. (*Walter R. Rainbow*)

XXXVb: The second anniversary service at Stopsley War Memorial on 11th November, 1921. It was conducted by the Revd. Ernest T. Leslie a few days before he returned to Australia. A portable harmonium provided the music. Behind can be seen cottages, now demolished, in Bury Road and the old Baptist Church. There are glasshouses to the right of the church: the precursors of those used by Ernest Simpkins from the 1930s to 1960s. (*Author's collection*)

XXXVIa: Winifred Gilbert, the Vicar's wife, organised a series of entertainments during her husband's incumbency. This Gypsy Fair was held at the Vicarage on 16th June 1923, to raise funds for the Church Institute. Mabel Mardle (née Dawson) is the central figure beneath the 'Spring' sign.

XXXVIb: Fay Weighell (née Fryer) was crowned village May Queen by the Mayoress, Mrs (later Lady) John Burgoyne, in the Ashcroft Road Recreation Ground in 1943. She is seen here on a float provided by farmer, Frank Boulter, surrounded by her Maids of Honour. (*Luton News*)

XXXVIIa: Stopsley Senior School pupils visited the Houses of Parliament on 15th June, 1948. William Warbey, MP for Luton, is in the centre of the back row, together with Winifred Froud, Mr L.C. Benson (Headmaster) and Ivor Moyle. (*Walter R. Rainbow*)

XXXVIIb: The Stopsley Ladies' Association's New Year's Eve party, 1946-7, in the Church Institute. Guest of Honour was Dr Charles Hill, MP, seen left of centre behind the fairy, with Mrs Hill to his left. (*Luton News*)

XXXVIIIa: Members of the 1st Stopsley (St Thomas') Guide Company, led by Captain Joan Cox, photographed outside the church, soon after their formation in 1939.   (*Myrtle Cox*)

XXXVIIIb: Members of the Stopsley Brownies and Girls' Life Brigade competing for glory during a wartime May Day entertainment in 1943 or 1944. The same game is still played today. (*Luton News*)

XXXIXa: On 19th September, 1970, Lady Patience Baden-Powell opened the Girl Guide Centre at Haverings. On her right is Leslie B. Sell who gave the land for the Centre (and also land at Ross Park for the Scouts). Ruth Halsey, County Commissioner for Guides, is on the right. (*Luton News*)

XXXIXb: Stopsley Council School's last senior netball team in 1947, prior to the opening of the Secondary Modern School. *Back row*: Eileen Flecknoe; Brenda Simpkins; *Front row*: Doreen Kavanagh; Isabel Duffy; Barbara Cole; June Draper; Peggy Dearman. (*Luton News*)

XLa: The 1st Someries Scouts enjoying an adventure day at Barton Springs in 1976. Kath. Davis, the Assistant Cub Leader is demonstrating a Tarzan swing for the benefit of Scout Leader, Clive Wheeler and the troop. (*Cynthia Sutherst*)

XLb: The Stopsley Company of the Boys' Brigade in their Centenary Year, 1983. They are being inspected in the old Baptist hall by Squadron Leader Mike Warwood. (*John Rowlands)

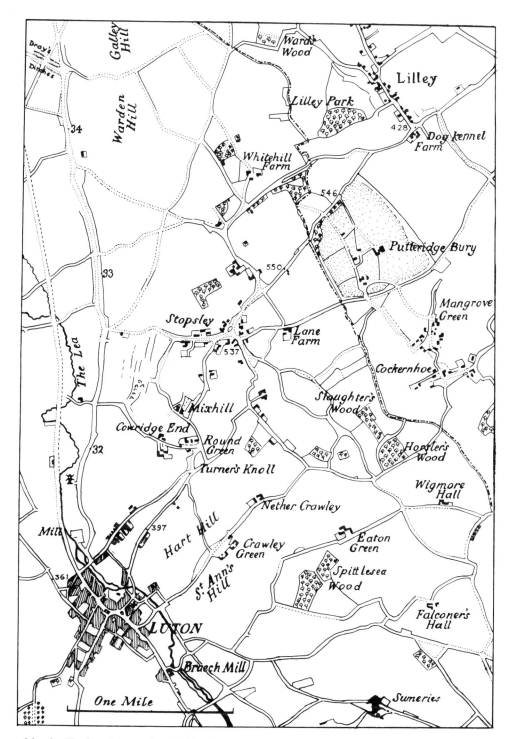

Map 5: The Stopsley area about 1900, redrawn from the Ordnance Survey map, to approximately the same scale as Maps 2 and 3.

107

Chapter 10

Stopsley During the 2nd World War 1939-1945

On 30th September 1938 the British Prime Minister, Neville Chamberlain, returned from meeting Hitler in Munich, waving a sheet of paper and proclaiming "It is peace in our time... He has given me his promise." Those words had a hollow ring, and almost too late, Britain began to stir itself in case of war. Already the A.R.P. (Air Raid Precautions) and Civil Defence organisations were making preparations, and early in 1939 Luton's recently appointed Director of Education, Mr. E.O. Cutter, in his capacity as Billeting Officer, began to muster local teachers and others, to prepare for the possible arrival of evacuees. On 25th April, 1939, Stopsley School was closed for the day, so that the staff could canvas the district looking for surplus rooms. In Luton as a whole, some 22,000 rooms were found.

On 1st September, 1939, there began a mass exodus from the East End of London of mothers with children, and the elderly. Trains arrived at intervals over the next three days bringing 12,285 people to Luton Station; 5,381 of them tired and frightened children, clutching a single bag of possessions, and wearing conspicuous name-tags around their necks. 276 blind people also arrived in the town.

Long crocodiles of children made their way from Station Road to the reception centre at Dunstable Road School. From there they were dispersed on foot or by coach to fifteen centres around the town. One of these was at Stopsley (Infant) School, where they were met by the Headmaster, Mr Tom Whalley, assisted by John Bavister, Albert 'Billy' Williams, Ivor Moyle, Mabel Knight, Hilda Kiddy and others, who acted as local billeting officers. The visitors were fed and then given medical examinations. Meanwhile Stopsley folk congregated at the School gates for the ignominious selection of the nicest and cleanest looking children. Eventually, even the ducklings were found a home. At 11 am on 3rd September, a state of War with Germany was declared.

The Village School, plus the Methodist Chapel Hall opposite, was already full to bursting point in 1939. More than sixty pupils in a class was not unusual. Now it was called upon to accomodate even more children. Classes had to be split into parts and a shift system was put into operation, most children receiving only two days teaching each week. After only three weeks the situation was slightly eased when about half the evacuees decided to return home, considering that London was as safe as Luton. Two small boys who were billeted in Venetia Road with school teacher John Bavister, returned to their London school. Some time later they were both killed when the building received a direct hit from a bomb. Shortages of materials soon befell the school. Pencil stubs were glued onto the end of sticks so that they could be used to the end. Sheets of white wrapping paper were begged from Frank Brightman who worked in A.E. Fisher's Stopsley butcher's shop. Text books, if they existed, were ancient, dilapidated and shared between a number of pupils. The central (Infant School) hall accomodated at least a hundred children, two teachers, and the

Headmaster with his desk at the front. Seating for the children was partly on forms, and spilled over onto the top of cupboards and P.E. apparatus. Toilet facilities were hopelessly inadequate, and stood on the far side of the playground. A new problem occured in October 1939 when it was decided that for safety reasons only 100 children would be allowed in the school building at one time.

During the uneasy peace of late 1938 and early 1939, Stopsley, like the rest of Britain, prepared itself for war. Aerial attack was particularly feared, with so many engineering firms around Luton potential targets. Attention was given to the construction of air raid shelters. In many streets two or three neighbours worked together to dig a large rectangular hole in the tenacious Stopsley clay. This they would line and roof with timber and corrugated iron, before covering it with a mound of earth. Inside were packed wooden bunks, tables, oil-lamps and stoves, together with bedding, water and supplies of canned food. No one knew for how long the shelter might be occupied. In many cases days of hard work during the summer were frustrated by heavy rain in the winter which flooded the shelters making them uninhabitable.

In time the Government came up with three shelter designs which were very popular in Stopsley. All, unless they suffered a direct hit, proved highly successful. Brick-built, above ground shelters, appeared in some streets and many back gardens. One, largely demolished, in Stapleford Road in 1993, had brick walls 35cms (14 inches) thick, with a ridged concrete roof. It took three days to knock down manually 54 years after it was built. The Anderson shelters consisted of arched sheets of corrugated iron, bolted together, and set about a metre into the ground. Covered with a layer of soil and turf, they proved very effective, and were most popular in the village, where a few survivors can still be seen. Many owners decorated the interiors and fitted them out very comfortably; though few wanted to leave their warm beds for a flight down the garden path on a cold winter's night. A count taken in Luton on 2nd October 1940 showed that 1277 people were sleeping in underground shelters, 404 of them children. The Morrison shelter was a different concept. Assembled in the home, it consisted of a large steel-constructed box the size of a king-size bed, with a flat table-top-high roof and wire mesh sides. The family slept inside it and theoretically ate their meals off the lid. Its advantage was that it proved adequate protection without the necessity of leaving the house.

Public shelters were constructed in the parish, both above and below ground, including two large underground ones which still survive on the eastern side of the Ashcroft Road recreation ground, and another at Turner's Knoll, Round Green. Two still exist under Stopsley Junior School playground, where they are used by the Fire Brigade for training purposes from time to time. Originally lit by oil lamps, electric light was installed in September 1941. With access steps at each end (now removed) and two escape hatches, they still remain dry after half a century.

At the sounding of the air raid siren situated on a pole above the Police Box on the Village Green, most people trooped to their shelters. However, as the war dragged on, after many false alarms, lots of adults became rather blase and seldom made the effort.

"Still falls the rain"

Stopsley was lucky to escape most of the Luton bombing. During the first months of the war explosives seemed to be deliberately dropped in the open countryside. It was suggested that this was the work of German anti-Nazi pilots who had no desire to destroy human life. But this rapidly changed. Soon, night after night, the people of Stopsley could see the orange glow of London burning on the southern skyline. There were no street lights to distract from the horror.

Many incendiary bombs fell in our area, including a large 'bread-basket' which did little damage on open land north of Whitehill Farm in October 1940. The largest bomb to explode near the centre of Stopsley fell, in the same month, into a disused clay pit at the rear of 11-13 Lothair Road, some 200 metres from the houses, on what is now the Regional Sports Centre playing field. Luckily, by falling into a pit, some of the blast was diminished. Even so, many windows in Lothair Road were blown out, including Police Sergeant Fryer's French windows at No 29, which had been boarded up to prevent just such an occurrence! The only direct hit was a high explosive which demolished a house in Turners Road (South) on 15th November, 1940. An unexploded bomb in a garden at the south-west end of Mixes Hill Road was detonated by a controlled explosion. On 21st June, 1944, a flying-bomb or 'doodlebug' fell on allotments just south of Sowerby Avenue. There was considerable blast damage to bungalows in the road and a rest-centre was set up, although most of the occupants declined to leave their homes. A colourful elderly couple, the Abrahams, were found dazed and wounded amongst the wreckage of their house together with a cow. Milk was rationed during the war!

It was practically impossible to purchase any food without a Ration Book, unless you grew it yourself. Villagers wanting to shop in Stopsley village had to be registered with one of the four local grocers: the Co-op, John Cox, Percy Osborne or Ken Fryer. Similarly for meat they needed to shop with the Co-op or at A. E. Fisher's. Shop windows tended to be filled with faded cardboard 'dummies' of popular pre-War items, that had long been sold out. Whenever possible, householders stocked their gardens with vegetables, and kept chickens and rabbits that were fed on scraps, before ending up on the dining-room table. The older children at the School had instructions in rabbit keeping, and throughout the war Rabbit Shows were a regular form of entertainment in the village. Clothes and household goods were also subjected to rationing.

Petrol was also strictly rationed and was only available for essential war work. Private cars were stored for the duration of the war, either at the Stopsley Garage on the Green, or in back gardens, where the tyres perished and the chassis rusted. Doctor Anderson had a small petrol allowance, but other Stopsley residents, like the wholesale grocer, Leonard Hedden, had to walk to their work in Luton each day.

One of the first demands on the villagers was for a total blackout. Not a trace of light was permissible, as it might give German night-time pilots a clue to their whereabouts. Powdrill's brickworks in St Thomas's Road, and possibly Bennett's in Ashcroft Road, were major casualties: the flames shooting from their open-topped kiln chimneys at night could be seen for miles, and so they were forced to close.

Household blackout ranged from brown paper, cardboard, linoleum and old blankets to fitted wooden shutters. Blackout fabric was at a premium and could only be purchased with special coupons or on the black market. Car headlights were fitted with slotted masks that only permitted a narrow beam to fall on the road immediately ahead. Hand torches for pedestrians were essential if you were to avoid hazards, but they, too, had to be dimmed with brown paper masks.

Visibility was made even worse by artificially produced smoke-screens on moonlit nights. At first sawdust and tar blocks were burnt. Later they were replaced by smoke-screen generators: oil burning canisters that stood every few yards along Hitchin Road as it passed through the village. Motorists in the blackout tended to run into them, knocking them down like a row of ninepins. The smoke left houses and clothes lines coated with a smelly, oily deposit.

The only permitted lights were searchlights, which swept the sky, seeking enemy planes. The main local light was based at Offley, with half a dozen others in a ring around it. One of these, together with a rest-hut and ablutions, stood beside the old school at the corner of Butterfield's Green Road, almost opposite Cannon Lane. It was operated by seven or eight members of the 93rd Searchlight Regiment, which included Mrs Muriel Hill of Ryecroft Way, (formerly Mrs Bob Warner). Their jobs included operating the light and maintaining radio contact with headquarters, as well as cooking and maintenance.

Civil Defence

Everyone from 18 to 60 was compulsorily enrolled in some form of Civil Defence unless they had special exemption. Each night the Home Guard and the A.R.P. Wardens were on patrol. Today we laugh at the antics of 'Dad's Army', yet at the beginning of the War the Stopsley Home Guard were drilling with wooden pikes and World War I Canadian rifles, and crawling along the hedgerows and ditches of Stopsley Common and Warden Hill on manoeuvers that usually ended up at *The Sportsman* or *The Lilley Arms*. Air Raid Wardens, led by teacher John Bavister, walked the streets, wearing tin helmets and carrying rattles. They had bases at the rear of the Wesleyan Chapel, the old School at Swift's Green, and the Round Green Skating Rink. They were trained to deal with all kinds of incidents from unexploded incendiary bombs on roofs, to the indentification of poisonous gases, first aid and emergency rest centres. Fire Watchers, under Rex Clayton, had shelters on street corners, from where they were prepared to deal with any emergency, working shifts from 10 pm to 2 am, and 2 am to 6 am. High points, like the School roof, were manned as observation posts for sighting enemy aircraft and missiles. The Woman's Voluntary Service provided First Aid posts, often in individual homes; they operated mobile kitchens to feed the hard-pressed Civil Defence workers, and the casualties of bombing. The new Senior School was scheduled as an emergency feeding centre. Large supplies of food were locked in one of the store-rooms there: this caused problems as the main access for Fire Watchers to the roof was through the same cupboard. In October 1943 the Headmaster recorded "The Food Stores in this school were removed today. They have been neglected for a very long time and were in a disgustingly filthy state, reeking of mice. The filth has been left for the school to remove, together with 20 dead mice." The bicycle shed became a Rest Centre kitchen.

Stopsley housewives worked in the munitions factories, hat makers sewed servicemens' hats or camouflage nets, others drove buses, delivered letters, emptied dust bins and swept the streets: there were two lady street cleaners in Stopsley who kept the village looking a lot cleaner than it does today! Women with young families looked after the children of working mothers in dozens of unofficial crèches. Many younger girls joined the armed services or worked on local farms as members of the Women's Land Army. Collections for the Red Cross were organised on a regular weekly basis, and women (including the author's mother) went from house to house with collecting tins, or helped make up parcels of 'comforts' which somehow managed to reach British prisoners-of-war.

Even before the War started it was feared that the Germans might attack with poisonous gas. Consequently everyone was issued with a black rubber gas mask (respirator). Tiny babies were placed inside their masks. Small children had brightly coloured Mickey Mouse designs, which were supposed to calm those who found the devices frightening. Everyone carried their masks in cardboard boxes wherever they went. At the School respirator drill was frequently practised, and the A.R.P. checked that they fitted properly.

On the streets stacks of sandbags protected shop windows and vital doorways. One of the most odorous signs of war in Stopsley were the pig-bins chained to lampposts at intervals along the streets. Into these the householders were expected to tip certain items of waste food, which could be converted into pig and poultry fodder. Residents soon learnt that pigs would eat bread and vegetable scraps, but were not too keen on tea leaves or rabbit bones.

A variety of salvage schemes operated in Luton. Families were encouraged to save waste paper, and most children carried bundles of newspaper to school each week. Newspapers were rationed to a single fold sheet. The schools were paid for the paper they collected, which supplemented their meagre funds. Inter-school competitions were organised to see who could collect most - Maidenhall Junior Boys held the record with 23 tons! Special Salvage Weeks were held in Luton and children went around collecting tin cans and scrap metal. In November 1942 workmen removed most of the iron railings from around the Stopsley Schools, from the gardens in Hitchin and Putteridge Roads and from beside the Green. These, together with thousands of others, were intended for recycling, but few were ever used as the metal was unsuitable. Along with old aluminium pots and pans, it was largely part of a morale boosting exercise: most of the railings were dumped in the Thames estuary!

At a number of points in Stopsley iron tank-barriers were prepared, but fortunately never used, in combat. These were large angle-irons, a metre high, made from old railway lines. They slotted into square sockets, spaced about a metre apart, across the road. When the irons were not in place the sockets were sealed with wooden blocks which expanded when it rained, and were practically impossible to remove. One such barrier of irons ran across Ashcroft Road from the front door of No.96 to No.85 or 87 opposite. Another barrier stood outside Pond Farm beside the Green. In operation, they would have delayed progress to or from the Hitchin Road, south to Luton Airfield, Vauxhall Motors and London. None were ever set up, except for practice purposes, and they remained stacked in rusting piles for many years after the War.

One reminder of wartime defence does survive. Behind the Wigmore Hall hotel is a brick-built pill-box, carefully positioned (at TL:126222) to survey the airport landing ground.

At night the drone of British aircraft on bombing sorties to Europe was commonplace. More frightening was the sound of air raid sirens, followed by the throb of German planes, and later the whine and thud of flying bombs. Quite often all eyes would be turned skywards to watch an exciting dog-fight between allied and German planes. Barrage balloons might break loose around London and drift northwards to Stopsley. These could prove a hazard to British aircraft. One was shot down in the Putteridge area of the village. Fay Weighell (née Fryer) recalls "A Wellington bomber made a forced landing in a field north-west of Hayes Wood (now the Regional Sports Centre playing fields). It was quite intact and taped off, and there was no sign of the crew. No one seemed to know how it got there or how it was taken away. I was allowed to peep inside, it seemed very cramped and uncomfortable."

When the War began in 1939, Stopsley was alive with troops, much as it had been in 1914. Convoys often passed through the village and stopped for a break under the shade of the trees on the Hitchin Road at Arsley Bottom, between Round Green and Lynwood Avenue. The village women would make them cups of tea and chat to them. Their movements were supposed to be secret but the slogan 'Careless talk costs lives' was not always taken to heart. One well-known Stopsley lady (Mrs A. Gibson) wrote to her relatives in Ireland, mentioning the troops. Her letter was opened and censored, and she received an official reprimand from the War Office.

Wireless bulletins and newspapers were subjected to censorship and government propaganda. Nothing was broadcast that might demoralise the nation. Consequently those people who wanted to hear news of enemy action in Britain tuned in to the German propaganda programme 'Germany Calling'. This was not because they supported the enemy, but because they heard details of air raids against Britain (often exaggerated) that they could not hear from the BBC. On 5th September 1942, for example, Stopsley people could hear the German radio gloating over the bombing of the L.M.S. Railway Goods Depot in Midland Road, Luton, long before any mention of it appeared in a British newspaper. Another source of up to date news were the Railway passengers, freshly arrived from London, who brought first-hand accounts of events they had witnessed in the city that day.

Prisoners-of-War

On 10th April 1941 a German Heinkel 111 was shot down as it was returning from a raid on Coventry. It crashed near Breachwood Green, its crew having baled out between Harlington and Mangrove. One of the crew was taken prisoner near the entrance to Putteridge Bury, and a bus was commandeered to take him, accompanied by an R.A.F. officer, to Luton Police Station. That night the bus passengers found themselves walking into Luton.

There were a number of Prisoner of War camps close to Stopsley. One comprising 14 Nissen huts stood on the west side of the drive leading to Putteridge Bury house, to the north of the former cricket pitch. Early in the War this was occupied by Italian prisoners, who were given a relative amount of freedom and were allowed to work around the village in twos, where they proved quite popular, helping with gardening and general repairs: something useful, when many of the local men were serving in the Forces.

Later the Putteridge Camp was used for German prisoners. These were under much stricter guard until the war was over. Then they were allowed to come into the village, where they successfully sold a variety of objects that they had made, including carved wooden pecking chicken toys and 'slips' - slippers made from the side of old car tyres with knitted uppers.

The main Prisoner of War camp was opposite the entrance to Luton Airport, where Chertsey Close and Lalleford Road run today. It was occupied by Italian prisoners, a number of whom were employed after the war in the construction of the B.I.S.F. (steel) houses at Ramridge. Other prisoners camped on the Recreation Ground in Lilley and at Breachwood Green.

V.E.Day (Victory in Europe), the 8th May 1945 was celebrated with an improvised bonfire on the village green and, inexplicably, a noisy torchlit march across the fields to

Mangrove. Parties were held on street corners and in the Church Institute and Chapel halls. Jellies and tins of fruit that had not been seen during the years of austerity, suddenly appeared and never tasted better. Services were held at the church and chapels, where attempts were made to comfort families who had sacrificed fathers, sons and daughters.

Many Stopsley people have vivid recollections of the first Christmas after the War, when Sunday School children performed a Nativity in the Church Institute and the Prisoners of War were invited to attend. At the end of the performance the children quietly sang 'Silent Night, Holy Night' and gradually the Germans joined in 'Stille Nacht, Heilige Nacht' - and soon almost everyone in the Hall was in tears. At the Baptist Church a few nights later a German prisoners' choir led the singing, with a similar result.

There is no accurate record of how many Stopsley men and women served in the Armed Forces during the 2nd World War, or of the ordinary men, women and young people who served on the Home Front. According to official lists, some 29 men and 1 woman from the parish lost their lives: about a dozen less than in 1914-1918. Eleven of those served in the Army, eleven in the Royal Air Force, four in the Royal Navy, three uncertain and one, a civilian. Seven died in the Far East at the hands of the Japanese, four were lost at sea and nine died in the air.

The names below are taken mainly from the official War Office list of those killed during the 2nd World War, it is unlikely to be complete. Regretably, no details have been found of three of the men:-

Abbott, Leslie Charles, 134 Turners Road. Pte. 4th Royal Norfolks. Killed in action, Paula Uban Island, Singapore, 8th February 1942

Armitage, Harold William, 8 Hayes Close. Able Seaman R.N. *H.M.S. Cornwall.* Died of wounds, Bay of Bengal, 5th April 1942

Armstrong, Percy, 1 Hayes Close. Gunner. R.A. Lost at sea while prisoner of Japanese, 8th November 1942

Butler, Thomas Walter, 11 Applecroft Road. Cpl. K.R.R. Killed in Egypt, August 1941

Cain, Leslie, 81 Ashcroft Road. Tpr. 142nd Regt. R.A.C. Died of wounds, Algiers, 2nd July 1943

Card, Francis Austin William, 506 Hitchin Road. Sick berth attendant, R.N. on *H.M.S. Curacoa.* Lost at sea, 2nd October 1942

Chamberlain, Ernest John, 31 Cannon Lane. Pte. 5th Battn. Beds. and Herts. Regt. Lost at sea as prisoner of Japanese, 21st September 1941, aged 24.

Church, Frederick James, 89 Putteridge Road. A/Seaman R.N. *H.M.S. Isis.* Died on war service from exposure at sea, 20th July 1944

Clark, Thomas Plato, Hitchin Road. R.A.F. Killed in ground accident whilst on active service, 18th June 1942

Conisbee, Gordon H.C., 95 Ashcroft Road. Sgt.(N) R.A.F. Killed on active service, Walney Island, Barrow-in Furness, 30th September 1944

Dearman, Derrick Roy, D.F.C., 93 Putteridge Road. P/Officer, R.A.F. Killed on operations, Paris, 21st April 1944

Eaton, H.W., No details

Edwards, Robert, 23 Chesford Road. Pte. Died in Burma, 22nd May 1944

Edwin, Edward Francis, 131 Turners Road. Sgt/Pilot R.A.F. Died on active service, 15th November 1940

Gibson, William Maurice, 543 Hitchin Road.   Sgt. Rear Gunner, R.A.F. Killed in action whilst returning from operations over Nuremberg, Germany, 3rd March 1944

Gilbert, Frederick Charles, 66 Wigmore Lane.   Killed by German action at Vauxhall Motors Ltd., 30th August 1940

Hadaway, Norman Jack, 38 Ryecroft Way.   Pte. Beds. and Herts. Regt. Died 30th December 1939

Hill, Lewis Albert, Flt/Sgt. R.A.F.   Killed in flying accident at R.A.F. Lichfield, 18th October 1941, aged 21

Horton, Derek Basil, 1 Cannon Lane.   Pte. 5th Battn. Beds. and Herts. Regt.   Died as prisoner of Japanese, No. 2 Camp, Siam. 13th August 1943

Housden, Phyllis May, (née Lampard), 24 Applecroft Road.   Pte. A.T.S.   Died on active service. 14th July 1945, aged 21

Ibbotson, William, No details

Jackson, Francis Charles, D.F.M., 23 Felstead Way.   Sgt. Flt. Eng. R.A.F.   Killed on active service, December 1942

Large, Leslie William, 88 Stapleford Road.   1st Class Stoker, R.N.   Killed by enemy action in northern waters, 13th November 1944

Lawrence, Archie, No details

Matheson, David Black, 218 Ashcroft Road.   Pte. R.A.S.C. Lost at sea with *H.M.S. Ceramic,* Atlantic, 6th December 1942

Pain, Ronald George, 38 Clevedon Road.   Sgt. 35th Sqdn. Pathfinder Force R.A.F. Missing, presumed killed, on operation over Keil, Germany, 26th-27th August 1944

Pain, Stanley Edward, 38 Clevedon Road.   Pte. 2/7th Queen's Royal Regt. Killed in action, Forli, Italy. 27th September 1944

Wilcockson, Robert, 29 Felstead Way.   Sgt. R.A.F. Killed on operations, North-West France, 1943

Williams, Glyn, Putteridge Park.   F/Officer R.A.F. 140 Wing 2nd T.A.F. Missing, presumed killed in action over Holland. 3rd December 1944

Wright, Jack, 3 Clevedon Road.   Pte. Highland Light Infantry. Killed in action, Germany, 14th February 1945

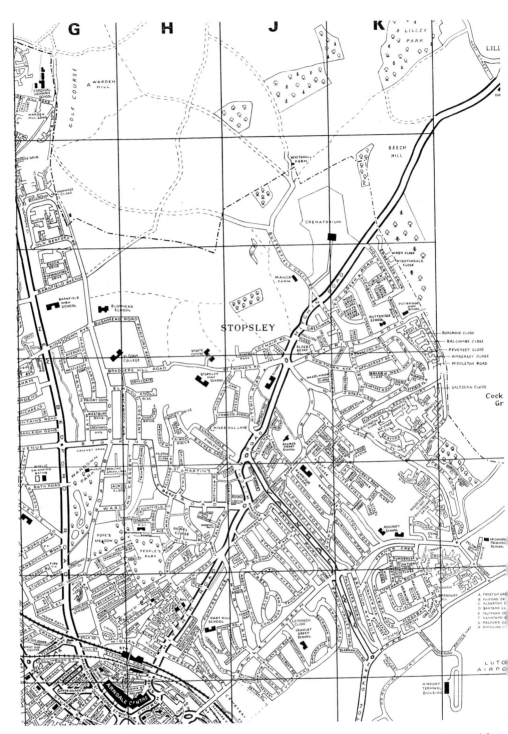

Map 6: A street map showing the growth of Stopsley by 1985. Practically the whole of the parish south of Manor Farm has been built over, mostly since 1930. Additional development in the Wigmore Hall area was completed by 1995. Taken from the *Map of Luton* by permission of the White Crescent Press.

116

Chapter 11

The Growth of Post-War Stopsley

At the outbreak of War in 1939 a number of new roads in Stopsley were under private construction. All work on them stopped for the duration of the War, and did not resume until 1946. Amongst these, the major development was at Ramridge. The carriageways of Clevedon, Yeovil, Williton and Burnham roads had all been laid out by 1938, but house building had only begun at the northern end of Clevedon Road and on six houses in Burnham Road. Preliminary work had also begun on Upwell Road. Similarly, the carriageways of Eaton Valley Road and Falconer's Road, Abbey Drive and Cowridge Crescent had all been prepared. In east Stopsley work on Chesford Road (beyond Nos. 94 and 103), Peartree Road and Rochester Avenue all came to an abrupt halt. Their layout would have been somewhat different had they been completed at that time.

Once the War was over, hundreds of returning soldiers got married and there was an urgent need for new houses. Luton Borough Council sought to provide good quality, cheap homes as quickly as possible. In April 1946 Councillor Geoffrey Hey, Chairman of the Highways, Town Planning and Estates Committee, submitted a plan to compulsorily purchase the 24 acre Ramridge building site, where the roads were already in place, and construct 200 permanent steel homes. The buildings in question were known as B.I.S.F. houses (British Iron and Steel Federation), and had been designed and promoted to provide a substitute for timber construction when forest products were in short supply. The architect commissioned was Frederick Gibbard, who was later the architect-planner of Harlow (Essex) New Town and Liverpool Roman Catholic Cathedral. Unlike prefabs of the single storey bungalow type which were intended originally to have a life of about 15 years, the B.I.S.F. houses were expected to serve twice that span, being regarded as 'permanent'. Councillor Hey, who had inspected examples of the houses elsewhere, said that he was quite satisfied, particularly with the inside fittings and the layout, and would welcome the opportunity to leave his present house [162 Old Bedford Road] and go into one of these, because they were superior. Councillor H. C. Janes, the local builder, criticised the expense of the scheme, saying privately built houses would cost the Council nothing whilst the B.I.S.F. houses would set them back £22 per house annually for the next 60 years. The Council passed the scheme, estimated to cost around £250,000 by 22 votes to 3. The Ramridge 'steel' houses were completed by the end of 1949 and extended to include Hartsfield Road and Dovehouse Hill. They were built using a work force which included large numbers of Irish immigrants and unrepatriated prisoners-of-war. The use of the latter was the subject of some local ethical criticism. Since they were built the original inner wall linings, which were of hardboard, have had to be replaced to meet updated insulation standards, and other modifications have been made. The original ox-blood coloured external walls have been painted in attractive alternating pastel shades, and the houses, now 50 years old, seem likely to well out-live their 30 year shelf date!

By 1948 Council house building was well under way on the Abbey Drive area of Hart Lane; on the first Wigmore development on the Ramridge End Farm site between Wigmore Lane and Ashcroft Road; and near the Airport off Lalleford Road. Chesford Road, Applecroft Road and Peartree Road, all started before the war, were completed with various additional Closes and joined to Sowerby Avenue. Private house building extended between Putteridge Road and the Hitchin Road at Wood Green Road and Crowland Road, and along Cannon Lane and Greenways. More infilling took place on the former allotments site around Langford Drive.

Each of these new developments stretched existing amenities to the limit, and in the late 1950s and early 1960s small shopping centres were built in Putteridge Road, Wigmore Lane, Yeovil Road and Abbots Wood Road. These were quite inadequate for the rapid growth in population, and it was necessary to provide a larger shopping development in the centre of Stopsley. Similarly the existing educational institutions were quite unable to cope with the vast influx of children, initially of infant age, and new schools opened at Ramridge, Crawley Green, Putteridge, Ashcroft and Stopsley. Medical facilities were faced with similar problems, and the number of doctors in the area grew rapidly by the 1960s and a Clinic was set up in Abbots Wood Road. Public transport increased from a single bus route from Luton to Stopsley Green via High Town, to another from Park Square to Crawley Green Road and Ashcroft Road, servicing the Ramridge and Wigmore estates on the way.

A major problem by the 1960s was the amount of traffic from Luton to Hitchin that passed through the centre of Stopsley village. Almost as bad was the traffic passing along Ashcroft Road from Vauxhall Motors and the Airport to join the Hitchin Road at Stopsley Green. The logical solution seemed to be the implementation of the pre-war plans, and the construction of the long-awaited by-pass between the Hitchin Road on the north-eastern side of Stopsley and the New Bedford Road south of Streatley; and linking it with a continuation of Eaton Valley Road from Vauxhall to Arsley Bottom, Bradgers Hill and Old Bedford Road near the South Bedfordshire Golf Course. The matter was thoroughly mishandled, and instead of moving traffic out of Stopsley, in 1968 a dual carriageway was directed straight into the centre of the village. This necessitated the destruction of the village Green, and created enormous traffic hazards, with two dual-carriageways and three other busy roads all converging onto what now became a traffic island. Little thought was given to pedestrian safety. The village centre was cut neatly in two. To get from one side to the other walkers had (and still have) the choice of either risking the badly sited underpass, subject to frequent vandalism, muggings and flooding; or using a pelican crossing and hoping the traffic would stop. No provision was made for the large number of pedestrians (mainly schoolchildren and the elderly) trying to cross either Putteridge Road or Ashcroft Road at the roundabout.

It was shortly prior to this in 1959 that permission was given to build the monstrous Jansel House. Historic Pond Farm was replaced with a six-storey steel-framed office block, totally out of place, scale and sympathy with its surroundings. Completed in1961 it brought together the scattered offices of the building firm, H. C. Janes Ltd. under one roof. Herbert Charles Janes, who had been born in Luton in 1884, built a number of estates around the town, including the Lane Farm development off Putteridge Road in the 1930s and after the war (Stapleford, Chesford, Applecroft and Peartree Roads). His firm went on to build all over England south of Leicester. A member of the Luton Town Council from 1942, he served as Mayor in 1953-4. An ardent Baptist, he was President of the Baptist Union of Great Britain in 1956-7. (see page 166). Fifteen years after the offices were built H. C. Janes Ltd. was taken over by Barratts. The ground floor of Jansel House is occupied by shops which initially included a supermarket: Bishop's Stores Ltd., Houghton Newsagents, Bobbies Hairdressers, and from 1974 the village Post Office. Inspite of the attraction of a large car-park, the majority of shoppers are drawn to Jansel House only by the necessity of having to visit the Post Office. This is no reflection on the quality of the other shops; they simply have the misfortune to be on the wrong side of the Hitchin Road to attract maximum trade.

It was a combination of the building of Jansel House and the row of village centre shops on the south side of the High Street area of Hitchin Road, together with the construction of the dual carriageway, that began the savage decimation of Stopsley. Within the space of the ten years between 1960 and 1970 the village lost its innocence, and was irreparably destroyed by unsympathetic developers who had no feeling for its past heritage, and whose eyes were firmly distracted by mammon. Sadly for them, mammon can have done them few favours. More sadly for Stopsley is the total lack of a planning policy for revitalising the village in the future.

Shopping in Stopsley Village Centre - 1930 to 1980

Prior to 1930 in the old village centre (the High Street between the Green and St Thomas' church) shops were limited to three general stores and a bakery. Ownership varied from time to time. The oldest was associated with the Harris family, whose shop stood beside the former alleyway between the Green and Lothair Road known as Harris Lane. Farm labourer William Harris was living there by 1841, but he and his wife did not open their grocery shop until the 1850s. Thomas Harris held it in 1891, and by that time it was primarily a bakery, with groceries and coal deliveries available. On Sundays and special occasions the villagers would take chickens or meat to the bakehouse where Harris would cook it for a penny. It had become a butcher's shop run by Mr Davis by the early 20th century. The other grocers were the Hucklesby's in Bury Road (St Thomas's Road, see page 82) and Jabez Cook at 630 Hitchin Road, opposite the modern junction with Venetia Road.

A number of travelling tradesmen with carts visited the village daily (milkmen), weekly (hardware, paraffin, etc.) or occasionally (haberdashery, rag-and-bone). Amongst these, older residents recall the baker's carts of Redrup and Starkings and Emery's (both from High Town); Hughey Smith the greengrocer; Mr Cain's milk round; Johnson of Lilley's milk cart with its churns and cans, followed later by Frank Boulter and Charles Fitzjohn; Frank Draper's groceries and household goods; the Holly Laundry and the Okey Pokey ice cream vendors.

The shops along the north side of the Hitchin Road were built in the 1930s, and have continued to be used to the present day, although a number have been extensively updated and enlarged from time to time. John Cox moved from Park Street, Luton in 1935 to open a high-class grocery shop at 617 Hitchin Road. Due to his failing health, he sold it to the Luton grocers, H.Inwoods Ltd. in 1945. It was almost immediately acquired by the W.H.Cullen grocery chain, and in 1966 was extensively altered to become the Midland Bank. Next door, R.A.Hopkins, the Chemist, is the only shop to have remained in the same family ownership since 1936. Today it incorporates Cecil Halsey's gentlemen's hairdressing saloon, which stood beside it for more than 30 years. The shop at the corner of Venetia Road (611 Hitchin Road) was opened by Frederick Darvell about 1935 as the 'Devonshire Dairy'. Harry Robinson converted it into a fish shop in 1938. In turn Rudd's acquired it as their second hardware shop, which they sold to Albert and Stanley Toyer after the War.

On the opposite corner at 609 Hitchin Road a newsagent and confectionery shop was opened by Joseph Smith. In a varied career, his daughter Kathleen Smith became an actress, Deputy Governor of Holloway Prison, and a successful novelist and TV script writer. During the War the newsagents was run by Percy Pheasant, and his wife who mesmerised small children as she peered at them over the top of her spectacles! It was next run by Ball and Parish, before being acquired by Fred Henderson in 1966. Next door at 607 Hitchin Road Sidney Mardle owned a haberdashery store. This was later acquired by Sydney Ashton as a toy and bicycle shop, before becoming an Estate Agent and then a hairdressers. Stopsley Branch Library was next door at 605, with the (Ashcroft Road) Park Keeper, Fred Clarke and his family living above. It became the Post Office in 1946, run by Bob Warner and his wife, and after 1954 Hyde and Sons, bakers. Today it is a Travel Agent. Ernest Simpkins, a builder by trade, built 603 and 605 Hitchin Road in 1933. He ran a grocery store from 603, selling fresh fruit and vegetables grown in his own greenhouses in Tancred Road. In due course the shop specialised in his greengrocery products. It remained in the family until 1983. Later it served as a haberdashery, before becoming a bakers.

On the opposite side of the road at 630 Hitchin Road was a general stores and at one time the post office. This was Jabez Cook's shop in 1891. It changed hands a number of times and it is difficult to trace the succession of owners. In the 1920s it belonged to Jim Leggett. Harry J. Beckitt acquired it in 1929 and a few years later he became Postmaster. Donald Thomson was in residence in 1939, followed by Kenneth Fryer and his wife. They relinquished the post office in 1946 but kept the general store until 1948. Robert (Bob) Yeomans ran the shop until it closed, prior to demolition, in 1960. Further east at 644 Hitchin Road was the Stopsley shop of A.E. Fisher, the Luton butcher. It was established in the mid 1930s and served the village well. It was taken over by R. Gunner Ltd, also butchers, around 1950. In 1938 the Luton Co-operative Wholesale Society built a branch at 598-602 Hitchin Road. This was the forerunner of the supermarket, with grocery, bakery, greengrocery, and hardware sections, and a separate adjoining butcher's shop.

Next door to *The Sportsman* Walter Lawrence had his shoemaker's shop. An old Stopsley schoolboy, he had a wealth of information about Stopsley, and bitterly resented having to leave school at an early age to take up a shoemaking apprenticeship, when he longed for higher education. On retirement he purchased the complete *Chambers' Encyclopaedia* in an effort to increase his knowledge. As a shoemaker he was an expert, and in later life he turned his precision skills to prize-winning model engineering with considerable success. Shortly before his retirement, about 1965, Lawrence was joined by a partner, Ray Stimpson. By then shoe repairing was on the decline, and Wally despaired at the poor standard of quality and craftsmanship in the shoe manufacturing industry. He died in 1985, aged 82, and is buried at The Vale.

On the corner of Lothair Road and St Thomas' Road stood the Stopsley Branch Library from 1946-7. Later this was Chapman's fish and chip shop, and by 1965 Hensome Ltd, Turf Accountants. On the opposite corner at 10-12 St Thomas' Road stood the first Rudd's hardware shop. By 1965 this had become Eveling's, and then Cunningham's haberdashery. The early history of Hucklesby's shop at 13 St Thomas' Road was described in Chapter 7 (page 82). It was a grocery shop run by Percy

Osborne throughout the 2nd World War, followed by a widow, Florence Dunham. It was acquired by Robert Yeomans when his Hitchin Road grocery store was demolished in 1960. Later it sold motor cycles, before being converted into a private house. Rose Cottage, opposite the War Memorial at 1 St Thomas's Road was converted into a bakery shop for Redrup and Starkings in the 1950s. It is appropriate that today it is a flower shop.

Along the Hitchin Road at Dropshort (roughly between 542 Hitchin Road and 97 Stopsley Way) was a Nursery Garden founded about 1880 by Robert Sharp. By the 1891 Census Return it was being run by a Scotsman, Lewis Dunbar, aged 56, and his sister Margaret. Dunbar described himself as a Nurseryman and Florist. Around 1895 the business was acquired by Watson Kime, formerly head gardener to Lord George Cavendish of Ashford Hall (Ashford-in-the-Water) in Derbyshire. When Watson died in 1920 his grandson, William Arthur Kime, carried on with the business, specialising in salad vegetables and tomatoes. George Draper owned it in 1939. The Nursery and its three adjoining glasshouses were demolished shortly after the construction of Stopsley Way in 1959. Watson Kime had three sons, one of whom, Percy Smith Kime was the village grocer and postmaster, who married Sarah Ann Godwin, niece of Elizabeth Hucklesby, the former postmistress. Mention has already been made of Ernest Simpkins who grew his own greengrocery produce in Tancred Road. At the foot of Bradgers Hill Road (No. 46) Mr A.M. Shore had a smallholding with a large greenhouse. There he attempted to grow a variety of garden plants on a commercial scale. He enjoyed only moderate success due to the poor chalky soil.

In the 1930s other corner shops appeared around Stopsley. Some in permanent premises like Reg Markie's newsagent and confectionery shop at 82 Putteridge Road or Frank Draper's grocery store at 2 Sowerby Avenue struggled to survive during the 2nd World War. There were others such as 2 Hawthorn Avenue, set-up in the front rooms of private houses. At 56 and 97 Ashcroft Road lean-to sweetshops were built on the side of the houses. The former catered for children going into the recreation ground. At the latter Charles Butler and later E. A. Williams must have found it hard to make a livelihood from a small stock of sweets and groceries. Another temporary shop stood in Putteridge Road opposite the former Vicarage where H. G. Cleaver had a tiny general store housed in a barn which stocked everything from Zebra grate polish to Lyons tea and Plummers mineral waters. Like many other local stores it operated a Christmas Club, and a 'slate' for those unable to pay immediately. From the front room of 25 Wigmore Lane, Albert Windsor ran a shoe repair business, whilst Hilda Wheeler cut hair for a few pence in the scullery of 78 Ashcroft Road. Her husband, Alfred, delivered coal with a horse and cart direct from the L.M.S. goods yard.

With the creation and expansion of the Wigmore estates in the 1970s and 1980s a shopping centre was created close to Wigmore Hall, with a large supermarket and a range of smaller shops, health clinic and library. With its ample carparks it caters for mobile shoppers as well as local residents. Being 1½ miles (2.5 km.) from Stopsley centre, it is no substitute for the shops or their customers living in the older parts of the village. The elderly find it quite inaccessible, and threats to close Stopsley village library during 1998 on the grounds that that at Wigmore is adequate are the views of cloud-cuckoo bureaucrats.

In December 1988 the Mayor of Luton, Alderman Mary Brash opened Mixes Hill Court, Warden controlled sheltered accomodation for the elderly, on the corner of St Thomas' Road and Mixes Hill Road: the site of the former Bury Farm orchard. Other housing for older residents had already been provided by Luton Council at Bray's Court in Ashcroft Road, and in Wigmore Lane.

Some mention must be made of the changing population of Stopsley, which began to increase rapidly during the 1930s. As a result of the great depression an influx of work-seekers and their families from north-east England, Manchester and Liverpool, moved into most parts of the village, particularly the newer Putteridge and St Martin's Avenue districts. Wartime evacuees temporarily swelled the numbers, but very few families stayed on after he war. From 1946 opportunities in building work brought large numbers of Irish immigrants to Luton and many settled in the Ramridge and Wigmore areas, where the Sacred Heart Catholic Church and Hall were built to cater for their religious and social needs. Prior to the mid 1950s there were very few families in the parish from outside the British Isles. Of about 440 children at Stopsley Junior school in 1964, only two were of Indian and two Caribbean parentage. By contrast, in 1997, out of 792 pupils at Stopsley High School, 80% of the pupils were registered as white, 15% Asian, 1·6% black African and 1·5% black Caribbean. In fairness it should be noted that some of the pupils who attended the High School lived outside Stopsley parish. The number of families who have lived in Stopsley for more than fifty years is now very limited, 10% being a rough and probably high estimate.

Population of Stopsley: 1861 - 1931

The Census Returns give the following figures for the population of Stopsley hamlet between 1861 and 1931. After 1933 they are absorbed into the figures for the Borough of Luton. The sharp fluctuation in the figures is best explained by inconsistencies in the choice of outlying settlements included in the catchment area.

1861 - 793
1871 - 956
1881 - 741
1891 - 801
1901 - 787
1911 - 943
1921 - 1140
1931 - 1474

XLIa. Members of the Girls' Life Brigade and the Boys' Brigade taking part in a wartime Joint Churches Service Parade in 1943. In the background is the *First and Last* with its doors protected by bomb-blast shields. Alongside the road are rows of smoke-screen generators: oil burning canisters that were ignited on moonlit nights to create dense clouds of foul-smelling oily fog. During the nights of blackout they were a hazard to pedestrians and drivers alike. (*Luton News: Luton Museum Collection.*)

XLIb: The remains of a pill-box behind the Wigmore Hall Hotel. It was set-up at the beginning of the War as part of the defences around Luton Aerodrome. (*James Dyer*)

XLIIa: The end of the 2nd World War was celebrated in halls and streets throughout western Europe.   The residents of Wigmore Lane, Mayfield Road and Hazelwood Close held their party in the Church Institute on Saturday 12th May, 1945   (*Luton News*)

XLIIb: An open-air VE Day party at the corner of Ashcroft Road and Wigmore Lane on Wednesday 9th May, 1945.   Trestle tables were hastily knocked together and benches were borrowed from the Wesleyan Chapel.   Long-rationed food appeared as if by magic, and disappeared just as quickly.   The White family are prominent at the end of the table on the right.   In the background, one house (No. 66) has managed to produce some home-made bunting.   (*Frederick Dyer*)

XLIIIa: When the children of St Thomas' Sunday School performed their Nativity play at Christmas 1945, German Prisoners of War were invited to attend.   The audience was moved to tears when English and German voices joined in singing 'Silent Night' at the end of the performance.   Janet Johnston and John Massey played Mary and Joseph.   (*Luton News*)

XLIIIb: British Iron and Steel Federation (BISF) houses under construction on the Ramridge Estate at the Hartsfield and Yeovil Road junction in 1947.   (*Stuart Smith*)

XLIV: Luton Airport in 1946, still camouflaged after the War. In the centre of the picture, beyond the Eaton Green Road, can be seen the enclosure containing the huts of the Italian Prisoner of War Camp (around present day Chertsey Close). Many of the prisoners helped to build the Ramridge Estate, whose white roads can be seen in the background (left). H.C. Janes used the huts as offices for a time. Slaughter's Wood (Haverings) is on the right. (*Luton News: Luton Museum Collection*)

XLV. The Stopsley Way dual-carriageway nearing completion in September 1968. This aerial view is dominated by Jansel House in the foreground. The Ashcroft Road Recreation Ground is clearly visible with its pavilions and enclosing path. The new shopping centre replaces a row of 19th century cottages. Overcrowding at Stopsley Infant and Junior schools is attested by the large number of hutted classrooms. The Lady Zia Wernher School is top left, and the Sacred Heart Schools top centre. *(Luton News: Luton Museum Collection)*

XLVIa: Jansel House, the headquarters building of H.C. Janes Ltd., under construction in 1957. This view also shows 19-21 Ashcroft Road on the right. (*Basil Cheverton*)

XLVIb: Once built, Jansel House dominated Stopsley and the old village Green, now reduced to a traffic roundabout. The open countryside of Butterfield's Green is clearly visible in this photograph of 1989, taken from an extending ladder above Stopsley Fire Station. (*James Dyer*)

XLVIIa: Hitchin Road (or Main Road) in 1938.   The shops on the left are still recognisable, but the hedge has been removed to build flats.   The cottages on the right have given way to the shopping centre development of the mid-1960s.   The old Vicarage dominates the hill in the distance.   Freda Miller and Dorothy Hedges (on cycle) chat in the empty road, watched by Alice Claridge.   Down the road, Freda's brother, Frank, delivers milk from Johnson of Lilley's milk cart.   (*Author's Collection*)

XLVIIb: John Cox's grocery store opened in Stopsley in 1935.   In 1945 it was sold to H. Inwood's and shortly afterwards to W.H. Cullen.   In 1966 the building was extensively altered to become the Midland Bank.   Notice the white telephone box.   (*Myrtle Cox*)

XLVIIIa: This vulnerable little wooden shop was owned by H.G. Cleaver. In the 1920s it stood on 'the Bank', almost opposite the old Vicarage in Putteridge Road. Amongst the many posters, one advertises 'Barratt and Co's, Christmas Club Boxes - join at once!' (*Author's Collection*)

XLVIIIb: The old Vicarage in Putteridge Road, photographed in September 1972, prior to its demolition. In spite of its solid appearance the building suffered badly from dry rot and had become a liability. Elderberry Close has been built in the Vicarage garden where a number of the original trees survive. (*James Dyer*)

Chapter 12

Stopsley and its Farms

In an earlier chapter we saw that Stopsley was one of a number of daughter-settlements in woodland clearings. These developed in late Saxon times, as part of the process of clearing mature forest to create new agricultural land. At the centre of each was a farmstead, a few cottages and sometimes a subsidiary manor, subservient to the Manor of Luton. Each needed pasture, arable and woodland, and each was linked by trackways to the others. The main concern of the farmers was to produce food and wring a living from the land. Until their crops were safely harvested, they never knew if they and their families would starve or survive for another year.

During the middle ages the Stopsley region contained more than twenty farms and half a dozen subsidiary manors. In some cases the same person owned more than one farm, which he or she let to a tenant. Close to many of the farms were 'greens', frequently the result of assarting or forest clearance, which gave rise to such place-names as Butterfield's Green, Swift's Green, Round Green, Eaton Green, Crawley Green, Bleak Hall Green and Crouch Green.

Around each farm or manor were open fields. No one is sure when the open field system of agriculture began, though many consider a late Saxon origin most likely. Tenth century charters from Oxfordshire show that open field terminology was in use by AD 962. The medieval landscape that resulted was reminiscent of the broad, treeless prairie landscape of north-east Bedfordshire that emerged in the 1950s. It was very different from the patchwork of hedged fields with scattered trees and woodlands that most of us think of as traditional today. Most of the countryside was wide, open and arable, lacking trees and hedgerows, but with occasional woods for pannage and estover (foraging by pigs for acorns; gathering firewood). Permanent pasture usually existed next to streams. In Stopsley, where streams were absent, ponds took their place. The arable was usually arranged in two or three large open fields, divided up into many long strips, demarcated from each other by earthen baulks. Each strip was as much as a man could plough in one day. Villagers usually had a selection of the strips in each field which were changed by rotation annually, thus giving them a fair share of the best and poorer soils. One field was left fallow each year. It was in everyone's interest to make sure that no animals trespassed on the cultivated land until the crops had been harvested. By mutual agreement all the strips were ploughed, sowed and harvested at the same time. Occupiers of strips had the common right to depasture their cattle and sheep over the open fields during the winter months and on the fallow field all the year round (allowing them to manure the land). In Chapter 1 we mentioned Juliana Balle, who claimed a number of strips in Stoppeslega in 1219. That is our earliest known reference.

Sheep farming increased during the fifteenth century. It was soon seen as a means of acquiring wealth. Consequently some villagers attempted to keep more sheep than the land could sustain, and efforts were made to control the number of animals allowed to graze.   In 1518 John Crawley of Stopsley exceeded the limit and was excluded from Blackwater Field and Bridge Field, both water meadows beside the river Lea.   In 1537 it was announced that 'no inhabitant of Stopsley shall have common grazing of sheep in West Croft or Old Croft up to the Feast of St Edward.'   Stopsley folk had a common right to graze their sheep at Lammas (after the harvest) beside the river Lea between Stockenbridge and Sheepbridge [Stockingstone Road and Mud Arches at Kingsdown Avenue].   They also had grazing rights on Little Moor, which were exchanged in the 1860s for a piece of meadow called Harper's Mead, which was in the vicinity of the West Side Centre in Dunstable Road.

Today in Stopsley all signs of the open fields have vanished, but study of the 1844 Tithe award map suggests where some of them may have been.   In a *Court Roll* of 1518 John Crawley and Thomas Shilbarn [Shelbourne?] were excluded from 'North Field' in Stopsley.   This can probably be identified with the area occupied by the vast playing fields of the Regional Sports' Centre.   Now treeless, it probably looks much as it did in the middle ages.   North Field would have been bounded by St Thomas's Road, the escarpment of Bradgers Hill, and Butterfield's Green Road.   There may have been a South Field south of St Thomas's Road, roughly bounded by Birchen Grove, Turners Road and Ashcroft Road.   To the east of Stopsley Green another large field lay between the road to Hitchin on the north and Sowerby Avenue on the south.   This was probably the remains of the field called Darley referred to in a will of Thomas Holmes dated 1707.

Whilst this may have been the case in the northern part of Stopsley, it may be too simplistic a picture for the whole parish.   When one considers the multitude of farms, some within half a mile of each other, it seems likely that at times, smaller, more close-knit groupings would have been more rational.   The Chiltern escarpment to the north of our parish has long been seen as a divide between the classic three-field Midland system of agriculture (as practiced in mid-Bedfordshire), and the more complicated farming landscape found on the hills to the south.   The Chilterns formed one of the two great woodland areas of south-east England, and large areas remained forested well into the fourteenth century.   Instead of the large two and three-field systems of the text books, farms could be found surrounded by some ten to twenty relatively small common fields, most of which had been cut out of the surrounding woodland.   The three-field rotation system was still followed, with a third of the fields sown for example with autumn wheat, a third with spring barley, and the remainder fallow.   The peasants would have their strips spread amongst the fields.   Since there was a tendency to want strips close to home, some peasants might find themselves with an excess of strips in one field which was growing barley and none growing wheat.   This could usually be balanced, since most peasants also held their own closes in which they grew what they liked.   Similarly, the demesne lands of the manors were grouped together in closes near the manor house.

That the Chiltern system was practiced in south Stopsley, is perhaps borne out by an incomplete rent-roll from Haverings Manor (situated near the Wigmore Lane and Crawley Green Road junction) dated 1544.   It contains the name of seven tenants who held strips of land in various fields of the manor:-

Thomas Jakys, lands in Eveley Field, Howfield and Darleybrake Field,
    all in Stopsley.
Edward Spycer, land in Howfield.
Robert Perott, land in Ramridge Hill Field.
William Arden, guardian of ..... Thrale, daughter and heiress of George Thrale,

land in Ramridge Hill Field.

Thomas Kilby, and enclosed pasture called Bromyscrofte.

William Smyth, a house and garden, land in Ramridge Hill Field.

John Crawley, land in Eveley Field.

In some parts of south Bedfordshire, around Hockliffe and Potsgrove for example, the ridges and furrows of the medieval strips can still be seen when the lighting is appropriate. Not so in Stopsley, where deep and frequent ploughing in recent times has removed every trace.

Groups of strips actually survived on the western edge of Stopsley until the middle of the nineteenth century. These lay on the very different terrain of Stopsley Common at the foot of the Bradgers Hill escarpment, and are now covered by the Sixth Form College and Bushmead estate. They are recorded on the 1844 Tithe Map, and on a plan of the proposed Cambridge to Oxford railway (1845). One stretch of 19 strips was unequally divided between six owners: Frances Chase owned 6, Thomas Sowerby 5, Charles Cox 3, Francis Butterfield 3, George Ashford and Daniel Brown 1 each. In turn they rented 10 of the strips out to Elizabeth Butlin, 3 to Richard Stokes, 3 to William Clark, and one each to Ann Clark, John Dix and Robert Dimmock. One more-recent owner in Bradgers Hill Road refused to sell the final surviving strip until the 1930s, delaying building development and eventually securing a handsome sale price.

Although there were survivals like those listed above, the majority of open fields, where they existed in Luton and Stopsley, had been enclosed well before the beginning of the 18th century. Enclosure usually required an Act of Parliament. The only Luton Enclosure Act (of 1808) was passed after most of the land had been returned to enclosure. Such enclosure must have been done by mutual agreement between the owners, but no records exist to prove the point. Poorer members of the community who owned only a few strips, sold their land to their richer companions and took pay as labourers on the larger farms, or found casual employment in Luton and neighbouring towns.

One of the earliest enclosed fields of which we have details was the one mentioned above called Darley. Eighty acres in extent it was bounded roughly by Putteridge Road, Stapleford Road, Chesford Road (southern section) and Selsey Drive. On 17th August 1600 it was sold by Richard Crawley (yeoman) to William Bigge (yeoman) of Stopsley (Ramridge End) and his sons John and Richard Bigge for £25. (also spelt Bygge and Bigg). Two years later on 23rd July 1602 the Bigge's sold a ten acre portion of the same field adjoining 'the lane called Sea Lane and abutting on Braye's Lane' [in the vicinity of Peartree Road] for the sum of £40 to Richard Franklyn of Willesden, Middlesex, clearly making a considerable profit.

Improvements in the quality of cattle, sheep and geese produced in the Midlands and East Anglia meant a steady flow of animals passing along the drovers' roads to markets in London and southern England from the late eighteenth century. The Icknield Way along the northern limit of Stopsley parish provided a major east-west routeway between Norfolk and central southern England, whilst minor drove roads ran north and south from the Icknield Way using the Hexton 'highway' across Stopsley Common to Luton and St Albans. Another route from northern England and central Bedfordshire passed through Butterfield's Green, Stopsley and along Wigmore Lane, enabling stock to be driven by a direct route, provided with known watering places, through Chiltern Green, Kimpton and Wheathampstead to the London markets.

There can be no doubt that Stopsley farmers would have used the same drove roads and bridleways to take their animals to markets in Luton, Hitchin and beyond.

Manor Farm (TL:105245)

Manor Farm, in Butterfield's Green Road, was built about 1870. It occupies the site of the former Manor of Hayes (also called Hooburne or Hoo Barn Manor). The first mention of the overlordship is in 1487 when it was held from John Rotherham, Lord of the Manor of Luton, for a rent of 50 shillings. The de la Haye family held property in Luton during the 12th century and they may well have given their name to the manor. In a Feet of Fines (or land conveyance) of February 1198 John de Sandon [Herts.] transferred a quarter of a virgate of land (about 8 to 10 acres) in Luton to Reginald de la Haye and his heirs, and the family are mentioned in connection with Luton and Stopsley in conveyances dated 1275, 1296 and 1390. As landowners John, Geoffrey and Thomas de la Haye were summoned to parliament during the reigns of Edward II and Edward III. The *Return of the Gentry of Bedfordshire* of 1433 includes John Hay of the Manor of Hayes and Hoo Barn, who achieved fame locally by carrying out major repairs at St Mary's church in Luton.

There is uncertainty about the manor's history until 1475 when, under the name of Hooburne Manor, John White recognised the right of Sir John Catesby, one of the Justices of Common Pleas, to the property. His son Humphrey succeeded him in 1487. After his death in 1504 it passed to his wife Grace, followed by their son Anthony (aged 49) in 1534 and his son Thomas in 1554. Finally George Catesby sold the manor to Thomas Cheyne for £830 in 1598.

When Thomas died in 1612 Hayes Manor passed to his younger son George who, in turn, seems to have transferred it to his son Robert in 1645. Amongst the Sowerby papers in the Hertfordshire County Record Office is a document of 1649 in which George, and Robert his son, declare that they have sold 48 acres, comprising Great Hayes and three closes called the Frith, Felmore and Dame Close, to Thomas Docwra of Putteridge Bury.

Robert Cheyne transferred the property in 1652 to John Howland of St Albans. He in turn sold it to Samuel Starling who had been born in Stopsley about 1628 and was destined to become Lord Mayor of London (see pages 27-8). Hayes Manor may well have fallen into disrepair during the Civil War. It was a period when Bedfordshire farms suffered badly, often having troops from both sides quartered upon them. Horse teams, wagons and tools could be commandeered without warning, and labourers might by conscripted as soldiers, causing hardship and general disruption to farm routine, with serious loss of harvests and fodder. Hayes was probably in a bad state and was sold cheaply. After the restoration of the monarchy in 1660, the sale of land made during the interregnum was confirmed and Samuel continued to hold the manor until his death, having paid tax on its eight hearths in 1671.

After Starling's death at Enfield in 1674 the company of Brewers, in which he had held the office of Master, administered the Manor during the minority of his nephew and heir, another Samuel, and it is recorded that the Court of the Company visited Luton a number of times on the business of the estate. The younger Samuel died before inheriting and eventually the property passed to Samuel senior's great niece Jane, wife of Anthony Ettrick, of Bishop Wearmouth (now Sunderland). After Jane's death, seven years later in 1716, her husband sold the Manor to Benjamin Morris.

William Gordon's map of Bedfordshire drawn in 1736 shows the only known representation of the original manor house. It is doubtful if it is a true likeness. A document held by the Crown Estate Office records that under the will of Martha Morris Ashford, dated 1791, an annuity was paid out of the rents of Manor Farm (Hayes Manor) to Luton Parish Church to educate 12 poor scholars. According to the Census John Waller was Bailiff at Manor Farm in 1841, but his place had been taken by William Irons when the 1844 Tithe Assessment was made. The Morris Ashforth family continued to hold the manor of Hayes, and John Ashforth farmed some 400 acres with the assistance of 12 labourers, until about 1868 when it was bought by Colonel George Sowerby and became part of the Putteridge Estate.

The Tithe Map of 1844 shows that much of the land north-west of the farmstead was still worked in long narrow strips, but with the purchase of Manor Farm, the Sowerby family, who already owned Whitehill Farm and Little Whitehill, now had a monopoly of the land and soon bought out most of the remaining small landholders. They then set about organising it into compact units by building a completely new farmstead on the old common fields, Stopsley Common Farm, and grouping the rest of the land round Manor and Whitehill Farms. Manor Farm was largely rebuilt soon after its purchase by the Sowerby family, probably about 1870. There is a map amongst the Sowerby papers showing the new Manor Farm and the cropping programmes for all the fields from 1873 to 1879. At that time the farm was run for the Estate by Thomas Russell. He and his wife Mary had seven children. In 1871 they employed four servants and a nursery maid in the house, and the 1,005 acre farm was worked by 27 men and 9 boys. Russell also had farming interests in Essex.

George Shaw became tenant farmer in 1888, assisted by his brother Thomas. Another brother, Charles Hugh Shaw, from Whitwell, took over in 1902. Charles Hugh Shaw was joined by his sons Cyril Hugh Shaw and Thomas Cecil Shaw in 1930. They acquired the tenancy when Charles died in 1934. Thomas left in 1937 and Cyril was joined by his two sons Patrick Hugh and John during the 2nd World War. Prior to Cyril's death in July 1960 the two sons ran the farm in partnership and were joint tenants from 1960 until 1987. John lived at Manor Farm, whilst Pat, having also acquired the tenancy of Whitehill Farm in 1967, moved to the latter in 1968. The two farms were then amalgamated. John left the business in 1987, and his place was taken by Pat's son, Lionel Hugh Shaw. With Pat's sudden tragic death in an agricultural accident in November 1989, the tenancy was acquired by Lionel.

Manor Farm remained part of the Putteridge Estate for the first third of the 20th century, passing through the successive ownership of the Sowerbys, the Clutterbucks (1908-19) and the Cassels (1922-35), until the Crown Estate Commissioners bought all the outlying farms in 1935 and formed what is known as the Putteridge Bury Estate.

Manor Farm gradually lost land to various urban needs over the years. The brickyard in St Thomas's Road (later owned by Powdrill's) was already in operation by 1875 and in the mid-1930s Luton Borough Council bought all the meadows between the farm and Stopsley village as a potential site for Luton Airport. Cox Croft and the Meadow (to use the 1873 field names) became playing fields, but Rough Pightle, Clay Croft and Middle Wood Field continued to be cropped until 1965 when they, too, were required for playing fields. Nails Hill Common, Dirty Acres and Oziers were sold away from the Estate, together with Stopsley Common Farm, in 1935 and 1937, but continued to be worked with Manor Farm until 1961. On the credit side, when another Crown farm became vacant in 1964 there was a reshuffling of land between tenants to increase the size of the holdings and Stone Field, Siberia and

Middle Field, all on the eastern flank of Galley and Warden Hills, were added to the northern extremity of the Manor Farm land.

The Tithe Map suggests that the original Manor House may have stood in the orchard between the present farm house and the eastern pond. The 1870 farmhouse is squarely built with a narrow passage from the front door, facing the road, to the coal barn at the back, and a broader passage at right angles to it from the yard door to the garden door. Four large, lofty rooms occupy the front part of the house, with the kitchen, pantry and dairy at the back. Beneath the front stairs is a cellar; whilst on the first floor are eight bedrooms, one now converted into a bathroom. Two outside privies, built back to back, served the family on one side, and the servants at the other.

The buildings were laid out in a model square fashion, with four cattle yards divided by a central passage, and surrounded by stables on the north, two long, low buildings on the west, a big Barn on the south and a range of sheds and horse boxes facing the farmyard on the east. A cartshed and an iron Dutch barn run parallel to the big Barn. The Dutch barn was built in 1950 to replace one at the Chalk Pit, (some 600m. north-west of Whitehill Farm), which was burnt down in the hot summer of 1949. The western part of the big Barn seems to have been part of the earlier farmstead and has been added to in height. The cartshed may also be part of the original farm, foundations of which were noticed beneath one of the cattle yards fifty years ago. A well (covered over) in one of the outbuildings is extremely deep 'with room at the bottom to turn a waggon and horses'.

Fred Gutteridge was horsekeeper at Manor Farm about 1900. He was paid 14s.0d (70p) a week to look after 16 horses. He got up at 4.30 a.m. in summer to prepare them for the labourers' who arrived at 5 a.m. He would be in bed by 8 p.m. tired out.

One unusual employee of Manor Farm is worthy of note. Harry Toyer was born at Lilley Bottom Farm in 1868. Photographs show him as a smart young man with receding wavy hair and a fine moustache. Like most country boys he worked on the land but, when he was 26, he went off to Russia. His passport, signed by the Earl of Kimberley, was issued on 23rd July 1894, and was reissued over the following three years. It is unclear why he went to Russia, though family tradition said that it was to learn farming. He may have travelled to the Congress of Agriculture held by Prince Shcherbatoo in 1894 in the wake of the severe famines of 1891 to 1893. There were about a dozen Farming Colleges in Imperial Russia at that time and it is possible that Harry attended one of them. When he returned to England he married and worked for the rest of his life at Manor Farm, Stopsley. He lived with his wife and three daughters, Ethel, Lillian and Celia at 20 Wigmore Lane. How he coped with the Russian language is not known. In 1990 Celia recalled that he had lived near St Petersburg, and suffered from a frost bitten left ear all his life. He sometimes amused the family be requesting caviar for breakfast, and at Easter treating them to the Orthodox Russian greeting. A photograph still exists showing him riding through the snow on a sleigh. He died in 1953, aged 85, and is buried in St Thomas' churchyard.

Swifts' Farm   (TL:106244)   'School Farm', 'Allwyn's Farm'[?]

Swifts' Farm stood midway between Manor Farm and Hitchin Road, on the western side of Butterfield's Green Road. The outlines of its foundations and associated buildings and paddocks could be clearly seen in the meadow before they were levelled to make the sports' field. When the car-parking area was prepared in 1973 a mechanical digger dug through the roof of a large brick-built underground chamber into what may have been a water cistern for the farm (see *Bedfordshire Archaeological Journal*, Vol. 10 (1975) p.84). Little is known about the property, but the name is almost certainly derived from the Swift family. John Swift farmed in 1830, and Edward and Mary Swift were there in the 1840s. A small Green faced the farm at the junction of Butterfield's Green Road and the Hitchin Road and was known as Swifts' Green. It was the site of the National School opened in 1858 and demolished in 1956: hence the alternative name of School Farm. It is possible that this was the property originally known as Bradways, but it is by no means certain.

The Tithe Award tells us that Swifts' Farm was owned by the Ashforths, who were related to the Morris family at the adjacent Manor Farm. John Allen from Woodhurst in Hampshire was the tenant farmer in 1861. The land, which was widely scattered around Stopsley and in the common fields, totalled some 190 acres. Colonel Sowerby seems to have bought Swifts' Farm at the same time that he acquired Manor Farm, and their lands were then combined. By 1871 the old farmhouse had been divided into four tenements, which were demolished by 1900. The small field to the south of Swifts' Farm was known as Dove House Close, and suggests the presence of a former dovecote.

Common Farm   (TL:097250) 'The Black Barns', 'The Flints'

There seems to be no record of this isolated set of buildings among the common fields until the Tithe Award map of 1844 which terms it 'barns with yard' and described it as part of the Manor Farm holding of Martha Ashforth.

Adjoining the barns were two semi-detached cottages built of partially knapped flint roughly coursed, with quoins, door and window surrounds of local orange brick. Although flint was a common building material in parts of the Chilterns, not many domestic examples have survived in the Stopsley area. Rebuilding of many properties by the Sowerby family may account for this. The first reference to the cottages comes with the 1861 Census Returns, when they were occupied by two farm labourers, George Worker and William Phillips and their families. The interiors were minute, with puddled-chalk floor and no indoor sanitation; yet Worker and his family had three children, and Phillips had a wife, three daughters aged 24,12 and 12, and three sons aged 20,14, and 9, all living together. In the 1930s an almost blind music teacher called Harry Spivey moved to Common Farm from 'The Elms' behind Green Farm. He used to walk to Cockernhoe each Sunday in all weathers to play the church organ. He made a little money by giving singing lessons. He also made and sold little packets of washing powder which he hawked from door to door. Croxford, a pigman, was his neighbour.

The cottages, later made into one, were always without gas or electricity, although water was piped from Manor Farm in 1938. A well still remains in the yard. From about 1938 their last occupant was Ada Perkins, a granddaughter of the Fundamentalist Baptist preacher, C. H. Spurgeon. After working on Manor Farm for most of his life, her husband, Jack Perkins joined the ground staff of the South Bedfordshire Golf Club. He was killed by a car in the Old Bedford Road. Together, he and Ada raised 9 children in the cottage, (and Jack had fathered 5 more by a previous marriage). Ada was a familiar figure in Stopsley pushing her weekly groceries in an old pram. Common Farm was pulled down shortly after her death in 1980. Mrs Perkins took great pride in pointing out the rare pasque flower *(Pulsatilla vulgaris)* that grew on the waste land at the side of the farm.

On the Tithe Map only two of the four barns were shown (in outline and not coloured like all buildings elsewhere) though the largest barn on the west was obviously of considerable age. The southern barn was a wooden structure with a king post roof, and its companion on the north had queen posts similar to those in the barn at Whitehill Farm. In 1902 an exceptionally strong gale blew down the fourth barn that stood at the eastern side of the yard, and pigsties were built in its place. An elderly informant recalled that all the barns were repaired at that time by jacking up the wooden sides and replacing rotting lower timbers with a brick foundation, and thatched roofs with corrugated iron. The woodwork was all coated with black tar: hence the most popular local name 'The Black Barns'.

It would be fascinating to know who built those great barns, and if at one time they were held in 'common'. As long as anyone connected with them can remember they were used to store the harvest from the fields lying away from Manor Farm, and after the Second World War they stored machinery and fertiliser also, but there seems no reason to think that Common Farm was ever a 'proper' farm. The barn adjoining the house was burnt down by vandals in 1981 and had to be cleared away. The Shaw brothers demolished the house and remaining barns shortly afterwards, using the bricks and timbers for renovating barns at Manor and Whitehill farms, and building the new porch on St Thomas' church.

The main access to Common Farm was from Butterfield's Green, down the hollow way long known as Oosey Hill. The adjoining field name is written as both Hosea and Osier, and Oosey is clearly a variation, possibly recalling the water that oozes through the chalk onto the road during the winter months. (There is a Doosley Pond in Lilley parish). A bridleway known as the Driftway linked Common Farm to the Old Bedford Road at the foot of Warden Hill. Minor problems arose in 1914 when the Golf Club tried to divert it without the consent of the Parish Council. The south-north track from Luton that crosses the Driftway at Common Farm and climbs the hill was called the Hexton Highway in the Parish Council Minutes. These old tracks were once the main arteries along which horse-drawn transport made its way from the Bedford Road to join the Hitchin Road at Swifts' Green or Lilley (via Little Whitehill and Lilley Wood) avoiding Round Green and Stopsley Village.

Little Whitehill (TL:105252) 'Old Farm' (1826)

Little Whitehill farmstead stood at the junction of the old road to Lilley (mentioned above) and the Butterfield's Green lane, directly behind the two modern 'Whitehill Cottages'. According to Davis's *History of Luton* (1855) it had been in the hands of the Pigott family for 500 years.

A survey of the lands of the Manor of Bennetts made in 1602 describes in great detail the land belonging to Francis Pigott then totalling 195 acres, much of it in strips of less than an acre, lying in common fields from Galley Hill to the south-west side of Stopsley village. Another Francis Pigott owned the farm in 1829. By 1844 the land then owned by Elizabeth Pigott had shrunk to 67 acres, mainly around the homestead. Elizabeth was styled a farmeress in the 1841 Census and by that time may have been living at Pond Farm. Little Whitehill was sold to Thomas Sowerby in 1850 and the land was absorbed into the Putteridge Estate. By 1881 it was described as a cottage, occupied by William Phillips, an agricultural labourer (aged 70) and his wife Elizabeth (69) a straw plaiter (formerly of Common Farm). Later known as Chapman's Cottage, it was pulled down about 1960.

Whitehill Farm   (TL: 106254)

Whitehill Farm stands near the site of the 'lost' Manor of Bennetts. The earliest reference indicates that it was in the possession of Thomas Rotherham at his death in 1504. It remained in that family until 1573 when George Rotherham transferred it to John Franklin and the property was referred to as 'the site of the Manor of Bennetts with lands in Stopsley and Luton'. Richard Franklin was the next owner, followed by his son Sir John Franklin who held the manor in 1622. A survey made in 1602 of the lands of the Manor of Bennetts lists the fields of Whitehill, and also records in detail the land held by Francis Piggott of Little Whitehill Farm, and other land in the parish of Shillington.

In 1671 Daniel Brace of Over Standon [Upper Stondon] in Bedfordshire bequeathed the Manor of Bennetts and Whitehill Farm to his son Thomas. In the same will he provides for the rest of his large family and apart from property in Shefford and Cambridge he mentions the following places at Whitehill:-

"to Francis my sonne, the greate severall [field] next Hexton [Way] wherein the great beech stands, the spinney to be measured as part of the said inclosure and the same to be fensed with a ditch sett by my executrix.

" to Daniel my third sonne, all that field at Whitehill now in my own hands with the most convenient way either to Luton or Hexton or both at all tymes.

"to Charles my sonne, all that inclosure next Hexton Way containing eleven acres and the inclosure adjoining it containing twenty-eight acres be it more or less.

"to Sarah Brace my daughter, all that close of twenty acres....being now sowne with the ashes but again to be fallowed....with free liberty of all ways and passages at all tymes to and from the same. Also all that piece of land that abutts upon the gate which is in my way from Hexton to my farm at Whitehill on which a great bush also now grows; and the said piece contains about 18 acres.

"to George Brace my sonne, all that greate inclosure that lies on the east part of the homestall closes containing 50 acres.

"those two little pitles of pasture ground belonging to my farm at Whitehill and the three acres of land now upon sale....to be sold to put my sonne Daniel apprentice.

"to Thomas my eldest sonne, all that my farm of Whitehill and the Manor of Bennetts (not before given).

"my wife Sarah to have power to fell £300 timber if she so pleases of my farm at Whitehill."

The 'greate severall' allotted to Francis can be identified with Great Field surrounding Goodman's Dell on the Tithe Map (now called Calves Pikel). A severall was land owned by one individual, as opposed to common land. Whitehill Wood has been extended to include Goodmandell which was a big chalk pit, but the aforestation bank and ditch surrounding the original spinney can still be seen. Charles and Sarah seem to have inherited the four closes, once in common, called Buxley according to the 1602 survey and which are identifiable as Little Peverells, Twenty-eight Acres, Eighteen Acres and Mushrooms on the Tithe Map. George's portion would be the Snarehill and Shortgrave of 1602, renamed the Great Field next Lilley by 1844. Daniel's share is too vague to identify with certainty - it might be Grubb's Bush, which became a famous partridge shoot in the nineteenth century, or possibly Deadman's Hole, the only remaining 'parcel' of any size in the 1602 survey, which lay between Galley Hill and the Icknield Way.

It seems likely that Thomas Brace bought out his brothers and sister. Under the terms of the will he was already given the option of paying his brother George £200 for the great inclosure east of the homestall. In 1678 he sold the whole property to Thomas Christie of Bedford. The sale document gives a striking impression of the place:

> "...all that scite Manor House and Demesne lands of the Manor of Bennitts and Farm of Whitehill or by whatsoever name or names the same was or were called or known situated lying and being in the Hamlet or Village of Stopsley in the Parish of Leviton alias Luton in the said county of Bedfordshire and also all Houses, Buildings, Barns, Stables, Dovehouses, Yards, Garden, Orchards, Backsides, Lands, Tenements, Heraditaments, Meadows, Pasture, Freebords, Feedings, Trees, Woods, Underwoods, Rents, Services, Commons, Common of Pasture, Ways, Easements, Mounds, Fences, and all other profits, Commodities, Advantages, Emoluments, and Appurtenances whatsoever unto the said Scite Manor House and Farm Lands belonging.... then in the occupation of one John Wells...."

In 1697 Thomas Christie bequeathed the property to his six nephews; one of whom, Christie Southouse, eventually inherited it. It remained in the family until William Southouse, a laceman, of Ludgate Hill, London, sold it to John Sowerby in 1797. The Whitehill lands then totalled 506 acres and were in the tenure and occupation of John Fowler who appears in the Jury Lists for 1791.

From this point Whitehill became part of Putteridge Estate and the ownership was the same as that of Manor Farm, but unlike that farm it was never run by the estate. Sometime after 1830 Daniel Gutteridge came from Wigmore Hall to run Whitehill Farm. Perhaps to mark his 50th birthday or his arrival at Whitehill, he left his initials and the date 1837 cut into a brick in one of the farm buildings. In 1861, aged 73, he was still farming 547 acres and employing 15 labourers and six boys. He was succeeded by Joseph Hopkins from Lincolnshire who brought his wife and a foreman with him. Hopkins became destitute after his entire crop of roots were destroyed by rabbits, and his sheep starved to death. In 1871 the farm was reduced to 400 acres and was worked by nine men and five boys. Francis Allingham ran the farm until 1921, when Cyril Hugh Shaw took it over for six years. Cyril Smith (from Radlett) worked it from 1927 until 1948. He owned one of the horse floats that provided a milk round in Stopsley. Douglas Jeffs held the farm until 1967, when the Shaws resumed control.

From 1967 Manor Farm and Whitehill Farm were worked together. Pat Shaw and his brother John, with four labourers, worked 880 acres. In 1997 Lionel Shaw and two men farm 1,070 acres, (some of it at Caddington and Barton). They are the only farming people left in Stopsley.

Whitehill Farm house is a jig-saw puzzle waiting for an architectural historian to sort out. It has been altered on numerous occasions, and internal plastering and external cement rendering make the task even more difficult. The writer claims little architectural knowledge, and what follows is open to speculation.

The original building seems to have been a hall of box-frame timber construction, two unequal bays in length. The wall panels were filled with horizontal brick nogging. This structure lies approximately east to west, and survives today as a kitchen and living room, with a large filled-in fireplace at the eastern end. Above are a bathroom and bedroom. Massive oak corner posts and tie beams are visible on both floors. It is possible that another bay existed to the east of the chimney, which was removed when the house was extended eastwards (over a cellar) during later alterations. The original front door would probably have been in the middle of the south face. Upper and lower brick-built passageways were built along the south front in the mid-19th century, making it possible to move along the house without passing through individual rooms, but cutting out much southern light. It is probable that the whole building was refaced in local brick, and that new windows and blue slate roofing tiles were added at that time. A brick-built wing projecting south was added to the south-west corner in the late 19th century. At the north-west corner is a single storey well-house covering a (filled-in) well; possibly that mentioned by Davis in 1855 as being 250 feet (76 m.) deep. In the early 1960s the eastern end of the house began to sink into the cellar, so it was demolished and the building reduced in length by some 15 feet (4.5 m.).

The farm buildings at Whitehill seem to have been little altered until quite recently, when a Dutch barn and cattle yards replaced old barns on the south side of the yard, and a cow-shed was built in what had been a small orchard. On the east side stands the brick barn which contains Daniel Gutteridge's initials of 1837. A low brick building runs from the barn towards the house, and according to 19th century maps, originally joined it. It may have contained stables. On the western side of the farmyard stand two wooden barns, the larger of which must surely be the one mentioned in the 1602 survey behind which 'Grovefield' lay. This barn used to measure 75 feet by 25 feet, (23 m. by 7.5 m.), but dryrot at the northern end necessitated the removal of some 15 feet (4.5 m.) and its replacement by a brick wall. The other barn is of similar area, but is not so high. Both have queenposts in the roof, and much of their original timber remains protected.

Until the late 1960s 'Grovefield', the meadow immediately west of the farmhouse, displayed a very uneven surface, with clear indications of medieval hollow ways and house platforms: almost certainly the site of the Manor of Bennetts. The western edge has been obliterated by a reservoir, and the field surface has been levelled by filling-in, but not destroying, the hollows. In 1966 the author conducted a small excavation and exposed the cobbled surface of Daniel Brace's 'way to Hexton'.

Stopsley Common Farm (TL:093243)

Still standing in Bushmead Road and surrounded by a modern housing estate, it is difficult to imagine that this was once a busy working farm standing in open countryside. The prefix 'Stopsley' to its name distinguished it from the older buildings known as Common Farm, a mile north-east , which were essentially a group of barns with two adjoining labourers' cottages, that formed an outpost of Manor Farm.

Stopsley Common Farm was created by the Putteridge Estate after 1868 on parcels of land that had previously belonged to Manor, Pond and Swifts' Farms. The farmhouse was built about 1870 in a style common to most of the Putteridge Estate houses. Like Whitehill, the farm does not seem to have been run by the Estate. It first appeared on the Ordnance Survey maps in 1879. There is no record of an occupier in the 1885 edition of *Kelly's Directory*, and it was vacant in 1888, but by 1891 Richard Osborne was farming there, and employing Charles Hutchins as a groom. Osborne moved to Dog Kennel Farm in Lilley. John Chennells was in control by 1898. In 1900 Private Wilson, a labourer of Stopsley Common, was serving in the Boer War. The farm, which stood on a slight eminence, was approached by a lane from the Old Bedford Road to the west, and consisted of a large south-facing house, not dissimilar to Manor Farm, with a square yard at the rear, enclosed by stables and barns. Two hundred metres to the east, beside the bridleway known as Hexton Highway, stood a stockyard enclosed by barns. For the first third of the 20th century until 1936 it was farmed by John Chennells, although it seems to have been owned for part of that time by Arthur Godfrey, landlord of the *First and Last* public house. With the rationalisation of the Putteridge Estate in 1935 Stopsley Common Farm was sold to Frederick J. Manning, W. R. Steel and Frederick Powdrill. It was their intention to develop the land, then known as the 'Old Bedford Road Estate'. Bushmead Road was constructed in 1937 and was eventually intended to extend over Bradgers Hill to Stopsley, forming part of a trunk road known as TP29 (Town Planning road 29) linking the Hitchin Road to the New Bedford Road. That is why it was originally wider than the adjoining Fairfield Avenue. The War intervened, plans changed, and a potentially useful by-pass for Stopsley was never constructed.

In 1935 Frederick Powdrill began farming the land from the neighbouring Waterhall Farm (a mile north-west), and continued to do so until the late 1950s, when F. J. Manning took it over. With the encroachment of Luton it had ceased to be a viable working farm by 1970, and its land was sold for development, (though it was still farmed from Waterhall Farm until that farm was sold in 1987.) The farmhouse was occupied by Major Curry until about 1946, when it was leased to the Kilby family. Since 1965 it has been the property of Mr John Young.

Bury Farm   (TL: 100237) 'Bleak Hall', 'Stopsley Farm'

Situated in Bury Road, now St Thomas's Road, the farm stood where the new Baptist Church and Mixes Hill Court now stand. The house was demolished about 1960 and the barns lingered until 1974, having been used for 26 years as classrooms for Stopsley Secondary Modern School.

Bury Farm has been identified as the original Manor of Norwood. The building is marked as Bleak Hall on Andrew Bryant's map of 1826, with Bleak Hall Green on the opposite side of the road. In his will of 21st October 1836 John Chase, Esquire, of Luton, left it to his son Frederick Chase. The Chase Family owned much of the land on the western side of the parish, including the adjoining Mixes Hill Farm. At the time of the Tithe assessment in 1844 it was rented to William Gillham. By the middle of the century it had been acquired by members of the Pigott family who owned Little Whitehill Farm, and were tenants at Pond Farm and Lane Farm. The farmhouse was rebuilt about 1870. Like most Stopsley farms it had a deep well beneath the kitchen floor, and a hand-pump to raise the water. Thomas Pigott and his wife Elizabeth moved to Bury Farm about 1850, together with their son Charles, and daughters Charlotte, Elizabeth and Clara. Thomas ran the farm of 94 acres until the 1880s, employing five men and a boy. The farm then passed to his son Charles, who died there in 1899 aged 68. Charles' daughter Helen (aged 43) inherited the farm. Almost immediately she married the chemist, George Duberly, in St Thomas' church. They lived there until 1907, when they moved to Bournemouth, leaving the farm in the hands of a tenant, Hugh Bond. Helen later married Henry Cook. When she died in 1930 she was buried with her parents in Rothesay Road cemetery. The farm was later acquired by Arthur and Ethel Woodfield. It was never a large farm; its land was bounded by St Thomas' Road on the north, the hill-scarp on the west, Hitchin Road on the east and roughly the line of St Martin's Avenue to the south. Gradually plots of land were sold for building on the south and east and it became uneconomical to run. The bulk of the land was earmarked for a northern bypass, and (after 1948) Stopsley High School playing fields.

Pond Farm (TL: 105238)

Pond Farm stood at the junction of Putteridge Road and Hitchin Road, on the south side of Jansel House. The farm got its name from two ponds, one of which lay between Putteridge Road and the village Green and the other on the north side of the farmyard, where Barratt's office block now stands. The Putteridge pond was a popular meeting place for mothers seeking a gossip, and a favourite spot with the village children for catching tiddlers. The youngsters also enjoyed a sense of adventure as they inched their way along the iron railings on the southern side of the pond until they reached the farm wall, where their elders told them there was a deep spring. There they climbed victoriously onto the road: no one came to any harm but they were all excited by the sense of danger. The pond was often polluted with rubbish and the Parish council were frequently asked to get it cleaned. Although both ponds had been filled in by the time Jansel House was built in 1959, both reappear in the car-park whenever there has been heavy rain.

Built of local grey bricks, with a slate roof, the farm house must have dated from the early-1800s. The kitchen had a large open chimney-corner, with a set of iron pot-hooks, as well as larger hooks on which to hang sides of bacon. There was an enormous stone sink with a pump beside it, which drew water from a well deep beneath the house. There were four or five other wells around the farm from which water had to be hauled by bucket. Below the kitchen was a large cellar, part of which was used as the dairy. Over the kitchen was a room which had reputedly been used as a doss-house (dormitory) for farm labourers. In order that these men did not go in and out through the farmer's private quarters, they had access to their room by means of an outside ladder. The farm land was widely scattered around the parish at the time of the Tithe assessment, but by 1914 it was mostly confined to the area between Round Green and Ashcroft Road, with a few fields where 'The Vale' cemetery now lies.

The early ownership of Pond Farm is not known. The tithes had been the property of Trinity College, Oxford, for many years and leased to the Marquess of Bute at Luton Hoo. By 1840 the farm belonged to Richard Oakley, and was leased to Elizabeth Piggott. A widow, and 55 years old, Elizabeth described herself as a farmeress. She was assisted by her twin children Henry and Elizabeth, both 25 years old. They employed four boys, and a woman, Sarah Norwood, to help in the house.

By 1862 William Queensborough had taken over the running of the farm. [In almost all documentary evidence relating to the extensive Queensborough family, including their signatures, their name is spelt as above. On the gravestones in St Thomas' churchyard, however, the names are all spelt 'Queneborough'. The reason for this anomaly if not known]. According to the 1871 Census Daniel Queensborough (then 56) was farming 56 acres in that year, assisted by his wife Charlotte (54) and their children, David (27), Emma (23) and Michael (17). When Daniel died in March 1882 aged 66, the farm was taken over by Daniel Benjamin Queensborough, aged 36. At that time it comprised 70 acres. The same Daniel was elected to the newly formed Parish Council in 1896 and in 1903 was its Chairman. He still occupied the farm on 13th June 1910 when its owners, the Allens, put it up for auction. According to the

Sale catalogue it contained an entrance passage, dining room, office, parlour and large combined kitchen and scullery, with four bedrooms and a box-room upstairs. There was a small garden facing Putteridge Road. Adjoining was a coach-house, stable for four horses, a large barn with a lean-to equipment shed, two cow-houses, three loose-boxes, a hen-house and a walled-in stock yard. Daniel Benjamin Queensborough died aged 67, in May 1911 and his wife Catherine (*née* Shaw) followed in 1914.

Jesse Boulter (aged 31), who had been the bailiff for a short time at Home Farm, Putteridge Bury, now took over Pond Farm, with the help of his wife Mary, and their son and daughter, Frank and May. In the late 1920s Frank worked at the Sawmill beside the old school at Swift's Green, until it closed down. Frank was a keen horseman and cut a fine figure dressed as a highway man, leading the village fancy dress parade from the Church Institute to the Vicarage garden each summer during the 1930s. In time Jesse Boulter looked after the farming, whilst May and Frank sold their home-produced milk, butter and eggs. Every morning and evening until the 1950s their cows regularly crossed Ashcroft Road, on their way to and from milking at the farm, to a long narrow meadow called Brays Close which stretched westwards from the road to beyond the present Stopsley Way. Jesse died in July 1961 aged 81, and Frank and May then concentrated on the dairy herd. Frank Boulter's milk-cart was a familiar sight around Stopsley. The milk was sold from churn to milk-can at each house, until Health regulations insisted on the use of milk bottles. He continued to deliver milk to his local customers until shortly before his death in 1989, aged 81. By that time he was living with his sister May at Mead Farm, Limbury.

The widening of Putteridge Road in the 1950s removed half the garden and some of the farm land. The farm buildings were condemned as unfit for cattle and the herd had to be sold, although it was still producing milk until Easter 1958. Drainage in the village caused the ponds to dry up in the summer, depriving the cattle of a water supply. It became impossible to operate a farm from a site that was being stifled by housing and increasing traffic. And so, like all the other old Stopsley buildings, it was demolished in July 1958; mourned only by those who remembered its friendly occupants and the lingering smell of the cattle as they made their way across Ashcroft Road to 'Boulter's Meadow.'

Green Farm   (TL:104232) 'Smith's Farm'

This farm, at 619 Hitchin Road, stood beside the village Green, until the last vestiges of the house were demolished in the 1970s. The farmhouse had been extensively altered in its later years, and when the author inspected it, shortly before its demolition, little of any antiquity had survived. Its original name had long been forgotten and even the oldest residents tended to call it after previous tenants. From 1930 a series of garages, petrol stations and car showrooms occupied the front garden.

Little is known of Green Farm except for one or two faded photographs and a few reminiscences of Ellen Barber whose grandfather, James Barber, lived there in the latter part of the 19th century. The house of local brick and tiles with timber framing was probably of 17th century date. It was set well back from the road with an extensive garden at the front. There were stables, cowshed and pigsties, an orchard and a meadow that stretched west from the farm to the Wesleyan chapel, where there was an iron gate. This field was used for the village flower show. Today it is covered by shops and Venetia Road.

There is little to suggest that Green Farm was a working Farm after about 1870. Maud Stronell, who was born a few doors away in 1884, observed that as a child she was sent to collect a can of milk each morning from Pond Farm or Manor Farm, never Green Farm. Ellen Barber recalled Lord George Sanger's circus parading through Stopsley on its way from Hitchin to a one night stand in Stockwood Park, Luton. The elephants put their trunks over the hedge of Green Farm and pulled up a row of cabbages. By the 1930s a blacksmith's workshop at the side of the farm was turned into a garage for tractor, car and cycle repairs. In 1936 it belonged to Jones and Barton Ltd. The front garden was replaced by a concrete forecourt with petrol pumps and a flag pole sporting the Union Jack.

The 1851 Census informs us that the farm with 10 acres of land, was occupied by Joseph Welch, a former publican turned farmer, together with his wife Charlotte and two of their four sons. Ten years later Joseph Welch was still at the farm (aged 74) and farming 25 acres, with the help of his son Benjamin (aged 28) and grandson Reuben (aged 11). Reuben's father, Levi (34) and mother Ann, lived in the cottage next door. Seven years later Levi and Reuben were both in Pentonville Prison. (see pages 46-7). When the 1871 Census was published Joseph Welch was registered as a 'former gamekeeper' and his son Benjamin a 'farm servant'. Joseph died in April 1871 aged 74 and was buried in St Thomas' churchyard, where Charlotte, his wife, joined him six months later. In 1881, when he was 50, Benjamin Welch styled himself a 'small farmer' with 20 acres. James Barber seems to have moved to the farm towards the end of the century.

Behind the farm in Harris Lane was a cottage once known as The Elms. Walter Kime and Annie Richards moved there after their wedding in 1903. Reginald Rainbow was living there between 1918 and 1926. He was followed by a music teacher, Harry Spivey, who moved to Common Farm after a minor scandal in the early 1930s. The Bandy and Draper families were the last to live there, before the house was demolished in the 1960s.

Stopsley Lane Farm (TL:109239) 'Park Road Farm'

Deriving its name from Park Lane - the lane leading to Putteridge Park, Lane Farm had a long history. William Austin identified it with the Manor of Plenties and the Crawley family. (see page 21). According to Austin the old manor house had been erected late in the fourteenth century, and members of the Crawley family occupied it for nearly a hundred years, selling it in 1568. James Malden and his wife Fanny were occupying the farm as tenants of Samuel Crawley of Stockwood in 1851. The Maldens raised three small children at the farm, and employed 9 men and 2 boys to work the 214 acres. The old house with all its buildings was completely destroyed by fire about 1860 when the house was occupied by Thomas Piggott and his family. This happened at the end of harvest and the entire crop was burnt. Lane Farm was rebuilt close to it original site, opposite the end of Cannon Lane in Putteridge Road. The new farmhouse was sheltered from the road by a row of barns which surrounded a large yard. In 1871 it was being farmed by William Clark who employed 15 men and boys to work 22 acres. *The Luton Reporter* recorded a sale of machinery, cattle, poultry and furniture at Lane Farm on 21st October 1874. Thomas Oliver ran the farm of 200 acres until the end of the century, followed by Maurice Titmus into the 1930s, then Adrian Hillhouse (who emigrated to Australia), and the Farnhams. Much land was sold for allotments in 1920 and more for building development in the 1930s. By the end of the 2nd World War the house had been divided into two flats, from one of which Hugh Farnham sold greengroceries. By 1960 it had been demolished.

Frederick Davis (1855) records that outside Lane Farm 'stood the trunk of a very old oak which measured 16.5 metres around the bottom part. It was hollow and nothing was left of it but the trunk and stumps of its branches, which were as large as a common sized tree. It was supposed to have been as old as that in the New Forest, against which the arrow glanced that killed William Rufus'. In all probability it was the last relic of the ancient woodland that once covered the area.

Mixes Hill Farm   (TL:099232)

This small farm of brick and flint construction, with labourers' cottages beside it, stood near the present south-eastern junction of Birchen Grove and Sunningdale. On architectural evidence it could be dated to at least the 16th century. A bridle road led past it to the Mixes Hill brickworks, and a right-of-way continued north to Bury Farm. It was one of a number of properties in Stopsley that John Chase owned in 1836, and on his death it was bequeathed to his son Frederick Chase and to Joseph Holden Turner. The family name was commemorated in a large house called 'The Chase', that was owned by Asher J. Hucklesby at the beginning of the 20th century, and lay between Mixes Hill Farm and the Hitchin Road. It was bequeathed to Hucklesby's three partners during their lifetimes and occupied by Stewart Hubbard, the dyer, from 1908, and later by Albert Wilkinson (Mayor of Luton 1901 to 1911, 1925 to 1928). After Wilkinson's death it was purchased by Mr Whitehouse, the husband of Asher Hucklesby's adopted daughter Constance. At the beginning of the 2nd World War it became 'The Chase Nursing Home', run by Mrs J. Healey and supervised by Dr Hegerty. It was purchased from Mr Whitehouse by Luton Corporation in March 1969 and demolished very shortly afterwards. The Turner name is probably perpetuated in Turner's Road and Turner's Knoll. The latter was 'Wheeler's Slip' in 1844.

William Irons farmed the property in 1855. Six years later his son, George Irons, styling himself a Yeoman, was in charge, assisted by his wife Mary, and their four children. Their youngest child, Charles, became a celebrated Town Crier in Luton. The *Bedfordshire Mercury* recorded that "On 20th March, 1881, a fire broke out at Mixes Hill Farm, doing damage to the amount of £80. A barn and two sheds were destroyed. The cause of the fire is unknown. The premises were insured in the County Fire Office." William Lawson was the tenant at the time. He seems to have had little immediate land to farm, but may have had pastures further afield. The Parish Council Minutes of 1898 mention Joseph Holdstock, who worked at Mixes Hill Farm, about 1860, driving stock along Mixes Hill Lane to reach grazing on Stopsley Common and the Lea water meadows. In 1911 Edward Barber moved to the farm from Cowridge End and his daughter Ellen recalled playing in the adjoining cornfields at harvest time. He was still there in 1934. (In 1938 Ellen Barber opened a popular 'Tiny Folks' Kindergarten' in Turner's Road using the Montessori teaching methods). Mixes Hill Farm and cottages were swept away in the mid-1950s building developments which attempted to link Round Green and Stopsley.

Cowridge End Farms (TL: 097228)

Frederick Davis in his *History of Luton* (1855) and *Luton Past and Present* (1874) suggests that the name Cowridge relates to its situation on the top of a hill, near the boundary of the township, and at the end of the common rights for cows; however the name can be traced back to 1196 in the *Register of Abbot John of Wheathampstead* when it was 'Curegge' meaning simply cow ridge (and can be compared with Ramridge a kilometre to the east). The name of John de Cowruge appears on a deed in the British Library dated 1257.

Upper and Lower Cowridge End stood on either side of Stockingstone Road, between Richmond Hill and Colin Road. In 1477 John and Laurence How of Cowridge End were wealthy enough to become members of the Guild of the Holy Trinity, a religious guild connected to a Luton church. In 1546 Edward Crawley purchased a large house with outbuildings and lands called 'Courgend' (Cowridge End) from Thomas Ramridge, (probably the nephew of Abbot Ramridge who owned Ramridge End Farm until his death in 1587). The estate was 'purchased of Thomas Ramridge for the rent of 13 shillings and 4 pence (2 marks) and one cock yearly at Christmas'. When Edward Crawley died he left Cowridge End to Thomas Crawley. In 1623 the Crawley's sold the estate to James Clarke.

Frederick Davis, in 1874, wrote "There were three farms [at Cowridge End] but the two small ones have been laid together, so that now there is only what is called the lower and upper farm; the upper farm has been a residence of a superior family, as the house is large, well built, and lofty," with gable ends and rooms in the roof. The timber beams were immense "painted red, with inscriptions on them in black letters." There was a big chimney corner. "The fireplace is raised above the floor, and cased and lined with Totternhoe stone. Over the front door is a carved oak board, with the initials 'W.H. 1609, J.H.'" Almost certainly these were the initials of William and Jane Howe. William Howe married Jane, a daughter of John Crawley of Nether Crawley and they were living at Cowridge End about 1586. A century later the property belonged to Jane Cart of Dunstable, who bequeathed it to Trustees on her death in 1736, as part of a charity known as 'Cart's Charity'. About 1795 the farm house was occupied as a pest-house (a hospital for infectious diseases) for private families during the time of inoculation for the disfiguring smallpox. The area is marked as Scourge End on Thomas Jefferys' map of 1765, and seems to be a corruption of Cowridge End.

Lower Cowridge End was bought by John Crawley M.P. in 1728. Daniel Davis was farming at Cowridge End when the 1851,1861 and 1871 Census Returns were collected. By each Census the farm had become smaller. There were 260 acres in 1851 and eleven labourers were employed. In 1861 it comprised 180 acres worked by Daniel, his son Edward, one labourer and three boys. Reduced to 160 acres in 1871, Daniel (then aged 79) employed seven men and two boys. The Upper Cowridge Farm building was demolished about 1874 when, according to Austin, "the present insignificant farm-house was erected in its place." That, too, was demolished and replaced by flats about 1970. The Census Returns do not differentiate between the Upper and Lower Cowridge Farms. John Smith is recorded for 1881, farming 80 acres and employing five men and one boy. Ten years later Alfred Barber was the tenant in one, the other was standing empty. He was followed in 1911 by the Bakers and Panters. Lower Cowridge was developed for housing from 1926, and Upper Cowridge by 1930.

The land of Cowridge End lay mainly south of Stockingstone Road. A large part of this belonging to Mr John S. Crawley, was given to Luton as 'The People's Park', together with Pope's Meadow and Bell's Close. This was the result of compensation for the loss of the southern part of the Town Moor which had been cut off by the construction of the Midland Railway in 1868.

Ramridge End Farm   (TL: 107232)

This farm lay east of Ashcroft Road, where Rickyard Close stands as a reminder today. It was demolished to make way for the Ramridge estate in September 1952. The name Ramridge first appears in an Assize Roll of 1227 as 'Ramrugg', and means either ram or raven - ridge. The original farm had been the property of the Ramridge family from the thirteenth century. In the fifteenth century it belonged to Thomas Ramridge, the 37th Abbot of St Albans (from 1492 until his death in 1519). The farm then passed to the Abbot's nephew, another Thomas. He was the last member of the family in the male line, and when he died in 1587 he bequeathed Ramridge End Farm to Robert Burr.

The Vicar of Luton, John Lammer, also held a farm somewhere between Stopsley and Round Green, possibly at Dropshort (the junction of Hitchin Road and Lynwood Avenue). On his death in 1477 it passed to the Guild of the Holy Trinity in Luton. Forty years after the dissolution of the Guild, in 1588, it was purchased by Robert Burr. Robert's sons conveyed both Lammer's farm and Ramridge End Farm to Edward Hubbard in 1593, and he and his son Francis Hubbard conveyed them to John Crawley and his son Thomas in 1596. Due to legal technicalities it was 1612 before the transfer was satisfactorily completed. William Bigge of Stopsley left his russet cloak to John Crawley's shepherd, William Cartright, in his will dated 1602. Bigge also left 10 shillings to his two nephews, Richard and John Bigge, the sons of William Bigge, yeoman of Ramridge End (see page 36).

The farm's fortunes for the next two hundred years are not known, although it was probably rebuilt at some time during that period. By the early 19th century it was a mixed farm of 84 acres and seems to have belonged to Martha Morris. Her tenants, William Barber, and then his son Joseph, kept two informative farm Account Books between 1816 and 1825, and 1833 and 1837. The Barber family had arrived in Stopsley from Biggleswade soon after 1800. We know nothing of William and Joseph's education, but both books were clearly written and the spelling was generally good, though sometimes phonetic. William's entries became more illegible and rather chaotic towards the end of his life, when Joseph took over on 24th September 1824. The books, of 98 pages and 48 pages respectively, list all manner of incoming and outgoing payments respecting the livestock, employees and activities of the farm. They probably present the best picture we have of the produce of any Stopsley farm in the early nineteenth century.

The writer has made only a cursory examination of William Barber's first Account Book, which commences on 12th August 1816. It records payments of the half year's rent at £61. 5s.0d, a property tax of £2.14s.6d., a year's tax for use of common land of 6s.0d, a highway tax of £2.10s.3d. and insurance of 14s.7d. William paid himself £18 for ten months labour, and also paid £28.16s.0d. for the 'Board of 2 Boys' [probably his grandsons]. He made frequent visits to London, Shefford and Biggleswade. His purchases included a mare for £14 and clover seed £9.14s.3d. He sold three pigs for £6.12s.8d., and received £16.7s.0d for pork that he sent to London. Three loads of wheat were sold for £7.16s.0d., and wool for £17.6s.6d. His wife earned between 8s. and 10s. each week making and selling butter. Other payments include rat-catching at 2s.11d; sieve-mending 4s.; chimney sweeping 1s.6d.; stone picking £1.1s.0d.; sheep shearing £1.17s.0d and a miller's bill for 12s.6d. Barber employed three labourers: Sharp, Gutteridge and James Bennet (born 1806), and a boy. Sharp's wages varied between 10s. and 15s. per week, Gutteridge 7s. and 8s. and Bennet 11s. to 12s. The boy received 2s.6d. each week.

A short inventory of the farm was made about 1824 when Joseph took over the farm. It reads:-

'A Statement of the Live and Dead Farming Stock on the Ramridge End Farm in the Occupation of Joseph Barber. Made by David Bradshaw and Joseph Barber.

3 Horses, 2 Colts, 4 Sturks [yearling bullocks or heifers], 5 Sows, 2 Yields [Gilts- young female pigs], 80 head of poultry, 5 Carts, Iron-rim Double Shaft Waggon, Gig Harness, 2 Ploughs, 3 Sets of 4 Beamed Harrows, Land Roller, 16 Dozen of Hurdles, 12 Sheep Troughs and 4 Pig Troughs, 4 Ladders, 2 Cow Cribbs, 4 Drags, Screen and Sieves, 3 Shovels and 3 Fans, 12 Forks. A Stack of Wheat about £40; ditto Oats about £20; half a Rick of Barley £10; A Stump of Hay about £5; twenty-seven and a half Acres of Wheat, twelve Acres of Clover, seventeen and a half Acres for Barley; ten Acres for Oats; three Acres of Beans; three Acres of Peas.'

The second Account Book, commencing in 1833, is in Joseph's handwriting and lists Nichols, Bennet, Lere and two boys as his regular labour force. At that time he was paying his men an average weekly wage of 10 shillings and the boy 4 shillings. In 1830 the Duke of Bedford had set a lead by paying his farm labourers 10 shillings a week. The Barbers were clearly generous employers. There are separate listings for 'Joseph Miller Horsekeeper Wagers [sic] £3; Samuel Cilbe [Kilby, aged 15] shephard Wagers £2; Joseph Barber Wagers £6.' In October an unspecified number of extra boys were employed to pick up potatoes for a total of 7 shillings. Other entries include 'Thatching the wheatcock and haycock, wagon hovel and hogsty £2.2s.6d.; Paid Parsons for pecking weeds in turnips 10 shillings; hoeing of turnips in Dulcut field £1; hoeing in Severels field and extra work £2.1s.4d.; Bought 8 bushels grain for 2 shillings; 2 barrels of Small Beer 9 shillings each; 14 Teggs bought at £1.2s.0d. each [a tegg was a hogget, or sheep in its second year]. Joseph also bought gunpowder to fill his own cartridges, and pitch to paint and preserve every scrap of wood on the farm. The fine barns were still painted with bitumen in 1952. At the end of 1834 his expenditure was £469.3s.1d. and his income was £461.16s.5d. 'Result misery', Mr Micawber would probably have said! Not so. When the Account Book finishes in 1837 the farm has grown turnips, wheat, barley, oats, potatoes, beans, peas, clover and trefoil, and stock has included horses, cattle, sheep, pigs and chickens, producing milk, butter, eggs, wool, pork and lamb.

William Barber's name appears as the owner of Ramridge End Farm in a Jury list of 1829, and *Cassey's Directory* records Joseph Barber still farming there in 1862. Three years later, when he witnessed his daughter's marriage to the future Mayor of Luton, Asher Hucklesby, he gave his profession as publican. Joseph's heirs were less successful; Alfred (born in 1846), after a period as a grocer at Round Green, was farming at Cowridge End by 1891, and his brother Edward farmed at Mixes Hill for a relatively short period.

By 1874 Ramridge End Farm had become the property of a bachelor farmer, Thomas Tomson. In 1891 Harry Eames, described as a 'working foreman' was occupying the house with his wife and five children. Henry Thompson was listed as the farmer in *Kelly's Directory* for 1898. John Holdstock took it over from a Mr Burgess during the 1st World War, and later his son Frederick Holdstock farmed it until its demolition in 1952. It remained a mixed farm to the end with cattle in fields adjoining the Ashcroft Road, and arable on either side of Wigmore Lane and south towards Crawley Green Road.

Other Farms in Stopsley Parish

On the periphery of Stopsley parish were a number of farms, the majority of which are no longer standing.

Of **Wigmore Hall Farm**, (TL: 125223) only the house survives as an hotel. We know that Daniel Gutteridge was farming there in 1829, before moving to Whitehill Farm a few years later. Wigmore Hall had to be rebuilt after a disastrous fire on 15th December 1843. Thomas Parrish occupied the new building in 1851. He employed 14 labourers to help him work his 258 acres. In 1885 James Owney was the farmer and James Oliver in 1891. Oliver styled himself 'a Machinist' and was working with agricultural steam engines by 1906.

A will of 1519 shows that John Crawley owned **Nether Crawley Farm** and left it to his son John. However, the son died a bachelor a few months before his father, in 1544. A rent book of 1811 shows it in the hands of Charles Tomson, whilst a jury list of 1829 list his son John Tomson as the farmer. By the 1851 Census Lititia Tomson, a widow of 47, (and perhaps John's wife ?) was in charge, with a bailiff, John Lines managing the 150 acre farm for her. Much later in 1891 Frederick Horesby was listed as the farmer and by 1898 Walter James Oliver. The Crawley family in the person of Francis Crawley still owned the farm in 1910, when it was occupied by the Hartop's. By 1910 the Hartop family held various farms in the Luton area, including William at Nether Crawley Farm (TL: 107223), and Benjamin and William at the large **Eaton Green Farm** (TL: 117217). In 1851 Kitty Wood, a widow aged 70, was responsible for Eaton Green Farm. Covering 258 acres, and employing 10 labourers, she needed her two sons, Thomas and William to manage it for her. The house and barns were rebuilt about 1870 'at a cost of about £5,000 with all modern improvements, for agricultural purposes'. William Mardle farmed there in 1891. It was bought in 1936 to provide offices for Luton Airport.

Falconer's Hall, [Faulkener's] (*c.* TL:126211) with 246 acres of land, was farmed by Hannah Davis, with the help of 5 labourers in 1851. By 1874 the house had been converted into two cottages and the land added to Eaton Green Farm. **Someries Farm**, (TL: 119203) on the southern extremity of Stopsley, covered 448 acres and was the responsibility of John How and 23 labourers in 1851. **Tinker's Hall Farm** (TL: 129205) the present **Chiltern Hall** in East Hyde parish, was listed as in Stopsley parish in the Jurors' List of 1829. Edward Dines was the farmer at that time.

The tiny hamlet of Crawley Green, containing some half dozen cottages and an inn called *The Tin Pot*, was dominated by **Crawley Green Farm** (TL: 104216). A deed of 1st July 1611 shows that Francis Crawley of Gray's Inn, London, Esquire, purchased a farm at Crawley Green from William Day and Edward Crawley. It consisted of a messuage (house), orchard, garden and 33 acres of land which ran down Hart Hill from Crawley Green to the river Lea. The farm adjoined land belonging to Francis' father Thomas Crawley. This confirms that there were originally two farms, dating from at least the 17th century. Thomas Smith lived in one in 1811, and his son, another Thomas, farmed 150 acres there, forty years later. Mary Cooper had the other farm with 134 acres of land. They were rebuilt as a single farm in the late 19th century, and it was altered a number of times subsequently. Alfred How held the farm between 1891 and 1898. By 1900 it was owned by Albert Wilkinson, six times Mayor of Luton, and was farmed by the Powdrill family on his behalf. On his death, Wilkinson left the farm to his son-in-law, Frederick Powdrill. His family continued to farm at Crawley Green until the mid-1950s. The farmhouse survives as the club house of the Royal Naval Association. Tin Pot Close (at the west end of Devon Road) was the traditional site used for bull-baiting.

At the bottom of Bradgers Hill lane, opposite the Sixth Form College, stood **Joey Dancer's Farm** (TL: 093236), with the house facing onto the lane, and a yard and barns to the south. At the western corner was a substantial pond. In 1845 it belonged to Frances Chase, widow of the Stopsley landowner John Chase, with the farmhouse (described as a cottage) occupied by Joseph Mann, and the adjoining barn, yard and field leased to Elizabeth Butlin. The last remnants of the farm were pulled down soon after 1946. One of the lynchets on the hillside above the farm was known as Joey Dancer's lince. Another, Nail's Hill Common, belonged to Matthew Dancer in 1844 according to the Tithe Map. Matthew Dancer was a Luton butcher, and had a brother William, who was a higgler. Who Joey Dancer was remains a mystery.

The Pollards managed **Wardown Farm** about 1914. It stood just north of the Old Bedford and Stockingstone Road cross-roads (TL: 092233). In 1845 it belonged to Jane Waller, and consisted of a barn, yard and buildings. The adjoining house was occupied by John Scrivener (aged 68). The 1851 Census records 'John Funnel, [or Fiennell] Old Barton Road, Stopsley, Farmer' with 58 acres and employing two labourers. Funnel was described as a bachelor from Eastbourne, living with his mother as his Housekeeper. Ten years later he was married (to Emma, aged 20) and farming 90 acres from what was then called the 'Farm House, Stopsley Common', with the help of four men and two boys. This was the Wardown Farm house, which was already occupied by John Scrivener (74) and his wife Mary. Later it was owned for a time by Albert Wilkinson. It was conveniently close to the Lammas lands which lay along the watermeadows of the Lea from Stockingstone Road (Clacks Lane) to Kingsdown Avenue (Sheep Bridge or Mud Arches). These were grass lands where Stopsley folk had common rights to graze their sheep after harvest each year.

Waterhall Farm in Old Bedford Road (TL: 088251) was yet another of the small late 19th century farms in the area. It belonged to the Powdrill family. Later it was used to rest horses. Further north **Warden Hill Farm** was in existence by 1844. Its last occupant was Frederick Toyer, who became Golf Course steward when the land was taken over by the South Bedfordshire Golf Club. Some of the farm's out-buildings were used for storing Golf Club equipment until about 1950.

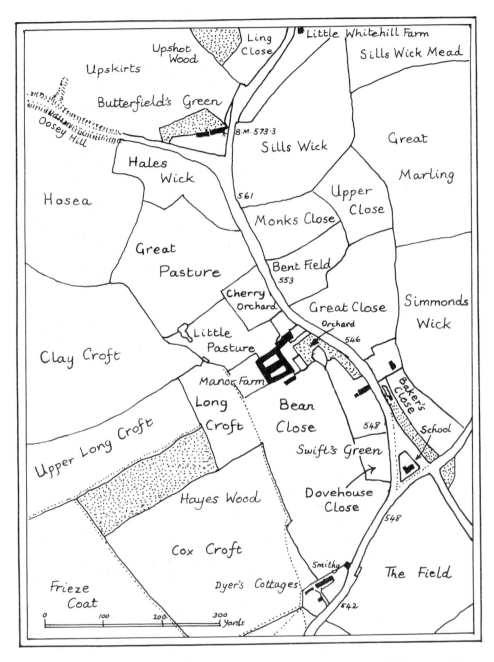

Map 7: The Butterfield's Green and Swift's Green area of Stopsley with its field names. Partly based on the Ordnance Survey map of 1881.

ILa: An aerial view of Manor Farm (about 1980) showing the square layout of the barns and cattle yards and the farmhouse of 1870. The ponds, fed by surface water, and used for watering the livestock, are clearly visible, as are old fruit trees surviving from a former orchard. (*John Shaw*)

ILb: Common Farm in 1959. Situated at the foot of Oosey Hill, it was the last surviving building constructed of knapped flint in the Stopsley area. As an outlier of Manor Farm, it consisted of two labourers' cottages (later knocked into one), together with three large barns and a stockyard. It was a familiar landmark recognisable by its creosoted 'Black Barn'. (*James Dyer*)

La: Pond Farm dated from the early 1800s. It stood between Jansel House and Putteridge Road, with a kitchen garden on the roadside. It had two ponds, one roughly at the present Ashcroft-Putteridge Road junction (plate I), and another in the forecourt of Jansel House. Mary Boulter and her daughter May are standing in the farmyard. (*Jeanne Powell*)

Lb: Farmer Frank Boulter and friend standing in the yard at Pond Farm (*Jeanne Powell*)

LIa: An aerial view of Whitehill Farm taken about 1960 during the tenancy of Douglas Jeffs. Modernisation under Pat Shaw included the removal of the right hand end of the farmhouse due to subsidence, the redesign of the farmyard and the erection of new barns. Undulations in Grovefield (upper left) indicate the presence of an earlier deserted medieval settlement. (*Lionel Shaw*)

LIb: The stockyard at the rear of Green Farm (compare plate IXa). James Barber is seen feeding his chickens, whilst his horse enjoys some hay. By the time this picture was taken, around 1910, Green Farm had more or less ceased to function as a viable working farm. (*Ellen Barber: Author's Colln.*)

LIIa: Lane Farm in Putteridge Road (Park Lane) in September 1956, shortly before its demolition.
It has been identified with the Manor of Plenties. The house in the picture was built after a disastrous
fire about 1860. It was from an earlier house on this site that Alice Crawley's bridecart carried her
dowry to her husband's home in 1560. (*Luton Museum: G. Rauston*)

LIIb: Joey Dancer's Farm stood in Bradgers Hill Road opposite the present Sixth Form College.
The lower slope of Warden Hill can be glimpsed between the buildings. The last vestiges of the
buildings disappeared in the 1950s. (*Luton Museum*)

LIIIa: The magnificent great barn at Ramridge End Farm. It was here that William and Joseph Barber farmed in the 19th century and preserved their barns with bitumen. This exhibition photograph by W.R. Lockey, taken in May 1926, was entitled 'After the day's work'. (*Mary Hall*)

LIIIb: A snapshot of Ramridge End Farm, in the process of demolition, to make way for Rickyard Close in September 1952. In the foreground are the foundations of 18-20 Bray's Road. (*James Dyer*)

LIVa: One of the oldest surviving Stopsley photographs showing the St Thomas' Senior Sunday School class in 1881. It may have been taken by the Luton photographer, Frederick Thurston. The clergyman would have been John Finch-Smith (Vicar: 1879-82) and some of the young ladies have been identified as: *Standing:* - ; Patty White; Clementine Pates; Miss Plummer (Mrs Toyer); Mrs Burkett; - ; Sarah Ann Godwin (Mrs Kime); Mary Ann Webster; *Seated:* Louie Allingham, Mr Finch-Smith; - . A note on the original observes 'average age 17 years'. (*Author's Collection*)

LIVb: St Thomas' Church opened in 1862. The growth of the yew trees and ivy suggest that this picture was taken about 1880. The only grave visible, beside the vestry wall, is that of Samuel Cumming, the baby son of the first vicar (*Author's Collection*)

LVa: St Thomas' Verger and Sexton, William Hill (1849-1925) with the church choir and Sunday School teachers.   Costume evidence suggests a date of 1898.   The absence of a Vicar would confirm this as the interregnum between the incumbencies of the Revd. J.H. Campbell-Cowan and Revd. Arthur E. Love.   Notice the old church porch and oil lamp.   (*St Thomas' Church*)

LVb: An interior view of St Thomas' about 1900, showing the church with its oil lamps, decorated for a harvest festival.   Above the chancel arch is the awesome text; 'Except that ye eat the flesh of the Son of Man and drink his blood, ye have no life in you'.   (*Leslie Church*)

LVIa: The old Vicarage in Park Lane (Putteridge Road) photographed in 1905 and used by the Revd. Walter Covey-Crump as his Christmas Card. Mrs Covey-Crump is seen with their eldest son Lewis. There is open countryside beyond the house. (*Michael Covey-Crump*)

LVIb and c: St Thomas' two longest serving clergymen: Revd. E. Denby Gilbert (1927-38) and Canon Francis A. Estdale (1961-95).

Chapter 13

The Churches in Stopsley

THE ANGLICANS: St Thomas's Church

The Manor of Stopsley was in the ecclesiastical parish of Luton. For centuries before the building of St Thomas's church in 1862, worshippers from Stopsley would have travelled to St Mary's church in Luton. Every Sunday and Feast Day, in all weathers, they would have made journeys of two or three miles along the narrow lanes to the parish church. They often took a snack with them, which they ate in the churchyard between services, or inside the church when it was wet and cold. Since the church was unheated and the roof often in disrepair they had little real choice!

It was normal for those who farmed in Stopsley to pay a tithe (a tax of one tenth of the annual produce of land and labour) to the Abbey of St Albans. After the Dissolution in 1539 these tithes passed to the Crown. On 8th March 1555 the Catholic Queen Mary Tudor granted the tithes of Stopsley (along with numerous other manors) to Sir Thomas Pope, who in turn gave them to his new foundation of Trinity College in Oxford. Amongst the Stopsley people who we know were paying tithes at that time were two farmers named Thomas Blake and Thomas Skipwith. Henry Cobbe, in his *History of Luton Church* (1899) records that the value of the Stopsley tithes rose from £24 in 1544, to £200 in 1642-48 and £820 in 1844. After 1836 tithes were converted into rent charge payments, and finally disappeared in 1936. For many years after Stopsley church was built, Trinity College gave it an annual donation (*e.g.* £10 in 1893).

Cobbe also recorded the presence of two 'wayside' chapels in Stopsley Parish. One described by Frederick Davis in *Luton, Past and Present* (1874) stood a quarter of a mile east of Falconer's Hall, in Round Wood (*c.* TL129213). There the foundations of a house and small chapel could be seen. Built of rough bricks and Totternhoe stone, they were surrounded by a moat. The place was still called Chapel Field, with Chapel Common next to it, in Davis's day. Its site was north-east of Luton Airport runway near the Wigmore Park recreation ground.

According to William Camden the abbots of St Albans had 'a little pretty place,' a summer residence with a chapel dedicated to St Anne on St Anne's Hill at Hart Lane (Rutland Crescent). It was built in 1121 and much of the surrounding land belonged to the abbey (see page 18).

By the beginning of the 18th century small groups of non-conformist worshippers were establishing themselves all over Bedfordshire and Hertfordshire, frequently meeting in each others homes or barns. For many in Stopsley this form of worship must have seemed more attractive than the long walk into Luton, and the Independent churches won many adherents. The Methodists opened their church in Stopsley in 1846, the Baptists in 1870. Village Headmaster Samuel Deane noted the result in the School Log Book as late as 1880 when he observed that 'the majority of the school children belong to the Dissenters'. By then the three churches in Stopsley vied with each other for custom, offering incentives like attendance medals and prizes, particularly to the children. Some villagers attended one church in the morning and another in the afternoon or evening. For many the warmth, companionship and refreshment offered was more important than the quality of the teaching.

In an effort to balance the situation, and to cater for the needs of the rapidly expanding parish of Luton in the mid-nineteenth century, the Anglicans decided to create new ecclesiastical parishes at Biscot, East Hyde and Stopsley, all within the diocese of Ely. In 1860 the Vicar of St Mary's, Luton, the Revd. Thomas Piele, voluntarily surrendered £203.1s.0d. which was part of the vicarial tithe rent-charges collected from Stopsley, to pay for the incumbent. The new ecclesiastical parish was created in February 1861 and building St Thomas's church began as soon as the designs had been drawn up. Mr Piele also sold the advowson (the right to appoint a vicar) and patronage of the new church to Colonel Thomas Sowerby of Putteridge Bury, the large estate adjoining Stopsley on the east, which lay in Offley parish and the diocese of Rochester. Probably on his Bishop's advice the Colonel appointed Samuel Cumming in 1861 to be Priest in Charge of the new church. Prior to its opening he held services in the school. In 1865 Cumming was promoted to Vicar of Stopsley, and in 1870 was joined by a Curate, the Revd. J. Hutchins. The latter is recorded as having visited the village school as Acting Curate on several occasions prior to his official appointment. The new church seems to have been completed by June 1861 when the first baptism was recorded. The Sowerby family retained a pew in the church until they left Putteridge Bury in 1908.

The New Church

St Thomas's church was consecrated on 2nd June 1862 by Joseph Cotton Wigram, Bishop of Rochester. It had been designed by the Luton architect, Henry John Pearson, and built at a cost of £1,150 by a local builder, E.O. Williams.. It was constructed of red-grey Stopsley bricks, with Bath stone and flint decoration, in the Early English style. It conforms to the standard church plan of chancel, nave, north transept (now housing the organ) and the vicar's vestry. The floor of the chancel was decorated with encaustic tiles by Maw and Co. Church music was provided by an harmonium until 1894, in which year an organ was acquired from Eustace Ingram of Holloway. It was replaced in 1931. A new choir vestry was constructed in 1973. The church is roofed in blue slate, and surmounted at the west end by a bellcote containing a single bell (muted during the 2nd World War). The original wooden porch with external oil lamp, was replaced in 1983 by the present one, constructed with old bricks from the former Common Farm. The tall lancet windows were all originally filled with plain or pastel-coloured 'cathedral-tinted' glass. In 1919 the East Window was replaced by one of stained glass as a memorial to those members of the Church who had died during the First World War.

The Revd. Samuel Cumming, M.A., the first Vicar, was 42 years old, and came from Westwell near Ashford in Kent. He was married to Mary Ann Stocker from Berkhampstead. When he first arrived he, alone, lodged with Francis Foster and his wife and four children in their house at 587 Hitchin Road, (later *The First and Last*). The Census records that Foster was a farmer and brickmaker. Later Mr Cumming rented Foster's house. As the first Vicarage in Stopsley was not built until 1882, we are not sure where the next five Stopsley Vicars lived. Elderly residents interviewed in

1966 believed that Stopsley House, next door to *The First and Last* was bought for them about 1868, but their names do not appear in any of the Census returns.

As well as attending to his parochial duties, Samuel Cumming had sufficient time to run the Collegiate School in Stuart Street, Luton. William Austin, author of the *History of Luton* (1928) and steward of the Manor of Luton, was a pupil of his and described him as an excellent master, respected and beloved by his scholars. Cumming's first child, Samuel Alfred, was born in Stopsley, but lived only 22 hours. He was buried at St Thomas's in May 1862, beneath a small stone, now lichen covered, beside the vestry door. Mr Cumming left Stopsley in 1871 to become Rector of Little Carlton in Lincolnshire.

The Marriage Register of St Thomas's Church commenced in 1862. On 2nd August James Phillips (aged 22) and Eliza Skeggs (aged 19) were the first couple to be married in the Church. Neither could write their names and so they both had to mark the Register with a cross, as did many couples who followed them. Similarly, since few villagers could read Marriage Banns posted on the Church door, the Vicar had to read them aloud: something he still does today! Quite remarkably, it was not until almost twenty years after the Church's consecration that it was discovered that St Thomas's had never been approved by the Ecclesiastical Commissioners for the solemnisation of weddings, and that all marriages that had been conducted in the Church prior to that time were illegal! Stopsley's own special Act of Parliament had to be enacted on 29th November 1883. Known simply as the *Act 47 Vic. cap I*, it legalised all the marriages that had been solemnised in St Thomas's during the previous twenty years, making it clear that there had been no deliberate default on the part of the persons married there.

We know remarkably little about the majority of the 20 clergy who have served St Thomas's since 1861. Village folklore speaks of one who had an Indian servant who caused a sensation by wearing flowing robes and a turban. In fact, this may have been the Revd. Ernest Leslie, who had come from India and enjoyed dressing up.

The Absentee Vicar

In 1872 Thomas Henry Papillon was appointed to the living, but he seems to have been conspicuous by his absence. Throughout his three years incumbency he conducted only one of the fourteen funerals recorded in the Burial Register and two weddings (all in December 1872). In 1871 the church-founded National School in Stopsley had closed, and its Trustees, who included the Vicar, seemed disinclined to do anything about it. However, the 1870 Forster Education Act had given local authorities the power to set up School Boards in areas where voluntary organisations failed to provide sufficient places for all children between the ages of 5 and 12. Elementary education was now to be funded with money levied from the Rates. A School Board was established in Luton in February 1874 after a long period of ignominious wrangling between the Anglican and Nonconformist bodies. Almost at once the Board began to interest itself in the unsatisfactory state of affairs at Stopsley, and enquiries were begun to see if they might take over the National School. Numerous letters were sent to Mr Papillon, who represented the School Trustees. They went unanswered. The Revd. E.R. Adams, Vicar of Biscot, and a member of the Board, commented: "I can hardly understand how things are at Stopsley. The Rector is in Paris, I believe. He is not seen in the village, and someone comes down on

Saturday night and goes away on Monday morning. This, I understand, is considered 'taking care of the parish'".

At the beginning of 1875 Mr Papillon was in Sweden and "regretted that the weather was too inclement for him to return". He was still there in September when a letter appeared in the *Luton Reporter* signed 'Parishoner Cello', complaining that "a temporary Curate of the runaway incumbent monopolises property of people to secure for himself lodgings, whilst doing duty here, and for whose convenience 200 children are barred from their rightful education." Papillon observed that the occupation of the School House by the Curate was a matter of benefit to the buildings, since it kept them aired and repaired. "Pray bear in mind," he concluded "that in every matter relating to the benefit of my parish and people, I am only too anxious to act for their best interest and the temporal good." Shortly afterwards he resigned the living. Why the Vicar of Stopsley spent so much of his incumbency abroad is not recorded. It is amusing and cynical to observe that 'papillon' is, of course, French for 'butterfly' and also French slang for 'flighty'!

A Curate, the Revd. James Joseph Frew, seems to have performed many of Papillon's duties for him from 1873, and was presumably the person living in the School House. At the end of 1875 he was appointed Vicar of Stopsley. Sadly, he was a sick man, able to take fewer and fewer services, and towards the end of 1876 he died: the only incumbent to die in office. Of his successors, Alexander Schwartz (less than a year) and George Henry Turner (1876-79) nothing is recorded, and neither of them conducted any weddings or funerals in the village.

The Revd. John Finch Smith came to Stopsley in 1879 and was immediately embroiled in the long-running School Board debate. It reached an acceptable conclusion in September of that year, and control of the School passed to the Luton School Board on 1st November, 1879. James O'Neill, Vicar of Luton, together with Henry Newland (Corn Merchant) and George Chambers (Oil and Colour Merchant) signed as the Trustees. John Finch Smith gave his assent to a resolution which stated that:

> 'At Stopsley School the Bible [will] be read and such explanations and instructions given by the Teacher or the Managers, in the principles of morality and religion as are suited to the capacities of the children attending such School. No attempts [will] be made in the School to attach children to any denomination; and further, that it shall be understood between this Board and the officiating Minister of the Parish of Stopsley that no further or other religious teaching than that referred to above shall be given to the children between the hours of 11.30 and 12 in the mornings of Tuesdays and Thursdays as named in the agreement between this Board and the Trustees of the School.'

According to the School Log Book, Mr Finch Smith's lessons at the School were somewhat erratic: often once a fortnight rather than twice a week. Perhaps this was not surprising bearing in mind Headmaster Samuel Deane's observation, quoted above, that the majority of the school's 99 pupils belonged to the dissenters.

Yew trees were planted beside the churchyard path shortly after the church was opened. They grew quickly and soon birds were scattering their berries all over the parish. A yew colony still thrives on Bradgers Hill. The Corsican Pines that front the churchyard were purchased as saplings in November 1880. They were transported by horse and cart from Luton Railway Station at a cost of 1s.2d. [about 6p], and men were paid 5 shillings [25p] for spending two days planting them.

A faded photograph, retrospectively dated to about 1881, belongs to this period and appears to show a young, bearded Finch Smith, seated book in hand, and surrounded by ten smartly dressed young lady Sunday School teachers. It was at the beginning of this Vicar's incumbency that William Hill began his 46 years association with St Thomas's Church as Sexton and Verger, serving faithfully under nine Vicars, almost until his death in January 1925, aged 76. Hill was a farm labourer who could neither read nor write. He was one of seven residents who marked a petition with a cross in 1907, requesting a gas supply. Finch Smith decided to exchange the Stopsley living with that of the Vicar of Edensor in Derbyshire, Paul Marland Walker. Walker had trained at Trinity College, Dublin. He became the new Vicar in 1882 and stayed for eleven years. During that time he was assisted by two Curates, the Revd. A.J. Wilson from 1888 - 1891, and a Scottish Curate, Alexander Sutherland (age 63) who was accompanied by his wife Elizabeth, and lodged with Elizabeth Hucklesby at the Post Office until 1893. Mr Walker set up a fund to build a Church Hall, a project that was to take more than 30 years to reach fruition.

The First Vicarage

In 1881 an acre of land known as "The Slipe" had been purchased on which to build a Vicarage. The building's completion coincided with Mr Walker's arrival. It stood on top of the hill in Putteridge Road (Park Road) where the Elderberry Close flats now stand. Some of the trees and bushes of the old garden still survive, especially on the west side adjoining the Working Mens' Club. The Vicarage was demolished in September 1972, at which time the Vicar moved to Dr J.G.R. Clarke's former house and surgery at 702 Hitchin Road. In 1885 the Stopsley living, with vicarage, had a gross yearly value of £203.

The old Vicarage was built of yellow East Bedfordshire bricks decorated with horizontal bands of orange bricks, and roofed in grey slate. It faced west, looking beyond Pond Farm towards the Church. The drive and front garden were lined with chestnut trees: ever popular with the younger parishioners. On either side of the front door was a large bay window, a plan repeated on the first floor. The central entrance hall had a decorated tiled floor. To the left, on entering, was the Vicar's study, and to the right the sitting room. Beyond was the dining room, and beneath the stairs a large cloakroom, formerly the Butler's pantry. A door cut off the rear of the house where there was a large kitchen, scullery and walk-in pantry, as well as Housekeeper's room. There was a cellar beneath the kitchen. On the first floor were five bedrooms and a bathroom, with two further servants' rooms at the rear. The builders had constructed the house to a high standard, with beautifully made panelled doors, high moulded skirting boards, and folding panelled shutters at the major windows.

At the rear of the Vicarage was the stable and coach house, recalling the days when the Vicar and his lady would traverse the parish in a pony and trap. Above it, and entered by an external staircase, was a large loft, (the Rover's loft) often used as a small meeting place. The large garden was a frequent venue for fetes and garden parties. During the Great War, one such fete was entertained by a concert party known as the Biscoteers, who were formed from soldiers camped at Biscot Mill, and reputedly included the comedian Max Miller. The Biscoteers also performed in the village School Hall on 2nd February 1918.

Unfortunately, by the 1960s dry rot was rampant in the Vicarage, and in 1972 it was considered most expedient to demolish it and sell the site.

It was during Mr Walker's incumbency in August 1887 that one of the few early acts of union between the Stopsley church and chapels took place: this was a joint Treat for all the village children to mark Queen Victoria's Golden Jubilee. It replaced that year's special Sunday School treats.

The Revd. P.M. Walker resigned the living in 1893, and was followed in August of that year by John H. Campbell-Cowan. We know little of his time at Stopsley, save that an organ was installed in the church in 1894, and that he fell foul of Headmaster Charles Breed at the school. The School Log reads:

> *"Tue. 21st Nov, 1893* The Revd. Cowan called 11.30 for Scripture. He has not called for more than a fortnight, and the result of his teaching has been that no less than 20 children claim exemption from his tuition. He admitted that he touched upon Church *v.* Dissent and said he should endeavour to make them good Church children. I advised him not to raise any bad feeling, but he replied, "Did I ask for your advice?" He kindly fell in with my suggestion that the Scripture lesson was best taken at 9.5 to 9.35 instead of 11.30 to 12.00.
>
> *Thu. 23rd Nov, 1893* Revd. Cowan cancelled engagement made as to time of Scripture".

His name makes no further appearance in the School Log Book.

In February 1898 Arthur E. Love became the Vicar of Stopsley. Again we know little about him, except what is recorded by Mr Breed. On 3rd February he was invited to the School "to witness a Bible lesson and school assembly. He expressed himself to the children as very pleased with their answers and singing of hymns. He evidently intends taking an interest in religious instruction." In October 1898 Mr Love used the School for the Sunday services whilst St Thomas's Church was undergoing repairs.

On 19th October 1903 a farewell social was held in the school to commemorate the Vicar's sudden departure from the village. Only two months earlier the Rural District Council had appointed him their representative on the School Managers. Mr Breed noted in the School Log Book about this time "Many people are leaving Stopsley to live in Luton", where presumably they were closer to their work and there were newer houses. The moves were reflected in the drop in school numbers, and attendances at all the village churches.

A Musical Family

When the Revd. Walter William Covey-Crump arrived in the village in February 1903 another welcoming tea and social were organised in the schoolroom. In October 1904 he was appointed the Education Committee's representative on the School Managers.

Because of his unusual name it has been possible to learn a lot about Walter William Covey-Crump. He was born Walter William Crump in Birmingham in 1864, and at the age of 14 was apprenticed to an evangelical printer who ran a Bible class for young lads. He attended night-school and was awarded a scholarship to Ayerst Hall in Cambridge, where he followed a three year degree course in mathematics. He took up residence in Cambridge with an elderly College Don who was going blind called Revd. Richard Covey. Walter became his amanuensis and turned his attention to ancient languages, including Hebrew, Sanskrit, Egyptian hieroglyphics and Greek. In 1891, with financial support from Richard Covey, he entered the Cambridge Clergy Training School (now Westcott House) and at 28 was ordained by the Bishop of Ely. Awarded his M.A. degree in 1895, he became Priest-in-Charge at Holy Trinity, Haddenham in

Cambridgeshire, where he developed a life-long interest in bell ringing. He changed his name by deedpoll to Covey-Crump on the death of Richard Covey, who had been a most generous patron. On 11th June 1903 he married Hilda Porter, the daughter of a local farmer and churchwarden. In 1903 he accepted the living of Stopsley which was then in the diocese and gift of the Bishop of Ely. The lack of bells must have been a sad disappointment to him! For three nights during Lent 1908 the church hosted performances of an oratorio: *The Story of the Cross,* with choristers.

Mr Covey-Crump was much moved by the death of King Edward VII on 6th May 1910. He recorded the event in capital letters across a double page of the Service Register. At noon on the day of the funeral (20th May) he held a memorial service in the church, and the Parish Council sent a letter of condolence to Queen Alexandra and King George Vth. Mr Covey-Crump was the only Vicar of St Thomas's to become Vice-Chairman of the Parish Council, much to the annoyance of some Nonconformists. One Councillor in particular, John Hill, was reprimanded for observing that the Vicar "would be casting a net to catch fish".

Whilst at Stopsley three sons were born to the Covey-Crumps, Lewis Charles Leslie (1904), Alwyn Thomas Lavendar (1907) and Leo William Rolf (1910). Walter taught the three boys himself, and each then went on to King's College Choir School in Cambridge, where they all sang in the world famous choir. Lewis sang treble until he was 17! His youngest son, and Walter's grandson is the internationally distinguished tenor, Rogers Covey-Crump. The Covey-Crumps were very popular in the village with their growing young family. Hilda played a full part in various womens' groups.

In 1910 Stopsley was transferred from the Ely to the St Albans diocese. Walter chose to stay in the Ely diocese, in order that he might maintain his connections with Cambridge and the University Library. This meant leaving Stopsley and moving to Friday Bridge near Wisbech. He had been a most devoted Vicar, and even won the approval of Charles Breed. In the School Log for 21st November 1910 Mr Breed wrote "Revd. W.W. Covey-Crump left Stopsley today. He has helped my school very much." Walter was a recognised authority on Masonic matters, and wrote a number of important books, including *The Hiramic Tradition.* In 1934, at the age of 70, he became Vicar of Newton in the Isle of Ely. He was an Honorary Canon of Ely Cathedral, and died in April 1949.

As Patron, the Bishop of Ely replaced Mr Covey-Crump with the Revd. Elleston Garside Alderson, who was instituted on 5th February 1911. Up to this time, members of the church living in Round Green walked to St Thomas's each Sunday to worship. In 1911 the first Wesleyan Chapel at Round Green 'established in 1865' became vacant. It had been built by Mr George Cox, a local Methodist hat manufacturer, and was leased to St Thomas's as a chapel-of-ease for its Round Green members. It was not the most satisfactory of buildings, and a contemporary report described it as 'small, badly lighted and ventilated and without a vestry or other necessary accommodation'. In 1914 the Bishop of St Albans, Edgar Jacob, dedicated the building to St John. It seated 100 people and was administered by the Round Green Mission Vestry. The Vicar of St Thomas's celebrated the Eucharist each Sunday morning after he had taken the service at Stopsley, whilst a lay preacher took an evening service. St John's stood on the present car park site at the corner of Hitchin Road and Ramridge Road and attracted a large number of adults. Most Round Green children continued to walk to Stopsley for Sunday School.

Mr Alderson attempted to make friends with the Headmaster, Mr Breed. He first visited the old Council School on 3rd February 1911. In June he photographed the school children who were preparing to celebrate King George Vth's Coronation. At 11.30 a.m. on Coronation Day itself, he held a special service in the Church. In November 1911 he was elected a Parish Councillor, and appointed a Manager of the School. He and his wife were present at the opening of the New Council School in the centre of the village on Tuesday 10th September, 1912. In September Mr Breed recorded that the school had a half-holiday in order that the "Vicar and vicaress [could] hold a jumble sale to raise funds for a parish nurse." At Christmas Mr Alderson presented a book each to the best boy and girl. He attended the school's Christmas celebrations on Christmas Eve 1913, and was also at a lesson on 4th February 1914 given by Mr Harold Gee of the *British and Foreign Seaman's Society*. He conducted his last wedding, that of school teacher Gertrude Hucklesby and Arthur Haines, on 1st June and then left the parish.

The War Years

Stopsley was without a Vicar when War was declared on 4th August 1914, but eight weeks later on 30th September, the Revd. G.H.C.Shorting, with his family, took up office.

At the beginning of the War many Territorial Army soldiers, followed by Royal Engineers and Staffordshires, were encamped in the fields north of Venetia Road (the Sports' Centre Playing Fields) and the Vicar was called upon to conduct open-air services, to which the villagers were invited. On 7th February 1915 the Royal Engineers filled St Thomas's Church for a special service before leaving for France.

In April 1915 the first Parochial Church Council for Stopsley was elected, with sub-committees to look after the churchyard and St John's Mission Church at Round Green. Amongst its first actions was to send copies of the Parish Magazine to all the Stopsley boys at the War Front. A determined effort was made to raise funds to build a Church Hall or Institute. In February 1917 Mr Lempriere gave a plot of land in Bury Road, that had formerly been used to grow osiers, as a Hall site. The church purchased an adjoining plot, giving a total area 40ft. wide and 84ft. deep. A building fund had been started in the1890s, and now whist drives, socials and dances were held to increase it.

With the opening of the new School in the centre of the village, the old one at Swifts Green became vacant, and the Education Committee ceased to rent it. It reverted to the Lady of the Manor, Lady Wernher, who offered it to the Church in October 1915 at a rent of £5 per year. This was accepted and the building was used as a Boys' Club and general meeting place. The Headmaster, Mr Breed, continued to rent the adjoining School House for the rest of his life.

As a School Manager Mr Shorting and his family attended the School's Empire Day celebrations, and insisted that it closed on Ascension Day each year. An ambiguous Log Book entry records '21st Sept. 1918: The Vicar and the Labour Party held a meeting tonight.'

Many people turn to the Church in times of stress, and the War years were no exception. At Easter 1917 more than 150 communicants attended Easter Communion. Throughout the War a number of special services were held for individual Stopsley servicemen who had been killed, including S. Peters, A.W. and H. Fensome, A. Cooper, A. Dawson, E.B. Angel, J. Bangs, G. Bigmore, A.T.Cain and J. Whittemore. Children's' services were held, to which eggs for sick soldiers were brought and sent to a London Hospital. There was a special Thanksgiving Service at 8 a.m. on Monday

11th November 1918 'to Almighty God on the signing of the Armistice at 5 a.m. this morning by the German plenipotentiaries.' On 6th July, 1919, a Thanksgiving Service was held for the men who had returned and their families. The Church was filled to overflowing, and lessons were read by two exservicemen, T. James and Arthur F. Cain. Mr Shorting suggested that the plain East Window in the chancel should be replaced by one of stained glass, to serve as a permanent memorial to those members of the Church who had died in the War. Once approved, it necessitated the removal of a painting of the Last Supper and some panelling which stood behind the Altar. A stained-glass artist, Mr Hubert Blanchford of Exeter, drew up the designs. In the centre light was a picture of the Crucifixion, with the figure of Mary at the foot of the Cross. To Christ's right was St Nicholas, patron saint of sailors, and to his left, St Alban, the Christian soldier and martyr, and patron saint of soldiers. A memorial brass with the names of the War Dead was placed on the wall beside the chancel arch. It was dedicated on Sunday 10th November, 1919. The cost of the new window was £100, with a further £7 for installing it. The money was raised by public donations; one anonymous parishioner giving half the cost.

The pine trees in the churchyard had grown very quickly, and in October 1918 Mr Shorting asked the Parochial Church Council to consider the advisability of having some of them cut down, with a view to providing extra fuel for the Church boiler during the winter, and by selling some of the logs, obtaining extra funds for the renovation of the Church windows. No action seems to have been taken.

Mr Shorting completed his Ministry at Stopsley on 20th July 1919, leaving to become Vicar of Kimpton in Hertfordshire. Amongst innovations during his time at Stopsley was the introduction of separate services for men and women (which were soon abandoned); social services for youth organisations like the Luton Troop Boy Scouts; and visits from musical groups such as St Hugh's Church Choir from Cockernhoe, who performed sacred cantatas at Easter on a number of occasions.

An Australian Connection

The Revd. Ernest Thomas Leslie's association with the village is more interesting than his brief stay might suggest. He was born into a Wesleyan family living at Mount Egerton, a gold mining town not far from Ballarat in the Australian State of Victoria, in 1897, where his father was a store keeper. He was educated at the local primary school, and then won scholarships to Wesley College and later, Queen's College, both in Melbourne. He became a Wesleyan Minister and went to India as a missionary, working as Superintendent of the Methodist Boys' Boarding School at Secunderabad, Deccan. There he met and married an English woman, Margaret Maggs from Melksham, Wiltshire. Their daughter Lillian was born in 1907.

In 1910 they travelled to Britain, having decided to join the Church of England. Ernest studied for a term at Wells Theological College before becoming a Curate at St Mary's Church, Hitchin on St Thomas' Day 1910. Two sons were born at West Hill, Hitchin: Kenneth in 1911 and Douglas in 1914. After serving as an Army Chaplain in Egypt, Palestine and Italy during the First World War, Ernest became the Vicar of Stopsley with Round Green on 18th October 1919. Of the three children, Lillian boarded at Bedford High School, and the boys attended the village school until they were confident enough to cycle to St Gregory's School in Downs Road, Luton.

During Mr Leslie's incumbency estimates were obtained in May 1920 for building a Church Hall in corrugated iron. These ranged from £800 to £1,662; none were considered acceptable and the matter was deferred.

In April 1921 the Round Green Mission Vestry decided to purchase St John's church, whose lease was to expire in September. They pressed the Parochial Church Council to ask the Diocesan Board of Finance for a grant of £100 towards the cost of £450. The Mission had already collected £250, and together with generous gifts and loans they commendably achieved their aim by the end of the year.

Mr Leslie's stay in Stopsley lasted only two years. He found the stipend for the incumbent quite inadequate, particularly in view of the high upkeep costs of the Vicarage and the needs of his young family. All Saints and St Matthews in Luton were guaranteeing their Vicars £300 and £100 per annum respectively. Stopsley was having difficulty in raising £30 from the congregation and Mr Leslie felt that £40 was the bare minimum required.

The Leslie's left Stopsley in January 1922 and returned to Australia. Older residents remember the auction of the family's furniture in the Vicarage garden. Mr Leslie became Vicar of Maryborough, New South Wales, and later Vermont in Melbourne, where he died in 1965, aged 88. His wife Margaret died in 1982 aged 102 years. Of the two sons, Kenneth was Bishop of Bathurst (100 kms. north-west of Sydney) from 1959 to 1981, and Douglas a very distinguished surgeon, being elected Vice-President of the Royal Australian College of Surgeons in 1977. Both brothers revisited Stopsley with their wives in August 1968 whilst Kenneth was attending the Lambeth Conference. Lillian and Douglas died in 1994. Bishop Kenneth (Ken) Leslie is still living in Kelso, New SouthWales, at the time of writing [1998].

Luton's Cricketing Vicar

The arrival of the Revd. Ernest Denby Gilbert in March 1922 marked a turning point in the history of St Thomas's church. He, and his energetic wife Winifred, with their two daughters, entered totally into the life of the village, and are still clearly remembered after sixty years. Educated in Bedford and at Queen's College, Cambridge, Denby Gilbert was ordained a deacon in 1908, and priest at Peterborough in 1910. From 1908 to 1915 he had been curate of All Saints, Oakham, in Rutland, before becoming curate of St Helen's, Wheathamstead. Soon after his arrival at Stopsley he joined the Luton Town Wednesday Cricket team; he also acted as captain of Stopsley Cricket Club, and organised the St Albans Clergy cricket team. Not surprisingly, he soon acquired a reputation as Luton's Cricketing Vicar.

During his 15 years at Stopsley much work was accomplished. Gas lighting was introduced into the church in late 1922. The Church Institute was finally built in 1927 (see page 86). The roof and exterior of the church were restored, and the interior was renovated. A 'new' organ was purchased for £150 from the old Wesleyan Chapel at Harpenden, and installed at a cost of £35.15s. Its official 'opening' on 1st March, 1931, was marked with a recital by Mr Billingham and his colleagues. An electric blower was fitted in March 1941. St John's Church at Round Green was sold in October 1933, but continued in use for a further six months. The groundwork was done for the building and opening of **St Christopher's Church** at Round Green on 5th June 1937, although by then Round Green had become a Conventional District (Sept.1935), with its own Minister, the Revd. Gerald Hawker, and power to elect a Parochial Church Council.

It was during Mr Gilbert's time that the Church Army made regular and popular visits to Stopsley. It met in a marquee on Church land in St Thomas' Road, until the Instutute was opened.

In 1931 Professor Albert E. Richardson was invited to prepare plans for a 'Children's Church' at Round Green, to be built 'by the prayers and offerings of children' and dedicated to their saint, Christopher. The initial design was considered too massive a structure for a children's church. It resembled a Cambridge college chapel and the cost of building would have been prohibitive. Richardson was asked to try again. His second building in domestic Gothic was 'constructed on cruck principles rather like a barn'. It had a low, sloping roof and wide, slightly pointed windows. The main feature was a spire based on Amiens cathedral, with a tapered flèche visible all over Luton. With limited finances, only the nave was constructed in 1936-7. More was added in 1958-9, but the spire has never materialised.

It was during Denby Gilbert's incumbency in October 1932 that Mrs Sarah Connor of Town Farm, Guilden Morden, died, leaving an estate of some £6,450. Of this she left "£100 to the rector and churchwardens of the Parish Church of Stopsley, for general charitable purposes, charged with the upkeep of certain family graves, and failing compliance with this condition, then the sum is to be paid to the North Herts. and South Beds. Hospital, Hitchin." A similar sum and conditions were imposed on St Peter's Church, Lilley. The Stopsley graves in question belonged to three members of the Allingham family; a farming dynasty once established in our area at Whitehill Farm, and still surviving in Lilley. The graves of Elizabeth Allingham (died June 1883, aged 36), her mother Hannah Allingham (died May 1905, aged 82) and Elizabeth's sister also Hannah (died February 1925, aged 80) are still maintained in St Thomas's churchyard and the remainder of the bequest is used for educational purposes.

Mrs Winifred Gilbert proved an enthusiastic vicar's wife. She was a member of the Parochial Church Council, superintended the Junior Sunday School, acted as enrolling member for the Mothers' Union, and supervised the voluntary workers at the Stopsley Child Welfare Centre, held in the Church Institute. She was also responsible for organising numerous fund-raising concert parties ranging from Children's' Operetta to Old Time Music Halls.

Mr Gilbert left Stopsley to become Vicar of Bromham and Oakley, near Bedford. He had grown up in Bedford, where his father had been Vicar of St Peter's for 18 years.

Albert Henry Willson Cleaver took up office as Vicar of Stopsley in March 1938, having been at St Nicholas church, Harpenden since 1931. He delighted local people by sending his two young sons, Geoffrey and Nicholas, to the village school. One of his first tasks was to oversee the installation of electric lighting in the church, together with an electric blower for the organ. This was carried out by the Luton firm of Cawdells at a cost of £20. During redecoration a large and threatening Biblical text over the chancel arch, painted on zinc sheeting in 1862, was found to be in a dangerous condition, and was removed. It read: 'Except ye eat the flesh of the Son of Man and drink his blood, ye have no life in you'. It was considered too expensive to replace. In the north wall of the chancel, a new stained-glass window depicting St Luke, the physician, (by Lawson of St Albans) was presented to the church in 1939 by Miss Clementine Pates, in memory of her sister Mary, who had died in June 1920. Both maiden ladies had lived most of their lives in a cottage called 'St Peter's', which stood beside a footpath that ran from the side of *The Sportsman* to Venetia Road.

The Second World War

With the outbreak of War in September 1939 a number of Government restrictions came into force. The church bell was silenced, only to be rung if an invasion was imminent. Blackout curtains were hung in the church and Institute, and the east window was covered over. During the winter months evening services were moved forward to 3.30 p.m. to avoid travelling to church in the blackout. In spite of spirited objections it was agreed that in the event of an air-raid, the service would be immediately concluded, thus allowing the congregation to reach better 'material' shelter than the church building could provide! The Halls belonging to the Nonconformist churches were commandeered for wartime service and the Church Institute was made available to their members.

Life for parishioners during the War years continued as near to normal as possible. With many men serving with the Forces, women were left to organise the Parochial Fetes and Sales of Work which continued to be held in the Vicarage garden, with home-produced concert parties and the Radio-Gram' to provide entertainment. In the Institute amateur theatricals, whist drives and jumble sales raised money for numerous wartime good-causes. When the new Stopsley Council School opened on 19th September 1940, the Vicar was amongst the guests present, to say appropriate dedicatory prayers. A number of joint church services were held at this time.

St Thomas's church celebrated the 80th Anniversary of its foundation in June 1943. To mark the occasion a new reredos was installed behind the Altar, and oak panelling was set around the Sanctuary at a total cost of £163. It was dedicated by the Bishop of Bedford on 6th June 1943.

On Tuesday 8th May 1945 a special service was held to mark the end of the War in Europe, and a more elaborate Thanksgiving Service was held on the following Sunday evening. Plans to erect a carved wooden memorial plaque to the members of the Church who had died during the War were discussed on a number of occasions from 1945 onwards, but nothing was done until November 1960 when an illuminated Book of Remembrance containing 15 names, scribed by Douglas Walden, was placed in the Church.

In July 1946 Mr Cleaver announced that he was resigning the Benefice, having arranged with the Bishop of St Albans to exchange livings with the Vicar of Potton, the Revd. H.T. Pimm. Mr Cleaver was to stay at Potton for five years, before moving to Barton-in-the- Clay.

Whilst awaiting the arrival of the new Vicar,the Parochial Church Council made sure that the Caretaker-Verger, Miss Elizabeth Hill received a fair reward for her work. She had looked after the Church for 18 years and was being paid £8 per annum, having only once (in 1931) had an increase of £1. The P.C.C. decided that it was time to pay her £19.10s.0d., a year. After she had retired in November 1947, her successor was immediately paid double that amount!

Henry Thomas Pimm was inducted at St Thomas's by Bishop Bernard Heywood on 14th September 1946. Mr Pimm had been Vicar of Selsby, near Stroud in Gloucestershire for 11 years, prior to becoming Vicar of Potton and Rector of Cockayne Hatley in north-east Bedfordshire in 1942.

St Thomas's churchyard had been full-up since 1940 and an extension was urgently needed. The alternative was to use the general Cemetery in Crawley Green Road. Having missed the opportunity to buy adjoining land in the 1920s, which by 1949 was built over, the P.C.C. turned its attention to the orchard belonging to Dr George

Garratt, the village G.P., who lived at Stopsley House, next door to *The First and Last*. However, the Doctor was adamant that under no circumstances was he prepared to sell his land, and the matter remained unresolved. In July 1954 The Vale cemetery was opened in Butterfield's Green Road. Laid out as a lawn cemetery, it was consecrated by the Bishop of Bedford and the President of the Luton Free Churches Federal Council. As Luton's principal cemetery, it was intended for use by every denomination. The Crematorium and Garden of Remembrance were added in 1960.

Nothing has been said of musical life at St Thomas's. It seems to have had a small choir since its inception. A photograph of about 1895 shows a choir of four boys and two men, together with ten young ladies, who were almost certainly Sunday School teachers, but may well have sweetened the singing. Throughout the later Second World War years from October 1942 John A. Cleaver, Head of Geography at Luton (Modern) Grammar School, had been the organist at a salary of £25 per annum. In April 1948 the Vicar appointed Walter Charles Kilby, who was to remain organist and choirmaster for 21 years, until his untimely death at the age of 52 in January 1969. Mr Kilby was an enthusiastic musician who created both Junior and Senior Choirs, which included girls and women as well as male voices. He raised the standard of the church's music to heights never before achieved at Stopsley. The choir's outings to such seaside towns as Eastbourne and Yarmouth became eagerly awaited annual events and usually filled two coaches. Mr Pimm acquired a set of hand-bells, and by 1948 he had trained four boys from the Youth Fellowship into a small ringing team. This was enlarged to eight the following year. The lads used colour-coded ringing charts, and soon became proficient, performing for charity at numerous venues including the Gaumont Cinema's Saturday Morning Film Club.

Troubled Times

From his very first meeting with the P.C.C. Mr Pimm was plagued by problems relating to the ownership of the Church Institute. Having established beyond doubt that it belonged to the Church Council, he insisted that Church organisations received preferential treatment concerning bookings and charges, but forbade them to use it for any social function during Lent. Non-church organisations could hire it, but not in Holy Week. Questions were raised in Stopsley as to what constituted a Church organisation. A letter sent to *The Luton News* in February 1950 claimed that the Institute had been built with money left over from the village War Memorial Fund (1914-18) and that consequently it should be available for use by *any* village organisation. There was no truth in the claim, but it was a rumour that proved hard to dispel. Charges and countercharges were made. The P.C.C. issued a definitive statement: "Any organisation claiming to be a Church organisation must acknowledge the authority of the Vicar and all things Spiritual. The Vicar must be an *ex-officio* member of its committee and notified of all meetings." The Girl Guides, the Stopsley Girls' and Boys' Clubs and the Stopsley Ladies Association were all barred from using the Institute, ostensibly for 'inappropriate use during Lent', which resulted in petitions to the P.C.C. signed by many prominent Stopsley adults and young people. The Girl Guides re-formed at Stopsley Secondary Modern Girls' School and the Vicar attempted to freeze their assests, claiming that they were registered as the 1st (St Thomas's) Stopsley Company. Eventually, he and the County Commissioner for Guides agreed that the school company should receive half the funds, but these, Miss

Millen, the Headmistress, declined. In September 1950 an attempt was made to restart the St Thomas's Company.

Mr Pimm announced his resignation as Vicar in September 1951. In a final message to the P.C.C. he thanked it members 'for their co-operation when they were up against difficulties, and for standing their ground against numerically superior forces.'

Mr Pimm was an ardent supporter of the British Legion, and had been a member for 21 years. In November 1946, at a meeting in the Church Institute, he formed a Stopsley and District Branch with 60 members.

A new Vicar, Gordon P.Owen, was instituted on 21st December 1951. He came from All Saints Church, Harpenden, where he had been Curate-in-charge. Eighteen months later he was joined by an Assistant Curate, Rodney Milton Stone, who moved on to south Lincolnshire in April 1955.

Mr Owen's incumbency was destined to become more stormy than his predecessor's. One of the first indications of trouble occurred in July 1952 when a belated proposal was made to provide a memorial in the church to Miss Elizabeth Hill, the late caretaker-verger. Mr Owen proposed that the memorial should take the form of a Sanctuary lamp. "It is desired to provide an Aumbury in the north wall.....and to place a perpetual Sanctuary Lamp before the door of such Aumbury to reserve the Blessed Sacrament." St Thomas's was traditionally 'low church' but Mr Owen was a high church man. A number of influential local people including some of the P.C.C. disliked this intensely, and resented his ministry virtually from the start.

In spite of this, much of what he said and did appealed to the general body of worshippers at St Thomas's. He socialised in the village and considered home visits particularly important. He dropped in on the elderly for a cup of tea, enjoyed a drink in the local pubs or Working Mens' Club, and worked extremely hard to encourage young people to come to the church. Under his supervision the Youth Fellowship flourished; he acquired an ancient motor coach and ran trips to ice rinks, London shows and even a Swiss holiday. The Church Lads' Brigade under Captain Bradbury, and the re-formed Girl Guides led by Mrs Collins became very popular. Some effort was made to heal the rift with the Stopsley Ladies' Association. In October 1953 a 'Mission to Stopsley' led by Capt. R. Williams of the Church Army provided a very successful recruiting campaign. Meanwhile Mrs Owen had been instrumental in founding a very popular Stopsley Young Wives Group.

By 1953 the P.C.C. were beginning to think of expansion. The Baptists were planning a new church hall and St Thomas's did not wish to be left behind. They had ideas for replacing the Church Institute with a more permanent brick-built structure. The Diocesan Reorganisation Committee was encouraging the Vicar to consider enlarging the church building, and architects had drawn up designs for an organ loft and choir gallery at the west end of the nave. The Vicarage was in a bad state of repair and had dry rot. It was proposed to sell it and the ground it stood upon, and to build a new one which would conform to modern requirements. In the enthusiasm, the complicated finances that were involved in all these proposals got temporarily out of hand. Unlike the Baptists, St Thomas's had no rich benefactors. In February 1955, before any major changes could be implemented, the P.C.C. were informed that the Church had serious financial problems, with £262 owing to various creditors.

Meanwhile, the Vicar's wife Elizabeth, had become seriously ill. At the beginning of 1955 she died, and the Bishop of St Albans conducted her funeral service in St Thomas's on 14th January. She was buried in the churchyard, and a silver ciborium was bought for the church in her memory. Mr Owen, who had nursed her throughout her illness, now became ill himself, and although he attempted to carry on with his duties as usual for some weeks, he found himself under great mental stress. His personal finances were in complete disarray, and he was called to appear at Luton County Court on 4th August to answer a judgement summons for unpaid debts. On 3rd August, after conducting Holy Communion and a funeral service at 11.00 a.m., he suddenly disappeared from the Vicarage leaving his schoolgirl daughter Gwyneth, a number of small unpaid debts, several about-to-be-married couples and a funeral without an officiant. The national press had a field day, and numerous inaccurate, damaging and wildly imaginative reports circulated around the village, almost all untrue.

Holy Communion on the following Sunday, 7th August, was attended by a large congregation and was taken by Canon William Davison, Vicar of Luton. In his address the Canon described Mr Owen's disappearance as "a great challenge to all of you to be faithful."

There was speculation for some days as to the Vicar's whereabouts, until a postcard with an Austrian postmark arrived at the Vicarage, addressed to his daughter Gwyneth. The message on it stated merely that Mr Owen would be returning, but gave no hint when that would be. Canon Davison, in a statement to *The Luton News* said that "the Vicar just could not face up to things. He asked me to look after his daughter who has now gone to stay with some friends in London. Mr Owen has undoubtedly been very harassed by the illness and death of his wife. He is very highly strung, and it probably preyed on his mind."

The Vicar returned to England at the end of August. He tendered his resignation to the Bishop, and visited Stopsley vicarage to clear up his affairs. At Canon Davison's instigation he then retreated to Mirfield in Yorkshire in an effort to regain his health and faith. The hostility towards him shown by some members of the P.C.C. must have been a contributory factor to his breakdown. He had needed help and sympathy from them but felt unable to ask for it when things began to get beyond his control. Malicious accusations of deliberate dishonesty with church funds which circulated in Stopsley for many years have been totally refuted by the church authorities. His successor, Canon Pollard, in communication with the author wrote: "There was muddle, yes, which had gone on for some time, but nothing more. After caring for his wife before her death, and coping as best he could afterwards, it was hardly surprising that administration suffered. The Bishop and Diocesan Office were very supportive of Mr Owen as soon as they became aware that there were problems. Both, in their different ways, did as much as they could to help, and that must not be forgotten."

For the next eight months church services were conducted by a large number of officiants, including H.T. Pimm and C.F. Pollard. A growing rift amongst members of the P.C.C. erupted in October 1955 when the Secretary and Treasurer resigned on the grounds that the Council failed to stand by its decisions, certain members failed to keep its business private, and that talk of high and low church was becoming prevalent. The task of finding a successor to Mr Owen was not made any easier by the unhappy rumours circulating both locally and nationally, and the benefice was offered to a number of clergy, before it was bravely accepted by Clifford F. Pollard.

Calm after the Storm

Mr Pollard had served in the R.A.F. in Britain and overseas for the five War Years, and had taken part in the siege of Malta. He was 25 when he began his theological training, and was ordained at Hereford in 1950 to serve at Leominster Priory. He came to Luton in 1953, officially as Curate of St Mary's, but in fact he became Priest-in-charge of St Paul's, New Town Street, Luton. He moved to Stopsley in 1956, being conversant with the parish and knowing much of what had been happening there. He was licensed by the Bishop of St Albans on 10th April 1956. At 35 he brought a wife and young family to the village and they were soon accepted by most of the community.

Congregations at St Thomas's were small and there was a good deal of pessimism, even amongst the loyalist parishioners. Divisions existed even between some of the stalwarts of the parish, but after a time most people were prepared to work with the new Vicar and virtually everyone who had left, came back again. Unfortunately suspicion of the Church and Vicar lingered in some quarters for a very long time, even being felt by Francis Estdale five years later.

The new Vicar was keen to restore a state of purpose at St Thomas's. He began by organising 'Operation Firm Faith' with the aim of introducing more systematic Christian teaching to everyone from 3-plus to man and womanhood. The Sunday School grew to over 400 children under the energetic Superintendent, Miss Myrtle Cox. For some years an over-crowded Ramridge branch met in the Ashcroft Café in Yeovil Road. It moved to Ramridge Infant School when it opened in 1951. At the same time Mr Pollard started a Church Fellowship and in 1958 the Stopsley Branch of Toc H, which met in the Loft above the Vicarage Coach House.

In order to facilitate the mowing of the grass in the churchyard, moves began in 1958 to level all the grave mounds that were no longer cared for. Twenty-three gravestones had either fallen down or were in a dangerous state. Some of these were repaired: others were laid flat. The work, by volunteers, was completed in 1960.

In July 1959, Church Councillor and Farmer, Patrick Shaw first mooted the idea of erecting an enclosed brick-built porch onto the church. The existing one failed to prevent heat loss and severe draughts in the colder weather. The cause was very dear to Mr Shaw's heart, and although he had to wait 24 years for it to materialise, he eventually saw it built with Stopsley grey bricks salvaged from his demolished Common Farm in 1983.

The second building stage of St Christopher's church at Round Green was completed in 1959 and it was consecrated on 12th September. As Round Green was still in the ecclesiastical parish of Stopsley, it was necessary to convey the site to the church Commissioners under the New Parishes Measure (1943).

In 1957 land was acquired off Carteret Road for a new church on the rapidly expanding Vauxhall Park estate (by then in the ecclesiastical parish of St Mary's). On 11th April 1959 the foundation stone was laid and the completed **Church of St Francis** was consecrated on 13th February 1960. Mr Pollard, representing the Parish of St Thomas', gave the new church an Altar Book. The architects of St Francis church were Peter Dunham, Widdup and Harrison. A feature of the church was the figure of St Francis in the vestibule window and the use of chunky glass in the other windows, designed by Pierre Fourmaintreaux and made by Powells at their Whitefriars factory. Behind the altar was a large mural 'To the end of time' by Mary Adshead. St Francis was created a separate parish in 1977.

Mr Pollard left Stopsley in the autumn of 1960 to become Staff Padre with Toc H in Kent, later becoming Rector of Mersham, near Ashford, and finally Director of Education for the Diocese of Canterbury: a post he held for 18 years until his retirement in 1987. The Archbishop created him an Honorary Canon of Canterbury Cathedral in 1972.

January 16th 1961 saw the induction of Francis A. Estdale, Stopsley's longest serving minister. He had completed 33 years when he retired in September 1994. Born in Kent in 1926, and educated in Essex, he worked for his father as a textile dyer, until he volunteered for the R.A.F. in 1944. Having run the local Youth Club and Sunday School whilst in his teens, it seemed natural, when he was demobilised in 1948, to train for the Church. He was ordained at Lichfield Cathedral in 1953, and became Curate at Penn, Wolverhampton and then at Christchurch, Watford. He had married his wife Marian, a nurse, in 1950, and they had two children, John and Julia. He was made an Honorary Canon of St Albans Abbey in June 1990.

Canon Estdale was responsible for some 2,500 baptisms at Stopsley, and roughly the same number of funerals and cremations, plus almost 1,000 weddings. Amongst his notable achievements was the introduction of a Stewardship Scheme. When he retired the future of the Ministry within the parish seemed secure, and the fabric of St Thomas's had seldom looked better. He and his family had moved to the new Vicarage in Hitchin Road in 1972. In the following year he saw the dedication of the new Choir Vestry, followed by the new porch and cloakroom in 1983, a new altar, complete redecoration by volunteer labour, the building recarpeted throughout and an audio system installed. His comments on retirement were that serving as a Parish Priest had been an abiding joy which he regarded as the greatest privilege in the world. "Plain, old-fashioned pastoral paternalism!"

In January 1990 a 110 year old Corsican pine tree in the churchyard was blown down, demolishing a car, parked in Hitchin Road, that had only just been vacated.

On 22nd August 1995 the challenge of Stopsley was taken up by the Revd. David Alexander. A married man, with three young children, he was the first incumbent to have grown up in the parish, having attended both Ramridge Junior School and Ashcroft High School.

THE WESLEYAN METHODISTS

John Wesley's family were Anglicans, and it was his original intention that Methodists should remain with the established church, attending parish church on Sunday mornings and chapel in the evenings. About 1750 a group of travelling Methodist evangelists held a meeting in Luton at a house on Market Hill which attracted a number of adherents. Wesley, himself, preached in the town at least six times. In January 1772 he wrote in his *Journal* : "I set out for Luton. The snow lay so deep on the road, that it was not without much difficulty and some danger, we at last reached the town. I was offered the use of the church [St Mary's]; the frost was exceedingly sharp, and the glass was taken out of the windows. However for the sake of the people I accepted the offer, though I might just as well have preached in the open air. I suppose four times as many people were present, as would have been at the room; and about one hundred in the morning. So that I did not repent of my journey through the snow."

In 1778 Wesley persuaded William Cole of Sundon to build a Methodist chapel opposite St Mary's in Church Street, and endow it with an annual sum of £10.10s.0d.

It had quite a small congregation at first, but after the Luton circuit was established in 1808 and under the energetic leadership of the Rev. Maximilian Wilson, it soon began to draw large numbers of followers, many from leading local families. In 1814 a new chapel was built in Hog Lane (now Chapel Street). Enlarged several times, it became the Luton Industrial College, and eventually closed in 1997.

A small society of Methodists had formed in Stopsley by the autumn of 1839. They met in a private house and were led by John Warner. Six of the congregation at the first meeting were practising Methodists, and nine attended the meeting on trial. By Christmas all 15 were full or class members (with their names entered in a Class Book), and during the following year, under the leadership of James Hawkes, numbers rose to 23. Unfortunately four back-sliders in 1841 reduced them to 19, and membership then fluctuated between 14 in 1842, 21 in 1843 and 24 in 1844.

During the period 1834 to 1846 eight new churches were established in the Luton circuit: one of these was at Stopsley. It was registered by John Crofts of Luton on 18th September 1846. A group of Trustees was set-up almost as big as the congregation. It included the local Superintendent of the Wesleyan Methodist connection, James Cook, and twelve other middle-class Lutonians, though no one living in Stopsley. They were:

Gustavus Jordan, draper	Joseph Hawkes, hat manufacturer
George Freeman, hat manufacturer	Frederick Davis, hat manufacturer
John Jordan, chemist	John Craker, carpenter
William Webb, hat manufacturer	John Waller, woolstapler
Thomas Hawkes, jnr. bricklayer	Francis Davis, jnr. grocer
George Hunt, hat manufacturer	John Webb, hat manufacturer

The Trustees bought 5 poles of land from the Quaker Daniel Brown, on 19th August 1844, and building soon commenced on a site to the east of *The Sportsman*. The church was registered with the Bishop of Ely as a place of worship on 23rd September 1846, and meetings began at once. Built of Stopsley bricks, the church cost £117.10s.0d., paid with a loan from central funds. Eight years later a debt of £38.14s.1d. was still outstanding, and the annual income was estimated at only £5.10s.0d. The interior was very plain, with pine benches for 90 people. Seating was increased to 120 when the building was enlarged to include a Hall in 1894. More land was purchased in 1924 for extensions which were never built: the same fate met plans to extend in 1962-63.

Plans were first announced in 1844 for a new Methodist church that would be the largest building in Stopsley. By 1845, led by George Butt, there was a potentially large congregation but only 22 who were prepared to become full members. When the new church opened in 1846 there were only 18 full (or class) members, and the numbers dropped annually to 13 in 1850. The following year George Butt was joined by Brother Bennett and numbers increased almost immediately to around 30. These figures are taken from the Quarterly Schedules preserved in the County Record Office. Figures given in the Ecclesiastical Census which was taken on Sunday 30th March 1851 record an afternoon congregation of 101 and evening of 108, as well as 40 Sunday School scholars. Again this indicates a large congregation, but only a small core of full members. The Census record was signed by James Godfrey, Local Preacher, of Pegsdon. In the 1860s during the Stewardship of William Dimmock and Thomas Wheeler the average full membership was 25. This figure was maintained during the Stewardship of John Bennett and E. Waller, rising to 26 from 1874 to 1878, but the last surviving recorded number is 22 in 1879. Unfortunately few documents are preserved covering the remaining years of the church's existence, although the Sunday School Minute Book survives from 1905 to 1948. In 1907 there were two classes each for young men, young women, boys and girls. Membership figures were only regularly entered in the 1920s, and show that the numbers of young people attending rose from 93 in 1921 to a peak of 117 in 1923, and then dropped steadily to 79 in 1927. In that year 42 of the pupils were girls and 37 boys, with a third of them attending the morning school, the remainder in the afternoon. In 1944 only 15 attended morning Sunday School and 20 to 23 in the afternoon. By 1974 it had fallen to single figures, although the Boys' Brigade was still a popular youth organisation in the village.

By 1930 the Wesleyan Methodists had two circuits in the Luton area: Chapel Street and Waller Street. Stopsley belonged to the latter, along with Waller Street, North Street, Central Hall and Round Green (all in Luton), and Barton, Hexton, Shillington, Gravenhurst, Lilley, Cockernhoe, Kimpton and Darley Hall and The Folly.

There are few records of personalities connected with the Methodist chapel. In his book *A Century of Methodism* (1908), A. E. Balch wrote that Stopsley was always associated with the name of Dimmock. In particular 'Mr William Dimmock (1860), the local preacher who read the *Day Star* and became so rapt in meditation, whether in the body or out of the body, he could not tell, and loved to ponder on those things "the angels desire to look into". He took his sons with him when he went to preach, and his sons (George and Arthur) learned to love the class meeting, and to use their gifts of thought and speech to win the ear and warm the heart of congregations both in town and country, as their father did.'

The Wesleyan chapel seems to have enjoyed a happy relationship with the village School during the Headship of Charles Breed (1893-1925); something apparently often denied the Baptist and Anglican churches. William Dyer was the Steward from the 1890s and Charles Breed attended his funeral in February 1916. Children from the village School often took part in evening entertainment's for the Band of Hope. The School log book records annual treats for all the denominations; the Wesleyans venturing as far afield as Felixstowe (1938) and Southend (1939).

In 1938 the Wesleyan Hall was used by the overcrowded village School as an extra classroom for 50 boys. With the outbreak of War the Hall was commandeered for the headquarters of the A.R.P., and on its termination a lengthy correspondence followed with the Ministry of Defence seeking compensation. The iron railings which surrounded the church were removed to be made into munitions. Most of them got no further than the back garden of 14 St Thomas's Road, where they still stand!

The *Statistical Returns* for 1940 record seating in the church for 150. In 1970 the *Returns* state 'Church seating 130'. Many non-members attended social activities organised by the church, but membership was dwindling. Between 1969 and 1972 extensive attempts were made to renew the life of the church. The building was in urgent need of repairs. Efforts were made to replace the school room floor and renovate the roof, but there were insufficient funds, and it gradually became clear that the building was no longer adequate. In spite of tireless work by a tiny group of stalwarts led by Arthur F. Cain, there was insufficient leadership available to revive the flagging church. Mr Cain died peacefully in the church during a Sunday service. Andrew Emerton was the last child to be baptised in the building on 18th February 1973. In that year Stopsley Methodist Church was faced with probable closure, and the Trustees met on a number of occasions to consider the situation. The fact that there was a lively Baptist Church on the spot and another Methodist Church in good heart not far away at Round Green, influenced their decision. On 6th January 1974 the Revd. Cecil Dawe, the Superintendent Minister for the Luton area, conducted the final Covenant Service at Stopsley. Three days later a Special Circuit Meeting ratified the decision to close the church. The Revd. Raymond E. Sargent, Minister responsible for Stopsley, conducted the Easter Services on 12th and 14th April. The final service was led by a Local Preacher, Stan Ward, on Sunday 5th May 1974, attended by a congregation of some two dozen members. As they left for the last time, 17 years old organist, Ian Cheverton, played them out to 'Lift High the Cross'. The Registration of the Church was cancelled on 22nd July 1974. The Trustees met on 13th September to dispose of the church property. Stopsley's oldest ecclesiastical building, and its most distinguished landmark, was unceremoniously demolished the following year.

STOPSLEY BAPTIST CHURCH

Mr G. C. Souster published his book *1869 -1969: A History of the Stopsley Baptist Church*, in 1969. Consequently, I have only outlined the church's story, and would refer the reader to Mr Souster's more detailed work.

The first Baptist community in south Bedfordshire was established in Kensworth Parish Church after Edward Harrison was appointed to the living in 1645. His followers flocked from thirty neighbouring towns and villages to hear him preach. As time passed by independent churches were set up at Luton, St Albans and Dunstable. The first Meeting House in Park Street, Luton "was erected by Richard Sutton of Tring, a collar maker, who sold it to the trustees on 28th July 1698 for the sum of five shillings." The Luton meeting was led by Thomas Marsom, a friend of John Bunyan, both of whom had served sentences in Bedford Goal for their faith. The church measured "about 32 feet by 26 feet [9.75m. x 8.00m.] with a vestry attached", and became very crowded, soon needing a gallery. In October 1707 there were 258 members of the church, of whom 99 lived in Luton, and four came from Stopsley. The latter are recorded as: 'Brother Henry Bradford and Sarah his wife,
Brother Thomas Horn and Lettis his wife.'

As numbers grew, village stations were set up wherever there were sufficient members. By 1815 meetings were being held at Mr Dimmock's cottage at Stopsley. In 1817 'Brother [Ebenezer] Daniel, of Luton, and members of his church, preached at.....Stopsley.' Candle collections were held during the winter of 1829 to pay for the cost of lighting the Stopsley meeting: 3s.8d. [c.19p.]. A few years later the Park Street Baptist Church account books also record:

April 1846:	One Quarter's Rent Stopsley Meeting and Candles	8 shillings [40p.]
23 Jan 1849:	Mr Dimmock One Quarter's Rent for Stopsley Meeting	6 shillings [30p.]
	Mr Dimmock Candles for Stopsley Meeting	2 shillings [10p.]

An Ecclesiastical Census of every church and meeting house in England and Wales was held on 30th March 1851. From this we know that the Stopsley Baptists were by then meeting at the home of William Dumpleton [an agricultural worker, aged 50], where there was seating [probably in a barn] for 60 people, although on the evening of the 30th March only 44 attended.

In 1869, during the Pastorship of Thomas Hands at Park Street, it was agreed that "on the request of three-quarters of Stopsley members when they numbered fifty, the village church should become independent of Luton". A letter to the Association of Baptist Churches of Hertfordshire and Bedfordshire dated 8th June 1869 tells us "at Stopsley the place of meeting has become so inconveniently crowded that it has become necessary to erect a Village Meetinghouse." Land in Bury Road was acquired from the Quakers, Mrs Lydia Brown and Miss Ann Brown, in November 1869, and work was immediately begun on building the first chapel: the cornerstones being laid by Richard and Henry Pigott on 9th November 1869, though neither Richard nor Henry were living in the village at that time. The Pigotts were an old and extensive Stopsley farming family who joined the Luton Baptists early in the 18th century. Francis Pigott had signed the application requesting the registration of the Park Street Meeting House for marriages in October 1839. Of the seven Trustees of the new building, the only Stopsley member was Charles Pigott, aged 38, whose address was given as Stopsley Farm House [Bury Farm]. The Clerk to the Trustees was Frederick Marsh, who walked to the Luton Meeting from Hitchin every Sunday, and later became a stalwart of the Stopsley Baptist Sunday School. It was he who proposed that the first Sunday evening in each month should be reserved for Stopsley's communion service. Sadly he died when he was only 30 years old.

The late William B. Fletcher recalled the first Stopsley chapel which he attended as a lad. It consisted of a single large open meeting room with a coke stove at the centre. There were hard wooden benches, paraffin lamps, and a small vestry at the rear. People from Luton and the surrounding farms came up to Stopsley for morning service, and stopped for afternoon Sunday School. At midday they all gathered round the stove to eat their lunches and enjoy the company.

Mr Fletcher also remembered the Sunday School Anniversaries, held on the second Sunday of July, which he attended between 1895 and 1911. As there were more than 100 children on roll by then, and their families, friends and other chapel members wished to take part, it was necessary to find more extensive premises than the chapel could provide. Consequently Charles Pigott lent his largest barn. each year. A platform was constructed on which the children sat, and the adults, some 200 strong, crowded into the body of the building or sat on the grass outside. Choral and instrumental music was provided by the Stopsley children and members of the mother church in Park Street.

Sunday School Treats were another highlight. On 7th July 1885 the meadow next to the chapel was the venue. The Methodists chose the same day, and the Headmaster at the Village School, William Johnston, recorded the worst attendance he had ever experienced! In 1886 the Baptists approached the Methodists and Anglicans with what would seem to have been the sensible idea of promoting a united Treat in Putteridge Park. Unfortunately the Anglican Sunday School was not interested and the matter was dropped. The School Board later decided that the village school would close on each of the three days of Sunday School Treats.

In its early days Stopsley Chapel had a number of inspiring Leaders, the first of whom was Frederick Pates (from 1869-86), followed by Harry Mander and T.G. Hobbs (between 1886-1901). Harry Mander went on to become Baptist Minister and President of the Baptist Union. T.G. Hobbs has become something of a legend in Luton history. He spent Sunday mornings at Park Street and in the afternoon walked up to Stopsley. A hat materials merchant by trade, he was steeped in the work of the Temperance Movement, and furthered its aims with highly popular lantern lectures.

He was a Fellow of the *Royal Geographical Society*, a highly accomplished photographer, organiser of coach and train excursions, and publisher of the local timetable, known to all and sundry as 'a Hobbs'. Letters addressed to 'T.G. Hobbs, Luton' always found him!

Rebuilding the Church

The Stopsley Baptist Chapel was rebuilt on the same site in 1902, with a vestry and an area of the meeting room which could be partitioned off for use as a school room. A plaque in the old chapel in St Thomas's Road reads:

This Chapel and School are erected to the Glory of God
and in Loving Remembrance of Charles and Sarah Pigott
the Dear Parents of Helen Duberly, 1902.

Helen Duberly carried out her father's wishes that a portion of his estate should be spent on rebuilding the chapel. During the following year the Duberly's built two rows of terraced houses in Bury Road, one called Marsom Place. It is reported that the weekly rental was 5s.0d [25p.]. For a short time she and her husband George Smith Duberly, a well-known local chemist (and partner in Duberly and White) farmed at Bury Farm. In 1907 they moved to Beach Royal, Bournemouth, whilst retaining ownership of Bury Farm. After George's death, Helen married Henry Cook. She died in 1930 and is buried with her parents in Rothesay Road cemetery, Luton.

By 1911 church membership was flagging, and Herbert C. Janes was sent to Stopsley as Superintendent. He found affairs in a very depressed state and immediately formed a Management Committee which set a programme of evangelism into motion. Soon numbers revived, only to be partially dashed by the departure of young men to the 1st World War. At that time there was a great influx of soldiers into the village with large camps in the surrounding fields. Both the Baptist and Methodist chapels were commandeered for military use. For the duration of the War all denominations used St Thomas's church, and the Vicar of Stopsley, the Rev. G.H.C. Shorting conducted open air interdenominational services for the soldiers and villagers. With the absence of so many young men, women began to play a more conspicuous part in chapel life for the first time. In the village, although sometimes at loggerheads with each other, all the denominations were again united when the War Memorial was dedicated in 1920.

Herbert C. Janes returned as Superintendent at Stopsley chapel in 1926, when the church was once more in need of revitalisation. He considered that one of the weaknesses at Stopsley was the lack of a full-time minister to hold the church together. In 1938 the Baptist Central Sustentation Fund agreed to grant £55 per annum towards a minister's stipend of £155. On 3rd September of that year Edwin Robertson became Stopsley's first Baptist Minister.

With the outbreak of the Second World War in 1939 the chapel had to be blacked-out and the windows boarded-up so that no stray light could be seen by enemy aeroplanes, and consequently evening services were held in the afternoon to avoid breaking the Ministry of Defence regulations. Church membership rapidly expanded and by 1940 wooden huts were needed to provide extra accommodation for a variety of church activities and youth organisations, such as the Boys' Brigade, Lifeboys and the Girls' Auxiliary which in 1941 became the Girls' Life Brigade. The school room was used as a canteen for men from the temporary R.A.F. camp in Putteridge Park in

1942. Consequently, after the War, plans were made to build a church hall. This materialised in September 1954 and was opened by Sir Herbert C. Janes. Not only did it serve the Chapel's own organisations, but others from the community as well, and for a time it was used as classroom accommodation for the rapidly expanding Stopsley Secondary Modern Schools.

On 1st January 1961, for the first time, Stopsley Baptist Chapel became an independent Baptist church, quite separate from Park Street, Luton. To give it a fresh start the interior of the church was completely renovated with new furnishings throughout. Two years later a house was built for the Minister on chapel land fronting onto Tancred Road. The church was attracting some 130 members by 1971 with as many more forming part of the congregation. Twenty years later numbers had more than doubled and negotiations took place over a protracted period to acquire land in St Thomas's Road for a new Stopsley church. By 1994 membership was in excess of 400 and at last it became possible to build a large multipurpose church, capable of providing both for its Baptist membership, and the wider secular community beyond. It was in this year that the Senior Pastor, Revd. Stephen Gaukroger became the third Stopsley Baptist to hold the office of President of the Baptist Union: (Sir Herbert Janes had been President in 1956). Appropriately enough, the site chosen for the new Stopsley Baptist Church was Bury Farm, the home of its benefactors of 1902, the Pigott and Duberly families. Built at a cost of £1.2 million, it was officially opened on 24th September 1994.

THE ROMAN CATHOLIC CHURCH AND SCHOOLS

There was no tradition of Roman Catholicism in Stopsley prior to the 2nd World War. In 1942 the Roman Catholic Priest in Luton requested permission to use St Thomas's Church Institute on Sunday mornings to celebrate Mass. Since neither the Anglican Bishop nor the Vicar had any objection, the Parochial Church Council was unanimous in giving it consent, at a rental of 7s.6d. per week.

In 1948 the Revd. George Joseph Walker was appointed as the first resident Catholic Priest in Stopsley. Born in 1911, he was educated and lived in France, from where he managed to escape in late 1940. He was ordained in the following year. He catered for the rapid post-war growth of Catholics in the parish, most of whom were freshly arrived from Ireland, assured of finding work in Luton's booming building trade. Father Walker continued to use the Church Institute each week, and orchestrated enthusiastic voluntary fund raising work which culminated on 26th November, 1950, in the opening of a new church in Ashcroft Road, dedicated by Bishop T. Leo Parker to the Most Sacred Heart of Jesus. The Revd. Walker was inducted as Parish Priest in 1953. Innumerable social and cash raising events followed in an effort to swell funds to pay for the church. Many parishioners felt that there was too much emphasis on fund raising, and that it hurt poorer families. The initial debts were eventually cleared in 1958. By that time the church was already too small, and there were chronic car-parking problems in Ashcroft Road.

A new Presbytery was opened in 1960, and authorisation was received to build a new Catholic Primary School. This was to be sited on the edge of the filled-in Ramridge End clay pits. The foundation stone for the school was laid by Bishop Parker on 24th September, 1961, and the two storey building was formally opened for

Junior classes by the Bishop a year later on 18th September, 1962, with Sister Columba as Headteacher.

During 1960-61 the church building was extended. A suspended ceiling was added, and an electronic pipe-organ was purchased. In Ashcroft Road the Sisters of the Sacred Heart took possession of No.124 and made it their Convent until it was sold in 1996.

By 1964 negotiations were taking place for the erection of a single-storey Infant school on the reclaimed land beside the Primary School. The building was completed by September 1967, but its formal opening ceremony, planned by Father Walker, never took place, due to his appointment to St Joseph's parish, Aylesbury. Sister Columba transferred from the Junior School to become Head of the Infant School, where she remained until she took up an appointment in Haverhill in 1974. Anthony Johnson was appointed Head of the Junior School: a post held for 27 years. (The second longest Headship in a Stopsley school). At that time there were 408 children on roll in the Junior school, with four classes being taught in temporary classrooms. Children leaving the school from September 1968 could transfer to the newly opened Cardinal Newman High School, in Warden Hill Road, on the extreme north-western edge of Stopsley parish.

Meanwhile by 1967 the Sacred Heart parish was again facing financial difficulties. It was unable to meet the repayment of loans raised for building works. Financial support came principally from the poorer Catholics. The great and good had stood on the fence from the beginning and, contrary to Father Walker's hopes, the benefit of Catholic schools in the community, did not seem to bring them any closer. A number felt that their own Catholic schooling in Ireland had been too repressive, and they wished to give their children the greater freedom that children in England received. Luton at that time seemed to be in the grip of a recession; people were not supporting fund raising schemes and Sunday collections fell far short of expectations. (This state of affairs seems to have been common to all denominations at the time). It was a great relief when the Diocese accepted responsibility for half of the loan payments.

After the arrival of a new Parish Priest, Father Patrick Oates, in January 1968 (until 1974), financial consultants were called in to advise on raising funds for the church. They found that many of the schemes enthusiastically pursued during the previous twenty years had produced little or no benefit to the parish, relative to the enormous amount of time and effort invested in them. In consequence, they were abandoned, and 'planned giving' and covenant schemes were actively promoted. The parish also severely limited its expenditure. Over the following years the financial crisis eased. The heady days of rapid development were over, and the more mundane era of everyday, ordinary parish life took its place. Fathers Eugene P. Connolly and John Breheny began their long association with Stopsley in 1976.

Sister Columba left the Infant School in 1974 to become Head of a school in Haverhill. She was briefly succeeded by Jane Kilkenny, until 1976 when Pat Tansley was appointed. She retired in 1997. At the Junior School a Youth Club was set up in 1968 to provide activities for former pupils. In March 1970 thirty children and five teachers made the first of a number of popular annual visits to France. Between 1975 and 1978 numbers on the school roll dropped significantly reflecting a national trend. By 1987, when the school was 25 years old, it had fallen into a poor state of repair. Parents, staff and children worked hard to raise money towards the total cost of putting the building to rights. The Head, Anthony Johnson, retired in July 1994, and was succeeded by Charles McNerney.

LVIIa: St John's Mission Church at Round Green. Formerly the old Wesleyan Chapel, it was leased to St Thomas' church as a chapel of ease for its Round Green members. This snapshot, taken shortly before its closure in 1933, shows the altar and stained glass window portraying St John. A carved chair on the left is one of a pair, now in St Christopher's Church. (*Derrick Hooker*)

LVIIb: The exterior of St John's Mission Church at the time of its demolition in the late 1950s. After the opening of St Christopher's Hall in 1935, St John's was used for various purposes, finally serving as the headquarters of the Stopsley and District Branch of the British Legion. (*Stuart Smith*)

LVIIIa.   A sketch showing Professor Sir Albert Richardson's original design for St Christopher's Church, with the transepts and spire that failed to materialise.

LVIIIb: A 600 strong procession progressed to the end of Felix Avenue where the Bishop of Bedford dedicated the foundation stone of St Christopher's church in October 1936.   In the background (top left) stands the old *Shepherd and Flock* which was rebuilt in 1937.   (*Luton News*)

LIXa: The retirement of Revd Clifford A Pollard in the autumn of 1960 was marked with presentations by the Church Warden, farmer Pat Shaw, and the Vicar's Warden, George Ring (left) (*Luton News*)

LIXb: Children of the St Thomas' Sunday School warmly wrapped up on a chilly Palm Sunday about 1928. Each child holds a palm cross. (*Barbara Peters*)

LXa: There was massive support for the village Baby Show, held in the Vicarage garden in 1934. It was there that the author made his first public appearance! (*Author's collection*)

LXb: The Vicar of Stopsley with the church handbell ringers, entertaining at the Gaumont Cinema's Children's Saturday Morning Cinema Club in 1950. *Left to right:* Barry Morris; David Scrimshire; Norman Edwards; Tony Clayton; David Burgess: Ronald Perry; Anthony Plumb; ? ; Revd. H.T. Pimm. (*Luton News*)

LXIa: Falling numbers and lack of funds to pay for urgent repairs forced the closure of the Wesleyan Methodist Chapel in May 1974. The building was demolished the following year, and the site was sold for the construction of flats. (*Bob Norman*)

LXIb: The interior of the old Baptist Church in St Thomas' Road. (*Bob Bristow*)

LXIIa: The old Baptist Chapel in St Thomas Road opened in 1870 and was rebuilt in 1902. On the right is the Church Hall opened by H.C. Janes in 1954, and in the far distance the new Church of 1994, built on the site of Bleak Hall and Bury Farm. (*James Dyer*)

LXIIb: Stopsley children assembled outside the old Baptist church in St Thomas' Road in 1947 after the Sunday School Anniversary Service. (*Author's Collection*)

LXIIIa: Bishop T. Leo Parker assisted by Revd. George Walker, laying the foundation stone of the Sacred Heart Primary School on 24th September, 1961. (*Luton News*)

LXIIIb: Revd. George Walker, the first resident Catholic Priest in Stopsley from 1948-67; Sister Columba, Headteacher of the Sacred Heart Primary School from 1962, and of the Infant School between 1967 and 1974. (*Sacred Heart School Archives*)

LXIVa: The original Stopsley National School, opened at Swift's Green in 1858. It became a Board School in 1879. This picture was taken in 1906 and shows an additional Infant classroom added in 1889. The policeman is likely to have been P.C. Walter Ernest Wood. (*Luton Museum Collection*)

LXIVb: The old School House at Swift's Green during demolition in 1956. The Headmaster and Clerk to the Parish Council, Charles Breed, lived there until his death in January 1948. Bricks from the walls of the old school were used to build the nearby *Thatched Cottage* in Butterfield's Green Road. (*Luton News: Luton Museum Collection*)

Chapter 14

Education in Stopsley

There was no provision for education in Stopsley prior to the opening of the National School in 1858. It is possible that a few boys may have attended schools in Luton, but no records exist. We know that the Hucklesby brothers, Asher, Eliah and Arthur attended the British School in Langley Street, Luton, from 1850. The St Thomas's Church *Register of Marriages* that commenced in 1862 shows that the majority of couples who married in the church before 1875 were unable to sign their names and had to make their marks with a cross.

The writer has described *The Story of the Stopsley Schools* in his book of that name, published in 1989. The early history is briefly outlined below, using new material where relevant. More attention is paid to the later 20th century schools.

Stopsley National School was built on a piece of ground described as 'waste of the manor of Luton', which was provided by John Shaw Leigh of Luton Hoo, the Lord of the Manor. It was situated at Swift's Green, a small triangle of land measuring some 53.5m by 43.5m by 54.5m. Today the site has been levelled and is landscaped with trees, at the entrance to *The Vale* Crematorium. The deed of Conveyance was signed on 4th February 1858 by Mr Leigh and the Vicar and Churchwardens of Luton. Whilst the Government provided half the cost of building the school, the remainder had to be raised voluntarily by the National Society, supported by the Church of England. The National School was generously endowed by John Sambrook Crawley of Stockwood Park and was administered by a group of Managers who included Mrs Crawley, the Vicars of Luton and (after 1862) Stopsley, and Thomas Sowerby of Putteridge Bury.

The original school building consisted of two rooms: a schoolroom measuring 33 feet by 18 feet (10m by 5.5m) and a classroom 10 feet by 18 feet (3m by 5.5m). A teacher's house was connected to the smaller room. The latter was enlarged and an infants' gallery was added in 1889. In the walled playground, which was divided between girls and boys, were three earth privies and a urinal that drained into an open ditch. The only clean water was pumped from a well beneath the school house. The building was heated by coal fires and a tortoise stove, and lighting was by oil lamps.

No Log Books have survived from the first ten years of the school's existence, so we know nothing of what went on at that time. The 1861 Census Returns tell us that John Stevens, a bachelor, was the Teacher in that year, and Georgina Menlove his housekeeper. By the time the 1871 Census was made, Miss Menlove had moved to the Tithe Cottage, near Stopsley Green, and John Stevens was boarding with her. At that time she was listed as a dressmaker (aged 57). In the 1881 and 1891 Census Returns she appeared as a school mistress, and Mr Stevens as an assistant master and then retired teacher. Together they set up a private school in Tithe Cottage. In 1874 two well-ventilated rooms housed 35 children aged 1 to 13 years. Mr Stevens taught reading, writing, spelling and grammar there until his sudden death in 1892, aged 68. Maud Stronell, interviewed in 1965 when she was 81, recalled that "Mr Stevens, who was a superintendent at the church, and Miss Menlove kept the school when I was five or six. We paid 3 pence a week. The classroom had a very low ceiling and we had low forms to sit on. We did very little writing, and didn't learn much there. I think there were about forty children. When it closed down we all had to go to the Board School. Mr Shoosmith was the Headmaster, with Miss (Bessie) Matthews, Miss Prycke and Miss Beryl". In December 1892 Fred Shoosmith wrote of Mr Stevens' ex-pupils in the School Log Book "Their ignorance, as a rule, is simply astounding. Some of them, 11 and 12 years of age, being unable to do simple addition or write correctly a line from a reading book. I am therefore obliged to form a Standard 0, as it is impossible to send such big children to the Infant room".

Following a long period of neglect the National School at Stopsley was taken over as a Board School in November 1879, with Samuel Deane as Headmaster. Few parents could see the need to send their children to school, in spite of the 1876 Education Act which made attendance compulsory for 5 to 13 year olds. Most parents were illiterate farm labourers or plait makers, wages were minimal and poverty was rife. It seemed more sensible to send a child to work or to make straw plait and let it earn its keep. In 1886 Headmaster William Johnston wrote, "There are many cases of dire poverty in the village." The Whittemore family were frequently mentioned, "One lad has been away for a fortnight thro' want of boots." It is scarcely surprising that as soon as he was able, the young Whittemore left home to seek a brighter future by joining the army, and to fight in the Boer War, and the Great War, where he made the ultimate sacrifice.

Fred Shoosmith taught at Stopsley from January 1887 until November 1893. He had learnt his profession in Luton, having trained as a pupil-teacher at Waller Street School: a breeding ground for quality teachers and the School Board's pride. He was paid £70 per year, and received half the School Grant (which was based on the number of pupils present at school). He had free use of the school house, fuel and lighting.

When Shoosmith arrived at the school, it was very run down, both academically and in the condition of the buildings. There were 114 children on the roll, with gross overcrowding, inadequate books and slates, and appalling ignorance, largely due to the frequent illness and loss of enthusiasm of the previous Head. The greatest problem was attendance and children used any excuse to be absent. In March 1893 measles broke out in several families and the attendance was very low. Shoosmith visited the absentees and found that quite a number of them were away for no reason whatever. William Plummer stayed at home for a fortnight "because Lizzie Hawkins has been away, and he has as much right to stay away as she has". All the Crook family were away for no reason at all, and the same could be said of Elizabeth Ball, Florrie and Agnes Wiseman and several others. In 1890 Ada Wear was absent for 40 days and William Toyer (aged 8) for four months for no good reason. Later the same Toyer had five weeks off to illegally work on Osborne's farm. (Stopsley Common Farm).

Fred Shoosmith introduced a system of giving marks throughout the school for good conduct, earnest work, and cleanliness. The results, especially in the latter, were gratifying. The marks were given with the intention of presenting prizes in the various subjects, good conduct and cleanliness, at the end of each term. By this means he hoped to improve attendance and reduce the need for corporal punishment. Sadly he was not always successful.

In September 1887 George Smith received a caning for gross laziness, insubordination and insolence. His parents considered that it served him right. He was caned again in December, together with Lewis Grundon, for dishonest work in arithmetic. "These boys and a few others persist in cheating at every opportunity, in spite of my appeal to their moral sense (which I am afraid is very low) and also of my warning as to the consequences if discovered". Lewis Grundon was in trouble again in 1889. He had taken a book from school in order to learn two verses of poetry. On the way home he had flung it across the road, and instead of returning it to school, had hidden it in a holly bush. "Expecting trouble he had filled his pockets with stones (and induced his friend John Blow to do the same), to throw at me in the event of my administering punishment. Having been informed of this, I felt bound to administer a very severe punishment to them both". Happily during his six years at Stopsley the standard of learning and discipline improved considerably, and on leaving Fred Shoosmith wrote "I feel bound to record that for more reasons than one I am sorry to be leaving Stopsley. It has been a good training in meeting, and overcoming, difficulties; a training perhaps that will stand me in good stead in my new schools" [initially Surrey Street, Luton].

Charles Henry Breed

One fine Headmaster was replaced by another. Charles Henry Breed came to Stopsley on 13th November 1893 and remained at the school for 32 years, and in the village for the rest of his life. He had been born at Sun Lane, Biggleswade on Christmas day 1864. His mother was Sarah Breed, aged 17, a straw plaiter. He was baptised at St Andrew's Church on 29th January, 1865. No father's name is recorded and no registration of his birth can be traced. He appears to have taken his mother's maiden name. Sarah later married Edward Lincoln, and the boy lived with them and his maternal grandmother. He attended Biggleswade Boys' Board School, where he became a Monitor in April 1879 when he was 14. In October 1880 he achieved 3rd class in the pupil-teachers' examination. His Headmaster noted that his papers were very creditably marked. Eighteen months later Charles was placed 1st class in the examination to the delight of his Master. On 11th February 1884 he left Biggleswade to become an Assistant Teacher at Waller Street Higher Grade School in Luton where he taught for ten years.

Charles Breed arrived at Stopsley in November 1893, aged 28. The painters were busy renovating the outside of the school. He spent a whole day moving into the master's house, and left Miss Spark in charge of the pupils. "The boys promised me to behave well in my absence, and I was extremely gratified in knowing that they kept it".

The writer has documented Mr Breed's years at Stopsley in some detail elsewhere and will not repeat them here. Suffice to say that he was a dedicated Headmaster. In many ways his teaching methods were ahead of their time. Although learning by rote was still fashionable, he added discovery methods, particularly in nature study, educational visits, musical and literary appreciation, and visits to concerts and the theatre. He was very active outside the school as Clerk and later Chairman of the Parish Council. At one time he was Choirmaster at Luton Parish Church and had been an active member of the choir since 1884. Only two years shorter than his choir record was his service to Luton Choral Society. He also sang in the Luton Hoo choir when it was in existence. At that time he struck up a friendship with the novelist, Joseph Conrad, who lived at Someries Farm between 1907 and 1909. They enjoyed playing chess together and discussions "over the coffee cups". Breed was naturally fond of reading, and when asked to choose names for new roads in the village, he suggested the titles of three of his favourite novels by Disraeli, namely *Lothair*, *Venetia* and *Tancred*. He also enjoyed the works of Sir Walter Scott, and toured Scotland (including Melrose) in search of places associated with the adventures. Books from his extensive library would eventually find their way into several Stopsley homes. He was fond of travel, both in Britain and Europe, and used his experiences to enliven his lessons.

For most of its existence the Stopsley School was overcrowded and understaffed. By October 1900 Mr Breed was trying to teach five standards (61 children) and his assistant, Miss Lily Tompkins, two standards (35 children). There was no one available to teach the remaining 49 infants when the two pupil-teachers were attending their weekly training centre. Mr Breed wrote "it is impossible for me and an assistant to do the work of three teachers, work which in former years really employed four. To take a big class and train every teacher on the staff is the work of a Hercules, especially as teachers are absent regularly and their classes as regularly present needy tuition. I feel most strongly that the lack of teachers at certain periods of the week is a great danger to the future welfare of this school". A few days later Breed developed influenza, leaving Miss Tompkins alone with 145 children in three classrooms: at midday she admitted defeat and sent the children home! The official capacity of the school was 147. It ceased to be a Board school in 1903, when it was renamed Stopsley Council School.

In February 1908 there were 153 children in the school; in May, "165 with consequent overcrowding". In September there were 172 on the books, but a new Infant School was being built. In June 1905 the Bedfordshire Education Authority had given notice to the Parish Council of their intention to build a new elementary school for 80 scholars in Stopsley. The cost of £1,698 worried the Council, who wanted to know from what source the money would come. To their horror, it appeared that the village would be expected to find three-quarters of it. However, since a new school was clearly needed, the decision was somewhat reluctantly accepted. The Infant School opened in the centre of the village on 12th January 1909 with 52 pupils and Charlotte Ethel Nott as Headmistress, assisted by Gertrude Newell. This left 115 children in the old school, to be taught by three teachers and a monitor.

In May 1910 the Parish Council were informed that the Education Authority intended to build a second new school, adjoining the Infant School, to accommodate 160 older scholars. The Vicar, Walter Covey-Crump proposed writing to the Board of Education to the effect that "as we are already saddled with the expense of a new Infant School yet unpaid for, that in the interests of the ratepayers we strongly recommend that the proposed new building be deferred. We consider it quite practicable to make existing buildings satisfactory and efficient".

One wonders what Mr Breed's feelings were at that time. As Headmaster he would clearly welcome a new school. As Clerk to the Parish Council he had to listen to their comments and minute them, but was officially not permitted to comment. In July he was asked to draw up a petition against the new school for presentation to the Board of Education. In October 1910 the Parish Council was informed that the petition had not been received within the three months legal limit, and on 5th December the Board of Education "saw no reason to interfere with the discretion of the Local Education Authority. The Board are satisfied that the existing Mixed School premises are inconvenient and unsatisfactory, and the site is insufficient to allow of any considerable enlargement of the school". Since the Stopsley rate payers were the most interested financial parties, it was agreed that a sub-committee of the Parish Council might meet in July 1911 with Mr Spooner, the Director of Education, and three members of the Education Committee to inspect the plans of the new school. At the same time they discussed the possibility of the County levying only half the cost on the parish, rather than three-quarters. As there was no decision about the village's share of the cost by

March 1912, they decided to write to Cecil Harmsworth, their M.P., who agreed to look into the matter if he were provided with the appropriate figures. The total cost of the new school, including the furniture, came to £2,470, to be repaid at three and a half percent over 30 years. The new Stopsley Council School opened on 10th September 1912. Standing in front of the Infant school, the new building was altogether superior and more convenient than the old one (except for Mr Breed, who would now have to walk a quarter of a mile to and from the school house each day!). It had a capacity of 158. By 1917 there were 189 children on the register! The debate about the cost seems to have subsided, and nothing more was recorded in the Parish Council minutes.

Mr Breed retired on 13th February 1925 after teaching at Stopsley for 32 years. He continued to take a keen interest in the schools. Every Christmas until his death he distributed newly minted pennies to the infants, and attended concerts and special functions, such as the opening of the Stopsley County Mixed School in 1940. He was Chairman of the Parish Council from 1928 until its demise in 1933. He died at the old school house at Swifts's Green on 31st December, 1954, aged 90.

Mr Breed's successor, Ralph Tom Whalley, enjoyed much popularity during his first ten years at the school, but by the mid-1930s problems began to develop which were not of his making, and were to cost him his Headship. During the 1930s Stopsley began to grow rapidly. Building in Ashcroft Road, Wigmore Lane, Putteridge Road, Hawthorn Avenue, Mixes Hill and the Round Green estates swelled the number of children entering the school. It should be remembered that it had been built for 158 scholars, and this was increased to 198 by partitioning off part of the hall. In October 1936 there were 298 children on roll and by August 1937 it had risen to 331.

In 1935 some 6 acres (2.5 hectares) of land off Ashcroft Road had been purchased from Messrs. W. and B. Hartop for £1,720, expressly for the purpose of building a new Stopsley School, but plans were constantly delayed. Mr Whalley was asked to accept the dreadful overcrowding and lack of furniture and equipment, which soon resulted in a breakdown in discipline, and general lethargy amongst the pupils and staff.

An unexpected Inspection in March 1938 was extremely critical of the school and the Headmaster. As a result fifty boys were moved into temporary accommodation at the Wesleyan Methodist Chapel opposite, and in modern parlance, a 'hit-squad' of three very experienced teachers was brought in to try and improve matters.

The War Years

By 1939 the new school, planned in 1935 and built by Messrs. Hansard Ltd for £18,092, was nearing completion, in a field between the Council school and the Ashcroft Road recreation ground. In July a double-shift system was planned to ease over-crowding in the infant and senior classes of the old school; half the children attending from 8.30 to 12.30 and the remainder from 1.00 to 5.00pm. The outbreak of War on the 3rd September threw affairs into disarray. The shift scheme was adapted to suit the whole school, since only 50% of the children were allowed in the building at one time, there being insufficient provision for their protection in the event of an air-raid.

Tom Whalley chose not to apply for the Headship of the new school. This was awarded to Leonard C. Benson, who commenced duties (in the old building) on 3rd June 1940. The move into the new building began on 25th July, and it was officially opened on 13th September 1940. It was designed to accommodate 370 children aged 7 to 14, yet when the autumn term began in 1940 that number had already been exceeded.

Consequently, the two youngest Junior classes had to be left behind in the old building, which was now designated Stopsley Infant School and had 189 of its own pupils.

Cooked school dinners were first provided for 59 infants and 92 junior children on the 17th May 1943, in order to allow mothers to take on war work whilst their children were at school all day. The meals were prepared in a central kitchen at Hitchin Road School, and then delivered by van, in steel containers, to be served by the prefects to the children of both schools in the Junior School hall. Eventually it was necessary to hold three sittings, virtually putting the hall out of school use for three hours each day, and longer on the many occasions when meal deliveries were late. A self-contained kitchen and dining hall, providing meals for both the Infant and Junior schools, was added in May 1961.

Gertrude Clarke remained the Infant Head until she retired in 1942, having completed 22 years, and improved the standard of infant teaching at Stopsley beyond all recognition. Miss Olive Branch succeeded her for the next seven years. When Dora Beighton took over in 1950 the school was considerably overcrowded due to the post-war 'bulge'. Infant numbers reached 411, but when Ramridge Infant School opened in 1951 Stopsley's numbers fell dramatically to 185. Mary Griggs, wife of the Ramridge Junior School Headmaster, ran the school from 1964 until 1971. The school was extensively modernised, with the addition of a prefabricated facade, in 1973, during Mary Thomson's Headship. Between 1981 and 1990 the school flourished under the guidance of Wendy Fry, who was sadly forced to retire due to ill health, and died shortly afterwards. Her Deputy, Sue Fuller, was entrusted with the difficult task of succeeding her. In 1997 the school had 180 pupils, including an active 4-plus and nursery unit.

Problems of Over-crowding

The new Stopsley Council Mixed School contained eight classrooms, four each for the Juniors and Seniors. An influx of evacuees in September 1941 inflamed accommodation problems, and two extra classes had to be taught in the Hall, and a hut was set-up in the playground for a third. By August 1944 there were 511 children at the school but desks for only 466. Although numbers dropped temporarily to 404 when many of the evacuees went home, the raising of the school leaving age to 15 in 1947 pushed numbers back up to 510, and 550 the following year.

Matters were eased somewhat when Stopsley Secondary Modern Boys' School opened in St Thomas's Road in September 1948 for boys of 11 and over, and four months later the senior Girls' School opened. Although this relieved matters temporarily for Mr Benson (at what was then renamed Stopsley Primary Mixed School), by 1951 the post-war birth explosion hit the school. New housing estates had proliferated in the Ramridge and Putteridge areas and their young children were pouring into the Stopsley schools. Mr Benson had classes of children in the Church Institute, the Baptist church and the Sacred Heart Church Hall. By 1953 there were 761 children on roll and by September 813!

In September 1954 Ramridge Junior School opened for years 3, 4 and 5 and Stopsley's numbers fell to 546, and from that time onwards it was possible to teach all the children on the village centre site.

For Leonard Benson, the early years at Stopsley must have been very difficult. Five years of wartime teaching with staff and equipment shortages were followed by nearly ten years of chronic overcrowding, and reorganisation after the creaming-off of the senior children in 1949. He weathered the storm, supported by a small core of loyal teachers which included Mabel Knight, Hilda Kiddy and Ivor David. Mr Benson retired after 26 years in 1966, and four years later married his former deputy, Miss Kiddy. They moved to Sway in Hampshire, where he died, aged 91, in 1992 and she followed, aged 81 in 1995.

Louis Martin, who succeeded Mr Benson in 1966, was born in East Bergholt, Suffolk, in 1917. At 23 he was conscripted into the Army and served in Egypt and North Africa. He was taken prisoner by the German Afrika Corp in April 1941 and was transferred to a prisoner-of-war camp in Italy until 1943, at which time he was moved to East Germany. He was released by British troops in March 1945. Whilst in Italy he developed an interest in teaching by working with other P.O.W.s, and upon demobilisation trained as a teacher at Wandsworth College. He taught at St Matthew's, Leagrave and Tennyson Road Junior Schools, before becoming Head of the latter in 1960. He was appointed Head of Stopsley Junior School in 1966 and retired in 1980.

Brian Gastell (1980-1993), and Michael Marsh have served successively as Headteachers. In January 1998 the school had 245 pupils, and intake numbers were once again increasing, necessitating more classroom accommodation.

The construction of a dual-carriageway through the centre of Stopsley in 1968 cut the Primary School grounds in two, leaving a substantial area of land, still the property of the school, between the new road and the bowling green on the north side of the Ashcroft Road Recreation Ground.

By the 1960s the Stopsley schools were enjoying a reputation for producing quality pupils, based on a firm foundation gained in the Infant School and nurtured in the Junior School. This flourished in the Secondary School under Dr Walter Roy.

Stopsley Secondary School was hastily built at Bury Farm in St Thomas's Road in response to the post-war birth explosion, and the extensive development of housing in the 1950s. The land had been bought for the purpose for £4,520 in 1937. It opened as Stopsley Secondary Modern Boys' School in September 1948 under the Headship of Harry J. Dawe, and a separate Secondary Modern Girls' School in February 1949 with Mary A. Millen as Head. Built initially for 200 pupils, numbers rose to a staggering 1,270 after the amalgamation of the two schools under Dr Walter Roy in 1960.

Born in Austria in 1925, Walter Roy came to school in England in 1938. He was evacuated the following year and then went to work after the war. He obtained an external B.Sc. Economics degree in 1951 whilst teaching in Welwyn Garden City. He became Headmaster of Old Bedford Road School in Luton in 1955. Four years later he moved to Stopsley School, and under his firm guidance it rapidly became one of the finest schools in the county, always in the forefront of educational developments. One of particular importance involved contacts with local industry. Stopsley initiated the scheme whereby senior pupils, particularly boys, whilst still at school spent a week at a time at Vauxhall Motors, Hayward Tyler, and occasionally with other employers whose feedback on the pupils was invaluable. At the time, this was an entirely new venture, although it is now commonplace.

Whilst at Stopsley Walter Roy obtained a Ph.D. for his study of *The Teachers' Union: 1950-1966*. He was a prominent member of the National Union of Teachers, serving on its Executive Committee from 1969 to 1986, and from 1976 was Chairman of its Education Committee. This brought him into largely confrontational contact with various national figures, in particular Margaret Thatcher, who was at that time Secretary for Education. In 1969 he moved from Stopsley to the Hewett School in Norwich, where his name is perpetuated in the Walter Roy Theatre. He was a founder of the International Sonnenberg Association and later its President. This is an association which promotes international understanding, particularly amongst young people. In December 1976, whilst Shirley Williams was the Secretary of State, he was awarded the CBE.

The opening of Ashcroft Secondary Modern Girls' School in 1960 seemed to have little impact on Stopsley's intake, though the effect of the closure of the Hitchin Road and Old Bedford Road Schools in 1967 was more noticeable. The Boys' department of Ashcroft Secondary Modern School opened with only one year of boys in 1966: the older lads continuing to go to Stopsley Secondary Modern School. For 26 years some of the old Bury Farm outbuildings were used as temporary classrooms and for a time housed a school 'farm'. The school was renamed Stopsley High School in 1966. In 1974 a new administrative block was built, incorporating a fine library. The opening of Putteridge High School on the eastern edge of the village in 1975 halved Stopsley High School's traditional catchment area and eased its crowded classrooms. During Peter Haydock's eighteen years as Head (1978-96) more children from High Town, Round Green and Bushmead came to Stopsley. In 1993 it was incorporated as a Grant Maintained School, with approximately 800 pupils. The present Head, Maureen Johnson, joined the school in 1996.

The Ramridge Schools

In 1946 construction work commenced on a large Council Estate of B.I.S.F. ('steel') houses between Ramridge End and Crawley Green Road. Young families soon proliferated, having the devastating effect on the accommodation at the Stopsley Schools already described. A special bus service carried children into Stopsley. There was parental opposition to a charge of 1½ d (less than 1p.) per single journey. A second Council Estate of more traditional brick houses was constructed between Ashcroft Road and Wigmore Lane in 1954. When Ramridge Infant School opened in 1951 its intake was mainly from Round Green, Crawley Green and the B.I.S.F. houses, whilst the Stopsley schools tried to accommodate the extra Wigmore children who remained in their catchment area until 1959.

Ramridge Infant School opened on 4th September 1951. Its Headmistress was Miss Joan Clarkson, aged 34, an enthusiastic graduate of Manchester University. The school immediately presented a challenge. It was built to hold 240 children in six classrooms. On the first day 205 children were admitted from Stopsley and Hart Hill Infant Schools, and a further 35 with no previous schooling. Twenty-five families were turned away. The following day extra chairs and tables were delivered and 26 more children were admitted. A hasty search for a teacher brought 69 years old, veteran Stopsley School teacher, Maud Hucklesby out of retirement. She was given a class of six year olds in the school medical room. The strain was to prove too much for her. After nine months she became ill and died exactly a year after her appointment.

By April 1952 the school had 340 pupils. It was officially opened on 6th May 1952 by Sir John Burgoyne OBE, Chairman of the Luton Education Committee. Two years later, as a result of the post-war baby 'bulge' the school was bursting at its seams with 459 children - most classes containing 50 pupils. Eight rooms were filled in the Infant School and two classes were in the incomplete new Junior School. Numbers dropped for a few years, only to peak again at 492 with the next bulge in January 1960. The situation was eased with the opening of Crawley Green Infant School in May 1960 and Sacred Heart Infant School two years later. Numbers then stabilised at around 320 pupils until the opening of the Wigmore and Someries Schools reduced the figure even further. In 1996, with nursery and 4-plus reception children, it stood at 270.

In January 1955 Ramridge was chosen as the school to pioneer an exciting, commercially backed, mathematical experiment called *Numbers in colour* or *Cuisenaire*. It was promoted and demonstrated by Dr Gattigno of London University's Institute of Education, and had been devised by M. Cuisenaire. A series of wooden rods of different lengths were associated with different colours, and were used to help early and slower learners to carry out basic arithmetical functions. Dr John Corbett, the Luton Borough Education Officer, and a number of H.M. Inspectors gave the scheme their blessing and it turned out to be a great success. It proved a very sound and useful introduction to mathematics if used properly. During the following ten years the school hosted a continual stream of visitors from schools, colleges and universities all over Britain and the Commonwealth. Miss Clarkson found herself lecturing and demonstrating from Bath to Birmingham, Oxford to Cambridge, and weekly for twelve months at the Putteridge Bury College of Education. By 1965 *Cuisenaire* was adopted throughout the majority of infant schools in Britain, and Ramridge gradually ceased to be the national showcase, much to the relief of most of the staff who were heartily sick of it! Attempts in 1966 by the same company to introduce a scheme called *Words in Colour* had little support at Ramridge.

In 1968 Miss Clarkson, influenced by her work at Putteridge Bury and supported by the College staff, introduced another innovation variously called 'vertical streaming' or 'family grouping'. Classes contained equal numbers of 5, 6 and 7 year old pupils who worked with the same teacher for three years, rather like a one-teacher village school. Cedric Griggs, Headmaster of Ramridge Junior School was not happy with the concept and considered that it caused reading standards to fall. A number of parents also expressed concern. Two Inspectors who tested the pupils in 1969 felt the results were 'neither startlingly good nor startlingly bad' and that it was too soon to tell. The class teachers working with family grouping liked it very much, provided class sizes were manageable: there was a continuity from one year to the next, not found with the traditional annual total change of class. A nursery for 4 year olds was established at the school in 1972. Joan Clarkson retired to Bromham in 1973, and Joyce Baldry took her place. Under the new Head the school gradually returned to more traditional methods and vertical grouping was phased out between 1974 and 1976. In 1981 Janet Tucker was appointed Headteacher, followed by Marie Heath (1989-1997). The school has since gone from strength to strength, adding a Nursery Unit for 3 year olds and a 4-plus reception unit in 1996, (officially opened in July 1997).

Ramridge Junior School was built to accommodate 320 pupils in six classrooms and two general purpose rooms. It was planned as an extension to the Infants' School, to which it was connected by a communal dining hall. Miss Ivy Christina Bates, formerly a Church of England missionary in Zanzibar, was the first Headteacher. The new building came into use on 7th September 1954. It was immediately filled to capacity with 387 children. All the 4th year pupils (Year 6) due to move to Ramridge, and some 2nd and 3rd year children, were retained at Stopsley Council School due to lack of space for them in the new building. Miss Bates had a staff of ten, with Mr Albert 'Billy' Williams as her Deputy.

The school was officially opened by Lady Zia Wernher of Luton Hoo on Wednesday 12th January 1955. It was still on the edge of open countryside and it is recorded that in its third week of existence Mr Williams took his nature study class to examine the wildlife of the hedgerows in Wigmore Lane.

On 24th February 1955 a cross-section of pupils and staff took part in a *Cuisenaire* demonstration organised by Dr Gattigno in the Infant School. Although Miss Bates supported Miss Clarkson's *Numbers in Colour* work, it was never very popular at the Junior School, and Cedric Griggs, Miss Bates' successor, actively opposed it.

When Ramridge Junior School opened for its second year in September 1955 places had to be found for 562 children. Four extra classes were accommodated in two new huts (the first of many) although new desks and chairs did not arrive until two weeks into term. The classes were divided into two halves for Assembly, as the hall could not accommodate the whole school at one time. At the end of the year Albert Williams left to become Head of Tennyson Road Junior School, and Mr W. Geoffrey Ley was appointed Deputy Head at Ramridge.

The exposed position of the school left it vulnerable to frequent burglaries and attacks of vandalism, which have continued to the present day, in spite of expensive security measures. In April 1956, for example, the football goal posts were broken-up and thrown into adjoining gardens.

School numbers rose to 651 in September 1956, and 691 a year later. Ramridge was hit badly by the influenza epidemic of 1957. On 27th September there were 166 children and 6 teachers absent; two weeks later the numbers had risen to 221 children, 6 teachers and the secretary. When the school opened for the autumn term in 1959 it had 727 children divided into 18 classes. It was wryly observed that the school had become a collection of temporary huts with a permanent annexe! Miss Bates retirement on 14th July 1960 was marked by a presentation to her by Alderman Bates, Chairman of the Education Committee. In poor health, she is affectionately remembered by pupils and teachers alike, for the flask of hot water that accompanied here wherever she went.

Ashcroft Secondary Modern School for Girls opened in September 1960 and 63 girls from Ramridge moved to the new building. 92 boys continued to go to Stopsley, whilst 28 children went to the Grammar, High and Technical schools.

On 1st September 1960 Cedric William Griggs became Ramridge Junior School's second Headteacher. He was a man with a considerable local and national reputation, being a J.P. and Chairman of the local Magistrates for many years. He was a member of the Burnham Committee which negotiated teachers' salary scales, a governor of the Cambridge Institute of Education and Putteridge Bury College of Education, and a member of the Primary II Programme Sub-Committee of the BBC (later called the Schools' Broadcasting Council). In spite of these commitments Griggs was a brilliant teacher and much preferred the classroom to his office. He knew exactly what went on inside his school, and was extremely supportive of his staff. Ramridge was seen as the ideal training ground for future headteachers. He was lucky to have strong support in the person of his Deputy, Gordon K. Toy (who would one day emulate him and become Chairman of the local Magistrates).

In September 1960 the Ramridge Junior School roll stood at 753 pupils divided between 18 classes. Fourteen of those classes had more than 40 pupils (three had 49). Mr Griggs was disappointed with parental response when, at the end of his first term, only a hundred parents attended the evening Carol Service. That was to change dramatically over the next ten years. Not only did he develop a strong home and school link, but also a closer co-operation with the local secondary schools.

In March 1961 the Police caught five boys who had broken into Ramridge Junior School, wrecking one classroom, damaging children's' exercise books and work, and stealing 28 fountain pens. Four were former pupils of the school then at Stopsley Boys' School, and one was still in the Ramridge 4th year. Dr Roy, the Stopsley Headmaster, sent his boys to Ramridge, where Cedric Griggs caned them and then set them to clean up their damage, humiliatingly observed by the junior school children.

In March 1961 the first television set was installed in the school. The following January the Mayor of Luton, George L. Matthews, and his wife visited the school and were interviewed about their work by eleven years old Paul Hancock. This was filmed by the BBC for a schools' television programme and broadcast on 26th January 1962.

Admission figures peaked at 800 in September 1961 when the school received 155 children from Ramridge Infant School and 53 from Crawley Green Infant School (opened 1960 under Mrs D. Bonner). This forced the creation of 20 classes, some with 48 pupils. In spite of the numbers the school established itself as a centre of excellence in many ways, often receiving visits from parties of student teachers in training. It was particularly prominent in sports and friendly rivalry developed with the larger schools in Luton. In Music the school choir won the Co-operative Society's Open Music Festival for Junior choirs in 1962, and the Recorder Ensemble was placed third.

School numbers fell for the first time in September 1962 when 65 children transferred to the newly opened Sacred Heart School (see page 168). An innovation in 1962 was the introduction of after-school French lessons for fourth year 'A' stream children. This was made possible by the presence of Edith Willis, a Belgian-born teacher, married to a Luton hat manufacturer, who taught the children to listen to the language and speak it as they did their native tongue, long before attempting to read and write it. With the help and support of Jill Naylor, French was soon being taught throughout most of the school and its success attracted the attention of teachers nationally and students in training, who made frequent visits to observe lesson in progress. As a result Mrs Willis took part in major courses and conferences, including one of three weeks duration in Paris. She also advised the BBC on the production of a schools French programme series.

Selective education was still in operation in 1964 when 11 boys and 2 girls passed the Eleven-plus examination for the Grammar and High Schools, and 5 girls and 1 boy for the Technical College. (In 1961 a total of 36 children had passed).

On 30th May 1964 the Lady Zia Wernher Spastic Centre was officially opened by Princess Marina, Duchess of Kent, in Ashcroft Road. For educational purposes the children and their teacher, Mrs B. Greenly, were placed on the roll of Ramridge Junior School. Thirteen children were admitted on the first day. Six weeks later a Fete was held at the school and £600 was raised for a swimming pool at the Zia Wernher Spastic Centre. It was opened by the childrens' television personality, Richard Hearne, 'Mr Pastry'.

In September 1964 81 Ramridge boys and 33 girls transferred to the Stopsley Secondary School, 49 girls to Ashcroft Girls' School and 19 to selective schools. On the Ramridge Junior School roll there were still 749 pupils. The following July saw the first of a series of seven annual school educational weeks in France. The Head and Deputy, accompanied Mrs Willis and Miss Naylor and 45 children to put their French lessons into practice. Travelling in different years by boat, aeroplane and coach, the parties stayed in a boarding school in Paris from where they visited Versailles, Fontainebleau and the Eiffel Tower, and in small groups put their lessons to good use in the local shops.

In February 1966 Messrs Pye Ltd. used the school to demonstrate closed-circuit television to George Humphries, Ron Swallow and Peter Hopkinson (Deputy Director of Education). Humphries was Principal of the new Putteridge Bury College of Education, and was keen to establish a television link between the College and a local primary school. It was considered that Ramridge would pose too many problems of installation, and thoughts were turned to incorporating it in Putteridge Junior School, under construction in 1967.

With the opening of the Boys' Department at Ashcroft Secondary School in 1966 it was possible to transfer 70 boys and 61 girls, reducing the number going to Stopsley to 37 pupils. The Ramridge roll still stood at 653, and was not to be substantially reduced until the opening of Someries Junior School in 1972. Cedric Griggs retired on 1st April 1971, and was presented with a radiogram from the children and staff. In September 1971 Emlyn Davies became Headteacher. Mr C. D. Powell succeeded him in 1982, followed by Hugh Wright from 1992 to 1997.

When Ashcroft Secondary Modern Girls' School opened in 1960 it was not possible to admit more than 300 girls to the lower three years. The number increased to 340 twelve months later. Mrs Dorothy Briggs was the first Headmistress. Ashcroft became Comprehensive in 1966, when the boys were phased into the school, one year at a time. In 1967 Hitchin Road and Old Bedford Road schools closed. A number of Hitchin Road School pupils transferred to Ashcroft swelling the numbers. At that time the school was situated in something of a wilderness, and pupils had little to occupy them during out of school hours. Consequently a strong and popular Youth Club was established at Ashcroft School. Mrs Briggs retired at Easter 1974 and her place was taken by Gerald Bowen until 1986. The following year Colin Griffiths became Headmaster. In 1993 the school became Grant Maintained and in October 1996 it attained Technology College status. At that time roll numbers had reached 974. Amongst the school's former pupils are the popular singer, Paul Young and the actor, Colin Salmon.

Putteridge College and Schools

In April 1966 Putteridge Bury College of Education opened in Putteridge Park as a non-residential teacher training college, in partial response to the dearth of teachers in Bedfordshire and Hertfordshire. It was initially directed towards mature students, many of whom might be teaching unqualified in schools, or to those suitably qualified ladies who wanted a change of career, perhaps after raising a family. These students were prepared for primary school work. Well-qualified ex-service personnel were also targeted for science teaching in secondary education. The College developed extensive contacts with schools in Luton, south Bedfordshire and north Hertfordshire. Children from Stopsley schools in particular, often visited the College for demonstration lessons and field work.

Putteridge Bury House had been acquired by Luton County Borough Council in 1965, together with 40 acres of grounds. It was administered jointly by the Hertfordshire and Luton local education authorities. The principal was George Humphries D.F.C., B.Sc., supported by a carefully chosen staff of 10 with primary school and teacher training experience. By 1974 this number had risen to 40. At its height the College provided training for 300 students per year. Luton lost its County Borough status in 1974 and the diversion of emphasis on teacher training turned towards colleges in Bedford. This led to the amalgamation to Putteridge Bury and the Luton College of Higher Education in 1978 and the end of teacher training in Luton. Putteridge Bury then became the Department of Business and Management Studies of Luton College, and eventually, in July 1993, part of the newly created University of Luton.

By the mid-sixties Stopsley's housing had spread eastwards, almost to the county boundary, and south to Darley Common. Lots of young families in the Putteridge area required school provision and as a result Putteridge Primary School opened to its first infant and junior pupils in September 1967. The school was of partially pre-fabricated construction, identical in design to Bushmead Junior School, (which also opened in 1967, in Stopsley parish, under Ivor C. Moyle), and cost £80,000. Alfred J. Mowbray was the first Headmaster. Eighteen months later a separate Infant School had been built, and Ruth Slack, the Headmistress, took her first 153 pupils on the 7th January 1969, with Mary Thomson as her Deputy. At that time Mr Mowbray received notice from the Education Office that his school would be closed for a day so that it could be officially opened as Putteridge Junior School! This happened jointly with the Infant School on 27th February 1969, the ceremony being performed by Madge Milner, Chairman of the Education Committee (and daughter of Luton historian William Austin), in the presence of the Mayor of Luton, Cyril Jephson and other local dignitaries.

The two schools were linked by their badges to Putteridge Bury College, where a number of the pupils' parents were training. Both schools and College utilised the *lion rampant* from the Sowerby and Clutterbuck family coats of arms. (Both families had lived at Putteridge Bury). They also worked closely together, the schools frequently providing pupils for work with the College students. Plans to link the two schools and College by closed circuit television were dropped due to financial restraints. Sadly, the Infant Head, Ruth Slack, died in 1980. Her successor, Jean Miller was appointed in September of that year, and retired in July 1998. Louis Fidge was Headmaster of the Junior School from 1987 to April 1990. He was succeeded by Steven Moreton in April 1991. Mary Rutherford acted as Head during the interregnum.

In 1972 part of a field called Purgemore, adjoining the Putteridge estate, was earmarked for a senior school. In September 1975 Putteridge High School opened, under the Headship of Albert Price, with some 300 pupils on roll. Due to its position between existing houses and the county boundary, the school site was restricted in size and there was insufficient room for a playing field. It was not possible to acquire green-belt land inside the adjoining Putteridge Park (Hertfordshire) for this purpose, so a compromise was reached when approximately 12 acres of arable land in Offley parish, adjoining Darley Common at the end of Selsey Drive, were acquired, some 450 metres walk from the school. With the opening of the Community Centre adjacent to the school on 3rd September 1977, (by Olympic swimmer Brian Brinkley) a fine Sports Hall, Swimming Pool and other sporting facilities became available to the school and the local community.

Putteridge High School soon became very popular, with an excellent academic record. Relaxation of rules controlling school catchment areas and application for entry from many parts of the Luton area, meant that the school rapidly became over subscribed. In September 1996 there were 1,125 pupils on roll: almost as many as at Stopsley High School in the 1960s. Putteridge High School took pride in the number of visually and physically impaired pupils who were fully integrated in the mainstream school. In 1986 David Young became Headmaster, to be succeeded in 1992 by the present Headteacher, Mrs Jacqueline Arkell.

Two further Primary Schools were built in Stopsley during the 1970s. Someries Junior School in Wigmore Lane opened in 1972 (officially March 1973) at a cost of £112,537. Initially it had four classrooms housing 65 children, but by 1996 there were 265 pupils on roll. David W. French was appointed as the first Headteacher, to be succeeded in turn by Louis Fidge (1983-1987), Peter Thorley (1988-1996) and Voytek Gabrys. A separate Infant School was opened in 1977 under the Headship of Mrs

Megan Mowbray. She retired in 1986, and Mrs S. Toyne was appointed as her successor the following year.

Wigmore Primary School was opened in Twyford Drive in 1982 with provision for children aged 5 to 11 years. Stephanie Noakes was the first Headteacher with an initial pupil entry of 60. After two years during which the school had been served by Brian Langley as acting head, David Hallett took over as Headteacher in April 1989. House building around the school had taken place at a tremendous rate during the 80s and early 90s. Consequently, by April 1996 there was a chronic accommodation problem, reminiscent of the Stopsley and Ramridge schools in the early post-war years. Almost 600 children were crowded into the school, many accommodated in prefabricated huts. In November 1997 an extension with five permanent classrooms was opened in an effort to remedy the situation.

Mention has already been made of the Lady Zia Wernher School in Ashcroft Road. which was built and funded by the Spastics Society (now renamed SCOPE). The first children were admitted on 11th May 1964. For educational purposes the pupils and teaching staff were initially on the roll of Ramridge Junior School. In 1974 the school became a centre for physically disabled children, between the ages of 2 to 11 years, in south Bedfordshire, under the auspices of the local Education Authority.

Luton Modern School

In September 1938 Luton Modern School for Boys opened its doors in Bradgers Hill Road, Stopsley. It had begun life in 1904 as the Luton Secondary School (for boys and girls), housed in a disused brewery at Park Square. A new building was opened in Park Square in May 1908, which was renamed Luton Modern School for Boys in 1919, after the girls' department had moved to a separate Girls' High School in Alexandra Avenue. The boys' school was grossly overcrowded, and students had to travel across the town to Chaul End Lane for playing field facilities.

A competition for designing a new school in the modern International style at Bradgers Hill had been won by Marshall and Tweedy, and it was built by Messrs. H.C. Janes. It was opened on 15th September 1938 by Alderman J.H. Staddon, High Sheriff of Bedfordshire. The Headmaster (since 1933) was Frederick E. Gauntlett, an unpopular appointment with both staff, boys and governors. He resigned in 1940 and was succeeded by Kenneth B. Webb. The school changed its name in 1944 to the Luton Grammar School, to avoid confusion with the proposed new secondary modern schools. Mr Webb remained at the school until it became the first Sixth Form College to open in England in 1966.

At the outbreak of war in 1939 the North-Western Polytechnic Boys' School from London was evacuated to Bradgers Hill, and the two schools co-existed until Whitsun 1945, sharing cramped accommodation, staff and fire-watching. Filled to capacity, classes were held in such diverse corners as the film projection room and cricket pavilion. The school started an Army Cadet corps, and part of the playing field was used for growing vegetables. A number of masters joined the armed services: one of them, Thomas Clark, a history teacher from Stopsley, died in a ground accident at his RAF station. Their places were taken by older men, some brought out of retirement. They included Dr F.W. Pick from Cologne who was, sadly, soon interned, and R.H. Squire who had at one time been a circus clown. In the immediate post-war years, parties of boys were seconded for weeks at a time to help out on local farms, like Manor Farm, with harvesting and potato picking, for which they were paid a small wage.

Throughout its existence, a steady stream of Stopsley boys made their way down Bradgers Hill to enjoy an excellent education at the Grammar School. A comparable number of girls had a much longer journey to the Girls' High School in Alexandra Avenue, outside the parish.

Amongst long serving masters at the Grammar School who lived in Stopsley and played a part in the life of the village were Cyril J. Godfrey (appointed 1918, became Second Master); Rex S. Clayton (1919, became Careers Master); Ronald Phillips (1927, English and Religious Studies) and John A. Cleaver (1926, Geography), who was also organist at St Thomas's Church.

The Luton Sixth Form College came into being in 1966, under the Headship of Brian D. Dance. From September 1966 to July 1968 it still contained Grammar School boys completing their 'O' level courses. Not until September 1968 did it house only Sixth Form students.

After becoming the Luton Sixth Form College, enormous structural changes took place and the original Modern School building grew almost beyond recognition, with little regard for the architects' original design. Today many boys and girls from the three Stopsley high schools complete their local education at the Bradgers Hill college.

Any history of local education will inevitably concentrate on buildings, staff and pupils. No study of Stopsley's schools would be complete without the mention of two exceptional ancillary workers who received MBE awards from the Queen for outstanding work as road-crossing patrol or "Lollipop" ladies. In 1995 Margaret Wiggett was rewarded for 30 years duty outside Stopsley Infant School, and in 1996 Violet Chater received her medal after completing more than 37 years at Ramridge School. Both ladies have continued with their work since the awards.

The provision of adult education and evening classes in Stopsley has been discussed in Chapter 8 on page 97.

Chapter 15

Stopsley at Work

The Brickmakers

The origins of modern brickmaking in England are closely linked to south Bedfordshire and the parish of Stopsley. Although the Romans used bricks, the art of making them was forgotten in Britain until the 15th century when it was reintroduced. Although we have no documentary evidence, one of the earliest surviving brick buildings in the country is Someries Castle, on the southern edge of our parish, which can be dated to about 1448. This is a remarkably sophisticated building for its period, with decorative corbelling at the main entrance arch and a cleverly constructed newel staircase. Only a ruined gatehouse and chapel survive, the remainder having been demolished in 1742. Terence P. Smith, who has written extensively on Someries Castle, believes that it was built by a small group of itinerant craftsmen, perhaps of Flemish or German origin, who were based somewhere on the Essex-Hertfordshire borders. In all probability clay for the bricks were dug from pits which can still be traced about 100 metres south-east of the present ruins, and were fired in temporary clamps. These produced mainly orange-red bricks, though a few vitrified in the firing, turning them blue-black. These latter were used to create decorative patterns on the building.

The Will of Thomas Butterfield of Stopsley made in 1720 refers to 'John Chalkley, brickmaker', but we do not know where he worked. It may have been at Butterfield's Green, mentioned below.

The earliest positive evidence we have for brickmaking in the parish is the Tithe Apportionment Map of 1844 which shows 'Brick Kiln Field' just to the north of the Hart Lane and Crawley Green Road junction, close to where St Anne's church stands. The actual kiln seems to have been defunct by the time the map was produced.

Earlier in this book I have described the occurrence of scattered pockets of brickearth in swallow holes across Stopsley parish and west on the hilltops around Caddington and Whipsnade. It is uncertain how the brickmakers discovered these pockets, since they are overlain by thick deposits of clay-with-flints. Whilst a trench for a water pipeline was being dug on the south side of Hayes Wood in 1992, archaeologists found a number of scoops dug into the clay, at least a hundred years ago, which may best be interpreted as trial holes, seeking brickearth. Other apparent trial pits were observed in the field opposite the row of cottages at Butterfield's Green called Great Pasture. One produced the base of an early medieval stone mortar.

The 1861 Census describes Francis Foster of Stopsley as a farmer and brickmaker. He owned a triangle of land between Hitchin Road and Bury Road (St Thomas's Road). In 1868 he sold his house (later *The First and Last*) that was occupied by Samuel Impey to William Lucas, the Hitchin Brewer for £450. It is possible that Foster dug the first clay pit in Bury Road which was certainly in use soon after 1860.

It was worked by Facer and Impey from about 1895 to 1901. The Ordnance Survey map shows the pit flooded at that time. John Facer and Son owned the site until around 1920. It has now been built over, and the bungalows at 38-42 St Thomas's Road, stand in the hollow created by the pit. A second much larger series of pits lay a short distance north-west of Facer's pit, at Bleak Hall Green, under what is now the municipal caravan site (laid out in 1963) adjoining the Stopsley Regional Sports' Centre. These pits, too, were in use by the 1870s and continued to operate until mid-1939 and the beginning of the Second World War. Owned by the Sowerby family at Putteridge Bury, they were worked by George Powdrill and Son Ltd. from at least 1914. Most of the clay pits, once abandoned, lay open for years. They were known to the local children as 'The Drinkers'. There they caught newts and tadpoles in the spring, and skated when they were frozen over in the winter. The pits were up to 40 feet (12 metres) deep and very dangerous, with edges suddenly shelving steeply downwards. On 18th May 1916, Edward Ashby, aged 8, drowned there.

The Mixes Hill clay pits, now covered by Birchen Grove and Sunningdale, were being dug by 1879, and according to Worthington G. Smith became disused in 1896. Former brickmaker George Souster said they were worked by the Scargills. It is worth noting that no brickmakers names are recorded for Stopsley in any Census before 1861. At that time Francis Foster (aged 39) is registered as a farmer and brickmaker, and his neighbours James King (25) and William Lawrence (26) as brickmakers. In 1871 the name of William Lawrence recurs, together with George Bunn (28), Alfred Garrat (37), Turner Whittemore (25) and George Whittemore (19), all living close to the village centre in Hitchin Road. Six names are recorded in 1881: George Whittemore, William Lawrence, Frederick Summerfield (26), Alfred Garratt (47), George Wiseman (20) and Robert Ford (52). By 1891 the number has dropped to three Stopsley residents: Alfred Garratt, George Wiseman and Arthur Walker (34). The Marriage Register of St Thomas' church records the names of six brickmakers at the beginning of the 20th century: Arthur William Plummer in 1903, George Whittemore (1904), James Whittemore (1905) and Frederick Summerfield, Alfred Plummer and Charles Cooper in 1906. The appearance of many brickworks on the Bedfordshire Chilterns between 1860 and 1900 is probably the result of the rapid expansion of hat factories and domestic housing in the Luton and Dunstable area, and the relaxation of taxes on brick and tile sizes. *Kelly's Directory* (1885) lists Smart Bros. as making bricks at an unidentified works in Stopsley.

The Turner's Knoll brickworks (Mardle's) at Round Green, situated in the triangle formed by Hitchin Road, Turner's Road and Ramridge Road, are the best recorded, since a series of drawings and photographs survive in Luton Museum, taken in 1909 for the archaeologist Worthington G. Smith. They show a circular domed down-draught kiln with a tall square chimney and a horse-operated trough-roller, as well as rows of drying 'hacks'. Round Green was worked by Alfred Mardle, a noted Luton builder. The works came to an end around the beginning of the First World War, possibly reflecting the steady national decline in house building from 1901. Smith records that whilst he was investigating the clay pits 'the sanitary authorities of Luton were all the while emptying the town refuse into the diggings to fill up the holes as soon as they were made.'

The fifth Stopsley brick and tile works was situated at Ramridge End, at the junction of Ashcroft Road and Turner's Road North, where the Lady Zia Wernher School now stands. The pits were described as being the deepest in the area, 'deep enough to take a double-decker bus.' They were filled with Luton refuse during and just after the 1939-45 War, and now lie buried beneath the Sacred Heart School playing field. The kilns stood at the Ashcroft Road end of the site in the forecourt of what is now the Lady Zia Wernher School.. Like the other Stopsley works, it began operating around 1870 and ceased prior to the Second World War. First worked by the Facer family, it was acquired in turn by Henry Impey, George Bartlett and eventually Sidney Bennett and Son Ltd. The latter was responsible for making the large quantity of high quality bricks between 1925 and 1927 needed to build 'Friends House', the Headquarters of the Society of Friends, in Euston Road, London. H. Lidbetter, the architect, considered that Stopsley 'grey' bricks complimented to perfection the Portland stone detailing of his Georgian design. Although the bricks were at first transported to Luton Railway Station by horse and cart, by 1925 Bennet's had acquired a Ford truck.

A map of 1879 shows the site of a brick and tile works at Eaton Green, (at TL 114217) to the south of Stopsley parish, which was covered with woodland by 1901. There is no known record of its owners, who might have been the Wood or Mardle families who successively owned the adjacent farm.

Although the Stopsley brickworks produced excellent handmade bricks that were used in many parts of Luton and its hamlets, these small works with a handful of employees and sharp, flinty clay, found it hard to compete with the mechanised Fletton brick industry of mid-Bedfordshire. The deeper bed of Oxford Clay, exploited by B. J. Forder (of Luton) at Wootton Pillinge and Elstow from 1900, produced raw material which could be crushed and pressed into brick shapes, fired almost immediately, used two thirds less fuel, and was far less subject to cracking and wastage. By 1910 Forders sold 48 million bricks a year at 13 shillings (65p.) per thousand. Stopsley bricks cost around 38 shillings (£1.90p.) per thousand at the same time.

In 1965 the writer tape-recorded an interview with George Souster, then aged 89, a former brickmaker at St Thomas's Road brickworks. Mr Souster began working at Stopsley in 1903 when he was 27. He recalled that in the 1920s and 1930s eight men were employed. They all dug clay from just before Christmas until April. From Easter until September five of them were brick makers and three fired kilns. For two months in the autumn the men were laid-off and did farm work. Workers hours were from 5 am to 9 pm in the summer with an hour's break. On Saturday the men finished at noon or 1 pm depending on the amount of work. The methods used for clay digging and brick making at Stopsley had changed little from medieval times. It was extremely difficult and hard work. George Souster quoted an old gypsy as saying "It's hard work leaning on the gate looking at it!" The clay was dug by hand using picks and spades whilst it was wet. It was then left in piles to be weathered by the rain and frost. This broke it down and softened it. After Easter the brick making could begin. First the clay had to be puddled: it was softened into a dough-like paste by adding water and stirring with spades or treading with the feet. A simple machine called a pug-mill was often used for this task, but when it was tried at Mixes Hill and Stopsley it didn't work satisfactorily. Apparently it packed the clay too tightly. At this stage the clay seems to have been stored in barrels. Souster spoke of forty barrels being turned four times to keep it soft. Eventually the clay was put onto a moulding table and pulled and rolled like dough, before being chopped into short lengths which were 'thumbed off': pressed into the sanded brick moulds, which were simple hollow oblong wooden frames which had a removable stock at the base This stock had a raised panel which produced the sunken frog on the brick: the frog is the hollow indentation in the top of the brick. A sharp knock released the brick from the mould The green (i.e. unbaked) bricks were coated with a mixture of road sweepings, dust and lime, and then placed on a flat topped barrow and wheeled away to be slowly dried on wooden racks or 'hacks'. They were loosely covered with wooden shutters when it rained. This drying process might take three or four weeks depending on the weather. When pronounced ready for firing, the bricks were loaded into the coal-fired kiln. They were then subjected to three days of slow baking followed by three days of intense heat, and then left for a week to slowly cool down. Drifting smoke and the smell of tar pervaded the village during the summer months. As the fires cooled they gave off sulphur fumes. In October 1913 the Parish Council were asked to consider the 'abominable nuisance caused by the smoke from the brickyards.' At that time there was little they could do, and no action was taken. There were two kilns at St Thomas's Road, both sunk into the ground with about 2.5 metres standing above. One kiln was always in use from April till August or September. Flames shot skywards from the adjoining chimneys when the kilns were being heated-up. It is believed that it was the possibility of these flames being seen at night by enemy aircraft, and used to guide them to military targets, that led to the closure of the works in 1939.

A good workman could make between 800 and 1000 bricks a day. George Souster claimed to make 1100. He was paid 6s.6d. per 1000 bricks, plus 6d. for each extra hundred. (i.e. 33p. per 1000). To make a 1000 bricks required 50 tons of clay. At its height the St Thomas's Road works produced about 20,000 bricks each week, and some 400,000 during the season. One man might make 100,000 a year. Souster claimed that the 'blue' clay from Stopsley produced the hardest bricks in the county. The traditional Stopsley and Luton 'grey' bricks get their silver grey, often lightly vitrified, finish from the presence of lime in the brickearth. The Stopsley brickworks also produced a range of colours from plum to orange-red, due to the abnormally high amount of iron oxide in the clay. Colour could be controlled by the length and heat of firing, the amount of oxygen present and a variety of 'secret' formulae. Builders often liked to use local greys with rubbed red brick. Good examples exist in the old Baptist Chapel (1902) and Marsom Place cottages in St Thomas's Road (built by George Duberly in 1903), the oldest parts of Stopsley Infant School (1909 and 1912), Jutland House (next to the school) and the wall around Putteridge Park, (although these might have come from the brickworks between Cockernhoe and Tea Green). Further afield, I have already mentioned the 'Friends House' in Euston Road, London of 1927.

In conclusion, mention must be made of a lime works that existed on the sharp bend, halfway up Bradgers Hill road. It does not appear to have been in existence when the Tithe Award map was drawn in 1844, and we do not know when it ceased to function, although it was possibly before 1879, when the large-scale Ordnance Survey map marks a lime kiln, apparently derelict. The grass covered hollows have provided an assault course for numerous generations of children. Lime was used in the brick making process, giving the grey bricks a silvery shine. It was also used for a variety of building and agricultural processes. Worthington G. Smith also refers to 'two small chalk pits that lie to the right and left of the lane that runs from Round Green to Ramridge End'. These are now built over, but lay on either side of Turners Road North, just east of the footbridge over Vauxhall Way. They probably provided lime for the Ramridge End brickworks. John Deller of Round Green was recorded as a lime burner in the 1891 Census return.

The Growth of Luton Airport

It was in 1934 that Luton Corporation began to show an interest in establishing an aerodrome near the town. The first proposal was to site it on Claycroft field (now the Regional Sports Centre) but the air currents were unsuitable. Instead an area of farmland in the south on the Stopsley-Hyde boundary seemed ideal for the flying requirements of the day. To that end in 1936 an initial 329½ acres of land were acquired for £32,950 from Benjamin and William Hartop at Eaton Green Farm. Its green meadows were soon to provide a runway, and its buildings became offices and workshops. Approximately 40 acres of land adjoining Kimpton Road were purchased from Davis Estates Ltd. to increase the area to 370 acres. At the same time the Corporation attempted to attract related industries to the site and Percival Aircraft Ltd., who made a three-seater aircraft called the 'Mew Gull', were the first to move into extensive new hangars at Luton early in 1937.

The Air Ministry gave official approval to the site in 1937, and soon afterwards Mr. R.H. Rushton was appointed as the first Aerodrome Manager. He was based in the farmhouse, which became Airport Headquarters, whilst the stables were destined to be occupied by the Luton Flying Club. A licence was awarded in April 1938, and three months later, on 16th July, Luton Aerodrome was officially opened by the Rt. Hon. Sir Kingsley Wood, Secretary of State for Air, accompanied by Luton's M.P. Dr Leslie Burgin, the Minister of Transport.. An impressive air display marked the occasion, which included a demonstration flight by Capt. Edgar Percival of a 'Mew Gull' monoplane made in his Luton factory, and Amy Johnson (the first woman to fly solo from England to Australia - in 19 days in 1930) glided in from the London Gliding Club at Dunstable.

The aerodrome had a grass runway until 1959, (on which John Cunningham safely carried out an emergency landing of the 'Comet' prototype). The original terminal was a wooden building, with passenger accommodation in the former Eaton Green Farm outbuildings. The first commercial flights began in 1939, but were almost immediately halted by the outbreak of war.

Percival Aircraft Ltd. immediately turned their attention to producing aircraft for the Royal Air Force: mostly trainers and small transport vehicles. Percival's built more than a thousand 'Proctor' and 'Preceptor' aircraft which were used for wireless and navigation training by the R.A.F. and Fleet Air Arm, and 1,300 twin-engined 'Airspeed Oxfords' for advanced flying training. They were also sub-contracted to produce 245 'Mosquito' fighters for de Havilland.

The flight testing of Napier aero-engines transferred from Northolt to Luton in 1940 with Mr C.L. Cowdrey as Manager and Mr Frank S.Lester responsible for the testing activities. During the 22 years of its existence the Napier Flight Test Establishment carried out thousands of test flights not only in support of Napier engines but also in investigating the serious problem of aircraft icing. Perhaps the highlight of these years was on 28th August 1957 when Mike Randrup and Walter Shirley took off from Luton in a Canberra aircraft additionally powered by Napier 'Scorpion' rocket motors and secured for Britain the World Altitude Record of 70,310 feet over the Isle of Wight. Frank S. Lester, a Stopsley resident for many years, was three times Mayor of Luton. In 1939, when a Sergeant in the R.A.F., he was given a special release to undertake his work at Luton Airport.

The only operational unit to be based at Luton during the War was B Flight of 264 Squadron, a day and night fighter unit, which flew Bolton Paul Defiants from Luton in the autumn of 1960.   In view of its military importance, all the aerodrome buildings were heavily camouflaged with khaki and green paint and netting.   Even so, they soon attracted German bombers.   A daylight raid during the afternoon of 27th August 1940 resulted in a string of bomb craters across the runway, but missed the factory buildings. At midnight on 24th September the Germans dropped two parachute mines, one of which damaged part of the Percival factory and wrecked a number of cottages in Eaton Green Road.   The second floated down to the main assembly shop and lodged in the roof.   It failed to explode.   Had it done so, the result would have been catastrophic, and resulted in a massive loss of life.   The two men who took charge of the dangerous situation, John Cunningham, Percival's security office, and Inspector Albert J. Sear of the Luton Police, were both awarded George Crosses.   The bomb was safely defused next morning by a Naval expert, Lieut. Armitage.

In 1944 Percival's was acquired by the Hunting Group of Companies and Hunting-Percival Aircraft Ltd. came into being.   They designed and built civilian and R.A.F. training aircraft at Luton until the early 1960s.   They then became part of the British Aircraft Corporation until 1966.   Other engineering and travel industries moved to Luton and a number still continue to use the airport site.

Extra land had been acquired for the aerodrome during the War and numerous hangars erected.   In the late 1940s Luton Council acquired these, with an eye to the future expansion of the site.   A major problem to development was the lack of Customs facilities.   In 1951 the airport was given a one year trial of such facilities. This was conditional on there being sufficient traffic passing through the terminal.   The trial failed and the facility was withdrawn.   During the next ten years Luton gradually increased its international traffic, and in 1960 the airport was granted full international status with 24 hours Customs facilities.   The following year a new terminal building was opened, to be replaced in 1966 by the present building.   This was soon found to be inadequate, and it was extended, reconstructed and enlarged in 1985.   By 1988 Luton was able to cope with 2,911,493 passengers and 68,371 aircraft movements.   In 1959 the first concrete runway was laid down, 5,432 feet long (1655m), 150 feet wide (46m) and 10 inches thick (25cm).   It took 7 months to build.   It was necessary to extend it to 7,000 feet (2133m) in 1964.   Radar was installed in the same year.   The first wooden control tower had been replaced in 1952.   That, too, was superseded in 1995 by a tower 164 feet high (50m), the highest in Britain.

For many people Luton Airport is synonymous with package holidays which began in the 1950s.   Charter flight firms such as Euravia (later Britannia), Autair (later Court Line), British Midland, Monarch and Dan-Air all flourished at Luton.   Occasionally there were major catastrophes, such as the collapse of Court Line in 1974.   Passenger numbers peaked at Luton in 1988-89, (see above).   After that there was a steady decline partly explained by cheaper competition elsewhere.   In 1993-94 the annual passenger figures had fallen to 1,836,183 and aircraft movements to 36,853.   Since then there has been a steady rise, with 3.4 million passengers in 1997 and a figure of 5 million passengers predicted for 2000.   There has also been a steady increase in freight traffic since the early 1980s.

This is not the place to say more about Luton Airport.   A definitive history has yet to be written.

VICARS OF ST THOMAS'S CHURCH, STOPSLEY
Church Consecrated: 2nd June, 1862

Year of Institution	Vicar	Years of Service	Patron
1861	Samuel Cumming	10	Colonel Sowerby
1871	Albert Aitkins	1	Revd. J. Gilman
1872	Thomas Henry Papillon	3	"
1875	James Joseph Frew (died1876)	1	"
1876	Alexander Joseph Schwartz	1	"
1877	George Henry Turner	2	"
1879	John Finch-Smith	4	M. N. Battenshaw
1882	Paul Marland Walker	11	"
1893	John H. Campbell-Cowan	5	Archdeacon Bathurst
1898	Arthur E. Love	5	"
1903-10	Walter W. Covey-Crump	8	Bishop of Ely
1911	Elleston G. Alderson	3	"
1914	G. H. C. Shorting	5	Bishop of St Albans
1919	Ernest T. Leslie	3	"
1922	E. Denby Gilbert	16	"
1938	Albert H. W. Cleaver	8	"
1946	Henry Thomas Pimm	6	"
1952	Gordon P. Owen (to 1955)	3	"
1956	Clifford F. Pollard	5	"
1961	Francis A. Estdale (Canon, 1990)	33	"
1995	David Alexander		"

STOPSLEY BAPTIST MINISTERS

Revd. Edwin H. Robertson	1938
Revd. Alan Funnell	1942
Revd. W. J. Crispus-Jones	1947
Revd. Ronald Rust	1951
Revd. S. A. Rooke	1954
Revd. W. R. Whitfield	1961
Revd. Norman Green	1970
Revd. Steven Gaukroger	1981-1995
Revd. Brian Doyle	1997

Mr William Hogg (Associate Minister) 1983 - 1988
Mr Andrew Hickford (Youth Minister) 1986 - 1996
Revd. David Warren (Associate Minister) 1990 -

LXVa: On 10th September 1912 Stopsley Council Mixed School opened its Senior department in the centre of Stopsley. This picture of all the pupils and staff was taken a week later. The boys are in their playground on the left and the girls segregated to the right. The school was built in front of the Infant department which had opened in 1909 (see plate XXIVb) (*Author's Collection*)

LXVb: On 18th July 1947 lads from Stopsley School descended on a farm at Northiam, near Rye in Sussex for their Harvest Camp. Accompanied by Headmaster L.C. Benson and parents, they picked fruit for three weeks as part of the government's 'lend a hand on the land' campaign. (*Tilly Hodgson*)

LXVIa: Stopsley Secondary Modern Boys' School took its first pupils in September 1948, and the Girls' School followed in January 1949. This picture shows some of the girls at the official opening of both schools by Minister of Education, George Tomlinson, on 25th May, 1949. (*Luton News*)

LXVIb: Leonard Benson was Headmaster of Stopsley Council (later County Primary) School for 26 years. His 21st anniversary on 21st June, 1961, was marked with presentations of camping equipment from his pupils. The House Captains in this picture (left to right) are Lesley Walker, Jill Burridge, Jennifer Robbins, David Hamel and Michael Jack. Hilda Kiddy (later Mrs Benson) stands to the left of Mr Benson. (*Luton News*)

LXVIIa: The separate Boys' and Girls' departments of Stopsley Secondary Modern School amalgamated in 1960 under the Headship of Walter Roy.   The school enjoyed considerable sporting success.   Here Dr Roy (on the right) stands with the Junior Cross-Country team in 1960.   Alan Slough (front row, left) became a professional footballer, playing for Luton Town from 1963-73, Fulham 1973-76 and Peterborough United. (*Luton News*)

LXVIIb: Speech Day at Stopsley Secondary Modern School in 1962.   Ronald Swallow, former Headmaster of Maidenhall School is presenting football trophies to Bruce Rioch and Ken Bevis Rioch went on to a successful career in football, which included playing for Luton Town, Aston Villa, Derby County, Everton, Birmingham, Sheffield United and Scotland, and managing Bolton. Middlesborough, Millwall, Arsenal and Norwich. (*Luton News*)

LXVIIIa: In 1955 Ramridge Infant School pioneered a revolutionary new method of teaching mathematics using coloured wooden rods, called *Cuisenaire*.   For the next ten years the school was open house to visitors from all over the world anxious to learn about the system.   By the time that this photograph was taken of Terry Gittins and Elizabeth Greaves using the rods in 1965, the method was soundly established.   (*Luton News*)

LXVIIIb: The staff of Ramridge Junior School in 1955.   *Back row:* Gordon Toy; Edna Mills; Joan Williams; Jose Commerford; Mabs Cleaver; Derek Tassey; Eric Cousens; *Front row:* Joyce Plummer; Albert (Billy) Williams; Ivy Bates; Olive Wilson; Jean Coombes-Goodfellow   (*Author's Collection*)

LIXa: Ramridge Junior School Choir with their Conductor, Neil Marsden, won the Co-operative Society's Open Music Festival for Junior Choirs in 1962. (*Luton News: Luton Museum Collection*)

LIXb: Two Stopsley Lollipop Ladies (crossing patrol wardens) received MBEs for their services to the safety of school children in the parish. Margaret Wiggett at Stopsley Infant School in 1995, and Violet Chater at Ramridge Infant and Junior School in 1996. (*James Dyer; Luton News*)

LXa: Like a scene from *Lord of the Flies*! Children from Stopsley schools often took part in demonstration lessons at Putteridge Bury College of Education. In 1970 pupils from Putteridge Junior School empathised with their prehistoric ancestors by constructing an 'iron age' hut, weaving, potting, cooking and casting metal axes, in the College grounds. (*Author's Collection*)

LXb: Luton Modern School for Boys opened in Bradgers Hill Road in September 1938. This aerial view, taken at that time, shows the award-winning design by the architects, Marshall and Tweedy. The extensive use of glass created problems during the War years, when blast walls had to be built and the windows criss-crossed with adhesive cloth tape to restrict flying glass. Air raid shelters were constructed beside the curve of the cycle shed on the right. Part of the playing field was ploughed up to plant potatoes. Traces of Dancer's Farm were still visible at the bottom of the picture. (*Author's Collection*)

LXIa: The two photographs on this page, enlarged from tiny snapshots, give an impression of the derelict St Thomas' Road brickworks about 1944.   The flooded clay pits, known as the Drinkers, were a favourite spot for catching tiddlers and sliding on the winter ice. (*Walter Rainbow*)

LXIb: It is possible to make out the wooden gantries along which barrows were pushed, in order to lift metal-bound buckets of clay from the pits below.   The pits rapidly became derelict after 1940, overgrown with hawthorn, and eventually back-filled with refuse.   Today a Caravan Park covers the site. (*Walter Rainbow*)

LXII: An aerial view of the centre of Stopsley village in 1994. In the foreground is the newly extended Working Mens' Club. Beyond are Jansel House and the Barratt office block on the sites of Pond Farm and Tithe Cottage respectively. In the distance are the new Baptist Church and Stopsley High School, and the Regional Sports' Centre to the far right. This photograph shows the heart of the village, and although a little remains, most of it has changed since the map of 1881 (on page 100) was drawn up. *(Herald and Post photograph)*

Select Bibliography

(*B.H.R.S.* = Proceedings of the Bedfordshire Historical Record Society)

Agar, N.E.   The Bedfordshire Farm Worker in the Nineteenth Century, *B.H.R.S.*
   Vol. 6 (1981)
Austin, W.   *The History of a Bedfordshire Family* (1911)
Austin, W.   *The History of Luton* (1928)
Balch, A.E.   *A Century of Methodism* (1908)
Barrow, T.J.   *The Story of the Bedfordshire and Hertfordshire Regiment* (1986)
Bell, P.   Bedfordshire Wills, 1484-1533, *B.H.R.S.* Vol. 76 (1997)
Brown, J.E.   Selections from Jury Lists, *B.H.R.S.* Vol. 4 (1917)
Bunker, S. *et al*   *The Changing Face of Luton* (1995)
Bushby, D.W.   The Ecclesiastical Census, 1851, *B.H.R.S.* Vol. 54 (1975)
Cirket, A.   English Wills, 1498-1526, *B.H.R.S.* Vol. 37 (1957)
Cobbe, T.   *A History of Luton Church* (1899)
Cox, A.   *Brickmaking: A History and Gazetteer* (1979)
Currie, M.L.   *Hospitals in Luton and Dunstable: An Illustrated History* (1982)
Davis, F.   *Luton, Past and Present* (2nd enlarged Edn., 1874)
Dony, C.M. and J.G.   *The Wild Flowers of Luton* (1991)
Dony, J.G.   *A History of the Straw Hat Industry* (1942)
Dony, J.G.   *A History of Education in Luton* (1970)
Dyer, J.   'Excavation of two barrows at Galley Hill' *Beds. Archaeological Journal*
   Vol. 9 (1974)
Dyer, J.   *Story of the Stopsley Schools* (1989)
Dyer, J. and Dony, J.G.   *The Story of Luton* (3rd Edn., 1975)
Fisher, J.S.   *People of the Meeting House* (n.d. 1988?)
Fowler, G.H.   Calendar of the Roll of the Justices on Eyre, 1247, *B.H.R.S.* Vol. 21
   (1939)
Gaydon, A.T.   The Taxation of 1297, *B.H.R.S.* Vol. 39 (1959)
Godber, J.   *History of Bedfordshire* (1969)
Hepple, L.W. & Doggett, A.M.   *The Chilterns* (1992)
Hunnisett, R.F.   Bedfordshire Coroners' Rolls, *B.H.R.S.* Vol. 41 (1961)
Lea, V.   'Luton Airport' in *Legacies* (1993)
Lunn, J.   *The Register of the Guild of the Holy Trinity* (1984)
Madigan, T.J.   *The men who wore straw helmets* (1993)
Marshall, L.M.   The Rural Population of Bedfordshire, 1671-1921, *B.H.R.S.*
   Vol. 16 (1934)
Richer, A.F.   *Bedfordshire Police, 1840-1990* (1990)
Rimmer, E.   *The Story of the First-Fifth Bedfords* (1917)
Smith, W.G.   'Human Skeletons of Palaeolithic Age' [Mixes Hill] *Man*, Vol. 6
   (1906)
Smith, W.G.   'Notes on the Palaeolithic Floor near Caddington' [Round Green]
   Archaeologia, Vol. 67 (1916)
Souster, G.C.   *A History of the Stopsley Baptist Church, 1869-1969* (1969)
V.C.H.   *Victoria County History of Bedfordshire*, 3 vols. (1904, 1908, 1912)
Welch, E.   Bedfordshire Chapels and Meeting Houses, 1672-1901, *B.H.R.S.*
   Vol. 75 (1906)

Index

194

197

199

Sewell field, 34
Sewerage, 66-8, 73, 185
Sharp, Mr. 141
Shaw family, 127, 130, 132, 136,
Charles Hugh, 102, 127; George,
65, 127; John, 127, 132; Lionel,
127, 132; Patrick, 2, 127, 132
Shaw, Mr. (Architect), 86
Shaw's Meadow, 87, 89
Sheep, 123-4
Shelborne, (Shilbarn, Shilborn),
Thomas, 33, 37, 45, 124
Shepherd and Flock, 13
Shillington, 41, 131, 163
Shires, 16
Shirley, Walter, 188
Shoosmith, Frederick, 92, 170
Shops, 52, 82, 119-21; Shopping
Centre, 118-119
Shore, A.M., 121
Shorting, Revd. G.H., 86, 101,
152-3, 166
Sibley, John, 34
Sickness, 48, 62, 69, 102, 170,
178
Simpkins, Ernest, 120, 121
Sims, Alec, 106
Skefko, 85
Skeggs, Elizabeth, 147
Skipwith, Thomas, 145
Slack, Ruth, 181
Slaughter's Wood, (Slater's), 8,
9, 94
Slipe, The, 149
Slough, Alan, 90
Small Holdings, 81, 86
Smart Bros., 18
Smith, Albert, 103, 104; George,
170; Henry, 91; Hughey, 119;
James, 47; John, 139; Joseph,
120; Kathleen, 120; P., 103, 104;
Samuel, 42; Terrence P., 184;
Thomas, 31; Thomas, 45, 143;
William, 45; Worthington G.,
12-13, 14, 185, 187; W.R., 95
Smith's Farm, 136-7
Smith's Meadow, 87-8
Smyth, William, 125
Someries, 29, 32, 171;
Castle, 184; Scouts, 94
Somme, 104
Souster, George, 13, 51, 94, 95,
99, 164, 185, 186-7; William,
105, 106
South Beds. Golf Club, 89, 129
South field, 124
Southouse family, 132
Sowerby Avenue, 74, 81, 110,
118, 121
Sowerby family, 21, 28, 40, 42,
47, 57-59, 126, 181, 185;
George, 57, 73, 127, 129; John,
57, 132; Thomas, 57, 125, 130,
146

Sparke, Miss, 171
Spira, Dr M., 72
Spittlesea, 18, 50, 68, 69
Spivey, Harry, 129, 137
Spooner, E.K., 92
Sport, general, 23, 51; archery
34; athletics, 90; bowls, 88-9;
cricket, 154; cross-country, 89;
football, 87-8; golf, 89, 118, 143;
greyhound racing, 89; horse
racing, 40; Rugby football, 88;
shooting, 59, 62, 63; swimming
pool, 51-2, 181; tennis 88
Sportsman, 47-8, 91, 111
Spufford, Anne, 29
Spurgeon, C.H., 129
Spycer, Edward, 124
Squire, John, 80; R.H., 182
Squires, John, 42
Staddon, John H., 182
Staffordshire Regt., 152
Stapleford Road, 84, 109, 118
Starling, Richard, 28; Sir
Samuel, 27-8, 31, 126
Staunton, William, 31
Steel houses, 113, 117, 176
Steel, W.R., 134
Stevens, John, 169, 170
Steppinge, Robert, 38
Stiles Wood, 8
Stimpson, Ray, 120
Stockenbridge, 124
Stockingstone Road, 1, 8, 15, 139
Stockwood Farm and House, 20,
56; Park, Museum, 3, 82, 137,
High School, 97
Stokes, Richard, 125
Stondon, Upper, 131
Stone, Revd. Rodney M. 158
Stoppelee, John de, 6
Stopsley family, 26; Alexander,
20, 21, 24, 25; Alice, 27;
Dennis, 25; Hugh, 25; John, 22;
Lucia, 22; Matilda, 24; Richard,
26; William, 25
Stopsley and District Football
Club, 87; Athletic Football Club,
88; Bowling Club, 89; Common,
9, 15, 111, 125, 133, 143; Court,
90; Cricket Club, 88; Farm, 134;
Stopsley House, 70, 79, 96, 101,
147, 157; Ladies' Assn., 87, 95,
105, 157, 158; Lodge, 62;
Manor, 20; Regional Sports'
Centre, 89; Tennis Club, 88;
United Football Club, 87; Young
Wives Group, 158
Straw Hats, 42-44; plait, 42-44,
171; dealers, 43
Streatley, 41
Strike, General, 84
Stronell, Maud, 90, 137, 169,
W.B., 105
Stronnell Close, 8

Stump, R.M., 15
Summerfield, Frederick, 185;
Frank, 83
Surgery, Stopsley Green, 71-2
Suvla Bay, 103-4
Surrey, Thomas, 37
Sutherland, Revd. Alex., 149
Swallow, Ronald A., 179
Swift family, 129; John, 45
Swift's Farm, 2, 128-9
Swift's Green, 45, 123, 169, 173
Sworder, Clara, 57; Herbert, 57
Sybley, John, 19

T
Tallebosc, Ralf, 17
Tancred Road, 8, 138, 171
Tansley, Pat, 168
Tatman, William, 46
Tavener, Joyce, 95
Taxation, 21-22, 24, 31, 45, 145
Taylor, A.J.P., 98; Jean M., 61;
Nicholas, 31
Tea Green, 41
Tebold, Ralph, 23
Teck, Duchess of, 58
Telegraph, 83-4
Tennant, Thomas, 96
Tennis, 88
Territorial Army, 152
Thame-Stevenage link, 10-11
'Thatched Cottage', Butterfield's
Green, 78
Thatcher, Margaret, 175
Thompson, Henry, 142; Ian, 90
Thomson, Donald, 83, 120;
Mary, 174
Thorley, Peter, 181
Thorne, Dorothy, 62; Mr. 62
Thrale, George, 124
Thrussell, William, 45
Thurcatel, 16
Tidnam, Harry, 90
Timber, 37, 131
Tin Pot Inn, 142, 143
Titchmarsh, James, 83
Tithe Cottage, (Tythe), 78, 90,
98, 101, 169
Tithe Map, 90, 124
Tithes, 145-6
Titmus, Maurice, 137
Toc H, 95, 160, 161
Toddington, 103
Tompkins, Lily M., 172
Tomson family, 45, 142
Toy, Gordon K., 178
Toyer, Albert and Stanley, 120;
Alfred, 80; Ethel, 128;
Frederick, 143; Harry, 128;
Lillian, 95, 128; William, 170
Toyer's Cottages, 79-80
Toyne, Mrs. S., 182
Trades, blacksmiths, 37, 42, 75,
80, 91, 137; bonnet sewers, 42;

Subscribers

to 1st August 1998

George Adams
Mrs J. Adams (née Peters)
Mrs Elsie Aldridge
Revd. David Alexander
Anne Allsopp
Peter Appleby

Bernard and Eunice Bachini
Steve Bachini
Mrs P. Baker
Jay Bardwell
Jack Beane
Mr P. Bebb
Bedfordshire and Luton
  Archives and Records
  Service
Patricia Bell
Mrs Maureen Bennett
Mrs B. M. Benson
Denis Beswetherick
D.J. and P.M. Biddle
P. R. Biggs
Josephine Blackburn (née
  Halsey)
Gordon Blockley
Ann and Malcolm Boddy
H. E. Bodsworth
John Boon
Mrs Jackie Brennan
Margaret Britton (née Pigott)
Mrs V. Brown
Mr K. W. Burchett
John Frederick Burley
Melvyn Butcher

Mrs P. Cannadine
Eric and Barbara Cannon
Jeffrey Cannon
Jacqueline. Paul and Ruth
  Carter
Cynthia D. Cartwright
Michelle Catlin
T. A. Catlin
K. J. and P. M. Chalmers
M. J. Chamberlain
Joy Chapman
B. T. and R. E. Cheverton
L. Church
Janet Claridge
Raymond A. Clements
P. J. Clorley
Mrs I. G. Collier
David and Doris Collom
Christine Conley

Ealey Conquest
Michael J. Cook
James and Maureen Cook
Terry and Leslie Cooper
Barbara F. Cox
Myrtle E. Cox
Mr E. A. Coxall
David J. Craddock
K. Crampton
Doreen Crawley
Jane Creasey
Eileen and Michael M.
  Crowe
Lilian Cunningham
Maria Curtin

Betty Dalton
Jane Dear
Kevin Dooley
Richard L. Dooley
Lucy Draper
Josephine Driscoll (née
  Fisher)
Mr R. E. Dumpleton
Jacqueline H. Duncan
Frederick Dyer
Mr and Mrs M. and L. Dyer

Mr C. J. Ebbs
R. P. Edwards
Mr and Mrs B. J. Emerton
Canon Francis Estdale
Charlie Evans
Vivienne and Lew Evans

Mr David Farish
J. E. Farrer
Bruce Faulkner
John Fennell
Christopher Fildes
Ruth and Jim Fisher
Iris and Ron Fletcher
Tim and Marion Franklin

Jim and Beverley Gabriel
William L. Gates
Alan and Jill Gibbs
Kathleen Gibbons
Jean Gicquel
Mr and Mrs J.J.M. Gillespie
F. W. A. Godfrey
Marjorie A. Gosbee
Eddie and Rosemary
  Grabham
Mr and Mrs P.M.W. Greaves
Bert Green
Richard Green
Brin Griffiths

Mrs A. Gudgin
Ronald B. Gutteridge

Gerald and Eunice Hale
Mrs D. Hall
Christine Halsey
Cynthia Handscombe
Irene F. Harris
Dave and Joan Haynes
Kathryn Hewitt
Mrs Muriel Hill
Mrs M. J. Hill
Patricia Hinds
Tilly Hodgson
Geraldine and Richard Hogg
Richard Holt
Mrs K. M. Horne
Emma and Sophie Howarth
Mrs June Howarth
Miss C. J. Howe
Ernest and Gillian Hughes
Julie A. Hughes
Mrs Melita A. Hughes
Chris Hunt
Mr and Mrs G. Hunt
Paul Hunt

Mr Ray Impey
Mr Ron Impey
Mrs J. Ingram
John and Doris Irons

Pam and Denis Jack
Eileen Jasinski
Alan and Janet Jones
Doreen and John Jones
Mansel Jones
Miss V. Jones

Mr and Mrs J. Kairis
Mr K. J. Kilby
Mrs V. Kilby
John D. Kingham
Mary Knight
Rob and Pam Knight

Mr Derrick Lack
Mrs M. Large
Mrs Gloria Lathwell
Mr Blyth Latimer
Ronald G. Lawrence
Mrs M. Laycock
Anne Lewis
Freda Lewis
Mrs Phyllis Luck
Luton Libraries Service
Luton Museum and Art
  Gallery

Helen Lyle-Ross
Mary and Bernard Mace
Sarah Jane Maddick
O. G. 'Boxer' Maddox
Dave Manning
Mr J. Manton
David and Peter Martin
Louis Martin
Molly-Joy Massey
Betty Matthams (née
  Akerman)
Evelyn Maughan (née Shaw)
Paul and Teresa McCarthy
J. M. McCurdie
Kathleen and Richard
  McLeod
M. G. Miles
Mary Moatt
C. R. and P.J. Montague
Mrs Brenda H. Morgan
Cynthia Morris (née Breed)
R. Morrison-Chapman
Geoff. and Win. Mullis
Mr and Mrs K. E. Munslow
Christine Murray

Mrs H. Norman
Mr O. Norman
Paddy and Bob Norman
Patricia Nye (née Faulkner)

Mr Brian John O'Dell
Mrs Eileen Odell
Joe O'Dell
Margaret E. O'Dell
Mr D. Ogden
Hazel and Philip Osborn
Kathryn P. Osborn
Victoria Osborn
Mr and Mrs W. Owen

Audrey Palmer
Gill and Tony Palmer
Jean and Roy Palmer
Mr A. W. Parkins
Brian and Valerie Payne
Mrs J. Payne
Mrs Muriel Peace (née
  Fisher)
Anne, Andrew and Robert
  Pearce
Roy Perry
Miss B. R. Peters
Mr M. S. Peters
Mr S. J. Peters
Jean Phelps
Alan D. Philp
Mr and Mrs D. W. Philp

Dr Graeme S. Philp
Freda and Norman Pinney
Mrs A. Pinnock
Mrs C. Pinnock
Mr and Mrs M. and E.
  Playle
Malcolm, Shirley, Katie and
  Stephen Plummer
Christopher Pollard
Canon Clifford F. Pollard
Mark J. Pollard
P.A. and B.M. Porter
Jeanne B. Powell
Putteridge Junior School

Wally Rainbow
T. C. Ray
Mrs J. Reid (née Impey)
P. C. Richardson
Derek Robins
Geoffrey Robins
Margaret Robinson
Brenda Roe
Mrs J. Roe
Mr D. A. Rouse
Dr Walter Roy

Reg Saunders
Dick Savage
Mr and Mrs A. and C.L.
  Scarpa
David J. Scrimshire
Joy Sendall
Miss B. J. Sewell
Miss Deborah Sewell
Janet and Bryan Sexton
Spencer P. Shane
Betty Shaw
Christine E. Shaw
John Shaw
Katharine Shaw
Lionel H. Shaw
Barbara and Derrick
  Simpkins
Colin Maurice Simpkins
Sylvia and Barbara Simpkins
David Skinner
Michael Skinner
D.M. and E.W. Slater
Ann and Dave Smith
Barry Smith
Mrs D. Smith
Joan, Win. and Roy Smith
Stuart Smith
Miss W.G. Smith
Someries Junior School
Christy and James Sparham
Dr M. Spira

Mrs J. Sterry (née Peters)
T. W. Stevens
Paul Stevenson
Jane and Alec Stewart
Doris Stock
Stopsley Infant School
Stopsley Junior School
Stopsley High School
J. Stubbs
Janice Swan

Alan Thayne
B. Titley
Mr and Mrs F. Towner

Walter Upton

Brian and Jill Waller
Philip and Ann Waller
Geoff and June Wallis
Andrew, John and Michael
  Walsh
Jenny and James Walsh
Mr and Mrs M. and A.
  Warner
David M. Warren
Norma and Rowland Watson
Beryl A. Webb
Michael and Sheila Webb
Stephen Webster
Sheila Mary Weedon
Fay Weighell (née Fryer)
Carole and David Wells,
Darren Wells
Jemma Wells
Russell Wells
Stacey Wells
S.M. and J.G. Westmore
Mrs J. White
Margaret White
Paul C. Wightman
Mrs J. Wilkins
Miss M. Williams
Sylvia Williams
Carole Wood (née Morgan)
Rosemary Wood
Keith John Woods
Stewart Woolsey
John A. Worby
Albert Wright
Nicholas Wright

Kath Yeomans

Books Published by THE BOOK CASTLE

COUNTRYSIDE CYCLING IN BEDFORDSHIRE, BUCKINGHAMSHIRE AND HERTFORDSHIRE: Mick Payne.
Twenty rides on- and off-road for all the family.   1 871199 92 1

PUB WALKS FROM COUNTRY STATIONS: Bedfordshire and Hertfordshire: Clive Higgs.
Fourteen circular country rambles, each starting and finishing at a railway station and incorporating a pub-stop at a mid-way point.   1 871199 53 0

PUB WALKS FROM COUNTRY STATIONS: Buckinghamshire and Oxfordshire: Clive Higgs. Circular rambles incorporating pub-stops.   1 871199 73 5

LOCAL WALKS: North and Mid Bedfordshire: Vaughan Basham.
Twenty-five thematic circular walks.   1 871199 48 4

FAMILY WALKS: Chilterns South: Nick Moon.
Thirty 3 to 5 mile circular walks.   1 871199 38 7

FAMILY WALKS: Chilterns North: Nick Moon.
Thirty shorter circular walks.   1 871199 68 9

CHILTERN WALKS: Hertfordshire, Bedfordshire and North Buckinghamshire: Nick Moon.   1 871199 13 1

CHILTERN WALKS: Buckinghamshire: Nick Moon.   1 871199 43 3

CHILTERN WALKS: Oxfordshire and West Buckinghamshire: Nick Moon.   1 871199 08 5
A trilogy of circular walks, in association with the Chiltern Society.
Each volume contains 30 circular walks.

OXFORDSHIRE WALKS: Oxford, the Cotswolds and the Cherwell Valley: Nick Moon.   1 871199 78 6

OXFORDSHIRE WALKS: Oxford, the Downs and the Thames Valley: Nick Moon.   1 871199 32 8
Two volumes that complement Chiltern Walks: Oxfordshire and complete coverage of the county, in association with the Oxford Fieldpaths Society. Thirty circular walks in each.

JOURNEYS INTO BEDFORDSHIRE: Anthony Mackay.
Foreword by The Marquess of Tavistock, Woburn Abbey. A lavish book of over 150 evocative ink drawings.   1 871199 17 4

JOURNEYS INTO BUCKINGHAMSHIRE: Anthony Mackay.   1 871199 14 X
Superb line drawings plus background text: large format landscape gift book.

BUCKINGHAMSHIRE MURDERS: Len Woodley
Nearly two centuries of nasty crimes.   1 871199 93 X

HISTORIC FIGURES IN THE BUCKINGHAMSHIRE LANDSCAPE:
John Houghton. Major personalities and events that have shaped the county's past, including a special section on Bletchley Park.   1 871199 63 8

TWICE UPON A TIME: John Houghton.
Short stories loosely based on fact, set in the North Bucks area.   1 871199 09 3

MANORS and MAYHEM, PAUPERS and PARSONS: Tales from Four Shires: Beds., Bucks., Herts., and Northants.: John Houghton
Little-known historical snippets and stories.   1 871199 18 2

MYTHS and WITCHES, PEOPLE and POLITICS: Tales from Four Shires: Bucks., Beds., Herts., and Northants.: John Houghton.
Anthology of strange, but true historical events.   1 871199 82 4

**FOLK: Characters and Events in the History of Bedfordshire and
Northamptonshire**: Vivienne Evans.   1 871199 25 5
Anthology about people of yesteryear – arranged alphabetically by village or town.

JOHN BUNYAN: His Life and Times: Vivienne Evans.
Highly-praised and readable account.   1 871199 87 5

THE RAILWAY AGE IN BEDFORDSHIRE: Fred Cockman.
Classic, illustrated account of early railway history.   1 871199 22 0

GLEANINGS REVISITED: Nostalgic Thoughts of a Bedfordshire Farmer's Boy:
E W O'Dell.   1 871199 77 8
His own sketches and early photographs adorn this lively account of rural Bedfordshire.

FARM OF MY CHILDHOOD, 1925–1947: Mary Roberts.
An almost vanished lifestyle on a remote farm near Flitwick.   1 871199 50 6

BEDFORDSHIRE'S YESTERYEARS Vol 2: The Rural Scene:
Brenda Fraser-Newstead.   1 871199 47 6
Vivid first-hand accounts of country life two or three generations ago.

BEDFORDSHIRE'S YESTERYEARS Vol 3: Craftsmen and Tradespeople:
Brenda Fraser-Newstead.   1 871199 03 4
Fascinating recollections over several generations practising vanishing crafts and trades.

BEDFORDSHIRE'S YESTERYEARS Vol 4: War Times and Civil Matters:
Brenda Fraser-Newstead.
Two World Wars, plus transport, law and order, etc.   1 871199 23 9

DUNSTABLE IN TRANSITION, 1550–1700: Viviene Evans.
Wealth of original material as the town evolves without the Priory.   1 871199 98 0

DUNSTABLE WITH THE PRIORY: 1100–1550: Vivienne Evans.   1 871199 56 5
Dramatic growth of Henry I's important new town around a major crossroads.

DUNSTABLE DECADE: THE EIGHTIES: A Collection of Photographs:
Pat Lovering.   1 871199 35 2
A souvenir book of nearly 300 pictures of people and events in the 1980s.

DUNSTABLE IN DETAIL: Nigel Benson.
A hundred of the town's buildings and features, plus town trail map.   09509773 2 2

OLD DUNSTABLE: Bill Twaddle.
A new edition of this collection of early photographs.   1 871199 05 0

BOURNE and BRED: A Dunstable Boyhood Between the Wars: Colin Bourne.
An elegantly written, well-illustrated book capturing the spirit of the town over fifty
years ago.   1 871199 40 9

ROYAL HOUGHTON: Pat Lovering: 0 9509773 1 4
Illustrated history of Houghton Regis from the earliest times to the present.

THE STOPSLEY BOOK: James Dyer.   h/b – 1 871199 24 7; p/b – 1 871199 04 2
Definitive, detailed account of this historic area of Luton. 150 rare photographs.

THE CHANGING FACE OF LUTON: An Illustrated History:
Stephen Bunker, Robin Holgate and Marian Nichols.
Luton's development from earliest times to the present busy industrial town.
Illustrated in colour and mono.   h/b – 1 871199 66 2; p/b – 1 871199 71 9

THE MEN WHO WORE STRAW HELMETS:
Policing Luton, 1840–1974: Tom Madigan.
Meticulously chronicled history; dozens of rare photographs; author served in Luton
Police for fifty years.   h/b – 1 871199 81 6; p/b – 1 871199 11 5

BETWEEN THE HILLS: The Story of Lilley, a Chiltern Village: Roy Pinnock.
A priceless piece of our heritage – the rural beauty remains but the customs and
way of life described here have largely disappeared.   1 871199 02 6

KENILWORTH SUNSET: A Luton Town Supporter's Journal: Tim Kingston.
Frank and funny account of football's ups and downs.   1 871199 83 2

A HATTER GOES MAD!: Kristina Howells.
Luton Town footballers, officials and supporters talk to a female fan. 1 871199 58 1

LEGACIES: Tales and Legends of Luton and the North Chilterns: Vic Lea.
Twenty-five mysteries and stories based on fact, including Luton Town Football
Club. Many photographs.   1 8711199 91 3

**LEAFING THROUGH LITERATURE: Writers' Lives in Hertfordshire and
Bedfordshire**: David Carroll.   1 871199 01 8
Illustrated short biographies of famous authors and their connections with these counties.

A PILGRIMAGE IN HERTFORDSHIRE: H M Alderman.   1 871199 33 6
Classic, between-the-wars tour round the county, embellished with line drawings.

**SUGAR MICE AND STICKLEBACKS:
Childhood Memories of a Hertfordshire Lad**: Harry Edwards.   1 871199 88 3
Vivid evocation of those gentler pre-war days in an archetypal village, Hertingfordbury.

SWANS IN MY KITCHEN: Lis Dorer.
Story of a Swan Sanctuary near Hemel Hempstead.   1 871199 62 X

THE HILL OF THE MARTYR: An Architectural History of St. Albans Abbey:
Eileen Roberts: h/b – 1 871199 21 2; p/b – 1 871199 26 3
Scholarly and readable chronological narrative history of Hertfordshire and
Bedfordshire's famous cathedral. Fully illustrated with photographs and plans.

CHILTERN ARCHAEOLOGY: RECENT WORK: A Handbook for the Next Decade:
edited by Robin Holgate.   1 871199 52 2
The latest views, results and excavations by twenty-three leading archaeologists.

THE TALL HITCHIN SERGEANT: A Victorian Crime Novel Based on Fact:
Edgar Newman.   1 871199 07 7
Mixes real police officers and authentic background with an exciting storyline.

**THE TALL HITCHIN INSPECTOR'S CASEBOOK:
A Victorian Crime Novel Based on Fact**: Edgar Newman.
Worthies of the time encounter more archetypal villains.   1 871199 67 0

SPECIALLY FOR CHILDREN

VILLA BELOW THE KNOLLS: A Story of Roman Britain: Michael Dundrow.
An exciting adventure for young John in Totternhoe and Dunstable two thousand
years ago.   1 871199 42 5

THE RAVENS: One Boy Against the Might of Rome: James Dyer.   1 871199 60 3
On the Barton Hills and in the south-east of England as the men of the great fort of
Ravensburgh (near Hexton) confront the invaders.

Further titles are in preparation.
All the above are available via any bookshop, or from the publisher and bookseller,
THE BOOK CASTLE
12 Church Street, Dunstable, Bedfordshire, LU5 4RU Tel: (01582) 605670